"WHAT SHALL WE DO WITH THE NEGRO?"

"WHAT SHALL WE DO WITH THE NEGRO?"

Lincoln, White Racism, and Civil War America

PAUL D. ESCOTT

UNIVERSITY OF VIRGINIA PRESS
CHARLOTTESVILLE & LONDON

University of Virginia Press

Printed in the United States of America on acid-free paper

First published 2009

1 3 5 7 9 8 6 4 2

Library of Congress Cataloging-in-Publication Data
Escott, Paul D., 1947–
What shall we do with the Negro?: Lincoln, white racism, and Civil War America / Paul D. Escott.
p. cm.
Includes bibliographical references and index.
ISBN 978-0-8139-2786-2 (alk. paper)
1. Lincoln, Abraham, 1809–1865 — Political and social views. 2. Lincoln, Abraham, 1809–1865 — Relations with African Americans. 3. Slaves — Emancipation — United States. 4. African Americans — Civil rights — History — 19th century. 5. African Americans — Legal status, laws, etc. — History — 19th century. 6. Race — Political aspects — United States — History — 19th century. 7. Racism — United States — History — 19th century. 8. United States — Race relations — History — 19th century. 9. United States — Politics and government — 1861–1865. 10. Whites — United States — Attitudes — History — 19th century. I. Title.
E457.2.E73 2009
973.7092 — dc22
2008034652

To David Wright Escott

“What shall we do with the negro?”

New York Times, 12 December 1862

CONTENTS

Part Three
Confluence

ACKNOWLEDGMENTS

UPON COMPLETION of a large project, one feels satisfaction and gratitude toward those who have helped him reach that point. Throughout my career I have been fortunate to receive enormous help and encouragement from Robert Durden, Raymond Gavins, Jeffrey Crow, and Emory Thomas. In polishing this book I have benefited greatly from the comments and advice of Ray Gavins, Jeff Crow, Bill Freehling, Michele Gillespie, and my editor, Dick Holway. I thank these individuals for their invaluable assistance and friendship. In addition, John David Smith and an anonymous reader for the University of Virginia Press provided extremely useful comments and suggestions. I thank Simone Caron, the chairperson of my department, for her steady support and two students, Katherine Powell and Amy Mueller, for research assistance. Any deficiencies of this text remain solely my responsibility.

INTRODUCTION

IN THE TRAGIC AFTERMATH of the invasion of Iraq, Americans began to reexamine basic assumptions about their nation's foreign policy. Several decades ago the diplomat George F. Kennan undertook the same task and reached important conclusions. Kennan identified a persistent, unrealistic strain of thought in American diplomacy. Throughout the United States' history as a world power, he wrote, Americans have been attracted to "professions of high moral and legal principle" as the basis of U.S. diplomatic practice. Kennan noted several ill effects of this attitude, among them a tendency to feel a "moral superiority" over other nations and the fact that these traits "work a certain abuse on public understanding of international realities."[1] The characteristics that Kennan regretted in foreign affairs also distort popular understanding of our nation's domestic history. They work an abuse on an informed understanding of our past.

The idealistic and celebratory character of American attitudes toward the history of the United States has deep roots. Puritan settlers dedicated themselves to the task of creating a model community—a "city on a hill." Many subsequent groups shared their idealism about the country and the sense, as Woodrow Wilson put it, that Columbus's discovery had given humankind "an opportunity to set up a new civilization." The United States, Wilson declared in 1912 as he campaigned for the presidency, was to be "a new human experiment . . . a new start in civilization . . . life from the old centres of living, surely, but cleansed of defilement." In Wilson's view, the Founding Fathers aspired "to bring liberty to mankind," to create on "consecrated soil" a new government that would be "a beacon of encouragement to all the nations of the world."[2] Wilson viewed himself as a *reformer* even though he extended segregation into the Federal bureaucracy. Still, though he was bent on correcting economic wrongs, he used history to argue that the United States was different from, *better than,* other societies. Generations of political candidates and officeholders have echoed the patriotic rhetoric of American exceptionalism, which gained further strength from the nation's increasing economic and military power and the arrival of millions of hopeful immigrants. Long ago, exalted patriotic images, rather than a realistic and factual appraisal, reflecting an awareness of societal shortcomings and difficulties, became the standard in popular culture for discussion of U.S. history. In public discourse about their history, Americans tend to emphasize only the nation's successes, hiding inevitable human failures or disappointments behind images of greatness.

This pattern has deeply affected popular understanding of the Civil War era. An internecine conflict that claimed 625,000 lives should be undeniable proof that all has *not* gone well, that U.S. history is not an unbroken record of success. Perhaps the very carnage of that era has impelled many to search for consoling arguments rather than realistic appraisals. In any case, inspiring myths and idealistic themes of progress dominate popular reflections on what was undeniably an era of widespread destruction, tragedy, and unsolved problems. A casual observer could be excused for concluding that the years in which the American political system broke down and citizens slaughtered each other on a huge scale were actually a time of unalloyed progress. For in many comforting and rose-tinted interpretations, Americans discovered a leader of timeless greatness, eliminated the scourge of human slavery, moved toward equality for all, reined in state particularism to forge a stronger nation, and perfected the Constitution for future generations. In crisis, citizens met the challenge and speedily laid the foundation for a brighter destiny.

Professional historians have, of course, produced a far more detailed, accurate, factual, and sometimes sobering account of the Civil War than the one that prevails in popular culture. But scholars, too, often emphasize the positive and minimize the negative. This seems to be especially true in contemporary treatments of Abraham Lincoln and racial issues. Lincoln is a mythical figure in American culture. His eloquent prose has touched hearts and minds more profoundly through later decades than it did while he was alive. Invariably, historians rate him as one of the greatest, if not *the* greatest, of chief executives. If some of his positions disappoint modern sensibilities, studies typically compensate by emphasizing change and growth in his views. This attitude allows readers to think that, had Lincoln lived, he would have come to hold views of which they could uniformly be proud. Not coincidentally, a positive depiction of Lincoln facilitates positive conclusions about matters of race, the most serious and enduring of all the nation's social problems. Scholarly studies generally focus more attention on wartime precedents for later progress than on the limitations and failures of that era's confrontation with racial prejudice.[3]

This book takes a candid approach to the struggle of Civil War governments, North and South, with the issue of race. My purpose is not to deny that any good came out of the Civil War or to attack the reputation of Abraham Lincoln, but rather to present an undistorted, accurate analysis of Civil War policies and thought that related to the future of race relations and the future status of African Americans. To address this subject, I look at developments in both the Union and the Confederacy. Although this book covers events throughout the war period, my aim is to illuminate attitudes and policies affecting the future status of the freed people rather than to focus on the decision to emancipate. As we shall see, there is less to celebrate on these matters than on the narrower—but still ambiguous and complicated—subject of emancipation.

In an effort to tell a more realistic and less celebratory story, I describe a divided and racist society both of whose sections traveled a conflicted and complex route before they could confront emancipation and finally, reluctantly, consider the future status of African Americans. Along that route white Northerners and Southerners gave priority to many other questions rather than address the future of black people. The movement away from reverence for state powers and state rights was limited, hesitant. More often than not, the agents of change during the war were events rather than wise and far-seeing leaders. Many outcomes that today are regarded as positive were largely undesired and unsought, and the progress that did occur left almost untouched a societal racism that would plague subsequent generations. In matters of race, the Civil War signaled a future of segregation and racial exploitation rather than equality, a future that soon became reality. Only by acknowledging this complexity can we gain a realistic understanding of one of the most significant periods in the history of the United States and of its racial problems.

EVIDENCE THAT EVENTS forced change and determined policies can be found, to cite just one example, in Abraham Lincoln's Second Inaugural Address. Its words capture something of the tumultuousness of the period for those who lived it. After almost four years of war, Lincoln reflected on the cause of the deadliest conflict in U.S. history. Slaves, he said, had "constituted a peculiar and powerful interest." That interest "was, somehow, the cause of the war." It is noteworthy that Lincoln used the qualifier "somehow." Even though he had played a major role in the events leading to war, Lincoln did not claim to know exactly how the slavery interest was connected to the vast and remarkable events that had followed swiftly upon his first inauguration.

At that time, four years earlier, his carefully chosen words upon taking office had been devoted "to *saving* the Union without war." He and his party had consistently "claimed no right to do more than to restrict the territorial enlargement" of slavery. But those he termed "insurgents" had sought "to strengthen, perpetuate, and extend" the slavery interest, and they had chosen to "rend the Union" to pursue their aim. "Both parties," Lincoln believed, "deprecated war; but one of them would *make* war rather than let the nation survive; and the other would *accept* war rather than let it perish." As a consequence, astounding things had occurred. Neither side had expected "the magnitude, or the duration" of their destructive war, and neither had anticipated that slavery "might cease with, or even before, the conflict itself should cease." Acknowledging his surprise, Lincoln then suggested that God might be balancing the nation's moral accounts, and he affirmed that "the Almighty has His own purposes." At the close of his brief address, Lincoln spoke of "malice toward none" and "charity for all." He invited his audience to help "to bind up the nation's wounds" and to care for soldiers and their widows and orphans, and he uttered his sincere desire for "a just, and a lasting peace, among ourselves." His attitude toward the "insurgents" with whom he would make peace also was indicated by his admonition, "Let us judge not that we be not judged."[4]

If we strip away popular culture's gloss on the Civil War and give credence to Lincoln's words, we begin to encounter the realities of that era rather than the myths our society has created about it. Lincoln stated clearly that he did not intend to destroy slavery and had claimed no right to do so; he wanted only to limit its "enlargement." His goal had been to save the Union without war. Emancipation was one of the unanticipated and astounding results of the war. He still desired strongly to restore not just the authority of a national government but peace and goodwill, marked by charity and an absence of malice, with the "insurgents." And although Lincoln discussed the end of slavery in the context of God's unknowable will, he said nothing either in general or in specifics about the future status of former slaves. Charity, one must assume, should be extended to them as to others, but reestablishing peace and union with those who had brought the war clearly was more important to him than elevating the status of the freedmen.

As we shall see, these attitudes had been strongly and consistently held by Lincoln throughout the war. They indicate a set of priorities different from those that popular culture normally associates with the Great Emancipator, and they suggest the importance of recapturing the contours of the mental world in which he operated. Not only had Lincoln not sought to attack slavery where it existed, but he had been willing to guarantee for all time its immunity from interference by the Federal government. Doubting the strength of the secessionists, he had expected a resurgence of Union sentiment in the South.[5] Even after years of war, he somehow continued to believe that the revival of loyal sentiments and loyalist governments in the South would not be too difficult. To restore the Union and reestablish peace and comity between white citizens of the North and South had always been priorities for him, whereas emancipation was an unintended consequence of the war. Although by 1865 Lincoln was committed to eventually bringing freedom to the slaves, we will see that his expectations for improvements in their status were modest and that the future status of black Americans was just beginning to appear on his and the nation's agenda. The uncontrollable forces of a great war had buffeted Lincoln the president and forced his policies in directions that he had not anticipated.

In the South, war-induced change had been even greater than in the North. Had Jefferson Davis been given to public reflection, he might have described a wartime political journey that was even more astounding than Lincoln's. For by early 1865 Davis, a large slaveholder himself and leader of an aristocratic slaveholders' republic, was advocating for the Confederacy an unpopular policy of arming and emancipating the slaves. And this was only the latest and most shocking of his administration's dramatic and unexpected innovations. The war had brought an avalanche of change to the South, and Jefferson Davis had adjusted to it and spurred it along in many areas.

Four years earlier, at the time of his inauguration, President Davis had hoped for and foreseen a Confederate nation drawing on tradition rather than change. Along with other white Southerners, he had expected it to be characterized by limited government, state rights, respect for slaveholders' rights and interests, and a fundamental consensus on social questions. Instead, the Confederacy had seen the rapid growth of a large and powerful central government, bitter controversies over state rights and national power, laws that coerced and regulated individuals in unprecedented ways, and deep social conflict both between classes and within the elite.[6] To fight the war, the Confederate government also took actions that interfered with slavery and damaged the interests of slaveholders. Steadily, the Richmond government claimed greater control over slaves, in order to serve the needs of the nation, until it arrived at its final and revolutionary proposal: arming and emancipating the slaves.

Enormous irony inheres in that proposal, which was at odds with the traditions and aspirations of the white South. In proposing emancipation, Jefferson Davis took political risks that were greater than any Abraham Lincoln had run and braved a storm of disapproval that was more withering than any Lincoln faced in the North. Davis also confronted more directly and outlined more specifically a racist answer to the question of what would be the future status of the freed people. The Confederate proposals and the reaction in the South to them shed further light on the power of racism in the nation and the moral challenges both sections were reluctant to face.[7]

This book will examine, without reliance on flattering myths, the evolution of wartime policies and racial thought in both the North and the South. The actions—and nonactions—of Union and Confederate leaders shaped the future of U.S. society. Their policies and the reactions of their citizens will often seem far more ambiguous and far less progressive than commonly thought, yielding a more realistic and less celebratory tale—one that is tragically consistent with the later narrative of Jim Crow segregation. But this story is important. It illuminates the answer that Americans of the Civil War era gave to the frequently asked question, "What shall we do with the negro?"[8] This question became unavoidable during the war. But it was a deeply flawed question, reflecting in its language the assumptions that African Americans were objects, not equals; that they were fundamentally different and outside the community; and that white people were entitled to decide their future. It foreshadowed later white complaints about "the Negro Problem." Both the flawed question and the flawed answers that were given to it aid our understanding of the troubled social relations that led to the age of segregation and Jim Crow.

"WHAT SHALL WE DO WITH THE NEGRO?"

PROLOGUE

FIRST DECLARATIONS

What was the Civil War about?

This simple question has produced an unending debate in American culture. Because so many soldiers died in the war, because the war left deep scars in the body politic, and because human behavior is inherently complex, it is not surprising that individuals argue passionately about the answers even today. Beyond these reasons, however, lies an intensely complicating fact: the institution of slavery—America's greatest civil wrong—was at the heart of the conflict. Abraham Lincoln reflected in his Second Inaugural Address that the slavery interest "was somehow the cause of the war."[1] Millions of Americans have agreed with his sure but imprecise judgment.

The centrality of the "peculiar institution" has made the Civil War eternally controversial. For if the bloodletting was about slavery, then the verdict of history and morality came down against those who defended human bondage and honored those who liberated the slaves. In that way, the war continued to produce winners and losers long after Appomattox. Once the conflict of arms ended, a battle of words began, as each section tried to persuade the public that its version of this shared and bloody history was correct. Southerners rejected the identification of their cause with slavery, insisting that they had fought for state rights and constitutional liberty. Northerners claimed the credit for emancipation, picturing themselves as proponents of freedom and human equality. Both oversimplified, and both contributed to a celebratory narrative, deeply rooted in the popular culture, that has distorted the truth, minimized the shortcomings of both sides, and exaggerated the progress and advances that came out of the war.

For the Civil War soon concerned more than the long-established institution of slavery. With the end of slavery would come the question of the future status of the freedmen. Taking this issue into account redefines the contest over credit and blame and points toward different conclusions. Focusing on how Americans addressed the future of the slaves yields a darker, more disappointing, and more convoluted picture than the triumphant national narrative about the breaking of bondsmen's chains. This other picture, though less flattering and less inspiring, is more accurate and more useful for understanding our nation's history. It reveals the extent of deeply engrained problems and expands the ground for understanding American society's long history of racial problems after emancipation. The unvarnished record is more significant and more informative than the myth.

In the Civil War era both Northern and Southern whites were creatures of their time and society, fallible human beings wrestling with the profound questions that the war raised about slavery and race. What would be the future of slavery? If slavery came to an end, what would be the future status of the slaves? What would become of them? As so many contemporaries put it, "What shall we do with the negro?" The answers of Northerners and Southerners to this racially biased question came reluctantly and imperfectly, under the pressure of war. When the fighting began, both sides agreed on the preservation of slavery. As to possible changes in the future, one section had a definite answer, while the other evaded or dismissed the question.

IN THE SECESSION CRISIS, as years of heated controversy culminated in precipitous action, the leaders of the South gave a clear answer to the question, "What shall we do with the negro?" These white men, predominantly slaveholders, assumed that it was their right to decide the future of black Southerners. Slavery was central to the decision to secede, and they did not shrink from acknowledging that fact. Unhesitatingly, they voiced their determination to preserve and maintain slavery, and as they reviewed history they recited a host of grievances that had a connection to the slavery issue. Although Southerners would later deny it, their leaders in the crisis of secession were explicit about what they wanted to do with African Americans: they wanted to keep them in slavery.

South Carolina seceded first, on December 20, 1860. Following the example of the Revolutionary patriots, its convention cited respect for world opinion as the reason to issue a declaration of the causes that justified secession. This document emphasized the constitutional history of the United States and argued that Northern states had broken the "compact" by refusing to honor their obligations on "rendition . . . of fugitives," the return of runaway slaves. The reason for this refusal to obey the Constitution was clear: "increasing hostility on the part of the non-slaveholding States to the institution of slavery." Shockingly, some Northern states had "elevat[ed] to citizenship, persons who, by the supreme law of the land, are incapable of becoming citizens," and a political party "hostile to slavery" now controlled the federal government. Because leaders of this Republican Party supposedly had announced "that a war must be waged against slavery until it shall cease throughout the United States," South Carolina concluded that it and other "slaveholding States will no longer have the power of self-government, or self-protection." Thus, secession was required to preserve slavery and the slaveholding society.[2]

Other Southern states were even more direct in explaining their actions. The leaders of Mississippi, after observing that "it is but just" to give reasons for such a "momentous step" as secession, immediately declared, "Our position is thoroughly identified with the institution of slavery—the greatest material interest of the world." Arguing that "none but the black race can bear exposure to the tropical sun," they wrote that "a blow at slavery is a blow at commerce and civilization." Rather than submit to the "mandates of abolition," Mississippians chose to leave the Union.[3]

In a similar manner, Georgia's seceders justified secession: "For the last ten years we have had numerous and serious causes of complaint against our non-slave-holding confederate States with reference to the subject of African slavery." The free states, they charged, had been weakening "our security" and attempting to "disturb our domestic peace." Now their votes had elected as president the nominee of a Republican Party that was "anti-slavery in its mission and its purpose." After reviewing political events and the progress of antislavery forces, the leaders of Georgia concluded that they had to secede "to avoid the desolation of our homes, our altars, and our firesides."[4]

Texas politicians noted that their state had entered the Union "as a commonwealth holding, maintaining and protecting the institution known as negro slavery—the servitude of the African to the white race within her limits—a relation that had existed from the first settlement of her wilderness by the white race, and which her people intended should exist in all future time." Unfortunately, they asserted, the majority controlling Congress had excluded Southerners from territory on the Pacific for the "avowed purpose" of gaining power that would be used as the means of "destroying the institutions of Texas and her sister slaveholding States." After reviewing other grievances, including violations of the fugitive slave clause and a failure to protect settlers in Texas from Native American tribes, the Texans justified secession with a ringing proslavery declaration: "We hold as undeniable truths that the governments of the various States, and of the confederacy itself, were established exclusively by the white race, for themselves and their posterity; that the African race had no agency in their establishment; that they were rightfully held and regarded as an inferior and dependent race, and in that condition only could their existence in this country be rendered beneficial or tolerable. . . . that the servitude of the African race, as existing in these States, is mutually beneficial to both bond and free, and is abundantly authorized and justified by the experience of mankind, and the revealed will of the Almighty Creator."[5]

The actions of the other Deep South states that led the secession movement were in a similar vein. Speaking in the Alabama secession convention, E. S. Dargan explained his fear of "the abolition of African slavery." It was "impossible," he said, to remove four million slaves from the South. But if slavery were ended "and our slaves turned loose amongst us without restraint, they would either be destroyed by our own hands . . . or we ourselves would become demoralized and degraded." Of these two possibilities, Dargan judged that the former would take place, thus driving slaveholders "to crime, to the commission of sin." He said that to avoid such an outcome, he would vote for secession.[6] A majority in the convention quickly formed, and Alabama's ordinance of secession declared that "the election of Abraham Lincoln . . . by a sectional party, avowedly hostile to the domestic institutions and to the peace and security of the people of Alabama" was "so insulting and menacing" in character as to justify secession.[7]

Unless secession threw a protective mantle around slavery, the leaders of Deep South states foresaw a racial cataclysm in the not-too-distant future. To make sure that the remaining slaveholding states were fully alive to the danger, they sent representatives to other conventions and legislatures to urge prompt action. Alabama dispatched Stephen Fowler Hale, a slaveholding farmer, lawyer, and legislator, to Kentucky with instructions to share with the Bluegrass State Alabama's views on the necessity of secession. The election of Lincoln, Hale asserted, was "nothing less than an open declaration of war" on slavery and the South. It would inaugurate "all the horrors of a San Domingo servile insurrection, consigning her citizens to assassinations and her wives and daughters to pollution and violation to gratify the lust of half-civilized Africans." Speaking particularly to nonslaveholding whites,

Hale declared that no Southern man would submit to "the triumph of negro equality" or to loss "of that title to superiority over the black race which God himself has bestowed." Consequently, "amalgamation or the extermination" of one race by the other "would be inevitable." Hale challenged Kentuckians to choose "self-preservation" so that "our civilization" would not go "down in blood."[8]

J. L. M. Curry, a congressman and Alabama's commissioner to Maryland, shared these violent forebodings. In November 1860 he had warned of "a saturnalia of blood" if the South acquiesced in Republican rule. Fearing "the abhorrent degradation of social and political equality," he predicted that Southerners would have to choose between "flying [from] the country" and facing "a war of extermination between the races."[9] Curry was joined by colleagues from Alabama who warned of a coming race war. In North Carolina, the Alabama commissioners Isham W. Garrott and Robert Hardy Smith declared that the South would have to abandon slavery or "be doomed to a servile war." Another commissioner from Alabama, William Cooper, traveled to Missouri and predicted that "the time would arrive when the scenes of San Domingo and Hayti, with all their attendant horrors, would be enacted in the slaveholding States."[10]

Even more apocalyptic was Henry L. Benning, chosen by Georgia's secession convention to carry that state's message to the vitally important Commonwealth of Virginia. A large planter and the youngest man in history to serve on the Georgia Supreme Court, Benning warned that it was "certain" that slavery would be abolished "if things are allowed to go on as they are." Then war would "break out everywhere like hidden fire from the earth." An army from the North would descend upon the South to help the slaves in rising against their masters. Benning's prediction of the results was dire. "We will be overpowered," he said, with white women suffering "horrors . . . we cannot contemplate in imagination" and white men "compelled to wander like vagabonds all over the earth." After Southern whites were "completely exterminated," the rich Southern land, left in the possession of the blacks, would "go back to a wilderness."[11] Similarly, Alexander H. Handy, a commissioner from Mississippi to Maryland, raised the threat of Republican agents infiltrating the South in order "to excite the slave to cut the throat of his master."[12]

Alarmist as these predictions may seem, many white Southerners felt these fears "in the marrow of their bones," as Charles Dew has explained. They imagined race war and "a saturnalia of blood" because in 1860 they could not conceive of any alternative to slavery and absolute white supremacy. "Our fathers made this government for the white man," William Harris told Georgia's general assembly. Whites had to be dominant, because African Americans were "an ignorant, inferior, barbarian race, incapable of self-government." Since no black person could ever be "entitled to be associated with the white man upon terms of civil, political, or social equality," slavery and racial subordination were essential to Southern society. Any departure from the racial status quo was untenable and therefore would lead to violence and ruin.[13]

For some white Southerners, of course, the events of national politics had not aroused this much fear, and Southern voters were not unanimous in favoring secession. Even among committed slaveholders there were those who believed that the best way to protect slavery was to remain in the Union.[14] Reluctance to secede was strongest in the Upper South, where the states of Virginia, North Carolina, Tennessee, and Arkansas refused to sever their connections with the Federal government until the outbreak of war forced them to choose sides. Before the fighting started, North Carolinians voted against holding a convention even to consider secession, but after Fort Sumter, slavery and regional identity combined to take these states out of the Union. As one Tar Heel put it, "War exists. In this emergency, North Carolina must and will dissolve her connection with the Federal Government."[15]

Even in the reluctant Upper South states many leaders were outspoken about the importance of preserving and perpetuating slavery. For example, North Carolina's governor, John W. Ellis, had strongly favored secession and saw the protection of slavery as paramount. When Ellis accepted the Democratic Party's nomination to lead his state in March 1860, he argued that the controversy over the territories was not the real national issue. The issue, he declared, was "whether African slavery shall be abolished here in the States, where it now exists?" Ellis urged his party not to be "deceived": "The abolition of slavery here at home is the design of our opponents. This is the bond that cements all the anti-slavery elements in one solid column against us."[16]

On top of these fears for the safety of slavery, there were other grievances, convictions, and principled emotions. Differences between North and South over the powers of the central government had their roots in the Early Republic. In President George Washington's cabinet, Thomas Jefferson and Alexander Hamilton had argued over the scope of the "necessary and proper" clause in the Constitution. Jefferson's preference for a small government of limited powers did not prevail in that argument, but it later gained strength and inspired other political thinkers, first in the Kentucky and Virginia resolutions and later in the writings of various Southern newspaper editors and officeholders. By the 1820s John C. Calhoun had begun his rise as the theorist of state rights and the compact theory of government, which made Southern interests and state governments paramount and erected barriers against central power.

Although these constitutional principles and theories initially focused on the debate about a national bank, and later had application to the federal tariff, they also served to protect slavery. Calhoun himself had acknowledged privately, in 1830, that he considered "the Tariff, but as the occasion, rather than the real cause of the present unhappy state of things." "The truth can no longer be disguised," he wrote, that the interests of the "majority of the Union" were a threat to "the peculiar domestick institutions of the Southern States." Accordingly, Southern leaders had to look to "protective power in the reserved rights of the states."[17] By the 1840s Calhoun was applying his theories with renewed creativity to the territorial conflict. When David Wilmot proposed that slavery be prohibited in any land won from Mexico, Calhoun invented a new theory that slavery could not be barred from *any* territory before that region became a state. His argument ignored key precedents, such as the Northwest Ordinance and the Missouri Compromise, in which Southerners had agreed to prohibit slavery in large portions of the territorial domain. But in the heated atmosphere of the late 1840s and 1850s it won the support of Southern politicians.

During controversies over the admission of California and the Kansas-Nebraska Bill, Southern politicians fought vigorously for what they saw as their rights in the territories. Then in 1857 the Supreme Court placed its imprimatur on both Calhoun's theory and doctrines of white supremacy. In the Dred Scott decision, Chief Justice Roger B. Taney wrote that black people could not be citizens and had been viewed by the Founders as "beings of an inferior order" with "no rights which the white man was bound to respect." Congress, Taney declared, could not prohibit slavery from any territory, and the Missouri Compromise had been unconstitutional. Although this decision remained controversial in the North, Southern politicians felt that the issue had been settled in their favor. Senator Albert G. Brown, of Mississippi, spoke for many others when he argued that slavery's right to go into the territories was now affirmed and protected. "The Constitution as expounded by the Supreme Court awards it," he declared. And he added, "We demand it; we mean to have it."[18]

Related issues aroused anger and resentment among proslavery Southerners, who felt that other rights to which they were entitled under the Constitution were not being respected. After the Compromise of 1850 produced a stronger fugitive slave law, Northern legislatures began to pass "personal liberty laws." These were designed to protect such rights as trial by jury for individuals claimed as fugitive slaves, but Southern slaveholders, reasonably enough, viewed them as designed to frustrate and undercut the national legislation. The increasing popularity of the Republican Party, whose main goal was to exclude slavery from the territories, in opposition to Justice Taney's ruling, seemed to be merely another proof of the faithlessness of the Northern public to the Constitution and to white Southerners' rights. Additional incitements, such as the praise of John Brown by some prominent Northern intellectuals, intensified Southerners' anger, resistance, and sense of grievance.

Southerner's belief that Northerners did not respect their rights added to the frustration of fighting against the steadily increasing numerical majority of the Northern population. The "culture of honor" that flourished in Southern society, and especially in Southern political culture, made leaders and officeholders extremely sensitive about their status and standing.[19] Northern opposition, in this arena of honor, amounted to a challenge to Southerners' manhood and social position. Such a challenge could not be ignored without loss of self-respect. Moreover, the pervasive sense among Americans of this era that they were heirs to the Revolutionaries of 1776 raised the expectations for political courage and leadership. Public figures, whether Northern or Southern, aspired to be worthy descendents of the Revolutionary generation, a generation that had refused to submit to Parliamentary laws it deemed destructive to freedom. Therefore, in 1860 many Southern politicians believed that they had to act, when their rights were in peril, to be "worthy" of the colonists who had acted when Britain threatened their freedom in the 1770s. They and others asked if it was possible to acquiesce in the Republican Party's victory without losing honor, political equality, and self-respect.

These powerful emotional influences affected almost every discussion of secession. In their declaration of the causes that justified secession, Southern states often referred to the humiliation or disrespect they felt they had endured. Mississippi's document charged that Northern hostility to slavery had "trample[d] the original equality of the South under foot." Georgians protested that a Northern majority that violated their rights was demanding "that we shall receive them as our rulers." Texans recited a long list of wrongs and then insisted that *"all white men are and of right ought to be entitled to equal civil and political rights."* They would insist on the equality to which they were entitled. The commissioners sent out by the seceded states spoke of the South's "equality of rights," guaranteed under the Constitution, and protested that this equality had been "denied us in the South"; that Northern perfidy had placed "the interest, honor, and safety of their citizens" in question; that "submission" to "despotism" was impossible; that "delay is dishonor"; and that Southerners had suffered "indignities and insults until they were no longer tolerable." Even a workingmen's association in North Carolina broke into applause when a speaker declared to them that "a Union of oppression or of inequality, I abhor, as our fathers abhorred the tyranny of England in 1776."[20] Such emotions helped to carry Southerners out of a Union that they had, in truth, revered.

Once secession occurred, Southern leaders took additional steps that identified their cause with the preservation and maintenance of slavery. Assembling in Montgomery, Alabama, they wrote a constitution that explicitly protected slave property, provided for the sure return of fugitive slaves, and addressed territorial issues by guaranteeing that in any Confederate territory, "the institution of negro slavery . . . shall be recognized and protected by Congress and by the Territorial government," with all inhabitants being entitled to take their slaves there.[21] It was, however, the vice president of the Confederacy, Alexander H. Stephens, who most visibly and notoriously identified the new Southern nation with slavery and white supremacy. In Savannah, Georgia, on March 21, 1861, Stephens delivered an address in which he boasted, "The new constitution has put at rest, *forever,* all the agitating questions relating to our peculiar institution — African slavery as it exists among us — the proper *status* of the negro in our form of civilization. This was the immediate cause of the late rupture and present revolution." Jefferson and other Founding Fathers, he noted, had erroneously believed that slavery was wrong. "Our new government is founded upon exactly the opposite idea; its foundations are laid, its corner-stone rests upon the great truth, that the negro is not equal to the white man; that slavery — subordination to the superior race — is his natural and normal condition."[22]

Southern convictions about the destiny of African Americans received enormous support because they formed part of an aristocratic social ideology and a religious vision of society. The leaders of the South proudly viewed themselves as aristocrats, and their aristocratic cultural values coexisted with a political system that allowed universal manhood suffrage for whites in most Confederate states. But an extended suffrage did not mean that the common man could, or did, rule. In some Southern states there were property qualifications for holding office or schemes of representation that gave an advantage to slaveholding districts. Throughout the South social norms and the customs of politics favored wealthy and successful men who were allied with the slaveholding interests, while ideology and religious beliefs buttressed the status quo. Elite Southerners affected an aristocratic lifestyle and values and saw their social system as fundamentally different from that of the North. They believed theirs was superior.

Southern leaders argued that the runaway democracy of Northern states was an unnatural and unhealthy development, and they blamed it for much of the conflict that eventually led to war. Northern society was unsettled and disorganized; it encouraged bizarre beliefs and undesirable reform movements. Abolitionism, socialism, women's rights, French theories of social reform known as Fourierism, and other kinds "isms" earned frequent denunciation by Southern spokesmen. The "fanaticism" that Southerners feared and deplored had been the inevitable product, they declared, of a radical democracy—a society that lacked structure, order, and deference and therefore could not be stable or sound. Even in an economically humble state like North Carolina, which had relatively few great plantations, the elite feared democracy or government by the common man and believed in rule by those of "intelligence, property, and virtue." The establishment of the Confederacy presented an opportunity to strengthen aristocratic and patriarchal influence in society, thus ensuring that Southern government was based on correct principles.[23]

Therefore, Confederates took pride in the notion that their new government was not a "popular government" but instead one run by the "intelligent and virtuous." The Confederacy, declared the *Southern Literary Messenger*, was "in a death-struggle with a radical democracy," and it needed a "bulwark against the encroachments of those tendencies to democracy which have been the Pandora's box of disintegration and ruin to all republics."[24] To be safe, the South must have a "Patrician" society, as opposed to "a system thoroughly popular." There was a danger, even within the Southern political system, that democracy might gain excessive influence, and therefore Confederates had to strive to maintain the "supremacy of property and education." Southerners must choose an "Aristocratic Republic" over a democracy. The threat of an "unbridled democracy" was something that could overwhelm the organic, traditional, and conservative polity desired by the Southern elite.[25]

This elite viewed slavery as the institution that would save the South and serve as its bulwark against the dangers of democracy. Writers in the *Southern Literary Messenger* saw slavery exerting its supposedly healthy influence in a number of ways. Slavery prevented "too heavy an influx from foreign shores of that class of population devoted to menial pursuits"; it was the basis of a social system that had "the dignity, and character of an Aristocracy"; and it imparted "homogeneity" and "community of interest." Slavery gave the South a naturally subordinate and docile menial class and formed "the cornerstone of our system." Accordingly, all were "interested in the security of that institution which creates the aristocracy." One author concluded that "the conservative institution of slavery alone, has saved us so far from as tamely surrendering our liberties as the people of the North."[26]

Supremely confident that their slave-based, aristocratic system was best, some influential Southerners identified their society and their new nation with the will of God. The editor of the *Southern Literary Messenger* asserted that governments were coming to be based on the scriptures and expressed his satisfaction that the Confederate government would "protect religion" and encourage morality. He expressed confidence that the outcome of the war "will, beyond a doubt, afford another striking proof of the existence of Providence in history." As to the substance of God's influence on the outcome, he had no doubt. "Sinful as we undoubtedly are, we can't be so utterly corrupt and heinous as our enemies . . . [or] deserve subjugation at the hands of a race so unworthy and ungodly as the Yankees."[27] This editor's faith that the Confederate government was part of a religious or divine plan was shared — and expressed with more fervor and authority — by prominent Southern clergymen.

"The doctrine of domestic slavery and the system of labor which time has built upon it are in a true sense divine," proclaimed Rev. William Hall in a lecture titled "The Historic Significance of the Southern Revolution." Slavery, he continued, "is an element of inestimable value in our political system. It naturally consigns the whole power of government to the hands of those who are best qualified to use it." Like Southern politicians and editors, Hall rejected the "dogma" of equal rights as "a fatal error." Individuals were entitled only to those rights appropriate for their "character and condition."

The African slave, he judged, was "unfitted in every respect" for any political role and therefore was "entitled" to be governed by "qualified superiors." The South had a "system of Bible, domestic slavery" that was not "oppression" to the slave but, instead, "his proper liberty," because it was the form of government "adapted to his nature and condition." Thus, the South's "revolution clearly aims to vindicate the word of God, which approves" the institution of slavery and "has wisely preserved it."[28]

Another Southern divine, Rev. Joseph R. Wilson, of Augusta, Georgia, published a sermon on slavery at the request of some of his parishioners in 1861. "It is surely high time," Wilson said in answer to their request, "that the Bible view of slavery should be examined" and that Southerners "meet the infidel fanaticism of our infatuated enemies upon the elevated ground of a divine warrant for the institution." In Wilson's view, God had ordained "slavery as an organizing element in that family order which lies at the very foundation of Church and State." Order and proper subordination were part of God's plan for humanity. "No household is perfect under the gospel," he wrote, unless it contains "all the grades of authority and obedience, from that of husband and wife, down through that of father and son, to that of master and servant." In the same way, society must have various levels and distinctions. Fourierism and other social experiments had "transgressed" the order decreed by God and thus had failed because they violated "a fundamental law." Slavery, sanctioned by the Bible, was a conservator of civilization. It saved the "lower race" from heathenism, while it served to "refine, exalt, and enrich its superior race."[29]

One of the South's most important religious leaders was Georgia's first Episcopal bishop, Stephen Elliott, who became the presiding bishop of his church in the Confederacy. Early in the war, Elliott reflected on why the United States had "degenerated and became corrupt in only 70 years." The answer, he asserted, lay in its "war against all authority" and an "impious" dedication to the idea of human equality. "All men were declared to be created equal, and man was pronounced capable of self-government," but "two greater falsehoods could not have been announced," Elliott thundered. These notions "denied the fall and corruption of man" and ignored the fact that "subordination reigns supreme in Heaven, and it must reign supreme on earth." He argued that man "is a fallen creature" and that the idea of human equality "is a miserable *ignis fatuus,* not worthy to be followed, even for the purpose of exposure." There have to be judges, governors, and other "necessary distinctions in a properly ordered, conservative society." Fortunately for the South, "the doctrine of State Sovereignty" and "the institution of slavery" preserved "a certain measure of conservatism." But he cautioned his congregation not to become complacent and instead to "reject as infidel . . . any idea that society or government can exist without due classification."[30]

If Elliott's sermon betrayed a small doubt that Southerners were fully attuned to God's plan, many other ministers discarded any concern whatever and identified the Confederacy completely with God's divine will. Led by their clergymen, Southerners readily adopted the view that they were God's people and the Confederacy the chosen instrument of his divine plan. For example, on the day of fasting and prayer called by Jefferson Davis for November 15, 1861, the Presbyterian minister Thomas V. Moore challenged his listeners to renew their devotion to God, accept the chastening that war brought, and end any sinful conduct, such as "buying up the very necessaries of life" to gain "enormous profits." But he offered forceful assurance as well that "God will maintain our cause!" Rejoicing that the Confederate army was pervaded with a "sense of the power of God," Moore declared that "a people who are fighting for their altars and their firesides, in the fear of God, can never, never be conquered." For Moore, slavery too was a fountain of strength, an institution whose "ethical nature" could not be questioned, since "God has recognized it twice in the Decalogue, and devoted an entire epistle to an incident connected with it in the New Testament, without hinting at its unlawfulness." Southerners, trusting "in the strength of our covenant God," were in a revolution untouched by the "infidelity and radicalism" of the French Revolution.[31]

Another Presbyterian clergyman, Rev. Thomas Smyth, affirmed the rightness of the South's cause, as well as God's support for the Confederacy, in a lengthy article in the *Southern Presbyterian Review.* Taking as his title "The War of the South Vindicated," Smyth argued that the war was fully justified as one of self-defense, based on American principles of liberty, and opposed to "fanatical abolition." Because the North was fighting against slavery, it was not only in "treasonable rebellion" against the Constitution, but also in rebellion "against the word, providence and government of God." Smyth declared that slavery was part of God's providential plan and that "God is working out a problem in the physical, social, political, industrial, and world-wide beneficial character of slavery," and the Confederacy clearly played a role in the plan. "In this war the South, therefore, is on God's side. She has His word, and providence, and omnipotent government with her." Whereas the North was fighting against God, Confederates could be sure that God "will . . . defend and deliver His people, who walk in His statutes and commandments blameless."[32]

Like Smyth, other prominent ministers reviewed both the moral issues and the political controversies that led to secession and found the South justified. On the eve of war, the well-known James Henry Thornwell, of South Carolina, reviewed the territorial controversy with the North and the slavery provisions of the Constitution. He concluded that Southerners should "be put upon the same footing" as the North with regard to slavery and that the federal government should "have no preference as to the character, in this respect, of any future States to be added to the Union." Not all Northerners were abolitionists, he admitted, but "the general, almost the universal, attitude of the Northern mind is one of hostility to slavery." Warming to his subject, Thornwell declared that with these attitudes the North was likely to make the South "a subject province" and "circumscribe the area of slavery . . . surround it with a circle of non-slaveholding States." This situation would lead to "the extinction of slavery," just as girdling an oak would kill the strongest tree. The South, he concluded, was "driven to the wall" and had no choice but to secede.[33]

Others justified the South's course with biblical as well as political arguments. In the view of Rev. Daniel Dreher, of Concord, North Carolina, the South's separation from the North, like Abraham's separation from Lot, was "inevitable" and necessary. Not only were the two sections different and antagonistic, but the North was guilty of beginning the strife. Its "murderous and licentious" troops were committing "heartless barbarities," and the North's action was "only a repetition of the conduct of Cain on an enlarged scale." God could be expected "to put His mark upon it, as He did on Cain." And Robert Newton Sledd, in Petersburg, Virginia, told his congregation that the leaders of Christ's church in the North had decided to "sacrifice the Word of God rather than the principle of abolitionism." Because they would not admit that slavery was right, they had destroyed the authority of the Bible. Confederates, on the other hand, as George F. Pierce pointed out to a Bible convention in Georgia, had acknowledged God in their constitution, and this recognition, "confessed by the chief magistrate, re-echoed by subordinate rulers, pervading the legislation of the country, presiding over public opinion, . . . will be a safe-guard in revolution, a guide in peace, a Pharos, beaming light and hope upon the future."[34]

Bishop Stephen Elliott proclaimed that God had a special mission for the South. God's word was spreading across the globe, except for Africa.

To convert that continent, God's plan called for a proselytizing agent that could "bear the burden of this work" successfully "through a like physiological structure, through a oneness of blood and of race." Elliott declared: "I find this agency in the African slaves now dwelling upon this Continent and educating among ourselves." Thus, Southerners had a vital role to play as slave owners in God's larger designs. "He has caused the African race to be planted here under our political protection and under our Christian nurture," Elliott said. Slavery in America would prepare them, "through a proper discipline, for the performance of this duty" of Christianizing Africa. It was up to Confederates to remember that "God has made us the guardians and champions of a people whom he is preparing for his own purposes."[35]

The emancipation sought by the North was an impious mistake, Elliott believed, for "the black race perishes with its freedom." The United States' rise to power had been swift, until it was "shatter[ed]" by abolition, the "heinous" sin of interfering "with the will and ways of God" toward slavery. By attacking slavery the North engaged in "bold defiance of the word of God, and of the principles of his moral government." Elliott saw "fanaticism and infidelity" in the North, which had "virtually dethroned the God of the Bible." Even in trying times he assured his listeners that the Confederacy was in the right. "We are resisting a crusade — a crusade of license against law — of infidelity against the altars of the living God." While he challenged Southerners to live up to their divinely appointed responsibilities, Bishop Elliott never doubted "that we were fighting under the shield of the Lord of Hosts."[36]

Thus, the political and religious leaders of the South entered the war with an avowed certainty that their section was right — right because it was a slaveholding society. Moreover, they believed they were blessed and supported by God, whose word and plans affirmed slaveholding and the South's role in human progress. The slaveholding purpose of the Confederacy was clear, and the Confederate elite had a ready answer to the question, "What shall we do with the negro?" Their answer was, firmly, to keep him in slavery.

IN THE NORTH debates about slavery's status and future were tied to the Republican Party. This new political organization had risen swiftly to become the nemesis of Southern slaveholders. They viewed this party — and Republicans viewed themselves — as antislavery. But in the United States of

1860, to be antislavery was very different from being abolitionist, and this distinction produced huge differences between Republicans and abolitionists as the secession crisis developed. That fact has been lost in the celebratory version of history favored by American popular culture, but it was a reality that produced surprising results.[37] For as the Civil War approached, Lincoln and his party firmly pledged themselves to maintain slavery, indeed even to guarantee it against federal interference, in every state where it was legal.

The Republican Party sprang up in the North as a result of widespread popular discontent over the passage of the Kansas-Nebraska Act.[38] During the winter of 1854–55 groups of citizens met and protested this law, which would allow settlers to introduce slavery into the new territories of Kansas and Nebraska. Leaving it to the settlers to decide on the status of slavery constituted the doctrine of "popular sovereignty." Stephen Douglas, the Democratic senator from Illinois, had won passage of this bill in Congress with the backing of the administration of Franklin Pierce, and Mississippi's Jefferson Davis, the secretary of war, had helped to arrange Pierce's support. But what made Douglas's bill so controversial was that it repealed the Missouri Compromise. The lands that would now be organized as the territories of Kansas and Nebraska had been placed off-limits to slavery in 1820, but under the new law slavery could be practiced there. Many Northerners did not want slaves and slave owners to compete in the territories with free settlers. Such competition was an alarming prospect to all those who viewed the territories as "places for poor people to go to and better their condition," said a concerned Whig named Abraham Lincoln. "This they cannot be, to any considerable extent, if slavery shall be planted within them." Like other Northerners, he agreed that "we want them for the homes of free white people."[39]

Thus, the Republican Party came into being as a party against the extension of slavery, even a party that wanted to exclude African Americans from the territories. Its core principle was opposition to the expansion of slavery, rather than action against slavery where it already existed. When the party ran its first candidate for president in 1856, its platform declared, in the opening sentence, that it was opposed "to the repeal of the Missouri Compromise; to the policy of the present Administration; [and] to the extension of Slavery into Free Territory." These founding Republicans believed that Congress had both the right and the "imperative duty" to prohibit slavery in the territories.[40] Four years later, when a stronger Republican Party contested the 1860 presidential election, its platform again denounced the offensive "dogma that the Constitution, of its own force, carries Slavery into any or all of the Territories of the United States." This idea, the platform declared, was a dangerous "political heresy" in conflict with the Constitution and "with legislative and judicial precedent." Republicans declared that the "normal condition of all the territory of the United States is that of freedom."[41]

By 1860 the new party also had expanded its platform, both to appeal to new and different sectors of the electorate and to assure voters that it was not a radical organization. Abolitionists, though growing in number, remained a small and widely despised group in the Northern states, and Republicans had always worked intently to separate their party from the radical claims for immediate abolition and racial equality. Moreover, by 1860 many citizens were increasingly fearful over the possible disruption of the Union, and Republicans were loath to present themselves as anything but devoted to its preservation. Accordingly, their platform stressed the continuity between the ideals and principles of the Founding Fathers and the Republican Party, and it expressed "abhorrence" for "all schemes of Disunion," which the party roundly denounced. Moreover, to make clear that the party was not a threat to the Union and that it deprecated John Brown's raid into Virginia, Republicans assured the slaveholding states that "the maintenance inviolate of the rights of the States, and especially the right of each State to order and control its own domestic institutions according to its own judgment exclusively, is essential to that balance of powers on which the perfection and endurance of our political fabric depends; and we denounce the lawless invasion by armed force of the soil of any State or Territory, no matter under what pretext, as among the gravest of crimes."[42]

As Lincoln sought his party's nomination for president, he was careful to make the same key point. During his rise to prominence in Illinois, he often sounded the theme that the only threat to the beloved Union was the effort of the South and its allies to extend slavery into new lands. Lincoln understood the importance of slavery, both in Illinois' past and to Southerners like his friends in Kentucky or his wife's family, many of whom were slaveholders. But like other Republicans, he insisted that the Founding Fathers had "expected and intended the institution of slavery to come to an end. They expected and intended that it should be in the course of ultimate extinction." Unfortunately, slave owners, wanting to reverse this expectation of "a peaceful end of slavery at sometime [*sic*]," had moved aggressively to overturn the Missouri Compromise and push bondage into new territories. Their action, and their action alone, threw a cloud over the Union's future. "Has any thing ever threatened the existence of this Union save and except this very institution of Slavery?" Lincoln asked. He presented Republicans as traditionalists who fully recognized slavery's "actual existence among us, and the difficulties of getting rid of it in any satisfactory way." Lincoln insisted that Republicans respected "all the constitutional obligations thrown about it."[43]

In 1860 Lincoln underlined these themes as he angled for greater visibility on the national stage. A great opportunity to gain exposure in the East arose when he was invited to deliver an address at the Cooper Union, in New York City. He arrived in the city nervous but intent on making a good impression. The tall and gangly Midwesterner had even brought a new suit, albeit an ill-fitting one. In his speech, he sought to justify the Republican Party by addressing a long closing section to Southerners—even though he did not expect that "they would listen."[44] In this section he argued that Republicans were not a purely sectional party and that they were, in fact, conservative. "We hold to no doctrine, and make no declaration," Lincoln said, that was not held and stated by the Founders. Moreover, Republican campaigns "are accompanied with a continual protest against any interference whatever with your slaves, or with you about your slaves." Republicans had no connection with slave revolts or with John Brown's attempt to incite a slave revolt. Letting slavery alone, Lincoln concluded, was the Republican policy, "because that much is due to the necessity arising from its actual presence in the nation."[45]

But in a more antislavery vein, Lincoln argued that the difference between North and South resolved itself into a difference over the morality and desirability of slavery. "Their thinking it right, and our thinking it wrong, is the precise fact upon which depends the whole controversy," he said. Republicans would and should consider Southern demands "and yield to them if, in our deliberate view of our duty, we possibly can." But that consideration could not extend to allowing slavery "to spread into the National Territories, and to overrun us here in these Free States." Lincoln endorsed the views of Thomas Jefferson on what might be the long-term solution to the problem: "In the language of Mr. Jefferson, uttered many years ago, 'It is still in our power to direct the process of emancipation, and deportation, peaceably, and in such slow degrees, as that the evil will wear off insensibly; and their places be, *pari passu,* filled up by white laborers.'" The emancipation referred to,

Lincoln hastened to add, was not emancipation by the federal government, but a decision undertaken by "the slaveholding States only."[46]

No sooner was Lincoln elected than the process of secession began, and before he could be inaugurated the new Republican president-elect faced a divided nation. Surely, this placed Lincoln in an agonizing situation, for he was emotionally devoted to the Union and to the promise of government by the people embodied in the U.S. Constitution. He had spoken frequently about his devotion to the Union. In an earlier phase in his career he had even declared, "Much as I hate slavery, I would consent to the extension of it rather than see the Union dissolved, just as I would consent to any GREAT evil, to avoid a GREATER one."[47] To justify his opposition to slavery's extension, he had denounced efforts to extend slavery as the source of threats to the Union. Yet Lincoln certainly knew that his brilliant leadership in arousing the Northern public and in defining the Republican Party's ideology had exacerbated the sectional conflict. Southern leaders feared Lincoln's influence and vilified his party as "Black Republicans." A president-elect who insisted that he loved the Union and regarded Southerners as no worse than Northerners would have been in their place, now had become a primary inciting cause for the apparent destruction of the Union. How could he hold the Union together and remain true to the anti-slavery-extension principles that were fundamental to the new party he had done so much to create?

Urged by many to make some reassuring statement to the South, Lincoln generally refused, explaining that all his statements were clearly on the public record and that new declarations were likely to be distorted or misinterpreted in the current atmosphere of crisis. But in a confidential private letter he could be more forthcoming. Alexander Stephens, soon to be the Confederacy's vice president, was someone with whom Lincoln had enjoyed cordial relations during his years in Congress. Writing frankly, Lincoln acknowledged that "the rub" between Northerners and Southerners lay in the fact that, "You think slavery is *right* and ought to be extended; while we think it is *wrong* and ought to be restricted." But Lincoln also asked his former colleague, "Do the people of the South really entertain fears that a Republican administration would, *directly*, or *indirectly*, interfere with their slaves?" Without qualification, Lincoln assured Stephens, "There is no cause for such fears."[48] This assurance, though consistent with the Republican platform, remained private and confidential.

Once Southern states had chosen to leave the Union, and gave no sign of recanting, the burden of decision fell on the North. In the words of Eric

Foner, would "the North refuse to let the South secede?"[49] Many voices cried out for a compromise. Even in the Republican Party, powerful forces, including the eastern business community, were pressing Lincoln to take action to defuse the crisis.[50] Faced with these tormenting pressures, Lincoln chose first the role of dependable party leader. He decided not to compromise on the issue of slavery in the territories — the question that had first brought his party into being and was vitally important to its most devoted members.[51] He held firm on that central tenet of the organization, but on other matters he was willing to be accommodating. In fact, as he held out an olive branch to the South, he proved willing to go very far indeed, and his desire to regain the understanding and cooperation of white Southerners would become an enduring hallmark of his policies.

In his First Inaugural Address Lincoln straightaway addressed the "apprehension" among Southerners that their "property, and their peace, and personal security, are to be endangered" by his administration. There had never been, he affirmed, any "reasonable cause" for such fears. Lincoln quoted from one of his own speeches: "I have no purpose, directly or indirectly, to interfere with the institution of slavery in the States where it exists. I believe I have no lawful right to do so, and I have no inclination to do so." He then cited a section of the 1860 Republican platform on which he had been elected. This was "a law" drawn by the Republican delegates for "themselves, and to me." That section, quoted above, promised to maintain "inviolate" all the rights of the states, "and especially the right of each State to order and control its own domestic institutions according to its own judgment exclusively." Although Lincoln declared that the Union could not be broken, and pledged to "hold, occupy, and possess" federal property and "collect the duties and imposts," he assured Southerners that "there will be no invasion — no using of force against, or among the people anywhere." Near the end of his address, he took note of the fact that Congress had proposed an amendment to the Constitution, "to the effect that the federal government, shall never interfere with the domestic institutions of the States." The intent, he explicitly observed, was to cover "persons held to service," or slaves. This proposal, which Lincoln had secretly had a hand in shaping, was already "implied constitutional law," and therefore he had "no objection to its being made express, and irrevocable."[52]

Thus Lincoln began his presidency with an offer to guarantee permanently the status of slavery in every state where it already existed. The existing institution, which he believed was "*wrong*, and ought to be restricted" from new territory, thus would have gained security for all time from federal interference. A disappointed Frederick Douglass, an ex-slave and abolitionist, wrote that the new president had declared "his complete loyalty to slavery in the slave States."[53]

Nor was Lincoln the only Republican willing to concede much to Southerners in the interests of avoiding war. In the closing days of the Republican-dominated Thirty-sixth Congress, legislators passed a bill organizing the Dakota, Nevada, and Colorado territories, with no mention of the idea that slavery should be excluded there.[54] And in July 1861, the Thirty-seventh Congress passed the Crittenden-Johnson Resolutions, which declared that "disunionists" had forced the war upon the "constitutional Government," which now fought only to preserve the Union. The North did not fight for conquest or subjugation or for any purpose "of overthrowing or interfering with the rights or established institutions" of the Southern states. Moreover, the Union that was to be preserved would respect "the dignity, equality, and rights of the several States unimpaired." As soon as the Union could be restored, fighting would cease.[55]

To Lincoln and the federal government the racist question, "What shall we do with the negro?" had not even arisen, because he and Congress had pledged that African Americans could remain in slavery, their bondage protected from interference by the federal government. Despite Lincoln's support for the Founders' hope that slavery might be on a path to "ultimate extinction," the initial policy of the Lincoln administration was to leave African American slaves exactly as Confederates wanted them: enslaved.

BECAUSE THE WAR changed circumstances and would alter policies, it is useful to examine more closely Lincoln's prewar statements about the future of African Americans. His views in the 1850s, developed over his life to that time, were the ground from which his wartime thoughts would grow, and though society would change, the key elements of his thinking did not disappear. What did Lincoln want for African Americans? How did he view their capabilities? Did he foresee a role for them in American society?

Race was a highly charged topic for any politician to address in the sectional crisis, especially a Republican trying to build support for his party in complex and highly contested terrain. The political realities were challenging. The political landscape was changing rapidly in the 1850s. Divisions between North and South were increasing ominously, and within the

North there was a yawning gap between the views of idealistic reformers and those of ordinary citizens. Republicans could gain strength by opposing the extension of slavery, but if they did so too stridently, they might arouse fears that they were endangering the Union. The young party needed to attract support from the ranks of abolitionists, but if it did so too effectively, it would damage its own prospects by appearing to *be* abolitionist. Similarly, Republicans knew they could benefit from increasing the Northern voter's dissatisfaction with the status quo, but if they criticized it too sharply, they might have to specify what would replace it. Abraham Lincoln became a leader in his party because he showed great skill in navigating these treacherous waters. As Richard Hofstadter observed, Lincoln creatively filled the role of political propagandist for his party.[56]

Lincoln was personally opposed to slavery. He felt that it was immoral and wrong. Slavery, he wrote in 1855 to his close friend Joshua Speed, "has, and continually exercises, the power of making me miserable." He recalled a journey in which he and Speed had witnessed "ten or a dozen slaves, shackled together with irons." That sight, Lincoln said, "was a continual torment to me." He empathized with the suffering of slaves and confessed that "I hate to see the poor creatures hunted down, and caught, and carried back to their stripes, and unrewarded toils."[57] For political reasons, Lincoln did not voice these feelings publicly, stressing instead slavery's ill effects on white Northern voters and on the nation, but they were real.

It probably was because of these strong moral feelings that in public Lincoln insisted on the basic humanity of black Americans. When referring to slaves in a legal sense, he preferred the phrase "persons bound to service" to the heartless word "property." Never was his emphasis on the African American's humanity more clear than in his Peoria speech in opposition to the Kansas-Nebraska Act. With this speech, in October 1854, he first stepped onto the national stage. In it, he strongly challenged those who viewed African Americans as things. The behavior of Southerners themselves, he argued, proved that they knew the truth of black people's humanity. Southerners had joined in declaring the African slave trade to be piracy, they "despise[d]" the slave traders among themselves, and they had voluntarily liberated property in slaves whose value ran into the hundreds of millions of dollars. What impelled Southerners to free slaves, "at vast pecuniary sacrifices"? Surely, it was their "sense of justice, and human sympathy," emotions that cried out that "the poor negro has some natural right to himself." Scorning those who felt that their "*perfect* liberty" involved "the liberty of making slaves of other people," Lincoln attacked Stephen Douglas's reasoning about popular sovereignty and "the doctrine of self government." In Kansas, the relevance of that doctrine "depends upon whether a negro is *not* or *is* a man. If he is *not* a man, why in that case, he who *is* a man may, as a matter of self-government, do just as he pleases with him. But if the negro *is* a man, is it not to that extent, a total destruction of self-government, to say that he too shall not govern *himself*? When the white man governs himself that is self-government; but when he governs himself, and also governs *another* man, that is *more* than self-government—that is despotism."[58]

By raising these questions, Lincoln suggested that black people were, indeed, human beings. The logic of American political values would then lead directly to Jefferson's "self-evident" truth that all human beings "are created equal" and possess God-given rights. But Lincoln shrank from asserting that African Americans were equal. Although he quickly proceeded in his Peoria speech to quote the Declaration of Independence, he emphasized its language about "consent of the governed," rather than equality. In racial terms, the idea of equality was politically dangerous ground for Lincoln, and time and again he avoided or rejected it. Only on rare occasions did he acknowledge that the logic of his thought pointed clearly in that direction. At Peoria, he briefly permitted himself to say, "If the negro is a *man*, why then my ancient faith teaches me that 'all men are created equal'; . . . Allow ALL the governed an equal voice in the government, and that, and that only is self-government." In Chicago, in 1858, he momentarily went still further—as far as he ever did in any of his public statements—and challenged his audience: "Let us discard all this quibbling about this man and the other man, this race and that race and the other race being inferior, and therefore they must be placed in an inferior position. . . . Let us discard all these things, and unite as one people throughout this land, until we shall once more stand up declaring that all men are created equal."[59]

These statements, however, were the great exception to Lincoln's public discourse about the status and future of African Americans. On many more occasions, he explicitly reiterated that he was not speaking in favor of any change in the social or political status of black people. In the Peoria speech, as soon as he suggested that "the negro" was "a *man*," he reminded his listeners that he was not "contending for the establishment of political and social equality between the whites and blacks." "My own feelings will not admit of this," he had stated earlier in the address, and "we well know that those of the great mass of white people will not."

Moreover, racial prejudice was not something that Lincoln imagined he could change. "A universal feeling," Lincoln declared, "whether well or ill-founded, can not be safely disregarded. We can not, then make them equals." In 1858, during one of his debates with Stephen Douglas, and in a district where antiblack feeling ran high, Lincoln made an uncompromising assertion of his own prejudice.

> I am not, nor ever have been in favor of bringing about in any way the social and political equality of the white and black races,— . . . I am not nor ever have been in favor of making voters or jurors of negroes, nor of qualifying them to hold office, nor to intermarry with white people; and I will say in addition to this that there is a physical difference between the white and black races which I believe will for ever forbid the two races living together on terms of social and political equality. And inasmuch as they cannot so live, while they do remain together there must be the position of superior and inferior, and I as much as any other man am in favor of having the superior position assigned to the white race.[60]

Rather than focusing on the status of African Americans, Lincoln found it more useful politically to emphasize the dangers to the North of the South's desire to expand slavery. The proslavery policy of Southern leaders had already captured the Buchanan administration and the Supreme Court. Slavery "soiled" the nation's "republican robe," deprived America's "republican example of its just influence in the world," gave white Southerners a new and unfair advantage over Northerners in representation in Congress, and spoiled the territories—which were supposed to be the great reservoir of opportunity for ordinary citizens—as "places for poor people to go to and better their condition."

Moreover, as conflict raised the stakes, Lincoln worked to persuade Northerners that they faced an even greater threat. In his famous "House Divided" speech, in 1858, Lincoln declared that the government "cannot endure, permanently half *slave* and half *free*. . . . It will become *all* one thing, or *all* the other." Worse than this troubling but vague prediction was the reality, he argued, that the demonstrable "*tendency*" was in the direction of universal slavery. Through the conspiratorial efforts of Franklin Pierce, James Buchanan, Stephen Douglas, and Roger Taney, slavery was controlling the government. In the future, Lincoln warned, "We shall *lie down* pleasantly dreaming that the people of *Missouri* are on the verge of making their State *free;* and we shall *awake* to the *reality,* instead, that the *Supreme* Court has made *Illinois* a *slave* State."[61] Such charges about an aggressive "slave power" did much to bring Northern voters into the ranks of the Republican Party.

If Republicans were to prevail, on the other hand, and if slavery were again "placed where the public mind shall rest in the belief that it is in course of ultimate extinction," then the question, What shall we do with the negro? returned. "Ultimate extinction" would raise the question: What status would freed slaves subsequently enjoy? On this issue, Lincoln offered one hint and a more definite answer. His most positive statements, such as the Chicago speech in 1858, carried the suggestion that African Americans, though not equal to whites, had some basic rights. In the Republican Party generally, concludes Eric Foner, a mainstream view was developing that blacks "were human beings and citizens of the United States, entitled to the natural rights of humanity and to such civil rights as would protect the natural rights of life, liberty, and property."[62] Lincoln expressed this as "the right to eat the bread" they earned by their own labor. The inalienable rights to life, liberty, and the pursuit of happiness, he argued, were not equally enjoyed in 1776 even by all white men, but the Founders meant to "set up a standard maxim for free society," and Lincoln hoped it would be honored and aspired to, rather than discarded.[63]

His other answer, stated much more frequently and prominently, was colonization—removal of African Americans from U.S. soil. Lincoln's interest in colonization was persistent during the prewar period and active far into his presidency. In the Peoria speech, though he acknowledged the difficulty of "get[ting] rid of" slavery, he stated, "If all earthly power were given to me . . . my first impulse would be to free all the slaves, and send them to Liberia." He went on to acknowledge that large challenges and practical difficulties rendered the "sudden execution" of this idea "impossible." But speed was not a top priority. He concluded this section of his speech by averring, "It does seem to me that systems of gradual emancipation might be adopted," and in later speeches he continued to return to the idea of colonization. In June 1857, for example, he stated: "The enterprise is a difficult one; but 'when there is a will there is a way'; and what colonization needs most is a hearty will. Will springs from the two elements of moral sense and self-interest. Let us be brought to believe it is morally right, and, at the same time, favorable to, or, at least, not against, our interest, to transfer the African to his native clime, and we shall find a way to do it, however great the task may be."[64]

President Lincoln's will was hearty enough to make him take practical steps to find a way. In April 1861, just hours before Southerners attacked Fort Sumter, Lincoln met and talked with a representative of the Chiriqui Improvement Company, an enterprise founded in 1855 with the idea of using freed slaves to develop coal and farm lands in Panama. This meeting marked the beginning of efforts by his administration to launch a process of colonization. In these efforts, Lincoln had the strong support of the influential Blair family. Its patriarch, Francis Preston Blair, had for decades been a leading Democrat in Washington before he helped to found the Republican Party. One of his sons, Frank, was a force in Missouri politics, and the other, Montgomery, was Lincoln's postmaster general. According to Lincoln's close friend Ward Lamon, Francis P. Blair and the president had "from the first to last a confidential relationship as close as that maintained by Mr. Lincoln with any other man. To Mr. Blair he almost habitually revealed himself upon delicate and grave subjects more freely than to any other."[65] Lincoln's will, and the Blairs' interest, meant that the Chiriqui company and other colonization ideas would receive serious consideration and active support in the White House.

Thus, as the war began, Lincoln's public record revealed an explicit but nuanced set of positions. They included a solemn inaugural pledge not to interfere with slavery in the South and a repeated preference for colonization in Africa or other areas abroad. Alongside these positions stood his belief that African Americans, though not equal, were human beings and should be entitled to some basic rights, if slavery were somehow to become "extinct." The historian and Lincoln biographer, Mark Neely Jr., has called Lincoln's "vagueness about the eventual 'extinction' of slavery . . . perhaps the most intellectually dishonest part of his program." The intellectual dishonesty stemmed both from his unwillingness to discuss how extinction might come about and from his use of this elision to evade questions about the status of free African Americans. Lincoln and the Republicans did not want "to deal with the question of race."[66] If freedom came, however, his preference for colonization of black Americans outside the United States was clear.

The tumult of war would quickly force change of many kinds on both North and South. The extinction of slavery and the status of African Americans in freedom moved from conjecture toward reality. Eventually, both the North and the South would confront directly the question, "What shall we do with the negro?" The dilemmas inherent in the question first confronted the North.

PART ONE

Northern Developments

ONE

THE NORTH CONFRONTS THE QUESTION

War is the preeminent agent of change, a potent force that alters institutions, beliefs, and social customs to create a new and unanticipated reality. The Civil War shook the bedrock of American institutions and beliefs, forcing both North and South to entertain ideas that had been unthinkable. Under the coercive force of events, leaders and ordinary citizens would resist the new and hang on to old ways of thinking, slowing but not stopping the current of change.

In the North the universal conviction that slavery in the states was not to be disturbed came under question with surprising swiftness. Only two weeks after Congress adopted the Crittenden-Johnson Resolutions, it passed a law confiscating slave property used in direct support of the rebellion. In less than six months many people throughout the North were asking whether slavery should be ended through the war. By early 1862, newspapers, periodicals, and policymakers were discussing the future location and status of black Americans if they became free. A more general discussion also developed about the different races of humankind, the nature and capabilities of African Americans, and how other nations experienced emancipation. Slowly, gingerly, and with ample attention to political interests, Abraham Lincoln entered the Northern dialogue, advocating the most conservative possible plan for abolition and urging colonization of African Americans outside the United States. Though offensive to Democrats, his initiatives lagged far behind the evolving views of many Northerners. By January 1, 1863, when the Emancipation Proclamation became final, the president and his allies had established these positions: that freedom was not an object but a means of victory; that colonization was a major goal; and that no ideas of racial equality were being entertained.

MANY NORTHERNERS had suspected that secession was a ploy designed to extract concessions from the North, and many more, including Abraham Lincoln, believed that Unionism remained strong in the South. But once the actual fighting began, a more sober and steely attitude began to develop. Less than three weeks after the surrender of Fort Sumter, an issue of *Harper's Weekly* announced that "the war has now begun in earnest." Moreover, this popular national journal, with 200,000 subscribers and an estimated one million readers, was in earnest about the means to prosecute the war. "The practical effect of a war in the Southern States," it warned, "must be to liberate the slaves. This should be well understood." The editors foresaw that many slaves would run away from their masters to enter Union lines. Although Union commanders initially were returning these fugitives to their owners, the editors promptly declared that it was not the duty of U.S. soldiers to catch and return runaways.[1]

In reaching this conclusion *Harper's Weekly* had anticipated the action of General Benjamin Butler by only a few weeks. On May 23, Butler, who had been a conservative Democrat and a supporter of the South's John C. Breckinridge, refused to return three fugitive slaves who had entered his lines. These slaves had been working on Confederate fortifications, and Butler declared that they were "contraband of war." He declined to deliver them back to the enemy, where they would be used against U.S. forces. News of Butler's action spread rapidly, providing an example for some other U.S. commanders and attracting approximately a thousand slaves to Butler's army within several weeks.[2]

Soon *Harper's Weekly* observed that Congress would have to face the question of what to do with runaway slaves, and the tone of its article clearly suggested that loyal citizens should not be taxed to defray the costs of identifying and returning slaves to rebellious owners. In July the *Atlantic Monthly* argued that the North should stop "conscientiously strain[ing] at gnats of Constitutional clauses" while Southerners did not hesitate to "gulp down whole camels of treason." Slavery was "the root of the rebellion," declared the magazine, and "war is proving itself an Abolitionist, whoever else is. Practically speaking, the verdict is already entered" against slavery. Looking ahead, the *Atlantic Monthly* foresaw "the adoption of the John-Quincy-Adams policy of military emancipation" as "an ultimate necessity." Black newspapers also argued for abolition, with the *Anglo-African,* of New York City, declaring that "liberty, universal and complete" was the only path to restoring the Union.

"Permanent peace cannot be restored," warned other blacks in a petition written by Dr. J. W. C. Pennington, until slavery was ended.[3]

Then, on July 21, 1861, at Bull Run in northern Virginia, the Confederate army inflicted a shocking defeat on Union forces. All Northerners, not just the terrified picnickers who had been compelled to flee back toward Washington, D.C., now had added reason to take the war seriously. Only two weeks earlier, Congress had officially resolved that the war was not being fought for any purpose of "overthrowing or interfering with the rights or established institutions" of the rebellious states. But in early August it passed its first Confiscation Act, which provided that the owner of any slave used in direct support of the Southern military forfeited "his claim to such labor, any law of the State or of the United States to the contrary notwithstanding." "During those two weeks," according to James M. McPherson, "the meaning of Union defeat at Bull Run had sunk in." At the end of August, a *New York Times* correspondent observed that "Public sentiment is undergoing a change."[4]

The same change of sentiment occurred rapidly in the army. "Soldier after soldier," concludes Chandra Manning, "began to insist that since slavery had caused the war, only the destruction of slavery could end the war." A Wisconsin soldier explained that "the rebellion is abolitionizing the whole army" and told readers of a newspaper back home, "You have no idea of the changes that have taken place in the minds of the soldiers." By the fall of 1861 enlisted men throughout the rank and file "championed the destruction" of slavery, "well before most civilians, political leaders, or officers did."[5] The seriousness of the rebellion was persuading many Northerners that "the abolition of slavery," not just a return to "the Union as it was, and the Constitution as it is," was needed.[6] This fact raised the question — which was a troubling conundrum for most whites — "What shall be done with the slaves?"

In the field in Missouri, one general had a ready answer. John C. Frémont, the Republican Party's candidate for president in 1856, declared martial law on August 30, and proclaimed that the property of anyone in arms against the United States was confiscated, "and their slaves, if any they have, are hereby declared free."[7] Public reaction outside the border states was largely favorable. The *New York Evening Post* said, "Mr. Frémont has done what the Government ought to have done from the beginning. War is war." The *New York Tribune* observed that if the slaveholders could be brought to reason, Frémont was "the man to do it." The *Albany Journal* wrote, "Gen. Frémont 'hits the nail on the head' exactly." The *Albany Statesman* said that Frémont's measures should have been applied to the whole South six months earlier. "It strikes the right note," judged the *Rochester Democrat.* The *Cincinnati Gazette* was pleased that "rebellion is to be treated as a crime." In the analysis of the *Cincinnati Commercial,* the rebels had brought this on themselves: "The secessionists themselves are the real abolitionists." The *Boston Post* agreed, arguing that rebel "defiance" was striking this blow at the slaveholders' beloved institution.[8]

The reaction of the *New York Times* was interesting and telling. The editor and proprietor of the *Times,* Henry Raymond, had played an active role in founding the Republican Party and would become chairman of the party's national committee in 1864. He reflected Republican thinking but also remained alert to defend the Lincoln administration when countering the main currents of criticism in predominantly Democratic New York State. Initially, Raymond's *Times* depicted Frémont's action as fully in tune with Congress's Confiscation Act and hailed the proclamation as "by far the most important event of the war." Although the United States had tried to be respectful of slaveholders' rights, the nation needed to "take from treason every weapon by which it can strike the deadly blow." If the rebellion continued, "slavery must inevitably perish," and the *Times* was glad that "hereafter, Slavery will not be allowed to stand in the way of a vigorous prosecution of the war." The paper also argued that because the war would, in fact, dissolve slavery, slave owners would recognize in Frémont's action a powerful "incentive to peace." But soon Raymond learned that Lincoln, anxious to avoid offending border state sentiment, was going to overrule Frémont. Then the paper abruptly changed its tune; it decided that Frémont had gone beyond the letter of the law and argued that Lincoln had to set the general's proclamation aside.[9]

The *Times*'s tactical retreat could not disguise the fact that an antislavery logic was moving public opinion. This logic flowed naturally from two widely accepted propositions. Northerners well understood, as Lincoln would observe in his *Second Inaugural Address,* that slavery was at the root of the conflict. Even more compelling was the fact that slaves and slavery were being used as assets to the rebellion. To strike at slavery was to wound the rebels' cause. Therefore it made sense to take action against slavery, if not for the slaves' or for humanity's benefit, then for the greater success of Union armies. The *Times* continued to acknowledge this fact even while offering support to a president who was proceeding at a different pace and with different priorities. Reacting to a speech in New York City by Charles Sumner in which the Massachusetts senator had emphasized that slavery must be ended to defeat the rebellion, the *Times* declared, "We have no shadow of doubt that Slavery will receive its death-blow in the progress of this rebellion." But the paper then argued that the practical realities of governing were complex, not simple, and that it was best to leave this outcome to the voluntary action of the border states.[10]

In taking this position, Henry Raymond's paper bowed to the analysis and differing priorities of the president. Abraham Lincoln believed not only that the Union had to retain the border states if it hoped to win, but also that the future cooperation of Southern whites would be essential for a successful reconstruction of the Union. To avoid offending whites, his administration had refused the help of black volunteers in Boston, New York, Philadelphia, and other cities. While hoping for an "ultimate extinction" of slavery at some time in the indefinite future, he had repeatedly pledged himself to respect the rights of his slave-owning countrymen, who, far from being evil, were "just what we would be in their situation." Long after his inaugural address, Lincoln continued to hope that "the mystic chords of memory" would draw white Americans together and restore good feelings between Northerners and the seceded Southerners, who were "not enemies, but friends" sharing "bonds of affection."[11]

These sentiments of identity with Southern whites and respect and fraternity toward them were sincere. They also had a personal dimension. Lincoln himself had been born in Kentucky; more importantly, slaveholding Southern whites were part of his family through his marriage to Mary Todd. The war tore the Todd family in two, with six children supporting the Union and eight the Confederacy. As Mary's husband, Lincoln offered positions to brothers-in-law who instead chose to side with the Confederacy. During the war Lincoln wrote passes for rebel Todds and welcomed into the White House Mary's grieving sister Emilie, widow of a Confederate general. The plight of Southern whites was not abstract to Lincoln, and his feelings of sympathy for them would persist to guide his actions throughout his presidency.[12] In the fall of 1861 they shaped his approach to slavery as forcefully as did his concern for the border states.

Before the year was out, Lincoln's first secretary of war had advanced the logic that the Union must attack slavery because the institution was a key asset to the rebels. In a well-publicized initiative, Simon Cameron (in what would be one of his last significant acts before he was replaced by Edwin Stanton) proposed that the federal government arm the slaves and use them to fight against the rebellion. Promptly Lincoln forced Cameron to withdraw his proposal. The president was far from ready to support either freeing the slaves or arming them.

A growing number of Lincoln's supporters reacted in dismay. The staunchly Republican *Chicago Tribune* declared that this latest of Lincoln's conservative decisions demonstrated that the president was not a bold leader but an "old fogy." The "four millions of black Unionists" were "ready to help us," declared the *Tribune.* They should be used to save the Union, even as James Madison in 1780 had suggested using slaves to win the American Revolution. In harsh language the *Tribune* declared that "Old Abe is now unmasked, and we are sold out."[13] If not betrayed, the paper was right to judge presidential policies as cautious.

Lincoln favored a conservative approach to the subject of emancipation. His views were grounded in acceptance of the power and scope of American racism and in the principles of voluntary state action and national responsibility. Acting on these principles, the president late in November drew up two bills laying out alternate paths to voluntary and compensated emancipation in Delaware, where slaves constituted less than 2 percent of the population. Both plans promised monetary compensation from the federal treasury. In the first, state legislators would decide to free one-fifth of Delaware's slaves each year until slavery ended in 1867; all minor children born to slave mothers would have to serve an apprenticeship, until age 21 for males and age 18 for females. The second plan—which Lincoln considered "better"—provided for a much slower process. Legal slavery would continue for thirty-one years, until 1893. After the date of passage of the act, however, those who reached age 35 would gain their freedom. So, too, would all those newly born to slave mothers, but these children would be required to serve an apprenticeship until age 21 for males and 18 for females, as in the first scheme.[14] Thus, as a practical matter, in the second plan most of Delaware's slaves would have to wait until age 35 to gain their freedom, and most black children born after passage of the bill would serve apprenticeships. The few unlucky individuals whose slave mothers gave birth to them near the end of the thirty-one-year period would still be bound as apprentices well into the twentieth century. Lincoln had his plan printed and distributed to members of the Delaware legislature. Within its general terms he was open to modifications of the effective date, but whatever date might be chosen, his plan envisioned a gradual emancipation, one in which slave owners would continue for many years to benefit from the labor of at least some of their slaves. Delaware's lawmakers did not act on his proposal.

A few days later, on December 3, in his first annual address to Congress, Lincoln put forward the other major element of his thinking about emancipation: colonization. He noted that Congress's Confiscation Act had liberated some individuals, who were now "dependent on the United States," and he speculated that some states "for their own benefit" might pass similar laws. Therefore, Congress should find some means to give the states financial credit for these persons, and "in any event" steps should be taken "for colonizing [them] at some place, or places, in a climate congenial to them. It might be well to consider, too,—whether the free colored people already in the United States could not, so far as individuals may desire, be included in such colonization." To make this proposal workable, Lincoln asked for funds to acquire territory and to facilitate the removal of blacks to it. Whites would benefit from these steps. To those who might object that "the only legitimate object of acquiring territory is to furnish homes for white men," Lincoln explained that "this measure effects that object; for the emigration of colored men leaves additional room for white men remaining or coming here."[15]

Then he argued that his proposal amounted to an "absolute necessity—that, without which the government itself cannot be perpetuated." The war was continuing, and he was "anxious" that it "not degenerate into a violent and remorseless revolutionary struggle." Apparently Lincoln feared that a deepening of the conflict would doom the government by making amicable reunion impossible. On the other hand, a policy of compensation and colonization would respect the rights of slaveholders and address their passionate objections to living in a country with freed slaves. Slave owners would be compensated, and freed blacks would be removed. The Union could be restored without a troubling black presence. The "integrity of the Union," Lincoln added, remained "the primary object of the contest on our part."[16]

Following up on this annual address, Lincoln asked Congress on March 6, 1862, to pledge its support for his proposed policy of gradual, compensated emancipation by the states. In providing "pecuniary aid" to a slave state, the nation would "compensate for the inconveniences public and private, produced by such change of system." Moreover, he argued, for the Union this was a measure of "self-preservation." The rebels hoped that the United States would eventually be forced to recognize the independence "of some part of the disaffected region," and they believed that once that happened, all the slave states in the Union would go over to the Confederacy. Preventing that event and "depriv[ing] them of that hope," however, "substantially ends the rebellion; and the initiation of emancipation completely deprives them of it, as to all the states initiating it." Again Lincoln emphasized that he favored "gradual, and not sudden emancipation" and that he claimed no right of the federal government "to interfere with slavery within state limits." In closing, he pledged that the war would cease "at once" if the rebels gave a "practical re-acknowledgement" of federal authority. He warned that "ruin" follows from war and indicated that it was his responsibility to use "all indispensable means" to preserve the Union.[17]

On the same day, Montgomery Blair, Lincoln's postmaster general, argued vigorously for colonization in a letter to a citizens' meeting at the Cooper Union, in New York City. "The difficult question with which we have to deal," Blair asserted, was "the question of race." White workingmen in the South and in the North would not tolerate "equality of the negroes with them, and consequently amalgamation." Their intolerance stemmed not from "bad passion" but from the natural and desirable "instinct of self-preservation." Blair insisted that Thomas Jefferson had been right to believe that separation of the races was essential. Whites should have "the lands intended for them by the Creator" in the temperate zones, where the black race "cannot maintain itself." It was not necessary to meet the challenge of "immediate, universal, or involuntary transportation," said Blair. If the government would merely announce a settled policy to remove emancipated slaves, "the more enterprising would soon emigrate, and multitudes of less energy would follow." In "but few generations," he predicted, whites would have "exclusive occupation" of the "temperate regions of America," and "the only obstacle to a perpetual union of the States" would be removed.[18]

Congress cooperated with Lincoln's request, passing a resolution early in April that stated its willingness to support his plans for colonization. Although Congress gave its support, many of the publications that normally backed Lincoln expressed doubts about his plan, wanting to move more vigorously against slavery and questioning the wisdom and practicality of colonization. Even the *New York Times* greeted those passages in his annual message to Congress that dealt with colonization with open skepticism. The president's proposal would be costly, observed the *Times,* and would not produce benefits comparable to the expense. African Americans were "imperatively needed" as agriculturalists, and the paper predicted that the government would see the need to keep them "*here,* at home." Early in 1862 the *Times* condemned colonization as "impracticable" as well as undesirable and added in patronizing words that this "humble, submissive, docile race" could certainly be useful in the United States.[19]

Harper's Weekly insisted that only the progress of Northern armies would bring emancipation, observed that "the Union party at the South" was dead, and said, in a section of editorial opinion, that Lincoln was "not a great leader." "Slavery in this country is doomed," declared an issue in February 1862, and Congress would soon have to confront the question of what to do with the freedmen. A few weeks later the paper recommended that Congress declare the slaves' freedom and then create a new "sub-department of the Interior" to oversee their situation, maintain order with the help of the military, and aid "their advance to citizenship at . . . graduated times." Although the slaves' future was a question "that most people wish to shut their eyes upon," *Harper's Weekly* asserted that the freedmen would progress to be useful citizens. "They would be at first like a mass of rude immigrants; but after due lapse of time they would be quite as competent citizens as many other immigrants." "Exportation," the magazine declared, "is not practicable." Although its columns became more complimentary toward Lincoln personally, *Harper's Weekly* continued to criticize the exportation of four million probably unwilling people as an immense, costly, and impractical undertaking.[20]

Within a few months *Harper's Weekly* went much further. It dismissed colonization as the benighted and favorite idea of western men such as Senator James Doolittle, of Wisconsin, and Representative Frank P. Blair, of Missouri. Their basic problem was prejudice, observed the weekly, for "Western men generally object as much to free negroes as to slavery." Although slaves were proving to be the only trustworthy friends of the Union army in the South, Lincoln and Montgomery Blair, Frank Blair's brother, continued to support an "insane" colonization idea that would "deprive the country of labor." Postmaster General Blair's position was that "the white people of the United States will not live side by side with black men as their equals." But in contrast to these views, wrote the editor, "we have got . . . to go on unlearning prejudices, acquiring toleration." The United States' "weakness" has been "not to be able to tolerate negroes, except as slaves." According to *Harper's*, the nation's "destiny" was "to show that an educated and humane people can rise superior to prejudices which have proved an insuperable obstacle to the besotted planters of the West Indian Islands. It is our business to demonstrate that two races which have lived peacefully and prosperously side by side under a system which was a compound of the most brutal selfishness, the basest cruelty, and the most outrageous injustices, can get along at least as well when the selfishness, cruelty, and injustice are replaced by humanity, kindness, and fair-dealing."[21]

The *Cincinnati Daily Gazette,* a Republican paper, featured a letter from Senator B. Gratz Brown, of Missouri, who contradicted the president and opposed removal of African Americans. Speaking for itself, the *Gazette* admitted that Northerners might find colonization to be "a very comfortable doctrine" but insisted realistically that at best it could result in the transportation of only a small portion of the black population. Moreover, black people were "the foundation of [the South's] wealth," and their departure would mean "ruin." The proper policy, argued the *Gazette,* was to protect freedmen "in the country where they are, and where their labor is vital to its prosperity." What was certain was that "the negroes must continue where they are." The *Chicago Tribune,* another strongly Republican paper, lamented that "suggestions of deportation and colonization endorsed by the Government, will only be fertile in fostering hostility and animosity between races." By making concessions to racism, the government nurtured the evil. Moreover, it was clear that "we cannot by any process get rid of them." Instead of that approach, the *Tribune* took a moral and idealistic stance. "We must, as a nation, look upon the black race as injured and wronged," wrote the paper. "The public mind must be enlightened and liberalized."[22]

Periodicals that were generally more conservative also were looking in directions different from those the president advocated. The *Continental Monthly* was a New York magazine pledged to independence and to speaking "in a tone [in] no way tempered by partisanship" that had spun off from the more literary *Knickerbocker Magazine.* In February 1862, while Lincoln was pledging not to interfere with slavery in the states, the *Continental Monthly* identified "the True Basis" of the war as a struggle between one society based on "a permanently sunken class" and another founded on "equal rights and free labor." Emancipation must be "demanded" as the way to win the war, and the magazine urged its declaration "as a military necessity." Another idea put forward was to limit slavery's expansion by purchasing the slaves in Texas and turning that state into a free-labor cotton producer that could demonstrate the superiority of free labor. The *Continental Monthly* also dismissed "the absurd assertion that the emancipated negro lapses into barbarism and will not work" and asserted that even in slavery African Americans displayed an "intelligence above a large portion of the white laborers of Europe."[23]

The *New Englander*, a journal published in New Haven, Connecticut, and influenced by the conservative theology associated with Yale, had condemned "the great evil of abolitionism" in January 1861. Later that year it rejected the idea of a "victorious and domineering North holding in forced and unwilling submission a conquered and subjugated South." But by January 1862 this magazine was celebrating the opportunity presented to end slavery "in accordance with the law of confiscation." Ignoring the idea of government-funded colonization, an article that month saw a different path to a solution of the nation's racial problem. An "aversion" to racial mixing would make "amalgamation" impossible, and it was untrue that slaves would "refuse to labor in a state of freedom." They would enjoy working in agriculture as free laborers more than as slaves. Over time, as emigrants from the North poured into the South, the freed slaves would "move on toward the tropical latitudes so much more in consonance with their nature and inclinations." Thus, over time, according to this article, "voluntary emigration" would remove "the larger portion of the negroes on this continent" and "deliver us from the incubus of a black population in our midst." Within several months the *New Englander* would adopt a still more progressive stance and conclude that colonization was "entirely unnecessary and altogether undesirable." Asserting that "the country needs their labor," in the fall of 1862 the magazine voiced its disapproval of the "senseless prejudice" of Northerners who wanted to remove African Americans.[24]

Meanwhile, Frederick Douglass, a determined advocate of equality, was criticizing and prodding the president. Before Lincoln's March 1862 proposal to Congress, Douglass had judged the president to be as "destitute of any anti-slavery principle or feeling" as James Buchanan had been. Douglass's newspaper also presented varied evidence that black people, once freed, would of course work. "That the black man in slavery shirks labor," wrote Douglass, "only proves that he is a man." To illustrate the effects of incentive, he cited the example of slaves in New Orleans who had performed prodigious labors in order to earn their freedom. He also reprinted reports from Hilton Head, South Carolina, that contrabands were laboring "willingly and satisfactorily." When Lincoln proposed compensated emancipation to Congress, Douglass wrote with pleasure that this was "more than I ever ventured to hope," but needless to say, he opposed removal from the United States.

In answer to the question, "What shall we do with the negroes?" Douglass regularly answered, "Do nothing with them . . . let them alone." He advocated giving black people their rights, treating them justly, paying them fair wages, and then letting them rise or fall on their own, just as other men did. As Douglass's paper also pointed out, "THE CONTRABAND WILL FIGHT!" and could be a military asset to the Union. Other black leaders agreed that the contrabands should be "called into service, and formed into a liberating army."[25]

Douglass's pleasure with Lincoln turned to bitter disappointment in April and May 1862, when the president overruled General David Hunter's antislavery actions in the Department of the South, which included Georgia, Florida, and South Carolina. Hunter first declared freedom for the slaves and then began organizing a regiment of black soldiers. Hunter had been planning to raise an African American regiment for some time. He had written to Lincoln's secretary of war, the Democrat Edwin Stanton, in January 1862, saying, "Please let me have my way on the subject of slavery." Hunter had promised to "bear the blame" of his actions, and Stanton had received copies of the general's orders to enlist black soldiers. These raised no problem for the secretary of war, for he was "far ahead of Lincoln in his thinking" about black troops. Stanton had already decided, as his judge advocate general recalled, "that the war could never be successfully closed for the government, without the employment of colored troops in the field." "Acting guilefully," the secretary of war was trying "to put the President in a position where circumstances might force" him to accept emancipation and African American soldiers. Yet Lincoln, who had other priorities, swiftly decided to negate both measures, and Stanton had to assist in drawing up the necessary document.[26]

Reacting to Lincoln's proclamation against Hunter's emancipation edict, Douglass charged that the president was still working "to shield and protect slavery" and lamented that the black troops had been disbanded just "when the blow was most needed, and when it was about to be struck." Philip Bell, the editor of a black San Francisco newspaper named the *Pacific Appeal*, denounced Lincoln's act as a "pro-slavery proclamation" and charged that he was "encouraging the Rebels in their efforts to overthrow the Union, and perpetuate slavery." More supportive of Lincoln, the *Continental Monthly* held that Hunter had acted prematurely and that "the Executive policy" was "gradual emancipation for the sake of the white man." But "sooner or later," this journal predicted, Hunter's plan "will be adopted." In support of Lincoln, the *New York Times* pointed out that he had always "refused to make this war one of emancipation." Meanwhile, Douglass reprinted General Hunter's assessment that the blacks he had armed showed "great natural capacity for acquiring the duties of the soldier" and had been "eager, beyond all things, to take the field and be led into action." From other officers in occupied coastal areas came reports that the contrabands were "far more intelligent than the 'poor whites,'" "have a strong desire to learn," and furnished trustworthy information to U.S. troops.[27]

Lincoln's actions in the spring and summer of 1862 revealed an evolving but still cautious and constrained approach to the use of federal power against slavery. While declaring General Hunter's actions "altogether void," the president changed his position—from his disavowal in March of any claim "to interfere with slavery within state limits" to a statement that "I reserve to myself" the decision whether it was "competent for me, as Commander-in-Chief of the Army and Navy," to declare slaves free as a "necessity indispensable to the maintainance [*sic*] of the government." He then used the rest of his proclamation against General Hunter's acts to remind the slaveholding states of his proposal in March and to "earnestly appeal" to them to act and not be "blind to the signs of the times." In language that he had drafted but did not include in his final text, Lincoln pointed out that "the strong tendency to a total disruption of society in the South, is apparent." He was appealing to slaveholders to avoid emancipation as a result of military action by choosing instead his gradual, compensated, voluntary proposal, which "would come as gently as the dews of heaven, not rending or wrecking anything."[28]

Then, in July, Congress passed a second Confiscation Act, and Lincoln reacted by raising a complicated constitutional scruple. The new law authorized seizing the property of Southerners who were in arms or merely "aiding or abetting" the rebellion and declared that the slaves of such persons would be "forever free" as soon as they came under Union control. Military officers were not to return any more slaves, and the law authorized the president to use blacks to suppress the rebellion "in such manner as he may judge best" and to pursue voluntary colonization "in some tropical country beyond the limits of the United States."[29] Before the bill was passed, Lincoln threatened to veto it on the grounds that its provisions on seizure of property would violate the Constitution's requirement that "no Attainder of Treason shall work Corruption of Blood, or Forfeiture except during the Life of the Person attainted." In order to obtain his signature, legislators then passed a resolution denying any intention to affect the heirs of rebels.[30]

Public debate followed on the question whether confiscation would violate the Constitution's provision relating to "Attainder of Treason." The attorney William Whiting, a special counselor and later solicitor for the War Department, in 1862 published a treatise on the president's war powers that included discussion of the Second Confiscation Act. Reviewing English law, Whiting wrote that bills of attainder were legislative acts condemning a person to death, usually for treason, without trial. He concluded that Congress had unlimited power under the Constitution to punish treason. The section and language that concerned Lincoln, wrote Whiting, "does not limit the power of Congress to punish, but it limits the technical consequences of a special kind of punishment [i.e., Attainder], which may or may not be adopted in the statutes." Since Congress possessed the power to punish treason by death or unlimited fines, why, he asked, would it be denied the power to take property in any other form? "Congress has the power, under the constitution" he concluded, "to declare as the penalty for treason the forfeiture of all the real and personal estate of the offender," and he specifically assessed the Confiscation Act of 1862 as neither a bill of attainder nor an ex post facto law. According to James M. McPherson, Lincoln accepted the argument that slave property, though not real estate, could be confiscated.[31] Thus, in a slow and complicated way Lincoln's policy was evolving as it followed legal opinion and much of public opinion toward emancipation. In the North generally, the number of citizens who had concluded that only strong measures could subdue the rebellion was rapidly growing. "You can form no conception of the change," wrote Senator John Sherman to his brother, William T. Sherman.[32]

WITH THE POSSIBILITY of emancipation now visible on the horizon, the literate public in the North embarked upon a discussion of the capabilities and future role of freed African Americans. In fact, from the outset of the war, books about race and racial issues had attracted attention. One of the first studies to occasion comment was Sidney Fisher's book *The Laws of Race, as connected with Slavery,* which was published in Philadelphia in 1860. Fisher, a lawyer and author, had an uncompromising belief in black inferiority and the necessity of racial domination. In a confident, assertive manner, he argued that "the white race must of necessity, by reason of its superiority, govern the negro, wherever the two live together." Although slavery contradicted American values and should not expand, it was unavoidable as long as the black race was present. Fisher also held that blacks and whites could never "amalgamate" to form "a new species of man"; individuals who were the products of race mixing soon died out, he believed, and could not propagate their kind. His book also advanced an idea of climatic suitability that seemed convincing to many: "Each race has a tendency," Fisher wrote, "to occupy exclusively that portion of the country suited to its nature." This climatic principle suggested to him that Africans would concentrate in the southernmost part of the United States.[33]

A reviewer in the *Atlantic Monthly* in 1861 was generally complimentary about *The Laws of Race* but challenged Fisher's estimate of black people. Whereas Fisher believed that African Americans were "incapable of such improvement" as to render slavery unnecessary, the *Atlantic Monthly*'s writer pointed out that white people had prohibited blacks from learning. Nevertheless, they were improving. This writer accepted that "some form of subjection of the negro may be necessary for a time that extends far into the future," but he believed it was "utterly untrue" that slavery was "the necessary result" of the African American's nature. Somewhat more approving was a commentary in the *North American Review*, which praised Fisher's "condensed and vigorous thought" and "close reasoning." But here too the reviewer questioned the immutability of the existing situation. Although he agreed with Fisher on "the native and essential inferiority of the negro race," he believed that blacks could improve in their intellectual abilities and in time deserve more influence over their own affairs.[34]

In this same article, the *North American Review* examined other theories and writings about slavery. The reviewer, who longed to see the Union restored, argued that all employers of labor tended to exploit their workers, and he sought to reconcile the views of North and South. Although he condemned racist apologists who showed a "complacent tolerance of American slavery as it is," he judged that "cruelty and harshness" were "the exception" in the South and criticized the abolitionists for causing "exasperation of feeling" among Southerners, while ignoring the "great problem" of deciding what to do with the slaves. There might be an "undoubted inferiority of the Africans," but this writer questioned whether that inferiority was "inherent and irremovable" or "the result of centuries of degradation." Urging greater Christianity to elevate both the powerful and the lowly, he predicted that slavery would be humanized before it eventually disappeared. "Its heart must be eaten out before its body dies." This reviewer also reported without criticism the views of a Reverend Hiller, who was a "zealous Colonizationist." Hiller (like Harriet Beecher Stowe) saw superior "moral susceptibilities" in the slaves and believed that the "design of Infinite Wisdom" was to allow slaves to be brought to the United States so that they could be Christianized and later, after gradual emancipation, sent home to evangelize and regenerate the land of their birth.[35]

The *New Englander* took a more scientific or anthropological approach to racial questions in an article in the fall of 1861. At some length it described and assessed the nature of African peoples on that continent. The resulting picture was one of astonishing diversity and a huge range of cultural attainments. In some areas the article reported "well organized communities, giving promise of an advancing civilization" and "great commercial centers," natives who were "generally quiet, orderly, industrious, thrifty," and tribes marked by "intelligence and morality." In other regions the inhabitants were "low in the scale of humanity, fierce in war, addicted to the slave trade, and some of them to cannibalism." The "prime cause of African degradation and barbarism," argued the *New Englander,* was the international slave trade, and it cautioned its readers not to judge Africans by "the most degraded portion" of that continent's population. It was a mistake to see "the enslaved and imbruted negro" as representative of the capabilities of the race. An adjacent article by Rev. J. M. Sturtevant, a Yale alumnus who was president of Illinois College, challenged Americans to treat African Americans with greater justice because they had some God-given rights, even if "the white man" was "the heaven appointed lord of our soil." At the same time, Reverend Sturtevant cherished hopes that the North would not exact "unwilling submission" from "a conquered and subjugated South" and that whites of both sections could be reunited in emotional reverence for the U.S. flag.[36]

Two publications that received some notice were aimed at a wider reading audience and had a seminovelistic form. Mary Lowell Putnam's *Record of an Obscure Man,* published in Boston in 1861, recounted the experiences of a fictional narrator on a visit to the South. There he encountered a scholar living in rural isolation who devoted all his spare moments to assembling reliable information about African peoples. Though there was almost no action in the novel, its long speeches and conversations presented the ideas that African culture was far less primitive than most whites supposed, that its customs bore a strong resemblance to those in ancient Europe, that cannibalism was a myth, and that prevailing views of Africans derived mostly from visits to the coast, where the corrupting influence of European commerce had been great. *Harper's Weekly* praised the book for its contribution to knowledge about "the actual historic capability and achievement of the African race."

A second book, which apparently sold well, was *Among the Pines,* an account of a pre-secession visit to the South written by Edmund Kirke, a pseudonym for J. R. Gilmore, one of the editors of the *Continental Monthly.* Gilmore's book was very critical of slavery and declared that the rebellion could not be "crushed till we have destroyed that accursed institution." Although the *Continental Monthly* strongly favored colonization, Gilmore had many favorable things to say about African Americans. He argued that enslavement dwarfed their nature, yet he regarded them as far superior to the poor whites and described one black man of "rare intelligence . . . fine traits of character, and . . . true heroism." Although some slaves were held down to the level of brutes, "a large body are fully on a par, except in mere book education, with their white masters," and Gilmore no longer doubted "the capacity of the black for freedom."[37]

The most ambitious scientific book to appear was Charles Loring Brace's *Races of the Old World: A Manual of Ethnology,* published in 1863. Brace's descriptions of the peoples of Africa seemed to be drawn from travelers' subjective accounts and surely were not the "most trustworthy" knowledge in any modern scientific sense. He depicted a great variety of African cultures and tribes, from those that were "savage and cruel" to others displaying "noble intelligence and poetic feeling." In his theoretical discussion of race and human variation Brace was more scientific; he employed Darwin's theory to explain how the varieties of humankind could have developed from a single origin. Acknowledging specifically that "barbarian human beings lived on the soil of Europe . . . hundreds of thousands of years before any of the received dates of Creation," Brace explained how naturally occurring variations, combined with differing environments, could produce "a new type." Skin color, he accurately reported, derived from the number of pigment-carrying cells in the skin, and he informed his readers that the brains and spinal cords of Africans and Europeans were the same in form, structure, and size. Moreover, he rejected the widespread notion that mulattos were sterile and could not reproduce. "All races of men, of all countries," he noted, "are fertile with one another."[38]

These were remarkably well-informed and progressive views, but unfortunately the comment they elicited was no more widespread than that for Fisher's *Laws of Race*. The *New York Times* endorsed the value of ethnology as a "descriptive science," but it drew conventional conclusions from Brace's work. "With a few exceptions," wrote the *Times*, "the Aryan races have been the governing people of the earth, and there is no chance of the scepter passing from their sway." Africans were among "the unhistoric races, whose influence has been minute and unappreciable" in the annals of human progress. Despite his scientific knowledge, Brace might not have disagreed strongly with this assessment, for he seemed to view Africans as less advanced overall. "The degree of civilization or barbarism," he wrote, "affects all the features of the body and face," and he described the black people of the "Northern United States and the West Indies" as a "low, barbarous type of one tribe . . . that of the coast negro of Guinea."[39]

Any negative assessment of blacks in Brace's work, however, paled by comparison with the virulently racist, pseudoscientific propaganda of J. H. Van Evrie, a New York doctor closely allied with the Democratic Party. His *Negroes and Negro "Slavery": The First an Inferior Race: The Latter its Normal Condition* was published in 1861 to incite "The White Men of America," particularly "the day laborer and working man," to resist any change in the racial status quo. According to Van Evrie, blacks were "a separate species" with primitive "cranial manifestation," a brain "ten to fifteen percent" smaller than the Caucasian's, and hair "so hard and wiry and in fact triangular in form, that a blow from the hand of a master would doubtless injure the latter vastly more than it would the head of the negro." Mulattos became sterile by the fourth generation, he declared, and blacks were created by God for the tropics and for slavery. It was cruel to remove them from slavery, for they were "child[ren] forever" and "incapable of comprehending the wants of the future." Reaching full mental development between the ages of 12 and 15, the African American could never be a genius, a "poet, inventor, or one having any originality of any kind whatever." He felt his "strongest affection" in "love for his master," and any attempt to force equality on the black race led to its extinction or destruction. Just as God had created woman to be the subordinate "help-mate to her husband," so he had made blacks to be slaves. Only in slavery could the heathen African become "an important element in the civilization, progress, and general welfare of both races." Van Evrie's book of more than three hundred pages warned repeatedly of the dangers of "mongrelism." The "'anti-slavery' imposture of our times" threatened the nation, and racial intermixture with blacks threatened "complete social destruction."[40]

No doubt Van Evrie's racism and pseudoscientific tone supported the visceral prejudices of many of his readers, but as the war caused increasing disruption of slavery and raised questions about its future, a different kind of discussion supplanted the ethnological or theoretical. As the possibility of emancipation became more real, attention turned to recent emancipations that had occurred in the West Indies. Four books on the emancipations carried out there by European nations were published and discussed during the war. The most influential of these was William Grant Sewell's *Ordeal of Free Labor in the British West Indies,* published by Harper & Brothers in 1861. Sewell's analysis, which had originally appeared in a series of letters to the *New York Times,* set the parameters of subsequent discussions. He tended to evaluate the success or failure of emancipation primarily in terms of agricultural output, but he demonstrated that the most significant declines in productivity had begun long before emancipation, and he regarded the black population as capable of improvement once they were free.

Sewell emphasized that the experience and conditions of each island in the British West Indies had been unique. Everywhere, though, a "battle" between free labor and former owners had taken place. Where resistance to emancipation "was feeble, all trace of the contest has disappeared, and prosperity has revived," whereas determined resistance to the slaves' freedom had left a pall of oppression on the people. In most of the islands exports had increased under free labor, and both commerce and society were in a healthy state. Giving figures, Sewell showed that sugar production had increased in Guiana, Trinidad, Barbados, and Antigua even though the agricultural labor force for sugar was now "scarcely more than half" of what it had been. Jamaica, where production of sugar had declined, was "an exception," and its decline "commenced before emancipation was projected, and can be traced directly to other causes than the introduction of freedom." Poor management by absentee planters and a failure to invest had brought about Jamaica's problems. As for the African laborers, Sewell judged them "inferior" to Europeans "in intelligence, in industry, and in force of character," but he emphasized that they had "progressed under freedom" and could not be blamed for "defects that slavery itself engendered." Sewell concluded that "freedom, when allowed fair play, injured the prosperity of none of these West Indian colonies" and that "if the people merit any consideration whatever," then the islands were "a hundred-fold more prosperous now" than in the heyday of slavery.[41]

When partisan newspapers debated the West Indian experience, they emphasized the experience of Jamaica or the other sugar islands. The Democratic *Cincinnati Daily Enquirer* focused on the decline of exports in Jamaica, dismissed prosperity elsewhere as due to imported coolie labor, and stressed that black people were inferior. "In all negro Africa," declared an article entitled "British Emancipation," "there is no such thing as a road, a bridge . . . a city." The *Cincinnati Daily Gazette,* on the other hand, pointed out that Jamaica's problems were of long standing and had preceded emancipation. With the progress in the other islands, "the truth has now become established in the minds of men who look at the evidence without a determination to distort it to a pro-Slavery result, that West India emancipation is a success." According to the *Daily Gazette,* it was difficult to criticize "negro capacity" based on the Caribbean experience, even in Haiti.[42]

When the *New Englander* considered West Indian emancipation in the fall of 1862, it agreed with Sewell's conclusion that outside of Jamaica "emancipation has been followed by a large and decided increase of the products of labor." Freedom had come without any violence against whites and without "the amalgamation of the races," which resulted from slavery rather than from freedom. "Because the African in slavery is thriftless, lazy, and improvident," observed this author, too many people had wrongly assumed "that he is always and essentially such in character." In fact, the increased production in most of the islands had come despite the departure of women from the fields and the arrival of only small numbers of coolie laborers. Thus, the record "proves unmistakably the industry of the negro in a state of freedom."[43] The same kind of analysis based on production figures appeared in an article in the *Continental Monthly* in 1862. While reviewing a pamphlet by "a Cotton Manufacturer"—Edward Atkinson—who had used Sewell's data, the *Continental Monthly* emphasized that Jamaica's problems had preceded emancipation, that elsewhere exports and food production had increased, and that the former slaves were living better than ever before.[44]

Because Sewell's book came first, it probably had more influence than more scholarly studies that appeared later and echoed some of its conclusions. Augustin Cochin, of France, published two books that would appear in translation in 1862 and 1863. *The Results of Emancipation,* a thoroughly researched examination of data from the colonies of France and four other European nations, had won a prize from the French Academy; *The Results of Slavery* focused on slavery's effects in various colonies as well as in the United States and Brazil. Cochin displayed a keen understanding of the various factors that produced variations in the experience of different emancipating colonies. The availability of land, for example, naturally affected freedmen's decisions about whether to remain on sugar plantations or seek farms for themselves. Cochin emphasized that five years after emancipation in the French Caribbean, production and commerce had returned to their previous levels, and they had increased since then. There was no economic ruin, little violence, and no regression of blacks to barbarism, while social progress was evident in the large number of marriages, stronger families, and crowded schools and churches. "The experience of the French colonies," he concluded, showed that "the best mode of emancipation" was "immediate and simultaneous emancipation."[45]

The Results of Slavery focused far more directly on American politics and on the future status of black people. Cochin argued strongly that Congress could abolish slavery. His views on the future status of African Americans borrowed from both abolitionists and racists. Although he challenged the view that Africans were hopelessly inferior and incapable of civilization, he advocated that "suitable conditions" be required for suffrage and made it clear that "the European surpasses all the races in reason" and is "destined by God to be the preceptor of the rest." Nevertheless, Cochin favored "social and civil equality, which should be decreed by law."[46]

In a review of Cochin's work, the *New Englander* noted that fears of emancipation in the French islands had been greatly exaggerated and that most freedmen proved "ready to work" and responsive to fair wages and treatment. Especially noteworthy was Cochin's demonstration that immediate emancipation was preferable to a mode "which is gradual or which interposes a state of apprenticeship between that of Slavery and Freedom." As Cochin put it, "By waiting, we obtain nothing; by venturing, we risk nothing."[47] The *North American Review* also credited Cochin with showing that "emancipation is entirely safe, productive in an economical point of view, and in a moral aspect of essential and vast benefit to both parties." The magazine felt these findings should have "momentous bearing" on events in the United States. It also reviewed a fourth book, *La question de l'esclavage aux Etats-Unis,* by an anonymous former official from the Dutch Indies. This book took a different position, arguing that immediate emancipation would be "injurious" and laying out a detailed plan for the gradual conversion of slaves to freemen through apprenticeship, education, and legal oversight. The *North American Review* reported these proposals respectfully but labeled them "impracticable . . . in the present disturbed condition of our affairs."[48]

These fact-based studies were influential among an educated and well-informed readership, but on the broader public they seemed to have less influence. Even many editors and writers continued to discuss African Americans' abilities and character in terms of established stereotypes and what people took to be common knowledge. Such notions often questioned the assertiveness and competence of blacks. *Harper's Weekly* reviewed the peaceful emancipation in the Caribbean and explained that "African blood is not fierce. It is a mild, patient race, although like all men they may be stung to vengeance." The *Atlantic Monthly* published an essay by Ralph Waldo Emerson that described black people as "a race naturally benevolent, joyous, docile, industrious, and whose very miseries sprang from their great talent for usefulness." The "simple sons of Africa," stated an article in the *Continental Monthly,* would need civil and religious instruction "under a proper system of APPRENTICESHIP" but would respond to "kind treatment and new hopes." Another article from that magazine in the spring of 1862 praised the efforts of missionary societies to imbue the contrabands "with notions of order, industry, economy and self-reliance, and to elevate them in the scale of humanity, by inspiring them with self-respect." In the fall of 1862 a writer in the *North American Review* still felt that the slaves were so unprepared for freedom that it would be "treason" to violate the state and federal constitutions "in order to give freedom at once to four millions of slaves, seven eighths of whom would not know how to use it." To the *New York Times* it seemed appropriate to publish an article by "A Veteran Observer," who described the African as "an *exotic*—a being whose proper soil and climate is the hot regions of the earth."[49]

The notion that climate determined or foretold destiny enjoyed a wide currency. Even the *Cincinnati Daily Gazette,* which opposed colonization and argued that "the negroes must continue where they are," occasionally made statements to the effect that "were there no Slavery, the tendency of the whole race in American would be Southward" and that there was a "natural drift" toward "the tropics."[50] The idea that black Americans should migrate from the United States to their natural home in the tropical regions had some very committed advocates among those close to and within the Lincoln administration. To the Blair family, particularly General Frank Blair and Postmaster General Montgomery Blair, the removal of African Americans to southern climes was a desired and essential element in racial and national destiny.

In 1859 Frank Blair had presented his ideas at length to an association of merchants in Boston. In his vision for the future, racism mingled with dreams of the prosperity that would follow construction of a transcontinental railroad. Although Blair viewed slavery as "a blot on the fair prospect of our country" and denounced Chief Justice Taney's opinion of black people's rights, he believed in racial inferiority. There were "indelible marks of difference" between whites and blacks, and the "sable race, bred in the pestilence of Africa," could not "assimilate with" the "superior and enlightened" whites. The presence of black people in America constituted an "unnatural connection" and threatened the development of a "hybrid" race that would "carry degradation alike into government as into communities." Blair believed that the races of humankind had a natural and differing "adaptability to the various climates of our earth" and that "whenever a region is acquired within our tropics to make a permanent home for our American freedmen, emancipation will take place rapidly" in adjacent areas. The federal government should support sending the freed slaves "to freeholds abroad." Then "removal of the enfranchised race to the tropics will follow, and the Southern States will fill up with people of our own race." In this way "a new empire" for commerce would develop, with whites spread "across the great temperate zone" and blacks enjoying their own government and homes "in regions congenial to their natures." This relocation of the races, Blair maintained, would "exalt the destiny of all the races of this continent."[51]

The claim that racial separation was in the interests of all was a tactic used by Blair's brother, Postmaster General Montgomery Blair. To Frederick Douglass he gave assurances (though his comments elsewhere contradicted him) that his advocacy of colonization was not based on a belief in the racial inferiority of blacks. Blair explained in the fall of 1862 that he was supporting the idea of Senator Samuel Pomeroy, of Kansas, to use African Americans to establish a "new empire . . . in Central America." But he insisted that this colonizing scheme was based on Thomas Jefferson's idea that "diversity, not the inferiority of race" was a problem for the United States. "Indelible differences thus made by the Almighty," contended Blair, created a "necessity for . . . separation" of the races. Saying that he did not expect black people to disappear from the United States for "many generations," Blair nevertheless argued that it was desirable to start an exodus to "intertropical America." As black people established a new government there, their success would supposedly benefit the United States, the remaining black population in the North, and even foreign blacks who came to universities in the United States.[52] To the

Blairs this tropical or Central American idea was a means to end slavery and remove African Americans from the United States while extending the nation's influence over a larger part of the Western Hemisphere.

Also advocating colonization, but with ideas for possible destinations within the United States, was the *Continental Monthly.* Consistent with its conservative racial views, this magazine held that slavery should be abolished but that emancipation "should be for the sake of the *white* man and the Union, and not of the negro." Moreover, it should be done "in such a manner as to cause the least possible trouble." Thinking that blacks might "ultimately go to the wall" and disappear, the *Continental Monthly* nevertheless saw a way to use them in the short run to suppress the rebellion. If colonies of white laborers were established in Union-held territories, such as Virginia and Texas, they could "persuade Cuffy [blacks] to become industrious" and thus hem the Confederacy in. With slavery abolished, immigration from abroad would soar and the Confederacy collapse. Then the freedmen should be put to work on Southern lands confiscated from traitors, and for four years their crops should be used to defray the war debt. After the fifth harvest, the blacks should be given the proceeds and sent to Texas or elsewhere to live by themselves. The *Continental Monthly* became more adamant in the summer of 1862 that "the South is inevitably to be 'Northed' or 'free-labored'" by the settlement of army veterans and immigrants. Soldiers would deserve reward for their service, and postwar reconstruction could not "be founded on reformed secessionists." To infuse the South with "northern blood, life, ideas, education, and industry," the only "effective means . . . will be to settle our Army" there.[53] But to make room for the white settlers and their positive influence, African Americans would have to go elsewhere.

THESE DISCUSSIONS in magazines and newspapers generated a variety of ideas for policymaking. But as Lincoln approached the end of 1862—the period in which he would issue his emancipation proclamations—colonization and a process of gradual, compensated emancipation remained very much on his mind. In July, before Congress adjourned and legislators left the capital, he invited the representatives of the border states to the White House. There he made a personal appeal to them to reconsider his March proposal. *They* had it in their power to end the rebellion, he argued, for if the border states accepted his invitation to adopt gradual emancipation with federal compensation, the rebels would see that they could not win. Moreover, he urged them to consult their interests. If they did not act, the "friction and abrasion" of war would ultimately destroy slavery, robbing the border states of slavery's "value" before they could "sell out" and let "the nation as buyer . . . buy [them] out." Emphasizing that he was speaking only of a "*decision* at once to emancipate *gradually,*" Lincoln added this assurance about colonization: "Room in South American for colonization, can be obtained cheaply, and in abundance; and when numbers shall be large enough to be company and encouragement for one another, the free people will not be so reluctant to go." In conclusion he observed that his repudiation of General Hunter's proclamation had caused much dissatisfaction, and he gently warned that "pressure" for emancipation "is still upon me, and is increasing." For all these reasons he appealed to their patriotism and "loftiest views."[54] The president believed that gradual emancipation by the states, with compensation and colonization, remained the best policy.

In August Lincoln sought an interview at the White House with a committee of black leaders. His purpose was to push them to support a colonization project that he and his cabinet had been discussing since October 1861. Congressional legislation had made six hundred thousand dollars available to support colonization, and Reverend James Mitchell, of Indiana, had been working for more than two months in the Department of the Interior on arrangements for a movement to the Isthmus of Chiriqui. By the time of this meeting, plans were in place to send Senator Pomeroy with "500 able-bodied negroes as the first colony." The exact site for settlement on the isthmus was to be selected by Pomeroy, and the administration hoped that an expedition would soon leave the United States. In his August 14 meeting with the black leaders Lincoln tried to persuade them to join his plan and to recruit others for the expedition.[55]

Raising first the question of why black Americans should leave the country, he bluntly told his visitors, "You and we are different races. We have between us a broader difference than exists between almost any other two races. Whether it is right or wrong I need not discuss, but this physical difference is a great disadvantage to us both, as I think your race suffer very greatly, many of them, by living among us, while ours suffer from your presence." No black man, Lincoln argued, was allowed equality with any white man "on this broad continent," and "I cannot alter it if I would." Now, because slavery existed, white men were suffering; they were "cutting one another's throats." Therefore, the president concluded, "it is better for us both . . . to be separated." Then, before touting the advantages of Central

America—with its location on a great ocean "highway," harbors "among the finest in the world," and "evidence of very rich coal mines"—Lincoln presumed to instruct the black leaders on their duty to their race. "There are free men among you," Lincoln recognized, who were not inclined to leave their country. These men could not see their "comfort" advanced by colonization and therefore preferred to stay in the United States. This, the president declared, was "an extremely selfish view of the case." The leaders among the black population, men who had elevated themselves despite adversity, now heard from the president that they should emigrate from their native land to set an example.[56]

Lincoln's words on August 14 were revealing of his views and priorities. He accepted as a fact that the racial problem in America was profound and intractable; he wanted to end the conflict between white Americans and reunite the sections; and he favored the removal of black Americans as a solution. In prescribing to his visitors what they ought to do, he gave little consideration to their rights or to how they might view their interests. Frederick Douglass was understandably offended. He protested that Lincoln showed "contempt for negroes" and gave "a weapon to all the ignorant and base, who need only the countenance of men in authority to commit all kinds of violence and outrage" upon black people. The president was "a genuine representative of American prejudice and negro hatred and far more concerned for the preservation of slavery, and the favor of the Border Slave States, than for . . . justice and humanity." George Vashon, another black leader and educator, assailed the "gross injustice" of Lincoln's request, which "may add fuel to the fire" of racism, and noted that America's problem was not the presence of African Americans but "the white man's oppression" of them. Even the Democratic *Cincinnati Daily Enquirer* took note of—and mocked—Lincoln's lack of concern for the aspirations of African Americans. In an editorial it scorned the hypocrisy of Republicans who favored abolition but "whose President has told a negro deputation that the African race can not be permitted even to live intermingled with his own."[57]

Yet in all this Lincoln was consistent. He had consistently appealed to Southern whites to remember the ties of common history that united them with Northerners so that they could be friends and brothers, not enemies. He had consistently denied any intention to interfere with the rights and institutions of the slaveholding states. He had repeatedly voiced the conviction that his purpose and his duty were to preserve the Union. As the *New York Times* declared on May 20, 1862, "From the beginning . . . he has refused to make this war one of emancipation." As he stood on the verge of military emancipation, Lincoln still hoped to reconcile the South with the North. In a letter to Maryland's Senator Reverdy Johnson, Lincoln noted the objections of people in New Orleans to Union forces but protested that "the people of Louisiana" knew "that I never had a wish to touch the foundations of their society." Indeed, "they forced a necessity upon me to send armies among them." Thus, there is every reason to accept Lincoln's statement of his priorities *and* to note his political adeptness when he responded in August to Horace Greeley's famous "Prayer of Twenty Millions." To Greeley's demand that he strike at slavery the president answered, "My paramount object in this struggle *is* to save the Union, and is *not* either to save or to destroy slavery. If I could save the Union without freeing *any* slave I would do it, and if I could save it by freeing *all* the slaves I would do it; and if I could save it by freeing some and leaving others alone I would also do that. What I do about slavery, and the colored race, I do because I believe it helps to save the Union."[58]

Lincoln endeavored to remain consistent even as he adopted the new policy of military emancipation. Historians know that before Lincoln wrote to Greeley, he had already decided to issue his proclamation, but he was waiting for a military victory to provide an auspicious occasion. That moment arrived when Lee retreated after the battle of Antietam, on September 22, 1862. Lincoln began his Preliminary Emancipation Proclamation with reaffirmations of his established policies. "Hereafter, as heretofore," he stated, "the war will be prossecuted [*sic*] for the object of restoring the constitutional relation" between the United States and the rebelling states. At Congress's next meeting he would "again recommend" his plan for voluntary emancipation, "immediate or gradual," by slaveholding states with compensation for any state not in rebellion. "The effort to colonize persons of African descent will be continued." Then, coming to the new element of his policy, Lincoln declared that on January 1, 1863, slaves held in any state whose people "shall then be in rebellion" against the United States would be "then, thenceforward, and forever free." To present "conclusive evidence" that it was not in rebellion, a state needed to send to Congress representatives elected by a majority of its qualified voters. Lincoln closed this proclamation by quoting from Congress's acts prohibiting return of fugitive slaves and confiscating and freeing the slaves of rebels, and he pledged to recommend compensation for loyal slaveholders.[59]

Thus Lincoln tried to move in two directions at once—toward gradual emancipation by the states and, if that failed, toward abolition through war.

Perhaps he still hoped, even at this late date, that Unionism might reassert itself in some parts of the South. Certainly his actions gave proof of his desire to continue to respect the rights of slaveholders as long as they were loyal. In addition, the structure of this step toward emancipation served an important political purpose in the North by giving Lincoln a shield against his critics. It put the responsibility for emancipation upon the rebels. It was a practical demonstration that "they forced a necessity upon me," as he had written to Reverdy Johnson. Amid the cascade of newspaper reaction, both celebratory and hostile, this message was heard.

On the positive side, the *Chicago Tribune* reported "Universal Acquiescence and Rejoicing," while the *Pittsburgh Gazette* declared "Thank God!"; the *Philadelphia Press* reported, "The Rebellion is at an end!"; the *Alton (Illinois) Telegraph* savored "a thrill of joy and hope through the hearts of all loyal men"; and the *New York Evening Post* proclaimed that "the chains of bondage were struck from the limbs of three millions of human beings." On the negative side, Democratic papers condemned the president's "extraordinary" and "unconstitutional" act, charged him with hypocrisy, concluded that a weak president had "given way" to radical pressure, and predicted that his action would unite the South and strengthen the rebellion.[60] But in addition there were perceptive reactions from a variety of journals.

An article in the *Atlantic Monthly* praised Lincoln's proclamation but went on to note that it was not at all an abolitionist document. This proclamation of emancipation was "not a threat, but a warning." It gave Southerners one hundred days to "make their election between submission and slavery and resistance and ruin." Writing in the same magazine, Ralph Waldo Emerson observed that "the President had no choice," an observation that surely would have pleased Lincoln. The *Cincinnati Gazette,* a Republican paper, accurately described the Preliminary Proclamation as a "lever to restore peace and the Union. The way to save Slavery is simply to submit to the Constitution. . . . The way to destroy it is to persist in rebellion." The immediate reaction of the *New York Times* was to emphasize that the war was "Still to be Prosecuted for the Restoration of the Union" and that gradual abolition and colonization were "Adhered to." The proclamation was "a weapon of warfare," an extraconstitutional war measure to preserve the Union. Later in the fall the *Times* would declare that "in no just sense of the term is this an Abolition war" and that the proclamation could not "be deemed an Abolition paper." If the rebellious states would return to the Union, "the war would stop instantly" and "slavery will remain untouched. . . . *They* can save slavery, if they choose to do so; if they refuse, they will have only themselves to blame."[61]

The prospect of military emancipation now gave added weight to the question, "What shall we do with the negro?" As various periodicals had noted, the events of war were disrupting and undermining the institution of slavery. Congress's Confiscation Acts and now Lincoln's Preliminary Proclamation confirmed that a dismantling of slavery was under way, not just as a result of the "friction and abrasion" of war but also as a goal of Union policy. The president's proclamation was irrefutably important, for it added powerful momentum to a process that was going to weaken slavery and give more opportunity to African Americans. But many questions remained. The legal power and scope of the proclamation as a war measure was unclear. Would it cease with the end of the war? To how many slaves would it actually bring freedom, and what would be the character of that freedom? The answers to these questions were unclear and uncertain.

Throughout the North others quickly began to ask what place the freed slaves would have in society. In the weeks after Lincoln's Preliminary Proclamation, Democrats worked to incite fears that a tidal wave of blacks would flood the North, overwhelming society and taking white men's jobs. The *Cincinnati Daily Enquirer,* for example, asked, "Do you want this country filled with negroes?" To "Workingmen of Ohio" it broadcast the warning that Republicans were "inviting the Negroes from the South to Come North and Compete with your Labor." "This was a nation of white men," declared the paper, and "our Government was a government of white men, for the benefit of white men," but now "Mr. Lincoln wishes to set loose upon the North millions of negroes, to be provided for by the white population." "Be Warned in Time," shouted a headline, of "The Negro Influx."[62] Republican papers and sympathetic independent journals set out to answer these charges both by denying them and by giving increased attention to colonization or to various means of containing free African Americans so that they did not injure whites. The basic assumptions of white racism were evident in these responses.

The *Cincinnati Daily Gazette* answered its local rival by insisting that blacks "will prefer to remain in the South." Relations between Southern whites and the freedmen would "adjust themselves," and even if some African Americans might need to be "disposed of in the North," that could be accomplished "without filling the actual want of labor." Besides, said the *Gazette,* the slaves would be unable to compete in "the most desirable kinds of labor," so Northerners would not be harmed. The *Chicago Tribune* argued reassuringly to Northern whites that "the Government must and will use them where they are, in the South as the home of the blacks." An article in the *New Englander* pointed out that it was unwarranted to assume that the North would be saddled with thriftless and improvident blacks. It was wrong to assume that just "because the African in slavery is thriftless, lazy, and improvident," he would "always and essentially" be so. The *New York Times* similarly blasted as "utterly unfounded" the Democrats' charge that "thousands" of free blacks would "*flood the North*" and depress wages. It reported that General Sickles had found that "nothing would induce the negroes to leave the South." The *Times* asserted that "*negro labor will always be more needed and more valuable in the Southern States than anywhere else; and therefore it will always remain there,*" and it endorsed the view of the Republican gubernatorial candidate in New York that "emancipation would not only keep the enfranchised slaves at the South, but would also draw thither the free negroes of the Northern States."[63]

The proadministration *Times* also became a leading advocate of specific schemes for internal colonization in the South. Although it blasted the Chiriqui plan, which was, in fact, abandoned due to the objections of Central American nations, the *Times* vigorously promoted other locations. Denmark, Haiti, and Liberia had all expressed interest in attracting newly freed slaves, according to the paper, but it favored an idea involving Florida that was being promoted by Eli Thayer, the inventor and former congressman who had led efforts to send antislavery settlers to Kansas. Thayer wanted the government to send free laborers to Florida, and Frederick Douglass was interested in the plan, predicting that thousands of Northern blacks would participate. Florida was quite unpopulated and had "a climate admirably adapted to African life and labor." The United States owned much of the land there, and "the whites have shunned" it, so the *Times* asked, "Why send away an honest, humble people . . . if we can give them a home on our own soil . . . without at all displacing, jostling or interfering with our white population?" A few weeks later the newspaper urged that "Florida and Texas are at hand, and a million free homes may be had in them for free blacks." On occasion the *Times* printed opinions of those who supported colonization abroad, but it criticized these views as "puerile," arising "because we are *prejudiced* against their color." It insisted that in the United States "the blacks are now precisely where their labor is needed most."[64]

Secretary of War Edwin Stanton spoke out publicly in favor of policy ideas that mirrored those of the *Times.* The productive place for freedmen was in the United States. Already in the occupied Sea Islands, he noted, black people were working productively, and with military protection they could "forever cut off from the rebellion the resources of a country thus occupied." Experience also showed that "no colored man will leave his home in the South" if protected there, so the danger of migration to the North would be avoided by "giving colored men protection and employment upon the soil." Florida and Texas, with their large amounts of open land, intrigued Stanton, and he wrote in an encouraging way about the possibility of settling thousands from the North and from western states on "vacant government lands" there.[65]

The *Continental Monthly* also campaigned for colonization, especially after two former governors of the Kansas Territory, Robert J. Walker and Frederick P. Stanton, assumed new editorial responsibilities. In November 1862, Walker argued in a substantial essay that "separation" of the races in North America "must be complete and eternal." The fundamental problem was "prejudice . . . against the negro race." According to Walker, this prejudice—already strong in the North and increasing with growth of the black population and with fears of "reduction of wages" due to "negro competition"—was a "far deeper" issue than slavery in the South, where whites of all classes feared and rejected "the intermingling and equality of the races." Only colonization abroad, he argued, could solve this problem, and he favored removal of African Americans to Africa, Mexico, Central and South America, the West Indies, or elsewhere. Walker particularly urged the "reannexation" of Texas, through which the black population would "recede," as if through a "safety-valve," into Mexico and Central and Southern America. Only in South America could black people escape being "a *degraded caste*" and enjoy the equality that "they can never attain in any part of this Union." To Walker it was necessary "to colonize beyond our limits the free blacks of *every State,*" because the "prejudice of race here is ineradicable."[66]

In December Frederick Stanton offered a more conservative plan based firmly on colonization but envisioning a slower process. Repeating some familiar racist stereotypes, Stanton described the slaves as unaccustomed "to take care of themselves," possessing "neither foresight nor enterprise," and imagining "in the glimmering twilight of their intellects" that liberty meant only "living without work." Due to these facts it would be necessary to tutor and prepare them before an "effective system of colonization" could be "gradually established." Moreover, the United States would need to increase its white population through European immigration or natural increase before the blacks could leave. Therefore, Stanton concluded, the freedmen would have to become "the wards of the government" and through "some system of apprenticeship" gain in civilization and education "as far as possible." Ultimately "the Africans will find their advantage in removing farther South, perhaps to Central America, possibly to Africa." For Stanton, immediate emancipation would be "inconvenient and, indeed, disastrous," and colonization would be delayed. But the eventual removal of African Americans was necessary.[67]

Lincoln seemed to agree. He used his annual message to Congress in December to argue again, and at greater length, for his plan of gradual, compensated emancipation by the states, accompanied by colonization abroad. He called on Congress to propose three amendments to the Constitution. The first would provide federal financial compensation to every state that abolished slavery in the next thirty-seven years, by January 1, 1900. Federal payments could be gradual or in one sum, depending on the timing of emancipation. Showing continued respect for state autonomy on slavery, Lincoln even allowed for a later state action "reintroducing or tolerating slavery," but at that point repayment to the federal treasury would be required. His second proposal would provide compensation to loyal slave owners whose bondsmen had "enjoyed actual freedom" during the war. The third explicitly authorized Congress to provide money or other aid "for colonizing free colored persons, with their own consent, at any place or places without the United States."[68]

Lincoln's arguments in support of these proposals were the lengthiest and most thorough of his presidency. To the foes of emancipation, he argued that the proposed length of time would "greatly mitigate" dissatisfaction and "spar[e] both races from the evils of sudden derangement." To the advocates of emancipation, he contended that the length of time would save slaves from what he casually assumed would be "the vagrant destitution which must largely attend immediate emancipation." He then demonstrated with statistics that compensation's financial burden on the nation would be very manageable, because in thirty-seven years the wealth and population of the United States would have increased dramatically. In regard to his second proposed amendment, he merely noted that loyal owners would deserve compensation, but he spoke at greater length, again, in regard to "the future of the freed people."[69]

"I cannot make it better known," Lincoln said, "than it already is, that I strongly favor colonization." But since colonization required the "consent of the people to be deported," some freed people might stay, and he offered two arguments in answer to those who objected to any African Americans' remaining in the country. Fears that black freedom would depress wages were mistaken, he said, because emancipation would change neither the number of jobs nor the number of workers. If any freedmen changed jobs, they would leave their old positions open to whites. If they worked less in freedom, as they "very probably" would, that would tend to raise wages for whites, and "with deportation, even to a limited extent" reducing the labor supply, "enhanced wages to white labor is mathematically certain." As for fears that "the freed people will swarm forth, and cover the whole land," Lincoln countered that a dispersed black population would be manageable and that freedmen would not come north but would stay in the South "till new homes can be found for them, in congenial climes, and with people of their own blood and race. . . . in any event, cannot the north decide for itself, whether to receive them?" In closing he voiced confidence that "timely *adoption*" of this plan "would bring restoration and thereby stay" both the war and the action of his Preliminary Emancipation Proclamation. Then he challenged his "fellow citizens" to give their support by noting that, "we *say* we are for the Union," and that "the world knows we do know how to save it," that is, by adopting his plan.[70]

Many Northern publications welcomed Lincoln's proposals, though they did not escape criticism. *Harper's Weekly* had taken an advanced position, arguing, "The prejudice against the colored race is one that we must overcome. To indulge it is to stab our fundamental doctrine to the heart." It also had condemned Lincoln's idea of colonization as "simply a shirk, not a solution." After the Preliminary Emancipation Proclamation, *Harper's Weekly* supported Lincoln by praising his act and insisting that emancipation was "a means of war" and "not abolitionism." It remained opposed and even sarcastic, however, on the subject of colonization. Few countries wanted to receive the emancipated slaves, and few American blacks wanted to leave. In fact, the "unreasonable" fondness that African Americans seemed to entertain "for their native country," observed the editor, "bears a remarkable resemblance to a sentiment . . . called by poets 'patriotism.'"[71] Frederick Douglass was delighted at the progress of Lincoln's policies, but he continued to attack colonizing schemes "urged on the ground that the white and colored people cannot live together in peace and happiness in the same country." Lincoln knew better, Douglass asserted. An article in the *New Englander* condemned colonization as a "senseless prejudice," argued that the nation needed its black population, and criticized the hundred-day delay built into Lincoln's emancipation policy.[72]

The pro-Republican *Chicago Tribune* reported that "radical Republicans are not particularly well pleased with [Lincoln's] lengthy argument in favor of compensated emancipation," but "secession sympathizers" were even more unhappy with his resolve to emancipate by executive proclamation. The *Tribune* itself proved willing to accept compensation to slaveholders in light of the many previous pledges that there would be no interference with slavery in the South. The *Cincinnati Daily Gazette* accurately described the Preliminary Emancipation Proclamation as an ultimatum, a measure "to *destroy the means of the rebels.*" Two months later it added, "If they persist . . . , they themselves have destroyed slavery." But the *Gazette* also criticized the "disease" of "*colorphobia*" that afflicted colonizationists and ridiculed Lincoln for thinking that "the colored people do not seem to appreciate the privilege of leaving their country for their country's good." Why should they want to leave "this most favored land," asked the paper? Its Democratic rival, the *Cincinnati Daily Enquirer,* continued to question the charity of Republicans who wanted to send freedmen to "the most pestilential regions" of Central America. It also scored heavily against the logic of Lincoln's economic arguments about jobs when it wrote, "It seems never to have occurred to the President that it would not be much consolation to the laborer in the North to be jostled out of his place by a Southern negro, because that left room for a white man in the South."[73]

At the end of one hundred days, late in the evening of January 1, Lincoln issued the final version of the Emancipation Proclamation. No rebelling states had responded to his warning, and voluntary emancipation had not begun, so he moved forward with military measures against slavery. His official text emphasized that emancipation was "a fit and necessary war measure for suppressing [the] rebellion," issued under his powers as "Commander-in-Chief, of the Army and Navy of the United States, in time of actual armed" conflict. It also "enjoin[ed]" the slaves to "abstain from violence," indicated that they would "be received into the armed service" to play supportive roles, and exempted from its effects those areas that were under Union control and thus not technically in rebellion. This "act of justice," Lincoln emphasized, was "warranted by the Constitution, upon military necessity."[74]

Opponents attacked the idea of emancipation and ridiculed the way in which it was implemented. The Democratic *New York World* noted critically that Lincoln had "purposely made the proclamation inoperative in all places where . . . the slaves [are] accessible" and declared "emancipation only where he has notoriously no power to execute it." Lincoln had, of course, exempted areas under Union control, but he had gone even further. He had also chosen to exempt from his "act of justice" Tennessee, even though many parts of that state were not in Union hands. Hoping to lure slaveholders back to support of the Union, the president had agreed with his war governor, Andrew Johnson, that the entire state would be exempted from the proclamation. The black *Pacific Appeal* criticized this "halfway measure" and insisted that "every bondsman" should have been freed and "every chain should have been broken." In England the foreign secretary, Lord John Russell, commented on the "very strange nature" of the document and noted that it did not declare "a principle adverse to slavery."[75]

This was, however, a characteristic of the document that Lincoln had purposely and carefully constructed. It gave him political shelter against charges of radical abolitionism, while it embarked on major change in the most conservative possible way. His proclamation expressed not merely his understanding of his constitutional obligations and the political forces that surrounded him but also the fact that his priorities were to end the war and restore the union between Northerners and Southerners. As Lincoln had stated in his public reply to Horace Greeley, his "paramount object" was "to save the Union," and "*not* either to save or to destroy slavery."[76] Nor was his paramount object to attack prejudice, to reshape social relations in the South, or to elevate the freedman. These issues, which were vital to the future of African Americans and the nation, were not addressed. Emancipation meant change, but it did not signal a new and racially radical direction in policy, for Lincoln's efforts to conciliate the South and Southern slaveholders would continue.

The *Cincinnati Daily Gazette* declared that Lincoln had given Southerners "full preliminary warning. . . . They themselves elected" to continue the rebellion and reject Lincoln's "amnesty." The *New York Times* also seconded and propagated Lincoln's message. It praised the measure, which it had consistently emphasized was a "*military expedient*," as one that would prove an effective war measure. Indeed, the *Times* noted that Jefferson Davis had already acknowledged its value when he denounced the proclamation and declared that slaves captured from the Union army would be turned over to Southern governors for probable execution. And though it frequently criticized colonization, the *Times* had no desire suddenly to change the status of African Americans. It feared a "disastrous shock" to "our whole civil and social system" if slavery were ended "too *abruptly* and *sweepingly*." It believed in "some gradual process" that would win "the cheerful concurrence of some, at least, of the Slave States." In the weeks immediately preceding Lincoln's final proclamation, the *Times* had published the opinion that African Americans could never rise "above the condition which the inferior castes of India have always occupied." It also had stated editorially that "it is not at all likely that the intelligent white proprietors [in the South] will ever be required or expected to live on terms of 'equality' with them." As 1863 began, with emancipation marking a new phase in the war, the paper even cast doubt on Lincoln's apparent assumption that freed slaves would know how to become free laborers. Vagrancy laws would be needed to make them work, said the *Times*.[77]

Thus, emancipation had arrived as federal policy. It now confronted Northerners with the question of African Americans' future status and role. Would they be successfully colonized abroad? If not, what would be their position in the United States? These questions had remained theoretical during 1862. After the emancipation proclamations they became tangible and real. The continuation of the war meant that additional hundreds of thousands of slaves would escape from their Southern owners. In areas throughout the South where the Union army was operating, they would come into Union lines and begin new lives as freedmen. Federal involvement with these freedmen inevitably became extensive, and this involvement would provide policymakers with abundant information relevant to the future if they wished to use it.

TWO

WAR'S PROVING GROUND

The North had no plan to discover the capabilities and preferences of the freedmen. Neither policymakers nor the public foresaw that the war itself would create a gigantic proving ground from which abundant and highly relevant information would be available. But while Abraham Lincoln gave thought to colonization efforts in Chiriqui and Haiti, extensive free-labor experiments came into being in the Southern states. Reacting to the pressure of events, government officials in the occupied South learned a great deal about African Americans as farmers, soldiers, and people. A multitude of reports and observations generated the raw material for intelligent policymaking, if leaders chose to use it.

It was the war that brought Northern generals, businessmen, reformers, and civil officials into contact with newly emancipated slaves in the Confederacy. Every time Federal armies made a significant advance, tens of thousands of slaves escaped from their masters and joined the contrabands within Union lines. There the government had to decide where to put the runaways and what to do with them. With some hesitation and much mismanagement, the government decided first to set them to work on the land and later to bring them into the army. The experience of dealing with the freedmen on plantations or in battle proved informative and even enlightening to those who had direct contact with the former bondsmen. Civilians and soldiers reported extensively on those they were trying to aid or supervise. They documented the actions and accomplishments of the freedmen, and they put forward their own impressions and theories about the abilities and character of African Americans. Taken together, their reports constituted a powerful brief for the abilities of African Americans and the contributions they could make to American society. They also accurately forecast the kind of exploitation that would develop if freedmen were not guaranteed their rights. But these data often were ignored; it was a struggle to gain recognition for this information against the weight of established stereotypes, racist beliefs, and political priorities defined in terms of the interests of whites. Whether these facts would be taken seriously by policymakers remained to be seen.

INITIALLY LINCOLN HAD PLEDGED not to interfere with slavery where it existed, and thereafter he consistently maintained that his goal was to preserve the Union. However much the necessities of war altered his plans, he remained eager to bring Southern whites back into a restored, peaceful, and united nation and to demonstrate his essential good faith toward those erring brothers, who, he had declared, must not be enemies, but friends. With these priorities in mind, President Lincoln did not hasten to disrupt the slave regime or disorganize it wherever an opportunity presented itself. Instead, if military conditions did not compel another approach, he left the institution as nearly untouched as possible. Thus, in the border states and in Maryland, local federal policy did little or nothing directly to promote free labor or undermine the system of bondage.[1]

On January 1, 1863, and later, many parts of Tennessee were outside the control of the U.S. military and thus were "in rebellion." But to avoid offending slaveholders and to cooperate with his Unionist military governor, Andrew Johnson, Lincoln refrained from mentioning Tennessee in his Emancipation Proclamation. For many months, the United States continued to recognize the legality of slavery there, and it delayed in establishing camps for escaped slaves or claiming them as contrabands. Similarly, long after army officers elsewhere were placing runaway slaves on abandoned plantation lands and leasing tracts to businessmen who wanted to hire free laborers, the government held back in Tennessee. Not until 1864, when the army recruited heavily for black soldiers, did government policy begin to seriously disrupt slavery in that state.[2]

Likewise, in Missouri, which fell under effective Union control early in the war, Lincoln's administration did not establish a single agricultural operation for runaway slaves or, later, freedmen. In the entire state only one contraband camp was established, and abolition did not occur until January 1865, by state action, because the administration was reluctant to alienate proslavery Unionists.[3]

Kentucky, though it was claimed by the Confederacy, sent more soldiers to the Union cause than to Jefferson Davis's army. But it also sent a delegation to Congress that was frequently adamant and outspoken in defense of slavery, and Lincoln's approach to that delegation relied solely on persuasion. Due to local resistance, little free labor developed in Kentucky until after the war ended, and that state proved to be the last of the border states to end slavery. It did not accept the death of the institution until the Thirteenth Amendment became a part of the Constitution in December 1865.[4]

Concern for loyal slaveholders also marked federal policy in Maryland. Though Lincoln used force to arrest pro-secession legislators of that state and keep it in the Union, he did not take strong action against Maryland's slaveholders. There were hardly any federally operated plantations or contraband camps in Maryland. In order to gain their freedom, many slaves chose to flee from the state in the days before its voters narrowly approved emancipation, just five months prior to the end of the war.[5]

Elsewhere, however, military action against the rebellion quickly produced increasingly large disruptions of slavery. Slaves poured into Union lines in Virginia and then along coastal areas as Federal forces mounted operations in North Carolina and South Carolina. To split the Confederacy in two, the Union launched efforts to seize the Mississippi River, and as Federal troops and ships first took New Orleans and then advanced up the river from the south and down the river from Missouri, their arrival attracted a flood of freedmen. As a result, 98,000 escaped from slavery in southern Louisiana, and the largest single concentration of freedmen within Union lines—125,000—was found in the Mississippi Valley. In all, almost 500,000 freedmen seized the opportunities presented by war to seek freedom within Union-controlled parts of the Confederacy. While the war continued, they lived and worked there. Approximately 271,000 were in Union-controlled areas of the Lower South, and 203,000 were with Federal forces in the Upper South. From both areas, but in large measure from the Mississippi Valley, more than 100,000 freedmen joined the U.S. Army and risked their lives fighting for the Union cause.[6]

As historian Willie Lee Rose has shown, Northern reformers and government officials recognized that in the area around Port Royal, South Carolina, the potential existed for an experiment in free labor.[7] There planters had fled, leaving their slaves behind. In the South generally, however, Federal officers were not thinking primarily of what could be learned for future policy. Rather, they were reacting, in a sometimes disorganized and ineffective manner, to the arrival of thousands of slaves and freedmen within Union lines. For military men, these African Americans were a problem and an unwelcome responsibility. Commanders did not want them to impede or interfere with military operations, nor did they want to shoulder the demanding job of feeding and taking care of them.

In the fall of 1862 the commander of the Department of Virginia, General John A. Dix, complained to the secretary of war that "the contraband negroes" were "a very great source of embarrassment" to his garrison at Old Point Comfort. He sought and received permission to ask the governors of Massachusetts and other New England states if they would receive a total of two thousand men, women, and children, "until peace is restored or a permanent Colony be established for their reception." Although the governor of Rhode Island was willing to cooperate, the other governors refused. Governor John Andrew, of Massachusetts, led the opposition. Objecting to "a swarm of homeless wanderers" whose freedom might become "license, corruption and infamy," Andrew declared that the former slaves should stay in the South. If Dix's fort were to be attacked, Andrew said, "let the blacks fight to preserve their freedom!" Such opposition, along with racial fears in the North, scotched this plan. Farther west, at about the same time, army officials actually sent a small number of contrabands to Cairo, Illinois, an action that ignited angry protests and dire predictions from Democratic newspapers in the state.[8]

Thus, it was clear that the men and women who escaped from slavery would remain in the South.[9] And if a growing number of former slaves were to gather in proximity to the Union armies, commanders had to find some practical solutions. One approach that proved unwise was to collect and settle the escaped slaves in hastily designed camps. Concentrated together in this way, the slaves often suffered from diseases that claimed many lives and became a serious concern. Therefore, to find some virtue in necessity, the military looked for ways to make the black population useful. Army officers hired blacks to perform work needed around the camps, set them to labor on abandoned plantations so that they could provide for themselves, and eventually began to recruit the able-bodied men into the army.

The army's record in dealing with the freedmen often was not good. Confusion, mismanagement, broken promises, and even harsh mistreatment occurred in many places. Early in the war, some commanders continued returning slaves to their masters well after General Benjamin Butler had pioneered the idea of retaining and using "contraband." Other officers did not know what to do with the contrabands who came into their camps and improvised poorly. Later, after policies to use and pay the freedmen became established, failure to pay the promised wages was a widespread and serious problem.[10]

For example, around Helena, Arkansas, in the winter of 1862–63, many escaped slaves did labor for the army but were paid nothing, because army officers failed to keep records of what was owed. At one point, a commander issued an order forbidding pay to these Arkansas freedmen because he feared that their owners might have a claim against the United States for the escapees' services. "Failure of quartermasters to enroll and pay the freedmen their wages" was a problem in the fall of 1863 in many places between Columbus, Kentucky, and Natchez, Mississippi. In May 1863, contrabands in the Department of Virginia were working for wages that were only one-fourth of those given to whites. At Norfolk, Virginia, in the same month, the superintendent of contrabands there complained that blacks were being paid almost nothing for work they did at Craney Island. Horace James, the superintendent of blacks in the District of North Carolina, reported in September 1863 that many of the freedmen under his supervision "have not been paid after having labored more than a year for the government." Three months later, that district's commander, Benjamin Butler, admitted that some workers had not been paid "for the space of more than two years." Even in the Sea Islands, pay or provisions sometimes were not furnished, and the commander of the Department of the South reported that the wages that were paid were too low. It was not surprising that, as Massachusetts businessman Edward Philbrick reported at the beginning of 1864, black laborers "lack confidence in our promises."[11]

Mistreatment also occurred at the hands of soldiers who were racist or, in some cases, merely determined to take care of their own needs, even if that caused the freedmen to suffer. In Arkansas, soldiers sometimes forced blacks who had come into Union lines to labor without any thought of pay. Worse, "sometimes they were shot down, and murdered with impunity." In the Sea Islands, Edward Philbrick, who was not indifferent to his own interests, lamented, "Our soldiers . . . are too apt to take advantage of [the freedmen's] helplessness." Philbrick also complained about a New York regiment that exploited its proximity to a well-stocked plantation to enrich its diet and supplement regular army rations. These soldiers, not atypically, slaughtered "some 80 head of cattle" and consumed most of the plantation's sweet potatoes, leaving the freedmen "barely enough for seed."[12]

After initial uncertainty, commanders in the Mississippi Valley and Louisiana took the lead in developing policies that featured free labor for the former slaves. However, there as in other parts of the South, policies "encouraged social stability and continuity rather than fundamental reform." General Nathaniel Banks, who commanded Federal forces in Louisiana from December 1862 on, required that African Americans work on plantations or public works with "subordinate deportment." In fact, he aimed for "respectful deportment, correct discipline and perfect subordination on the part of the negroes"—hardly a description of free labor. Most went to work for planters who paid a fee to the government, and a minority worked on farms run by the federal government. "Wages were largely illusory," concludes Louis Gerteis, and the freedmen found that army provost marshals "shared local prejudices against blacks." Even a friend of General Banks's described his "free" labor system as "something like a serfdom." Both Frederick Douglass and one of the members of the American Freedmen's Inquiry Commission, James McKaye, criticized these arrangements as suitable only on a temporary basis, but President Lincoln gave them his "full support."[13]

After the fall of Vicksburg, the army had to deal with a large number of freedmen in the Mississippi Valley. Its main effort was to put the former slaves to work on plantations that were leased to businessmen or speculators. Eager to gain quick profits from high-priced cotton, these lessees earned widespread criticism. Among those who assailed their low wages and treatment of the freedmen were Samuel Shepley, of the Friends' Association of Philadelphia, James E. Yeatman, of the Western Sanitary Commission, and General David Hunter. Admiral David Porter agreed, characterizing the lessees as "greedy adventurers" who "treat the Negroes brutally, and chastise them worse than their former masters did." In the District of Northeastern Louisiana, an inspecting officer reported that the lessees were treating the blacks very badly, with "utter disregard" for their rights and "even the commonest principles of humanity."[14]

These protests led to Secretary of War Edwin Stanton's assignment of General James Wadsworth to a fact-finding mission to the area. Wadsworth's report, in December 1863, lamented that the army had been unprepared to care for the large numbers of slaves who initially entered Union lines, and "a large mortality has been the result." He approved subsequent steps to move freedmen onto plantations, but argued that the lessees should be required to provide medical care, schools, and decent wages. Wadsworth also urged renting smaller plots of land to some of the African Americans so that they could "become Peasant Cultivators." If that was not done, he believed, the "great danger" would be "the tendency to establish a system of serfdom there."[15]

At this point, Salmon Chase, secretary of the treasury, attempted to intervene and implement the reforms recommended by James Yeatman. Because Congress had given the Treasury Department authority over abandoned lands, Chase felt that he could act, and his department tried to require a new standard of pay, with wages that were more than twice as high as those in effect previously. He also wanted to encourage leases and sales of land to African Americans. This reform effort was short-lived, however. Although Secretary of War Stanton "evidently" supported Chase's efforts, writes Louis Gerteis, "President Lincoln did not." For some reason, Lincoln perceived these reforms as too complicated, or perhaps he wanted to resolve bickering between army officers and Treasury Department officials. He instructed Adjutant General Lorenzo Thomas to go back to the Mississippi River and "take hold of and be master in the contraband and leasing business." Lincoln viewed the Treasury Department plan as "well intended" but destined to "fall dead within its entangled details." As a result, the large numbers of freedmen in the Mississippi Valley continued to work for low wages on plantations run by lessees who were motivated by hopes for a quick and large profit. The Treasury Department's reforms "had proved to be largely illusory," and the free-labor system remained "obviously repressive."[16]

The system also remained insecure because of the unpredictable changes in the military situation. General Lorenzo Thomas cited an example of this in October 1863 when he noted that "the necessity of withdrawing the troops from Louisiana to augment the forces operating against Vicksburg, left the line of plantations, some sixty in all, without adequate protection." Rebel raids drove off "the Negroes and stock" at a time "when it was important to cultivate the crops." This problem continued well into 1864, and historians have concluded that "only those estates near garrison towns or army camps were safe; elsewhere within Union lines, Confederate raiders and local guerrillas generally operated with impunity."[17] Both freedmen and lessees stood in constant need of greater protection from the military.

Early in 1863 the Lincoln administration became seriously interested in the potential contribution of the Southern freedmen as soldiers. In the fall of 1862, Lincoln had voiced skepticism about the idea of black troops, saying, "If we were to arm them, I fear that in a few weeks the arms would be in the hands of the rebels." The text of Lincoln's Emancipation Proclamation revealed some change in his position, but it spoke only vaguely about using freed slaves to "garrison forts, positions, stations, and other places, and to man vessels."[18] Such language suggested that their military role would be supportive, or behind the scenes. But in the spring of 1863, Lincoln decided to recruit among the freedmen in a major way. He sent Adjutant General Lorenzo Thomas to the Mississippi Valley with instructions to swell the army's ranks by adding black soldiers.

General Thomas "was a southern man, and his prejudices had been opposed to black enlistments," observed the *Chicago Tribune*, but now Thomas carried out his orders with determination. Upon arriving in the Mississippi Valley, he confronted directly the prejudice that was common among soldiers, many of whom came from the western states. Saying that "every officer and soldier should hear it from my own lips," Thomas addressed units in groups of 4,000 to 7,000 and then took questions and comments from the ranks. He "gave special orders that all negroes coming within the lines of the army should be 'kindly treated,'" for he had found that "instead of kindness," escaped slaves had met with denunciations of "the 'damned nigger'" and had been "kicked and cuffed in every direction." Thomas reported that the soldiers did not object to the government's new policy. They "only wanted to know officially what the government wished, and they were ready to do their part." The soldiers' ready cooperation may have derived from their desire to win the war and add more troops to the front lines, but some of the general's other comments may have helped. He declared that the former slaves would not be sent to the North, saying, "You all know the prejudices of the Northern people against receiving large numbers of the colored race." Thomas also threatened, in clear terms, to "dismiss from the army any man, be his rank what it may, whom I find maltreating the freedmen."[19] But whatever the reason, Thomas's clear stand had good results.

Initially this policy was controversial in the North, where it provoked a full spectrum of opinions. Democratic voices, like the *Cincinnati Daily Enquirer*, called black troops "*a disgrace to the Government that employs them—a reproach to our cause—calculated to bring upon us the shame of the whole world*. . . . The negro is a barbarian." Frederick Douglass, on the other hand, tirelessly urged men of color to enlist, for he believed that "once let the black man get upon his person the brass letters, U.S., let him get an eagle on his button, and a musket on his shoulder and bullets in his pocket, and there is no power on earth which can deny that he has earned the right to citizenship in the United States." Similarly, Henry Highland Garnet told a black audience, "We must fight! fight! fight!" and an editorial in the *Weekly Anglo-African,* of New York City, argued that the war was an opportunity "for reclaiming and holding our withheld rights." "What better field to claim our rights than the field of battle?" it asked.[20]

White supporters of the use of black troops sometimes combined racial self-interest with the cause of reform. George H. Hepworth, a Northern minister and army chaplain who worked with freedmen in Louisiana, published a book praising the capacity of African Americans for free labor and for military service. But Hepworth's interest in the freedmen was not wholly altruistic. He was glad that "the negro can be made to carry on this war," because "we need our boys at home." The *New York Times,* meanwhile, agreed that white troops needed to be relieved of some of the burden of fighting in the steamy South and stressed that the use of black troops was "a purely *military* question," and not a measure of reform. Military service did not imply equality to the *Times,* for it had continued to deny "that any portion of the Republican party or any but a very small and insignificant portion of the people of the North believe the negro race to be the equal of the white race."[21]

Regardless of clashing opinions, the wartime use of former slaves as free laborers and as soldiers continued. Against this background, it is remarkable that anything was accomplished, yet the results were striking. Despite the very unfavorable conditions under which African Americans first experienced freedom in the South, they seized their chances with alacrity. Voluminous and favorable evidence began to accumulate about their conduct as farmers and fighters. Indeed, government reports, testimony from missionaries and voluntary organizations, newspaper accounts, and books soon produced a wealth of information and analysis bearing on the qualities or character of black people and their capacity for freedom and citizenship. The authors of some of these reports may have been predisposed in favor of the freedmen, but most were not. A wealth of data came from agents of the federal government itself, such as army officers, as well as from the American Freedmen's Inquiry Commission, which was appointed by Secretary of War Stanton early in 1863. Despite the diversity of sources, the preponderant majority of reports agreed on major questions. Had there been a comprehensive effort designed to shed light on the question of African Americans' future, the government could scarcely have obtained more or better information.

One issue that immediately concerned Northerners was, as General Benjamin Butler wrote to President Lincoln, whether "black labor can be as well governed, used, and made as profitable in a state of freedom as in slavery." For generations, slaveholders had insisted that African Americans were congenitally lazy and would work only under the lash. Southern planters continued to assert that, in the words of Louisianan A. McCollam, "The negro has little, or no ambition to provide for the future. Hence corporal punishment is the only way to effect it."[22] But wartime experience rapidly convinced Northern agents and observers who were on the scene that the conclusion reached by Butler was right: there was "no doubt" that the freedmen would work, and work well.[23]

Early in 1862 favorable reports began to arrive from the Sea Islands. Special Agent Edward L. Pierce, for example, informed the secretary of the treasury that notions of their "general indolence" were untrustworthy. "I have seen them working faithfully and with a will," wrote Pierce, and "with proper motives set before them, they will as freemen be as industrious as any race of men are likely to be in this climate." Unfortunately, the army often failed to pay for work done or to provide needed provisions. Nevertheless, several months later, Pierce reaffirmed that when the former slaves "could clearly see that they were to receive the rewards of their labor, they worked with commendable diligence." Captain E. W. Hooper reported to the military governor in the Department of the South that, "I never knew a case where a man had reasonable security of getting wages, even moderate wages, that he was not ready to work." And a plantation superintendent from Ladies Island, South Carolina, testified that the freedmen worked "more industriously, thoroughly and energetically under the system of compensation than under the old system." The Massachusetts businessman and engineer Edward Philbrick pronounced himself "fully satisf[i]ed" with the freedmen's labor in 1863, and concluded, "The negro is actuated by the same motives as other men." At the end of 1864, Rufus Saxton, the military governor of the region, concluded that the "Sea Islands can be successfully cultivated by free labor moderately compensated." He added that on lands purchased or leased by the freedmen, they had "shown an industry, sagacity and prudence, that will not compare unfavorably in its results with white men in similar circumstances."[24]

From the Upper South came similar testimony. The Emancipation League published reports that "they are willing to work" and that no group was more "easily managed and kept at work." Captain C. B. Wilder, who superintended contrabands in Virginia, agreed that black people were disposed to work "if they could be reasonably paid." He admitted that their work and capabilities had exceeded his expectations: "I did not think they had so much brain. They have got as many brains as you or I have, though they have an odd way of showing it." Another Virginia superintendent of contrabands, Dr. Orlando Brown, testified that "they work well" and that this was "the universal testimony" of the overseers on farms. At the end of 1864, Brown reported that although many African American men were in the army, a smaller proportion of blacks than of whites needed government aid in his district. At the same time, Captain Wilder concluded that "the dogma . . . that negroes are very valuable as slaves, but when free, worthless, and unable to take care of themselves, is now exploded." He explained, "It makes all the difference . . . whether they are forced, or encouraged to work." Seventy-eight percent of the black population under his supervision was "now independent of assistance." Near Washington, D.C., an army quartermaster asked to replace his white laborers with African Americans, because the latter "are much superior workers."[25]

In Louisiana, government officials confirmed that the former slaves worked well and now were thinking and acting as free men. "On plantations managed by energetic men who desired free labor to succeed," reported the chaplain of a Connecticut regiment, "the negroes worked well," and they resisted "former overseers" who wanted to reassert a slavery-type control over them. H. Styles, an inspector of plantations for the Treasury Department, agreed: "These Negroes have succeeded beyond rebel Expectations in living without the assistance of white men." Colonel George H. Hanks, a superintendent of Negro labor in the Department of the Gulf, testified, "They are more willing to work and more patient than any set of human beings I ever saw." But he warned that planters were "even more rampant to enslave the negroes than ever before." Aware of this animosity, the freedmen insisted on their newly independent status. "The first moment you begin to talk to the slave of freedom, and tell him that in so many years he is to be free, or that his children are to be free, you spoil him for a slave," reported General James S. Wadsworth. Similarly, Provost Marshal John Ela observed, "The negroes come back on to the plantation, with altogether different feelings, from those of former times—They have obtained in the camps . . . and they exhibit a spirit of independence—a feeling, that they are no longer slaves, but hired laborers; and demand to be treated as such." These Louisiana freedmen proved "ready to work," but objected "to being hired out to the old slave holders,—very generally." Before long, some were petitioning "to cultivate the land on their own account."[26]

Federal officials filed the same kinds of reports from the Mississippi Valley, where conditions were often discouraging. An army superintendent of labor in Memphis admitted, in the spring of 1863, that many black laborers had been "most grossly abused . . . worked all day in water, drenched, nearly frozen, and then driven to tents for shelter . . . without covering, and almost without fire and food. . . . Wages seldom paid." Nevertheless, they performed important labor, such as "building fortification, cutting wood, rolling logs, running sawmills, and [working] in Quartermaster's Department and Hospitals." Other superintendents reported that the freedmen wanted pay for their labor. "Many if not most, have correct notions—believe they must work—anxious for pay," said a superintendent from Corinth, Mississippi. Those who leased plantations from the federal government, unfortunately, often ignored regulations and treated the freedmen very badly, showing "utter disregard" of their rights and of "even the commonest principles of humanity," according to Inspecting Officer Julian E. Bryant. Still, this officer added, "it has been demonstrated that the majority [of freedmen], if stimulated by the right kind of treatment, proper wages, and a prospect of bettering their condition, would labor faithfully and steadily: while some show a capacity for management and energy and executive ability that would do credit, to men of better education and a whiter skin."[27]

Some of the military's highest-ranking officers reached similarly positive conclusions. Adjutant General Lorenzo Thomas admitted that there had been many problems with the free-labor "experiment," which had been adopted "hastily and from necessity, with many misgivings." But freedmen's willingness to work was not an issue, and as early as October 1863 he pronounced free labor "a complete success." Admiral David D. Porter reported to Thomas that, "I have scarcely ever yet met with a Negro who has not been able to support himself, they are naturally astute at making money." His fleet employed many freedmen, including some of "our best mechanics," and he found that "the servants are all intelligent." Ben Montgomery, a former slave from the plantations of Joseph and Jefferson Davis, impressed Porter as being "as well educated as most white people and as sensible a man as I ever met with." General James Wadsworth reported to Secretary of the Treasury Salmon Chase in December 1863 that the freed blacks were "willing & anxious to continue to labor for their support." A few plantations had been leased to freedmen, and, "I found that the lands thus leased had been as well worked & that the laborers were as well cared for & as contented as on any Plantation leased by white men." John Eaton Jr., the general superintendent of freedmen in the Department of Mississippi and State of Arkansas, later agreed: "The Freedmen do best for themselves & the Gov't as independent cultivators of small farms[.] Those who warked [*sic*] for themselves, have raised on the average the most cotton per acre & have saved sums varying from one hundred dollars to ten thousand."[28]

Clearly, as army officers and Treasury agents worked with the freedmen, they developed a more informed opinion of their character, abilities, and culture. These white officials did not always view the freedmen in a favorable light, but their impressions of African American farmers and laborers were preponderantly positive. Viewed almost 150 year later, some of their comments reveal as much about the observers as they do about the observed; they also provided valuable information for wartime leaders about the former slaves and their surroundings.

Almost universally, officials praised the freedmen's desire for education and were surprised by the native intelligence they displayed. "They attended our free schools . . . regularly and with great earnestness," wrote Vincent Colyer from North Carolina. A Northern teacher in Virginia marveled that she "never saw such greedy people for study." Another visitor to Virginia found the schools "flourishing" and said that the children "have made at least as great progress as white children could have made in the same condition of life and under similar discouraging circumstances." One superintendent of Negro affairs in the Upper South said that "*all* engaged in teaching the Negroes" agreed that "they can learn to read and write as readily as white children," and another superintendent characterized black children as "smart, bright and quick to learn."[29]

In the Low Country along the southeast coast, "all" the adult freedmen "expressed a desire to have their children taught to read and write, and to learn themselves." Rufus Saxton, military governor for the Department of the South, felt in 1863 that slavery had degraded the slaves and "blunted their intellects" more completely on the Sea Islands than anywhere else, but he was confident that even there they could "make rapid strides toward improvement." One year later, he reported that, "They are intelligent, eager, and apt to acquire knowledge of letters, docile and receptive pupils." Likewise, in Louisiana, freedmen "manifest[ed] the greatest anxiety to educate their children."[30] Superintendents of contrabands in the Mississippi Valley, responding to a series of questions from their superior, John Eaton, described the freedmen in these terms:

> Far more intelligent than I supposed. Some are men of fine intelligence and correct views.
>
> Their common intelligence is good—much better than we had supposed.
>
> Exhibit intelligence greater than has been attributed to their race.
>
> House servants much more intelligent than field hands. All learn rapidly—are intuitive, not reflective—need line upon line.
>
> Higher than I had expected—keen and bright when they wish to understand;—stupid and idiotic when they do not.
>
> Better than many suppose, good as any could expect under the circumstances.
>
> As good as that of men, women & children anywhere, of any color, who cannot read.[31]

Reports also agreed that the South's African Americans were not quarrelsome or troublemakers, but well-behaved members of a community. "They were peaceable, orderly, cleanly & industrious," according to Vincent Colyer, whose report might have cheered a New England puritan. On Craney Island, in Virginia, Superintendent Orlando Brown reported very few disturbances or quarrels requiring an arrest. In North Carolina, Horace James reported that the freedmen were "happy and contented" except for the fact that the government was more than a year behind in paying their wages. Another official judged them to be "always more yielding to authority" than were whites, while in the Sea Islands, Edward Pierce heard little "profane swearing" and found that the freedmen were "not in any way inherently vicious." Rufus Saxton was confident that the blacks would be "provident" and quickly adopt "the social forms and habits of civilization." From his experience in Louisiana, General Wadsworth concluded that, "They will go on amicably with the whites. They are only too docile." Brigadier General John Hawkins affirmed that he "never saw people more willing to work and do what is right."[32]

The religiosity of the former slaves made a deep impression on Northern white observers. A superintendent of contrabands in the District of Columbia felt that the former slaves were "vastly more" religious than whites. "They are the most religious people I have ever had anything to do with, and are

Exceedingly devoted and fervent," he wrote. Edward Philbrick noticed their "religious trust" that "God has interfered to drive away their old masters and give them a chance for themselves." An observer on one of the plantations in South Carolina agreed that "They excel the whites in emotional religion," but he had some white, middle-class reservations about the fervor of their worship. "Their intellects need cultivation," he argued. "There must be education therefore to establish an equilibrium." To another white worker, "their religion" appeared to be "more a matter of *feeling* than of *principle*," and George Hepworth stated that the freedman's religion was "not always quite reasonable," but "an uncontrollable ecstasy." Others viewed the freedmen as not only "very religious," but "always orthodox," with "notions of doctrine better than to be expected." Some white observers in the Mississippi Valley found "their notions of the leading doctrines of the Bible" to be "remarkably correct" and their religious meetings "both solemn and interesting."[33]

Opinions about the freedmen's morality and their culture, which Northerners expected to be very different from their own, varied. Many observers assumed that there were deficiencies that would have to be overcome. For example, the Western Sanitary Commission urged the government to foster respect for "the institutions of religion, marriage, and all the customs of virtuous and civilized society," so that the former slaves would "become worthy of the blessing of a Christian civilization." A Northern teacher reported, "We found them docile but they are great liars and great thieves," and an army officer judged that "many are dishonest," because the slave system compelled them "to steal from their masters." Rev. J. B. Waterbury, of the American Bible Society, published a pamphlet called *Friendly Counsels for Freedmen* that was full of condescending admonitions, such as "Lying is a sin," "Cleanliness is very important," and "[Freedom] obliges you to seek a livelihood." A Northern abolitionist who visited occupied Virginia testified that former slaves' "opinions of conjugal fidelity" were "very loose." In the view of J. B. Roudanez, a Creole from New Orleans, the slave regime had undermined chastity, but African American females had become "more chaste" since the Emancipation Proclamation. In the Mississippi Valley, some superintendents of contrabands agreed that "their idea of the marriage relations" was "very low" or "all wrong." Others, however, took a more balanced view that considered the freedmen's past conditions. "Most of them have no idea of the sacredness of the marriage tie," said one man, but he added that marriage had "been impossible for them" and that for some black couples "the marriage relation exists in all its sacredness without legal sanction." Another official noted that the former slaves "have had no opportunity for correct notions and practices," yet many were "faithful." "Free and married," predicted one officer, "they will maintain the marital relations as sacredly as any other race."[34]

The cooperativeness or perceived pliability of the freedmen presented itself to some as a potential problem for peacetime. "They are much more docile and submissive than whites," reported a superintendent of contrabands in Washington, D.C., and General James Wadsworth exclaimed, "The docility of these people!" Based on his experience in Louisiana, Wadsworth feared that without proper government policies they might be "reenslaved," because they were "only too docile." Similarly, Colonel George Hanks argued that the former slaves had "been educated to a government of force; they are tractable, patient, and easily governed; if civil government be established here, and military rule withdrawn, there is the greatest danger that the negro would become subject to some form of serfdom." An inspector for the Treasury Department had a similar concern. "The Negro is Susceptible of flattery and Kind influence," he said, and would need more independence to withstand the "disposition among planters and Lessees . . . to make him More degraded and miserable, if possible, than under the old System of labor."[35] Here was a prediction, based on direct observation and accurate, of the oppressive white practices that black farmers would face in the postwar decades.

The same traits that aroused these fears also suggested to federal officials and others that the former slaves could be trained to be good soldiers. General Benjamin Butler believed that the "discipline" inherent in slavery meant an "advantage in favor of the negroes as soldiers." They had learned "to do as they are told" and did not question instructions or orders. Moreover, Butler was confident in May 1863, that there would be no need to draft freedmen into the army. "Give them *fair play,*" he argued, and let them have their own officers, and there would be ample volunteers. A superintendent of contrabands in Louisiana reported that the freedmen "often *beg* the privilege" of taking up arms, and he saw "no reason why they wo'd not become the best of soldiers for these times, & this region." Other officers in the Mississippi Valley readily agreed and gave their reasons, in answer to the inquiry from John Eaton Jr., the general superintendent of contrabands in the Department of Tennessee:

> I do not doubt he will make a good soldier. . . . Blacks have made better guards for our camps than whites.

> Should be at once armed. Many of them are bold—willing to fight, and are capable of rendering good service.
>
> Find they will unhesitatingly follow into any danger, so long as their leader exhibits no fear.
>
> I am confident, that with competent and brave white officers, they will make the best of soldiers.
>
> Policy and humanity say, Arm the negro.
>
> Yes, arm him! . . . These men will make good soldiers.
>
> Arm him—he is a man—he will fight—he can save the Union.[36]

On this question, of course, the Lincoln administration proved to need little prodding. Although the testimony of field officers in contact with the freedmen was certainly relevant, the needs of the military probably were more decisive. After two years of war and scores of bloody battles, the Union remained far from its goal of suppressing the rebellion, and any politician knew that the Northern public was not going to be patient indefinitely. Clearly, more troops were needed, and the freedmen were an obvious source for additional manpower. If Lincoln's doubts about the capacity of blacks to serve in the army had been substantial, he soon put them aside in order to try the experiment. The recruitment of freedmen under Adjutant General Lorenzo Thomas went forward swiftly, and tens of thousands of black men quickly entered the army. Many volunteered readily, eager to fight for freedom and Union, but the army also put heavy pressure on any others who came into Union lines but did not feel the urge to fight. As a result, most of the freedmen who farmed land within Union lines soon were women, children, and older or disabled males. The young and healthy men had shouldered rifles.

In a surprisingly short time, the hastily trained, raw black troops found themselves in the heat of battle, and contrary to the expectations of many whites, they acquitted themselves bravely. In May 1863 Federal forces sought to capture Port Hudson, on the Mississippi River, and African American troops were thrown into the assault. A dispatch to the *New York Times* bore the headline, "Great Bravery of the First and Third Louisiana Black Regiments: Six Distinct Charges Made by Them Upon the Enemy's Works." The *Times* correspondent, writing under the name Nemo, witnessed these troops "fighting most desperately." General Nathaniel Banks, in his official report, praised the conduct of the African Americans: "They answered every expectation. Their conduct was heroic. No troops could be more determined or more daring. . . . The severe test to which they were subjected, and the determined manner in which they encountered the enemy, leave upon my mind no doubt of their ultimate success. They require only good officers, commands of limited numbers and careful discipline, to make them excellent soldiers." The editors of the *Times* declared that this battle "settle[d] the question that the negro race can fight with great prowess. . . . It is no longer possible to doubt the bravery and steadiness of the colored race, when rightly led." The *Chicago Tribune* also published General Banks's report, along with a poem urging white soldiers never to "scorn the black regiment." The *Cincinnati Gazette* added that two-thirds of the 900 black troops "could not be accounted for" after their assaults. "It is said on every side that they fought with the desperation of tigers." Even Cincinnati's rival, Democratic paper, the *Daily Enquirer,* carried an article reporting the "undaunted bravery" of these African American soldiers.[37]

Quickly, more news of the bravery of black troops came from the South. Along the Mississippi River, African American soldiers again faced heavy fire in the attack on Milliken's Bend. The *Chicago Tribune* reported on the "Gallantry of our Negro Troops" and quoted an observer who said that "the negroes fought like tigers—better, in fact, than their white officers." The *Tribune*'s editors declared that the black man "has proved himself . . . and before the end of the war he will . . . have achieved a brilliant record." Then, in Charleston, South Carolina, Colonel Robert Shaw led his Fifty-fourth Massachusetts Regiment in a courageous but doomed assault on Battery Wagner. With undeniable courage, the black soldiers rushed the ramparts, only to be cut down in large numbers, many of the men dying with Colonel Shaw. The *New York Times* headlined the "Desperate Bravery of the Assaulting Party" and emphasized that the black soldiers were given "the post of extreme honor and of danger in the advance." They "gave a fierce yell and rushed up the glacis . . . gaining the parapet" before being cut down by the "murderous reception" of "grape, canister, and a continuous fusillade of small arms." By such bravery these soldiers showed that they were "entitled to assert their right to manhood."[38]

Such stirring reports forced some Democratic newspapers to complain that abolitionists were giving the efforts of black soldiers too much praise, while "the white soldiers must stand back." Yet even in Republican papers, white self-interest and a reluctance to recognize African Americans' claims to equality surfaced. The *Chicago Tribune,* which previously had declared that "the public mind must be enlightened and liberalized," now mixed praise for black courage with racially motivated observations. By previously excluding black Americans from the army, said the paper, "we have paid dearly . . . for our white pride." Though it urged the administration to "put every negro in the ranks at once," the *Tribune* argued that common sense, national interests, and the rights of the people indicated "that we should spare as much white blood as possible during the rest of the war." The *New York Times* reflected on the bravery of black troops in the South and concluded, "Being already acclimated and inured to hardship, they will be more available for service in this section than northern white soldiers, who . . . would undoubtedly suffer severely from the febrile and other deadly diseases that rage in the lowlands bordering on the Lower Mississippi." And, the *Times* added, the freedmen needed more "time and discipline" to become reliable soldiers.[39]

Henry Raymond's *Times* also was quick to deny that military service under the administration's policy would mean equal status for blacks in freedom. By an ironic coincidence, the news of black troops' valor along the Mississippi preceded the viciously antiblack draft riots in New York City by only a few weeks. Perhaps that shocking demonstration of Northern prejudice and racial hatred influenced the *Times* columns; nonetheless, it was true that the paper merely continued to state positions that it had clearly enunciated before. These conservative and racially prejudiced positions were that the administration's goal was to restore the Union; that emancipation was only a needed means to that end; and that the Republicans had no intention of revolutionizing race relations in the North or promoting equality in the nation.

At the end of July 1863, an article in the *Times* attempted to sum up what the war had revealed about African Americans. A number of "Humbugs" had been destroyed by the war, said the *Times.* It now was clear that slaves would not remain staunchly loyal to their masters; that they preferred freedom to slavery; that they would not rise in a bloody insurrection within the Confederacy; but that they could fight usefully in the army and, as soldiers, possessed their "share of combativeness and courage." Yet the paper hoped that more would not be expected of black troops than of white soldiers, and it cautioned, "We have yet to be convinced that the ignorant African can fight with the same effectiveness as the intelligent white man."[40]

Several days later, the *Times* addressed "The Social and Political Status of the Southern Negro." Its editors first rejected the claim that freedom would lead to racial amalgamation. Arguing that it was slavery that produced mulattos, they asserted that, in freedom, "it is notorious that the personal repugnance toward [black people]" was much stronger than in the slave South. Then the *Times* contemptuously dismissed the claims of "blatherskite" politicians that emancipation would lead to intermarriage and to the African American's becoming "a *voting* citizen of the United States." Assuring its readers that the *Times* opposed such an idea "as strongly as anybody," the paper declared that "for many generations to come," suffrage for freedmen would rapidly bring about "the destruction of popular institutions on this continent." The right to vote was a "privilege," and American democracy already faced "enough risk" from "the ignorance and corruption of white voters." History and the African character proved that blacks were "incapable" of exercising the right of suffrage, said the *Times,* "without danger to themselves and their neighbors." To think otherwise was "little short of insane." Although African Americans were people with human rights, they should be excluded from government as were women and Indians. Not only did the "vast majority" of freedmen have no knowledge of "the science of government" but they still needed to learn "the art of supplying their own daily wants."[41]

Such sentiments reflected the administration's political priorities and prejudiced Northerners even as they ignored facts that the *Times* had already reported and was soon to cover. In October 1863, the paper carried a news report entitled "The Southern Negro," in which a correspondent detailed how well and successfully former slaves were working as free laborers on a plantation in Louisiana. With pay, the freedmen were completing one-third more work than they had done as slaves. They were making money and attending a school and church. The writer admitted that he had assumed that it would take a generation for slaves to adapt to freedom, but the reality seemed to be different, as these blacks showed themselves to be responsible, thrifty, and industrious. This correspondent still believed that most slaves were "low, degraded, ignorant, and vicious," but he had learned that a hopeful future was possible if whites were not captured by "prejudice generated out of our passion and ignorance." One month later, the *Times* called for the establishment of a "Bureau of Emancipation" to help the freedmen move "from a state of dependence to one of self-supporting industry."[42] Beyond question, the future status of the freedmen was now demanding attention, for the events of the war obliged policymakers to consider this question.

At least two commissions established by federal authorities developed recommendations on policy toward the freedmen and the future status of African Americans. Both arrived at favorable conclusions. One of these, the American Freedmen's Inquiry Commission, originated at the cabinet level through appointment by the secretary of war, and it published its findings for all to read. The second was an investigative body for the army. In addition, a variety of individuals who were involved in some way with the free-labor arrangements in the occupied South spoke up, both publicly and privately, giving additional advice to government officials.

Early in the war, the opinions and recommendations that were formed often had a paternalistic flavor and were based on the assumption that the freedmen would need considerable schooling in freedom or civilization. But as time went on, the evidence from the South favorably impressed those who were observing the freedmen. A consensus began to develop that Southern blacks could manage well for themselves and needed only a fair chance. In order for them to have that chance, it probably would be necessary to arrange protection for the freedmen from the hostility of their former owners. But with an opportunity to rise or fall on their own, the freedmen could take their place as productive American citizens.

Early in 1862, an example of a reformist but paternalistic approach came from the South Carolina Sea Islands. Edward L. Pierce, a Harvard Law School graduate who was serving as a special agent for the Treasury Department, reported his impressions of African Americans to Secretary Salmon Chase. Pierce brought abolitionist sympathies as well as free-labor beliefs and assumptions to his work. Encountering many slaves of "low intellectual development" but others "who were as fine specimens of human nature as one can ever expect to find," he was optimistic about the long-term prospects for improvement among the freedmen. But he assumed that tutoring and guidance from idealistic Northerners like himself would be necessary. "As yet," he argued, the blacks of the Sea Islands were "in large numbers unprepared for the full privileges of citizens." He urged bringing in missionaries from the North and giving each laborer a "patch of ground on which to raise corn or vegetables for consumption or sale." His plan, he explained, "contemplates a paternal discipline for the time being" that would prepare the slaves for a brighter future. Thereafter, the market should govern. "As fast as laborers show themselves fitted for all the privileges of citizens, they should be dismissed from the system and allowed to follow any employment they please and where they please."[43]

Other observers were not able to combine these paternalistic and free-market ideas as easily as did Pierce. Notions of leaving the freedmen entirely alone, to rise or fall on their own, as Frederick Douglass had advocated, competed with the belief that a period of guardianship was essential. Edward Philbrick, the Northern investor active in the Sea Islands, was entirely devoted to the market and wanted to shun paternalism. "The negro is actuated by the same motives as other men," Philbrick wrote, and would respond to incentives. He established stores on the plantations and stocked them with inexpensive consumer goods in order to cultivate new wants. After the war, he insisted, there should be "no restrictions" on the African Americans' decisions about labor. "It must be *entirely voluntary.* Any half way system of pupilage or apprenticeship will fail, as compared with a perfectly free intercourse between Employer & Employed." On the other hand, Frederick Eustis, a plantation superintendent on the Sea Islands, believed "some system of guardianship" or "the apprenticeship system" was necessary, because the former slaves were "not prepared for freedom yet."[44]

Generals Benjamin Butler and James Wadsworth basically agreed with Philbrick but wanted to guard against Southern interference. Butler declared that black labor should regulate itself, just as white labor did, and "under the same laws." But given the destruction of slavery and the "disorganized state" of society, he favored a military, territorial rule for some years, to allow a transition in the society. General Wadsworth felt, on the basis of his experience in Louisiana, that the system of General Banks was controlling the freedmen too much. Wadsworth told the American Freedmen's Inquiry Commission that the government should help blacks make their first labor contract, "but just as soon as possible you must say to them, 'Now you must make your own bargains.'" He believed that if the "animus of the masters" proved to be virulent, the government would need to remain involved. Then, it could "exercise a certain guardianship" for protection, and "suspend reconstruction" until a thorough emancipation was a reality. Wadsworth expected that to require no more than three to five years.[45]

Another idea that gained some adherents was the linking of guardianship with white immigration to the South. Judge A. D. Smith, a direct-tax commissioner assigned to South Carolina, argued boldly that the freedmen should have "a homestead given to them—they *must have land, land.*" He told the American Freedmen's Inquiry Commission that every freedman should have the chance "to purchase from five to fifteen or five hundred acres." But all transfers of real estate should be sales, including sales "to white men," because "I want to have the examplar [*sic*] of white enterprise before the colored people." Success, he believed, required the "Anglo Saxon spirit of intelligence and enterprise to excite their emulation."[46] In northern Louisiana, Brigadier General John P. Hawkins reached similar conclusions. He advised the Northern abolitionist, Gerritt Smith, that there should be "no laws for the negro as if he were a child and had to be taught every thing," but Hawkins also believed it was essential to "get a large loyal population south." "We must have a large white population here," he said, and the solution was to divide the land into tracts of 80 to 200 acres and invite "the farmers of the north . . . to come down here and cultivate them." George Hepworth, in his book published in 1864, likewise argued that the North should "leave half our army to settle in the land they have conquered" and instill Northern values.[47]

Northern immigration to the South became a favorite project of the *Continental Monthly,* which promoted it frequently and vigorously as early as 1862. In April of that year, the magazine argued for apprenticeship, with "suitable instruction, civil and religious," supplemented by white settlers from the North, the West, and Europe. Later, its editors argued at length for "colonizing certain portions of the conquered territory with free white labor," which could instruct the black man and "contrive to persuade Cuffy to become industrious." The "'Northing' of the South" was the only solution, in the eyes of the magazine's editors, for there was "no hope of reconstruction to be founded on reformed secessionists." "Our only hope is in a complete reorganization of the South, by infusing into it Northern blood, life, ideas, education, and industry," they wrote. The history of emancipation in the Caribbean also proved, according to one article, that "European intelligence, European conscience, and European firmness of will are necessary to insure to the blacks the permanence of those rich blessings which emancipation has bestowed." Early in 1864, the *New York Times* supported a similar idea put forward by Senator Henry Wilson, who urged giving confiscated or abandoned Southern lands to U.S. Army veterans.[48]

One reason the *Times* gave for supporting Wilson's idea was that Northerners could support the freedmen against the hostility of their former masters. That idea began to be persuasive to a great many of the officials and volunteers in the occupied South who were observing the progress of the freedmen. As paternalism and condescension gave way to an enhanced respect for the ability and humanity of African Americans, the unyielding desire of Southern whites to control became more visible as a future problem. Colonel George Hanks warned the American Freedmen's Inquiry Commission that Southern planters were "even more rampant to enslave the negroes than ever before" and felt no loyalty to the United States. "With the present feeling of the Southern whites against them," Hanks warned, "to be left without national guarantees for the maintenance of their civil rights as freemen would be worse than Slavery." Several months later, in September 1864, a Treasury Department inspector informed his superiors that there was "a disposition among planters . . . to impress the Negro with a Sense of dependence, and to make him More degraded and miserable, if possible, than under the old System of labor." Southern planters who expressed an opinion did not hesitate to affirm that in their view the blacks could not provide for themselves and would not work without physical coercion. The freedmen themselves, of course, felt this hostility, and as a result they resisted the idea of working for their old masters. One group of blacks in Louisiana petitioned Treasury inspectors to be allowed to work "the Place among ourselves."[49]

Reports such as these constituted a treasure-trove of valuable information and advice for policymakers, if they chose to address the issue and give priority to it. What is striking is how little attention was paid to the recommendations and possibilities that emerged from these data. Not only was the amount of information ample and its scope far-reaching, but the raw information was analyzed, scrutinized, and digested by an official, high-level body, the American Freedmen's Inquiry Commission. The commissioners traveled widely, holding hearings in the North and in various parts of the occupied South. They interviewed scores of witnesses, from freedmen to generals, before writing their reports. Since this body had been appointed by the secretary of war directly, it was reasonable to assume that its findings and recommendations would carry great weight. Moreover, the commission put its conclusions before the general public, in addition to submitting them to government officials. The commission published a preliminary report in June 1863, and its final report in May 1864. Moreover, two of the three commissioners — Robert Dale Owen and James McKaye — published books in 1864 that drew heavily on the final report and expanded on its recommendations.[50]

The preliminary report of the American Freedmen's Inquiry Commission devoted much of its text to reporting on the former slaves who were coming into Union lines and to discerning their characteristics. It found that slavery had been more oppressive in South Carolina than in the Upper South or in Florida, and it identified a variety of social ills in the newly freed population.

These included lying, stealing, weak family relations, and ignorance, but observation of differences among the freedmen and of the changes taking place in freedom convinced the commissioners that the environment of slavery was responsible for the problems. The "vices" seen in the refugees were "such as appertain to their former social condition. Men who own no property do not learn to respect the rights of property. Men who are subjected to despotic rule acquire the habit of shielding themselves from arbitrary punishment by subterfuges, or by a direct departure from the truth. In the case of women living under a system in which the conjugal relation is virtually set at naught, the natural result is that the instinct of chastity remains undeveloped or becomes obscured." African Americans who had escaped from bondage and tasted freedom, however, were quickly adopting new and positive practices, showing that they were capable of great improvement. They placed "a high value both on education for their children and religious instruction for themselves." They showed "a strong sense of the obligation of law and of the stringency of any duty legally imposed" on them. They were laboring productively for wages and improving. Even in South Carolina, "the old habits are speedily yielding to better teaching," and the commission was confident that the former slaves could be "reformed" in "a comparatively brief period."[51]

The preliminary report noted certain characteristics that its authors felt set African Americans apart from whites. "As a general rule," they wrote, the freedmen were "more zealously devotional than the white race; they have more resignation and more reliance on Divine Providence. They have, also, more superstitions." The commissioners noted an "absence of revenge and blood-thirstiness" as a racial characteristic, but did not doubt that African Americans could act with courage. Another trait that had positive implications was their tendency to work docilely and be "easily managed" and "cheerful." In the virtues of "kindness and humility," stated the report, "we have as much to learn from them as they from us."[52]

Despite the preliminary nature of this report, the commission presented some strong findings and recommendations. The freedman definitely would work, and he "lack[ed] no essential aptitude for civilization. . . . There is little reason to doubt that he will become a useful member of the great industrial family of nations." The North would not be "flooded with fugitives fleeing from bondage," because former slaves would want to remain in the South. The United States should bring up to 300,000 black men into the army, where their service would be "advantageous." Every act of Northern prejudice, by discouraging such service, gave "aid and comfort" to the enemy. Refugees should be moved to plantations, where they could work for wages, draw their pay, buy, and save. In addition, a freedmen's bureau staffed by men of "comprehensive benevolence and humanitarian views" should be established, to guard the freedmen against prejudice and mistreatment. But this organization must not "become a permanent institution." Rather, it should aim at "even-handed justice, not special favor," and it should encourage "self-reliance and self-support" as soon as possible. The authors added that "the sole condition of permanent peace on this continent is the eradication of negro slavery."[53]

Eleven months later, after much additional investigation, the American Freedmen's Inquiry Commission issued a final report that was stronger and more decided in its recommendations. On no point, the authors declared, were they more convinced than that "the enfranchised negro is as capable of taking care of himself and his family as any other portion of our people." Thus, there was no reason to fear that "the result of emancipation will be to throw the negroes as a burden on the community." Nor was there reason to fear that great numbers of freedmen would move to the North or that the racial "amalgamation," so feared by racist propagandists such as J. H. Van Evrie, would occur. In fact, race mixing was the "offspring of slavery" and diminished in freedom. Turning to the Union's crisis, the commissioners affirmed once more that the freedmen had vital contributions to make to the war effort, but they emphasized that the nation had to treat these soldiers well and without discrimination.[54]

Impressions that the white commissioners had formed about racial traits were clearer in the final report, perhaps because they had pulled their ideas together into one concentrated portion of the text. Anglo-Saxons, they believed, had "great force of character, much mental activity, an unflagging spirit of enterprise, . . . a certain hardness, a stubborn will, only moderate geniality, a lack of habitual cheerfulness." They were a people more likely "to call forth respect than love; better fitted to do than to enjoy." Black people, on the other hand, were "the reverse": they were "genial, lively, docile, emotional, [and in them] the affections rule; the social instincts maintain the ascendant." The "African race" was "a knowing rather than a thinking race," and although it would find a respectable place in society, it would never "take a lead in the material improvement of the world." But black people excelled in "humility, loving kindness, resignation under adversity, reliance on Divine Providence," and the final report turned these differences to African Americans' advantage by asserting that, "As civilization advances, these Christian graces of meekness and long suffering will be rated higher than the world rates them now."[55]

"What amount of aid and interference is necessary or desirable to enable the freedmen to tide over the stormy transition from slavery to freedom?" asked the commissioners. Reaffirming their earlier recommendation, they urged a freedmen's bureau, but only to provide "temporary aid" and give protection to men who "for generations" had been "despoiled of their rights." Not only would the freedmen "soon take the labor and expense out of our hands," but "emancipation . . . should be unconditional and absolute." The commissioners rejected "apprenticeship" in any form, basing that judgment on the experience of the West Indies, and they insisted that "the freedman should be treated at once as any other free man." In its final report the commission adopted a position essentially the same as that put forward by Frederick Douglass. The nation should give the freedmen "a fair chance." Give them "civil and political" rights and a "fair and equal administration of justice"; "guard them against the virtual restoration of slavery in any form"; and then "let them take care of themselves."[56]

Without hesitation, the commissioners added recommendations relating to postwar reconstruction and the nation's future. They noted that the attitudes of Northern whites toward African Americans were "rapidly changing" and that the public was "fast approaching" a point at which it would support a constitutional amendment banning slavery. Hailing this development, the commissioners declared, "We need the negro not only as a soldier to aid in quelling the rebellion, but as a loyal citizen to assist in reconstructing on a permanently peaceful and orderly basis the insurrectionary States." Moreover, "short of entire justice there is no permanent security," for "in withholding from the freedman his civil and political rights we leave disfranchised, at a critical juncture, 4,000,000 of the most loyal portion of our population," with results that could be "disastrous." Therefore, all freedmen should be assured "equal rights," and those rights should be protected. This conclusion echoed the views of the *Weekly Anglo-African,* which judged freedom without the vote "a partial emancipation unworthy of the name."[57]

In his book, *The Wrong of Slavery and the Right of Emancipation and the Future of the African Race in the United States,* Robert Dale Owen explained this recommendation further, making plain that the right of suffrage should accompany freedom. He judged that "the eradication of . . . prejudice of race and color" would be a larger task than emancipation. Nevertheless, the freedmen were "the loyal half of a disturbed and disaffected population" in the rebel states, Owen wrote, and it would be a fatal mistake to leave that half of the population disenfranchised. He estimated that no more than one-third of the South's whites could be expected to be loyal. Consequently, representative and loyal governments could not be built on only one-sixth of the population. Moreover, he was convinced that the freedmen would rapidly progress and as voters would not be prey for demagogues, because as slaves they had learned to be wary and suspicious. Former owners would tend "still to treat them in an unjust and tyrannical manner," and for that reason as well the freedmen needed "those rights, civil and political, without which they are but laboring as a man labors with hands bound."[58]

Owen's fellow commissioner, James McKaye, made equally forceful recommendations in his book, *The Mastership and its Fruits.* McKaye declared that "the black man is not only capable of self-guidance and self-maintenance, but . . . under the influence of higher and nobler human motives and incentives, his progress in the arts and attainments of civilized life, is subject only to the same laws that control that of other races of men." The danger to America came not from the former slaves but from "the virus of slavery, the lust of ownership" that remained in "the hearts of these old masters . . . as virulent and active today as it ever was." To move the nation forward in the era of freedom, McKaye advocated policies that would:

—put "the civil right" of the freedman "on the same broad basis as that of the white man"
—protect the freedman's "civil and political rights," including "the right to the elective franchise, based upon the acquisition on their part, of such qualifications only, as are deemed essential in their white fellow-citizens," and
—by using "confiscated estates" or "forfeited lands," divide "the great plantations into moderate sized farms" for the benefit primarily of the "poor whites."[59]

In his support for confiscation and land redistribution, McKaye went even further than Owen, and McKaye's wording did not exclude blacks from that redistribution.

Thus, the official report of the American Freedmen's Inquiry Commission, and the books published by two of its members, forecast the danger of serfdom or racial oppression in the postwar South. The hostility of former masters and their determination to regain the racial and economic control of slavery cast a huge shadow over the freedmen's future. Unless the government took action, racism would produce a depressing continuity of oppression in the postwar South. The gains of emancipation, these reports warned, might become illusory.

A second commission produced valuable data speaking to the future of the freedmen. Reports that serious corruption had developed among army and government officials in the area of the Mississippi Valley forced President Lincoln to appoint a body known as the Smith-Brady Commission to investigate. The duties of this body were more limited in scope, and ultimately its findings were "hushed up," because they "indicated that the state governments set up by Lincoln in the Mississippi Valley were centers of vast corruption rather than renascent Unionism." But testimony before the commission generated information that was often consistent with the findings of the American Freedmen's Inquiry Commission. For example, according to one superintendent in the Bureau of Free Labor, the former slaves were "ready to work." Their reluctance to labor for "the old slave holders" and for some of the "new men" was due to mistreatment. Planters wanted to control their former slaves, and the freedmen were "treated worse . . . , if anything," by new lessees "than by their old employers." Other testimony indicated that experienced officials shared "the general impression" that the existing labor system should be set aside, "so as to let every negro hire himself at the best wages he could procure." If freedmen were protected in this right, "all would go on & be attended with a great deal better success than we are achieving under this system of [army] coercion."[60]

Thus, abundant evidence gathered on the ground in the occupied South pointed clearly to the ability of African Americans to become productive and independent citizens if given the chance. In freedom, the former slaves would work, support themselves, pursue education, and strengthen their families. Moreover, knowledgeable government advisers recommended that the freedmen gain the right to vote and possibly receive grants of land. These steps were necessary, the advisers argued, not merely to administer justice, but also to bring lasting peace to the nation and establish loyal governments in the heart of rebeldom. How would the administration deal with this gift of evidence and analysis that was highly relevant to policy?

THREE

AMNESTY, APPRENTICESHIP, AND THE FREEDMEN'S FUTURE

While war was creating major changes in the South, 1863 proved to be a crucial year for policymaking in Washington. Military events continued to be of primary concern, but the progress of the war was not the only issue on people's minds. President Lincoln was eager to begin the process of bringing rebellious Southerners back into the Union. In addition, that central and flawed question that troubled whites — "What shall we do with the negro?" — was forcing its way into public debate and into policy. Undeniably, the march of armies and the Emancipation Proclamation signaled a changed society for the South. As conflict undermined the institution of slavery and as freedmen played a greater role in the war, Northern citizens and policymakers looked toward the future. Clearly, major decisions were in order. Despite the importance of the issue, however, and despite the conflicting efforts of abolitionists, reformers, conservatives, and racists, the future of African Americans only rarely claimed center stage. Nevertheless, policy was being formed, and fateful decisions were being made.

In this process, the most influential actor was President Abraham Lincoln. As commander in chief, his views carried a special weight that no congressman or group of congressmen could match. Similarly, as the head of his party and its chief spokesman, he occupied a commanding position from which to respond to political tides and unexpected developments. Moreover, because Lincoln was in a position to initiate proposals and take executive action, his ideas tended to establish the context or set the boundaries within which discussion would evolve. Despite strong protest from Republicans in Congress, he issued proclamations that defined the government's approach to both white Southerners and the freedmen. Democrats, congressional Republicans, and various groups of citizens all would speak out on the future status of African Americans, but Lincoln's voice would prove most influential.

In 1863 and the early months of 1864, Lincoln gave careful thought to Reconstruction and the consequences of emancipation. On these issues, he developed strong but complex positions. Careful analysis of Lincoln's policies reveals that he continued to be deeply concerned, indeed solicitous, about the feelings of rebellious Southern whites. He seemed determined to find a way to bring them back into the Union on a cordial and cooperative basis after the fighting was over. In pursuit of that end, he was ready to offer them significant and attractive inducements, including inducements that came at the expense of the interests of the freedmen. Although he began to stiffen his commitment to emancipation, he showed Southern whites that he was not going to insist on anything approaching racial equality. The rights of African Americans in freedom was a topic he did not pursue in public, even when a test of his policy of colonization failed disastrously—and he barely raised it in private. Reunion was the compelling priority for him, and eventual emancipation for all the slaves was becoming nonnegotiable; efforts toward racial progress in postemancipation society were neither compelling nor nonnegotiable.

Lincoln showed little interest in the favorable reports about freedmen that were coming from the occupied South, and he repeatedly indicated that he was willing to constrict the future of African Americans as a means of gaining white acceptance of their freedom. Perhaps the president's heart was free of prejudice, as Frederick Douglass later commented, but Douglass also observed that Lincoln was "preeminently the white man's president."[1] Whatever the president's private feelings may have been, Lincoln chose not to take political risks to improve the future status of black people. He also showed little desire to educate the public away from its long established racism. An overriding devotion to reunion, a practical pessimism about America's racial attitudes, and the calculus of political advantage in American society convinced him that other goals were more feasible and more important. While many Democrats opposed any change in the status of black Americans, many Republicans in Congress and in the North expressed dissatisfaction with Lincoln's policies toward both the freedmen and Southern whites.

THERE IS A TENDENCY today to assume that Abraham Lincoln wanted to free the slaves long before 1863 and temporarily stayed his hand only because he wisely recognized that public opinion had not yet developed to the point at which emancipation would be politically acceptable. This view, however, contradicts Lincoln's own, consistent account of his actions. More importantly, it reverses a correct understanding of the priorities that he chose to follow as president. Lincoln explained to a proslavery Kentucky Unionist that "I have done no official act in mere deference to" antislavery feelings. He insisted that although he was "naturally anti-slavery," his oath of office "forbade" him to "indulge my primary abstract judgment on the moral question of slavery." Instead, Lincoln wrote, he had moved against slavery only when he saw "the indispensable necessity for military emancipation."[2] Lincoln's actions confirm that his first priority was always to restore the Union, and that meant reestablishing a government embracing the Southern slaveholders who had rebelled. Even as he moved forward with emancipation, he sought to mitigate the fears of slaveholders and conservative Northerners.

In the early months of 1863, Lincoln felt anxious and worried about his policy of military emancipation. He was troubled partly by the possible impact of the Emancipation Proclamation on racist and conservative Northern whites. He feared that this measure, though militarily necessary, might prove so divisive as to undermine the "paramount object," the restoration of the Union. James G. Blaine likewise feared that Lincoln's policy was "tending to a fatal division among the people."[3] Even among loyal military leaders there was serious opposition to his proclamation. During the previous year, General McClellan had made clear that he opposed Lincoln's approach to the war and the relatively mild steps that the president had taken to encourage action against slavery by the states. Now another general, the Illinois Democrat John A. McClernand, weighed in with new objections. In response to a letter from McClernand, Lincoln showed how far he was willing to go to constrain the future of black Americans in order to appease the South.

After denying once more that he wanted anything other than for the rebels to lay down their arms and "take their places, and their rights, in the Union," Lincoln noted that he had given the Southern states one hundred days to avoid emancipation. Since they had not ended their rebellion, this measure of "military necessity" had been taken and "must stand." But, the president went on, the rebellious states "need not be hurt by it. Let them adopt systems of apprenticeship for the colored people, conforming substantially to the most approved plans of gradual emancipation, and, with the aid they can have from the general government, they may be nearly as well off, in this respect, as if the present trouble had not occurred." Apprenticeship, like gradual emancipation, would enable the South to hold onto its slaves for decades. Lincoln himself had proposed a plan in which adult slaves would have to remain in bondage until age 35, with newborn slave children required to serve until age 18, if female, or age 21, if male. In addition, he had urged financial compensation from the Federal government to help slave owners mitigate their loss. This letter demonstrated that he continued to favor this approach after the effective date of his Emancipation Proclamation. To General McClernand he pledged that he remained ready to give governmental support to apprenticeship, which he also would refer to as "temporary arrangements." In closing, he even suggested, despite his statement that emancipation "must stand," that "peace upon the old terms" might be possible if rebellious Southerners "act at once."[4]

Meanwhile, civilian morale in the North was a great concern for Lincoln as he considered the effects of his policy of emancipation. As he later described it, when 1863 began, "the tone of public feeling" was "not satisfactory." The war effort had been going badly, both militarily and diplomatically. Then the Emancipation Proclamation, because it was controversial and unpopular with many, added to the uncertainty and debate, both at home and abroad. This unsettled situation constituted a "crisis which threatened to divide the friends of the Union." For some months, the president watched as "hope, and fear, and doubt" contended in the public mind and as the Union endured "dark and doubtful days."[5]

During this anxious time, Lincoln labored to keep the friends of the Union from dividing and to retain their support. Urging patriotism above party, he called on all Unionists to stand together. Repeatedly he explained and excused his Emancipation Proclamation as a necessary means to save the Union. For example, in June, in a letter to Erastus Corning and other New York Democrats who protested the arrest of Clement Vallandigham, Lincoln challenged his critics to meet him "upon a level one step higher than any party platform." Taking note of the fact that they had chosen to describe themselves "as 'Democrats,'" the president challenged them to rise to a higher plane. Corning and his colleagues would have done better to call themselves "American citizens," he asserted, for as patriotic citizens, Republicans and Democrats could work together through the nation's crisis. "We could do better battle for the country we all love," he argued, unencumbered by partisan habits or prejudices.[6]

Speaking more directly to the issues of slavery and race, in August Lincoln seized upon an invitation from Illinois Republicans to explain and defend emancipation as the policy of a Unionist, not an abolitionist. Regretting that he could not travel to Illinois to attend their planned "mass-meeting of unconditional Union-men," the president tendered "the nation's gratitude" to all those who put aside "partizan [*sic*] malice, or partizan hope" to support the Union. Then he wrote directly to "those who are dissatisfied with me." After arguing in several ways that they could not object to his approach to the rebels, he acknowledged frankly that most of their dissatisfaction was "about the negro."[7]

On the supposition that these "dissatisfied" Northerners did not want all men to be free, Lincoln insisted nevertheless that, "I have neither adopted, nor proposed any measure, which is not consistent with even your view, provided you are for the Union." They would have to admit that as commander in chief he had only used his constitutional power to do what "armies, the world over" do: take property that "helps us" and "hurts the enemy." Moreover, he had done so only after giving Southerners one hundred days to avert emancipation by "returning to their allegiance." Since January 1, 1863, black soldiers had helped the Union gain "important successes," at least one of which "could not have been achieved" but for their aid. Among the generals who agreed with this judgment were "some who have never had any affinity with what is called abolitionism, or with republican party politics." These battlefield commanders held their views on the importance of black troops "purely as military opinions," and those opinions gave the lie to charges that emancipation was "unwise" as a military measure or that it had not been adopted "as such, in good faith." Having made his point, Lincoln closed this letter by challenging the patriotism of white men who hindered the Union while black soldiers fought courageously to defend it.[8]

Northern Democrats had often charged that emancipation would embitter the South, making reunion impossible, and during the summer of 1863 there was a clear indication that they might be right. Jefferson Davis had issued orders that black men fighting for the Union would be enslaved upon capture, and the Confederate military now began to detain some black Union troops. In addition, Davis declared that the white officers commanding these men would be viewed by the Confederacy as leaders of a slave insurrection and thus would be subject to penalty of death. Lincoln had to protect the rights of his troops, and he denounced the rebels' plan as "a relapse into barbarism and a crime against the civilization of the age." Declaring that his government would "give the same protection to all its soldiers," he threatened to retaliate for any act of execution or enslavement. Yet, as William Gienapp has noted, "Lincoln wished to avoid retaliatory practices." He waited for hard proof of rebel actions before carrying out his threats, and then made a tepid response. Fortunately, "the Confederacy generally did not enforce its announced policy," although in fact some black U.S. troops were executed, others were treated as slaves, and wartime atrocities did occur.[9] To these persecutions Lincoln chose not to respond with general or harsh retaliation.

Lincoln remained determined to nurture loyalty among the rebels, whom he had called "fellow countrymen," and to facilitate the reentry of Southern whites into the Union.[10] He would not treat the Southern states as conquered territories, declared his adviser and postmaster general, Montgomery Blair. The ultra-abolitionists and their newspapers, Blair charged, were urging Congress to take charge of the rebel states and treat them as territories or as states that had committed legal suicide. Lincoln would not follow such ideas, said Blair, nor would he support "the Abolition party['s]" racial goal of "*amalgamation, equality,* and *fraternity.*"[11] Lincoln revealed his policy, as well as his desire to work with white Southerners to bring them swiftly back into the Union, through his approach to occupied areas of Louisiana.

In the summer of 1863, Lincoln instructed General Nathaniel Banks to begin the process of Reconstruction in Louisiana. Although most of the state remained under Confederate control, Lincoln wanted Banks to organize a loyal government, and he urged him to act promptly. By November, however, little progress had been made, and the president grew impatient. The process of registering citizens so that they could vote for a constitutional convention was supposed to have begun, but three months later the president learned that "nothing has yet been done." Saying that he was "bitterly" disappointed, Lincoln pressed Banks and provisional governor George F. Shepley to "go to work," and do so "without waiting for more territory." Lincoln wanted "a tangible nucleus" of white Louisianans who called themselves loyal to organize a pro-Union government. Revealing his continued belief that there was much Unionism in the South, he argued that launching such a government would allow "the remainder of the state" to "rally around" the new administration, "which I can at once recognize and sustain as the true State government."[12]

"Time is important," Lincoln stressed. If Banks and Shepley did not promptly establish an appropriate government, there was a "danger" that others would preempt them and claim to set up a state government that repudiated emancipation and reestablished slavery. Lincoln would "fall powerless" in any attempt to sustain such action, so it was essential that Banks make progress. To move the effort forward, Lincoln then offered a significant inducement to white Louisianans. In their new state government they could "adopt a reasonable temporary arrangement, in relation to the landless and homeless freed people," and Lincoln would "not object." The former slave owners of Louisiana would have to accept freedom for their slaves, but a "temporary arrangement," such as apprenticeship for the freedmen, was acceptable to the chief executive.[13] Louisiana whites certainly would understand these words to mean the continuation of important means of control over the former slaves.

This attractive inducement to Louisiana slaveholders contrasted sharply with the idealistic tone and spirit of Lincoln's remarks at the Gettysburg battlefield only two weeks later. While the offer to Louisiana slaveholders is little remembered, the Gettysburg Address remains the most famous of Lincoln's public speeches. It expressed, in general terms, the idealism about the United States that anchored Lincoln's hopes for the nation's future. In inspiring, allusive, but nonspecific language, the president ended his brief remarks by evoking a resolve "that these dead shall not have died in vain — that this nation, under God, shall have a new birth of freedom — and that government of the people, by the people, for the people, shall not perish from the earth."[14] In this elegant language Lincoln evoked freedom and the preservation of representative democracy as core values and goals of the war. But restrictions on freedom for the slaves and concessions to slaveholders remained integral to his thinking. Full freedom for African Americans remained a distant goal, something to be contemplated for the indefinite future rather than acted upon in the present, as Lincoln soon revealed in an important new policy.

Two and a half weeks later, on December 8, 1863, Lincoln delivered his annual address to Congress. Simultaneously, he issued his Proclamation of Amnesty and Reconstruction, which mapped out a process for the Southern states to reenter the Union. After arguing that he had power under the Constitution to pardon rebels and let them reestablish governments, Lincoln told Congress that he would acquiesce "in any reasonable temporary State arrangement for the freed people." His acquiescence was justified on the grounds that it could limit the "confusion and destitution" that, he claimed, would affect all, because of "a total revolution of labor." The concern he voiced here was primarily for Southern whites as they reacted to the loss of their slaves, and his goal was to facilitate reunion by allowing them to control black people longer through apprenticeship. As Lincoln put it, he hoped "that the already deeply afflicted people in those States may be somewhat more ready to give up the cause of their affliction, if, to this extent, this vital matter be left to themselves."[15] Slavery had led to rebellion and to the rebels' suffering; Lincoln was willing for them to extract some further benefit from slavery as the price of ending it.

On their part, Southern slave owners would have to swear to "abide by and faithfully support" Congress's acts affecting slavery and the Emancipation Proclamation, and Lincoln declared that this was right. Slaves who had trusted in his proclamation were aiding the Union, and it would be unwise and "an astounding breach of faith" to abandon them. He asserted that he would not be the agent for returning to slavery "any person who is free by the terms of that proclamation, or by any of the acts of Congress." But he added a caveat: compliance with these antislavery measures was required so long as they were not "repealed, modified or held void by Congress, or by decision of the Supreme Court." As president, he recognized a "modifying and abrogating power" in both Congress and the Court.[16]

One of the most striking features of Lincoln's Proclamation of Amnesty and Reconstruction was its liberality toward the rebels. His policy on pardons embraced not only those Southerners who might be only mildly Unionist in their feelings but almost any repentant rebel. He offered "full pardon . . . with restoration of all rights of property, except as to slaves" to all who would swear to be loyal "henceforth." Initially he excluded from the oath prominent Confederates—civil or diplomatic officers of the "so-called confederate government," high-ranking military officers, judges and office-holders of the United States who had left their positions to aid the rebellion, and also those who had mistreated Union soldiers. But his test of loyalty was to accept "as sound whoever will make a sworn recantation of his former unsoundness." This was surely a "sufficiently liberal" standard, as Lincoln put it. In fact, it was far too lenient for many Southern Unionists who were already cooperating with the administration. They feared that it would allow enemies of the Union to regain property and voting rights with no difficulty and then return to power at the polls. Moreover, in many subsequent statements Lincoln promised to pardon liberally, and he did so. He even sent his secretary, John Hay, to solicit oaths from Confederate soldiers imprisoned in Maryland. Elsewhere, Union officers began administering the oath to hundreds of prisoners, who then were released. After a few months, there were widespread complaints that these men were rejoining the Confederate army, and Lincoln then had to exclude imprisoned or paroled Confederate soldiers from his policy. But he remained committed to a very generous policy on pardons.[17]

To restore Southern states to the Union, Lincoln was ready to allow a small number of whites to set up governments that he would deem loyal and legitimate. As soon as pardoned individuals who had qualified as voters before the war numbered a mere one-tenth of the number of votes cast in a state's 1860 presidential canvass, they could "re-establish" a state government. Lincoln required no specific actions or policies from this new state government. Indeed, he made clear that he expected little change: boundaries, state constitutions, and "the general code of laws" could remain the same. As long as the reestablished government did not contravene the conditions of his oath, he would recognize it as "the true government of the state," entitled once more to its constitutional protections "against invasion" and "domestic violence." This Ten-Percent Plan, as it soon came to be known, thus required no changes in the reestablished state's electorate and minimal changes in state laws or constitutions. Under its terms, there was no possibility that freedmen would be able to vote and no requirement that their rights be broadly protected. Lincoln called only for a recognition of "their permanent freedom" and some provision "for their education" as part of the "temporary arrangement[s]" to which he would not object.[18]

THE IDEA OF apprenticeship, or "temporary arrangements," was an integral part of Abraham Lincoln's thinking about Reconstruction and the future of the freedmen — from his proposals for gradual emancipation by the states, to his Proclamation of Amnesty and Reconstruction, and, indeed, to the end of the war. Therefore, it is important to ask what this idea meant to him and to others. Was apprenticeship a benefit for Southern slaveholders or an opportunity for black freedmen? Was it intended to extend the dividends of slaveholding or to assist former slaves as they began their lives in freedom? How was apprenticeship commonly understood in Lincoln's time? What had it meant in the Illinois in which he lived his adult life and forged his political career?

The practice of apprenticeship began in the Middle Ages as part of the process by which guilds controlled the skilled trades and trained future artisans in their craft. In North America in the eighteenth century, apprenticeship continued to be a means for some boys to learn a skilled trade, moving upward from the status of apprentice to that of journeyman and craftsman.

Especially in urban areas, many a young man got his start in life by serving as an apprentice. Paul Revere's father is one example of a person who learned his craft and gained his start in life through apprenticeship; Benjamin Franklin is another. The prevalence of apprenticeships was diminishing, however, and after the beginning of the nineteenth century the importance of these arrangements faded rapidly.[19] Long before the young Abraham Lincoln arrived in Illinois, apprenticeship had ceased to be a widespread and valuable path to a rewarding occupation.

Apprenticeship had had an important role in Illinois' history, however. Rather than being a route to opportunity and upward mobility, apprenticeship had served as an instrument to extend slavery. This use of apprenticeship had been associated with the transition of Illinois from a territory to a state in 1818. Slaves had been brought into the area that became Illinois both before and after passage of the Northwest Ordinance in 1787. Although this ordinance seemed, on its face, to prohibit slavery and involuntary servitude, there was ambiguity in the statute, as well as a practice of successful evasion by early territorial officials. One section of the Northwest Ordinance provided that certain early French settlers, some of whom owned slaves, might retain their "laws and customs" in regard to the conveyance of property. A series of territorial governors, "especially Governors Arthur St. Clair, William Henry Harrison, and Ninian Edwards," also proved highly responsive to slave owners who wanted to retain human bondage. Not only did the proslavery elements petition Congress to repeal the Northwest Ordinance's antislavery language, but they succeeded in passing various laws governing "servants." By paying lip service to the Northwest Ordinance and avoiding use of the word "slavery," leaders such as Ninian Edwards correctly calculated that Congress would overlook the persistence of the institution in Illinois. As a result, writes Paul Finkelman, "slavery remained vigorous throughout the territorial period" in Illinois.[20]

However, as Illinois's entry into the Union as a free state approached, worried slave owners faced a new crisis. The arrival of statehood under a free-state constitution threatened to deprive them of the human chattel that they regarded as economically and socially valuable. The new state constitution allowed slavery to continue at the salt mines in Massac County and among some bondsmen introduced by the French, with freedom to come to the children of these slaves at age 18 for women and age 21 for men. Its language also could—and would—be interpreted to keep current slaves in bondage, but slave owners had no assurance of this as 1818 approached.[21] Drawing on ingenuity and past evasions, they launched a new effort to retain slavery, and the instrument chosen to achieve their purpose was indenture or apprenticeship. Records in the Illinois State Archives indicate that between 1722 and 1863 some 491 individuals were indentured, or legally bound to serve another person for a specified term of years. Fully 81 percent of these legal records were created between 1800 and 1817, and another 15.4 percent were created in 1818, just before Illinois became a free state. Although a few documents did not indicate the race of the individual, 95 percent of them explicitly noted that the person bound was "Negro" or "Mulatto." Thus, it is clear that black people were being indentured in anticipation of the change from a territory that retained slavery to a state in which bondage would be illegal.

Only a small number of records suggest that an individual was entering a status that would be equivalent to that of an apprentice. For example, in 1818 a man named Tilghman West indentured Delilah, a "Negro" woman aged 19, for a term of six years. Delilah was "promised clothes, a bed, and spinning wheel at end of term." Her case was very much the exception, however. Far more typical were the cases of Dilsey, a "Negro" woman aged 24, who was indentured to Francis Pulliam for ninety-nine years; Henry West, a "Negro" boy aged 16, who was indentured for seventy-five years; and Fanny, a "Negro" woman aged 22, whose indenture had ninety-nine years to run. Ironically, or mockingly, Fanny's record of indenture "promised $50 at the expiration of term"—when Fanny would have been 121 years old. The atmosphere in which these records of servitude were created was also revealed in some of the documents, such as the binding for fifty years of another Fanny, a 35-year-old "Negro" woman, in 1816. The county clerk of Edwards County noted that Fanny was "in a state of pregnancy and cannot travel to the county clerk's office and has agreed to the terms of service of 50 years." Clearly, ascertaining Fanny's willingness to spend the rest of her life in servitude was of little importance to the county clerk.[22]

Data on age and term of service often appeared in these legal documents. Among all those indentured, 57.5 percent were young men or women below the age of 20. Another 36.6 percent were adults aged 20–40. Few older people were indentured, and relatively few terms of service were short. Some 17.7 percent of the terms of service were for fifty years or more; 33.1 percent would run between thirty and fifty years; and another 22.6 percent were specified to last between twenty and thirty years. Thus, with 96.4 percent of the indentures being recorded before 1819, and considering that the life expectancy of slaves was not long at this time, it is obvious that most of those indentured were slaves who, under this legal arrangement, were going to have to serve the rest of their lives in bondage, even though they would live in a free state.[23]

Thus, slavery continued to exist in Illinois as Abraham Lincoln began his career there. Not only would he have seen indentured or apprenticed blacks who were in all practical senses slaves, but as a lawyer who rode the circuit and visited various courtrooms, he probably would have been aware of transfers of human property. Illinois' Servitude and Emancipation Records include a fair number of sales that occurred in the years after 1818. For example, in 1836 a woman named Caroline was sold for $100 by William Limm to Cassius Haskett. A year later, one Thomas Howel sold Harriet, a mulatto woman aged 27, to Anthony Butcher. Fortunately for Harriet, by 1840 she had been sold again to Griffin Yeatmen, who freed her.[24] Moreover, Lincoln's personal life brought him into close contact with individuals who were intimately connected with Illinois' history of slavery and black indenture. The former territorial governor, Ninian Edwards, held a number of indentured servants who probably spent their productive working lives in his service. For example, a mulatto boy named Anthony, aged 21, had been bound to Edwards in 1810 for a period of thirty-five years. In 1839, the governor's son, who also bore the name Ninian Edwards, was a leader of fashionable society in Springfield, and though he regarded Abraham Lincoln as "a mighty rough man," he included Lincoln, along with many lawyers and aspiring politicians, in the Sunday soirees at his luxurious mansion. There Lincoln met and began his courtship of Mary Todd, who was visiting her sister, Elizabeth Todd Edwards. Thus, when Lincoln married Mary, Ninian Edwards became his brother-in-law.[25]

For white people in Illinois, apprenticeship or indenture had almost completely died out. Only a couple of counties in the southern part of the state preserved any records of apprenticeship indentures from the 1830s to the 1860s. Jackson County recorded sixty-five apprentices between 1836 and 1860, and Perry County's records show thirty-three apprenticeship indentures between 1834 and 1865. In these two counties all of the individuals bound to service were minors, and only two were black. They were "orphants," "abandoned," "an infant orphan," "an orphan and liable to become a county charge," or children whose surviving parent felt unable to provide adequate care. County officials bound these young people to someone who pledged to teach them farming or housewifery and provide a rudimentary education. Typically, the males had to serve until age 21 and the females until age 18, and on completion of their service they might receive clothing or bedding, a Bible, a little money, and perhaps a horse, saddle, or bridle.[26] Such apprenticeship indentures were obviously a method of poor-relief or a means for the county to provide for homeless or helpless children, not an enviable route to a promising career.

From his experience in Illinois, Lincoln also knew well that prejudice against African Americans had remained strong. Early state laws prohibited black men from voting, serving in the militia, or assembling in groups, and immigration to the state was discouraged. Even after the state supreme court ruled in 1845, in the case of *Jarrot v. Jarrot,* that those slaves introduced by the French were entitled to freedom, many were still determined that Illinois should be a white man's state. In 1847, a new state constitution called on the general assembly to prohibit the immigration of free black people into Illinois and to bar slaveholders from introducing slaves for the purpose of freeing them. The legislature did not act until 1853, but then it passed a harsh "Black Law" that imposed numerous penalties on an African American visiting the state who remained for more than ten days. These Black Laws won strong support from the state's voters even during the Civil War, and they would not be repealed until 1865.[27]

Against this background, early in 1864 Lincoln showed remarkable optimism or a surprising continuing confidence in the Unionism of that "tangible nucleus" he was trying to organize in Louisiana. General Banks, after being prodded by Lincoln, had proceeded to organize a government, not with a new, antislavery constitution, but under the antebellum state constitution with its provisions on slavery declared "inoperative and void." Some Louisiana Unionists objected strongly to this decision. But Banks was afraid to offend the "self respect" of most white Louisianans by asking them to vote against the institution of slavery. Thus, even though voters swore to accept the Emancipation Proclamation, slavery could remain legal under Louisiana law if proslavery elements gained the upper hand.[28]

After a mere 11,000 voters elected Michael Hahn governor, Lincoln wrote to him in March. At this point, Lincoln felt added pressure to take some action to protect the rights of black Louisianans, for an impressive delegation of free colored men from New Orleans had visited Washington and petitioned for their rights. Noting that an upcoming constitutional convention would "define the elective franchise," Lincoln wrote to Hahn: "I barely suggest for your private consideration, whether some of the colored people may not be let in—as, for instance, the very intelligent, and especially those who have fought gallantly in our ranks." Doing this, he suggested, would add strength to the loyal elements "in some trying time to come" and thus "keep the jewel of liberty within the family of freedom." This idea was "only a suggestion," Lincoln emphasized, and it was offered in private rather than in public so as to offend no one. When it was ignored, Lincoln did nothing. The freedmen continued to work under harsh restrictions and enjoyed little autonomy under Banks's administration.[29]

Lincoln's desire to find an accommodation with slaveholders and prove his good faith to them was again on display the following month when he reviewed his policies in a letter to Albert Hodges, a Kentucky Unionist. Because Kentucky was within Union lines, slavery was in full legal force there, and Kentuckians continued stoutly to resist any interference with the institution. In answer to complaints from Hodges and others, Lincoln insisted earnestly and in detail that he had done nothing because of his antislavery feelings. His oath of office, Lincoln wrote, "imposed upon me the duty of preserving, by every indispensable means," the nation. He believed that unconstitutional measures "might become lawful" if they were indispensable to the preservation of the Constitution and the nation. After noting that he had overruled emancipation proclamations from Generals Frémont and Hunter and blocked a suggestion from Secretary of War Cameron to arm the blacks, the president pointed out that three times in 1862 he had asked the border states to favor compensated emancipation. When these efforts proved to be in vain, he had felt "driven to the alternative of either surrendering the Union, and with it, the Constitution, or of laying strong hand upon the colored element." Now, 130,000 black men were assisting the Union as soldiers, seamen, and laborers. Their support justified the decisions of an executive who had not set out to punish the South or free the slaves, but had been controlled by events. God would decide whether "we of the North as well as you of the South, shall pay fairly for our complicity in that wrong," slavery.[30]

The *New York Times* gave great support in this period to Lincoln's aim of reaching out for an accommodation with Southerners, and it was even more outspoken than he in its resistance to altering the status of African Americans. In August 1863, for example, the *Times* condemned Democratic politicians who cynically charged that emancipation would lead to intermarriage and then to every freedman's becoming a "*voting* citizen of the United States." It was slavery that led to racial mixture, said the *Times,* and "for a long, long time to come, suffrage for freedmen" would be impossible, because it would cause "the destruction of popular institutions on this continent." Voting was a "privilege," asserted the *Times,* and ignorant and corrupt white voters already constituted "enough risk" to democracy. History showed, according to the *Times,* that freedmen were "incapable of exercising [the suffrage] without danger to themselves and their neighbors." It would be "little short of insane" to think otherwise.[31]

In October 1863, a *Times* correspondent reported on the "Remarkable Success" of freedmen working as free laborers near New Orleans, but that did not change the paper's editorial opinion. Adopting the false Southern line that freedom meant idleness to African Americans, the *Times* would only say that "if they possess the elements of civilization," then they could work and stay "where they are."[32] Although black soldiers were proving useful, the *Times* ridiculed Wendell Phillips, the prominent abolitionist, as an extremist who sought "the enfranchisement, enrichment and elevation to supremacy of the negro race." It also criticized the political faction in New Orleans that favored rights for African Americans. Enfranchising the black man would mean "revolutionizing both sections of the Union," whereas the restoration of national unity required "the assent and cooperation of the great body of people in the rebel States." The *Times* even echoed the Democrats' argument that the "false clamor of negro equality" had driven many ordinary Southerners "into rebellion." On the last day of 1863 it emphasized once more that the government's first priority was to crush the rebellion, whereas emancipation and elevation of the slave's status were "incidents . . . secondary in importance to the salvation of the Union, and not to be sought at its expense."[33]

Early in 1864 when Wendell Phillips advocated requiring the rebel states to rescind all racially discriminatory laws, the paper saw an immense new danger — a danger to state rights. It charged that Phillips would "force New York" to abolish its property qualifications for voting and compel Southern states to "remit their entire civil control to the black majority now within their limits." Such a move would deprive "every State, loyal and disloyal," of all power to regulate its own most vital concerns. "General havoc is to be made among all the safeguards erected by our fathers against a consolidated Government. Principles which they treated [as] the very foundations of a Federal Republic, the broad corner-stones without which no stability or security was possible, are torn from their beds as if they were the very rubbish of the dark ages. . . . It is not in American nature to submit quietly to the overthrow of those sovereign rights of States which they were taught to regard as sacred and inviolable." Indeed, the "sovereign rights of States" were an essential aspect of "our Federal system." The *Times* predicted that, contrary to Wendell Phillips's desires, the system would be "preserved and perpetuated in its entirety."[34]

At the same time, the paper continued to assert that black people would not be moving to the North. When a small number of freedmen succeeded in buying confiscated land in South Carolina, the *Times* used this news to emphasize that blacks loved the South and would not "swarm to the North." In the Southern states where they would remain they would "take a long while" to "hold their own against their old masters," and few people now alive would ever see them take a place to which their numbers or virtues might eventually entitle them. That prospect apparently did not trouble the *Times,* nor would it trouble many Northern voters. Then, in March 1864, the *Times* quickly spoke up again when Lincoln's colonization experiment failed ignominiously. Using some of the $600,000 that Congress had appropriated to colonize free blacks abroad, the president had supported an expedition to Île à Vache, an island belonging to Haiti. After a year, many had died, and those emigrants who survived had returned in failure to the United States, having "suffered much hardship and misery." Now, the *Times* noted, Northerners were once again afraid "of being overrun by the emancipated negroes of the South." This was totally mistaken, the editors declared to reassure Northern racial fears. Black people were not swarming northward: "They stay, in the main, where they were 'born and bred.' "[35]

If the *New York Times* was unsympathetic to improving the status of African Americans, that was not the attitude of many of the so-called Radicals in the president's own party. They, along with many other Republicans and citizens, had been far ahead of Lincoln on the idea of emancipation, and after January 1, 1863, they continued to find fault with his approach to both the freedmen and the rebels. Although most of the Radicals reacted favorably at first to Lincoln's Proclamation of Amnesty and Reconstruction, they soon recognized its limitations and began to press on the floor of Congress for change. They wanted to confront the racism that long had prevailed in most sections of the North, and they believed that more ambitious action was necessary in order to end slavery forever and to protect the rights of black citizens. The priorities and political calculations of these men were on a collision course with those of the president. The collision would come over the Wade-Davis Bill and clashing visions of Reconstruction.

After issuing the Proclamation of Amnesty and Reconstruction in December 1863, Lincoln briefly enjoyed a rare phenomenon — universal approval from other politicians. In that moment, his proclamation found a path between the positions of conservatives and Radicals in Congress, while seeming to offer something to both. Most important to the conservatives was the fact that he continued to regard the war as a rebellion of individuals, not of states, and that he respected state boundaries, state laws, and the idea of a quick return to the Union. To those who disliked the Emancipation Proclamation, he had indicated that it might be subject to modification by either Congress or the Supreme Court. Radicals, on the other hand, were relieved and delighted that Lincoln seemed to stand firm on emancipation; he was insisting that Southerners accept it as a requirement for Reconstruction, and he had announced that he would not be the agent to return to slavery anyone who had gained freedom under the Emancipation Proclamation. Also, his policy on pardons seemed to reject the idea that Southerners had never compromised their status in the Union, and some even hoped that his statement that the South would have to "reestablish" governments meant that these states were in a condition analogous to territories. These features of Lincoln's policy seemed to provide an opening for Radical interventions in the South. The Democratic *New York World* commented that Lincoln the politician had shown "marvelous adroitness" in pleasing both wings of his party.[36]

This moment of good feelings, however, was fated not to last for long. The Radical Republicans felt a pressing need to deal with some of the fundamental racial issues that had led to the war, whereas Lincoln was focused more narrowly on restoring the Union. The direction of Radical Republicans' concerns began to be clear in Congress shortly after Lincoln's December address. Senator Charles Sumner, of Massachusetts, defined his role in 1864 as the championing of freedom and equal rights for black Americans, and he promptly succeeded in gaining the chairmanship of a special committee to consider "all propositions and papers concerning slavery and the treatment of freedmen." To this committee would be referred citizens' petitions favoring a constitutional amendment to guarantee freedom for all the slaves. Sumner and his allies in New England and the North intended to encourage a flood of such petitions. To further the process, Sumner introduced the text of a proposed constitutional amendment on February 8, 1864. Its wording placed primary emphasis on equality of legal status and derived universal freedom from that principle. "All persons are equal before the law," read Sumner's proposal, "so that no person can hold another as a slave."[37]

It also was Sumner who introduced a bill to secure equality before the law in the federal courts, but he was not the only Republican working toward such ends. Congress was debating a joint resolution to make the pay of black troops equal to that of white soldiers, and Senator Henry Wilson, chairman of the Military Committee, seized the opportunity to read a report from South Carolina praising the conduct of black soldiers. These troops had repelled an attack "with as much coolness and bravery as veteran troops" and had "entered into the engagement with enthusiasm rarely equaled and never excelled." In camp, they worked "with alacrity and good faith" and were "readily brought to the highest state of military discipline." Equal pay was their due. Whereas some senators had criticized the slaves for not showing enough manhood in resistance, this report warned that unless the black soldiers were paid equally, as justice demanded, "great difficulty" would result from their manly resentment of mistreatment.[38]

Another issue concerned discrimination against black people on streetcars in Washington, D.C. After hearing that some blacks had been ejected from the streetcars on account of their race, Sumner called for action to require a change. His argument for equality before the law won support from other Republicans and elicited a racist comment from a colleague from the slaveholding state of Delaware. About the same time, Senator Jacob Collamer, of Vermont, called up a bill to remove any disqualification of race from those carrying the U.S. mails. In order to allow African American mail carriers to testify about thefts, this measure also was drafted so as to prohibit any racial exclusion of witnesses in the courts.[39]

Sumner was not alone in his campaign for equal rights and emancipation through a constitutional amendment. Senator James Harlan, of Iowa, criticized and dismissed fears that "the immediate liberation of all the slaves in the United States" would disrupt society. "A vast majority of them are capable of taking care of themselves," he declared. "They have demonstrated it. . . . Nearly every soldier and officer that is now serving, or who has been heretofore serving in the rebel territory, has become convinced that a vast majority of the colored people are capable of providing for their own wants." Other senators objected to the wording of a bill to organize the Montana Territory because its text would allow only "white" residents to vote in the first election. Among these lawmakers was Senator John P. Hale, of New Hampshire, who argued that even if there were only a few African Americans in Montana, the federal government ought not to "educate the people to this absurd and barbarous prejudice." Senator Morton Wilkinson, of Minnesota, agreed, saying that he would not be governed "by that wicked pro-slavery prejudice that has ruled in the Congress of the United States for more than thirty years." He favored "strik[ing] out from the national statute-book everything which is inconsistent with the great truth of the equality of all men." One of the most radical Republicans was Senator B. Gratz Brown, of Missouri, who favored confiscation of land and other steps to change the whole social structure of the South. Brown also was quick to denounce those who raised fears of racial "amalgamation." If slavery had not feared amalgamation, he argued, freedom should not be a "coward," and he declared that the United States was already "an amalgam of all peoples."[40]

Conservative Republicans were not ready to go along with these ideas, and in some cases they openly voiced the racial prejudices of their constituents. Yet even in some of those statements, they indicated that Lincoln's approach to dealing with Southern whites was so mild as to be unrealistic. Senator James Lane, of Kansas, for example, proposed a plan to "set apart a portion of the state of Texas for the use of persons of African descent." Lane personally felt that the abilities of African Americans were "underrate[d]," but he was far more conservative than Sumner on racial matters. He had no intention of challenging the racial prejudices and the "repugnance to legal amalgamation" of "the people of the North and Northwest." Yet he also recognized that it would be unwise to leave the freed slaves unprotected in the South, where they would be surrounded by "an unfriendly people" who "will by all means in their power seek to undo what you and your armies have done." Southern whites would contest every effort of the former slaves to rise and improve themselves, he warned, and would try to reduce them to a condition like their former servitude.[41]

Many congressional Republicans also could not imagine that 10 percent of the prewar electorate was an adequate base upon which to build a new, loyal government in any Southern state. Nor did Lincoln's oath, which merely required supporters of a vast rebellion to say that they would "henceforth" be loyal, seem to have enough teeth in it. This standard for gauging future loyalty — a "sufficiently liberal" one according to the president — was much too liberal for most Republican lawmakers. Their objections seemed to be confirmed by the performance of Lincoln's "ten-percent" government in Louisiana. Not only had General Banks allowed the new and "loyal" Louisiana government to organize under its antebellum constitution, but a congressional investigation concluded that Reconstruction in Louisiana "has been a complete failure, and is regarded by the loyal people of the state as a vast scheme of fraud enforced by military rule."[42] Drawing the line against such results, both houses of Congress refused to seat newly elected lawmakers from Louisiana, and also from Arkansas. Moreover, it was becoming increasingly clear to Congress that Lincoln intended to run the process of Reconstruction himself, with the legislature playing no more than an ancillary role. On this point, many legislators were in fundamental disagreement with the chief executive, for they believed that Congress should have a major voice in the framing of Reconstruction policy.

For all these reasons, Congress soon came forward with its own plan for Reconstruction, embodied in the Wade-Davis Bill, which won the approval of both houses and was sent to the White House on July 2, 1864. This bill duplicated some of the provisions in Lincoln's plan, such as the prohibition on political participation by high-ranking Confederates. But it was both more specific and more exacting than Lincoln's proclamation in several important ways. First, as part of a thorough enrollment procedure directed by a U.S. marshal, a *majority* of the white male citizens of a state would have to take an oath to support the U.S. Constitution. The oath required was the same one specified in the Second Confiscation Act of 1862, a sworn declaration that one had never voluntarily borne arms against the United States or aided the rebellion. Here, plainly, was a much more rigorous standard than Lincoln's requirement that rebels recant their past unsoundness and promise future loyalty. In fact, it may well have been unrealistically high, just as Lincoln's was unrealistically low. Since most Confederate soldiers were volunteers, not conscripts, they would automatically be excluded unless some qualified voter would testify that their service had not been voluntary.

Second, when qualified voters had chosen the members of a state convention, the delegates to that body would be required to take certain actions, after again swearing their allegiance to the United States and declaring the state's "submission" to the Federal constitution and laws. Delegates would have to alter the state constitution to require that no high-ranking Confederate officers, civil or military, were allowed to vote or serve as governor or a member of the legislature; that involuntary servitude was prohibited forever and all persons' freedom guaranteed; and that state or Confederate debts contracted under the rebellion were not recognized or paid. The revised state constitution then would have to be submitted to the voters for approval. If that endorsement was obtained, Congress would have to approve the document before the new state government was recognized. Only then could senators or representatives be sent to Washington. Should the convention fail to comply with the specific requirements of the bill, it explicitly directed the provisional governor to "declare it dissolved," and the state would remain without a "Republican Form of Government" until sentiments altered. During such a period the freedom of the slaves would be protected.[43]

With this plan, Congress indicated to President Lincoln that much more was required than his Proclamation of Amnesty and Reconstruction envisioned. The lawmakers used a higher standard to define both republican government and loyalty. They were unwilling to put as much faith in the good intentions of Southern whites as did the president, and they were more concerned with protecting the future of African Americans. Congress also would insist upon vital changes to the new state constitutions, to give these changes a permanence not even envisioned in Lincoln's plan. As the first session of the Thirty-eighth Congress came to an end, lawmakers sent the Wade-Davis Bill to the president.

When Lincoln pocket-vetoed this proposed legislation, he encountered a fierce protest from leaders of his own party. His comment that their bill represented "one very proper plan for the loyal people of any State choosing to adopt it" assuaged no one's anger, for he also made his opposition to Congress clear. He resisted seeing his governments in Louisiana and Arkansas "set aside and held for nought." Congress's bill, he said, would have the undesirable effect of "repelling and discouraging the loyal" Southerners who had set up governments under his Ten-Percent Plan. Moreover, he accused Congress of unconstitutionally assuming a "competency . . . to abolish slavery in the States" by law instead of by a national constitutional amendment, which Lincoln favored.[44] That comment clearly challenged the legislators' idea of the kind of role they were entitled to play in Reconstruction.

The conflict between the president and Congress was clear, and Benjamin Wade and Henry Winter Davis quickly responded in protest with a fiery manifesto. Lincoln's governments in Arkansas and Louisiana, they charged, were mere "shadows of governments," so lacking in legitimacy and support that both houses of Congress had "repelled" their elected senators and representatives and "declared formally" that they would have "no electoral vote for President or Vice President." Valid state governments could not be created by "a handful of resident citizens" acting under military direction. Acknowledging the validity of Democrats' criticisms, the manifesto declared that such governments were not Republican but "mere creatures" of the president's will, "mere oligarchies." If Lincoln served his "personal ambition" and tried to benefit from the electoral votes of such shadow governments, his opponents for the presidency could not be expected to acquiesce. Moreover, only Congress's bill would require changes to the state constitutions to ensure future loyalty, while Lincoln's plan did nothing to secure "these guaranties." What would happen, Wade and Davis asked, if the one-tenth in Lincoln's reestablished rebel state governments later allowed "the other nine-tenths" to "succeed to the control of the State"? Pointing out that Lincoln's Emancipation Proclamation covered only some of the South's slaves, rather than the institution, the manifesto even charged that "every constitution of the rebel States at the outbreak of the rebellion may be adopted without the change of a letter: for none of them contravene that proclamation; none of them establish slavery." In closing, the congressmen warned, "Our support is of a cause and not of a man," and "The authority of Congress is paramount and must be respected."[45]

Although the words of Wade and Davis were fiery, outside of Congress the abolitionists were arguing with an even stronger voice for black rights. To men like Frederick Douglass, Wendell Phillips, and their associates belonged the distinction of speaking out uncompromisingly for the rights of African Americans. Theodore Tilton declared in 1863 that the Union's war was a fight "for social equality, for rights, for justice," as well as for freedom. Moncure Conway asserted that in addition to having the goal of liberty, "it is a war for Equality." Rev. Horace Hovey, a Congregational minister from Massachusetts, preached that "the negro has the same right that we have . . . to obtain a first-rate education . . . to rise in social position according as he rises in worth . . . to vote" and to hold office. Rev. George B. Cheever, when he was invited to speak in the Hall of Representatives in the U.S. Capitol, expressed amazement that the government could consider denying "the rights of representative government on account of the color of the skin." A "republican form of government," he declared, could not "exclude the loyal citizens" from their rights and "hold them down forever as an inferior, oppressed race." In full agreement, the Massachusetts Anti-Slavery Society resolved that the black man was entitled to "an equal share with the white race in the management of the political institutions for which he is required to fight and bleed."[46]

Frederick Douglass had a ready answer to white people's question, "What shall we do with the negro?" He had declared in June 1863: "There is but one way of wisely disposing of the colored race, and that is to do them right and justice. It is not only to break the chains of their bondage and accord to them personal liberty, but it is to admit them to the full and complete enjoyment of civil and political Equality." This meant that black Americans should have "all the rights, privileges and immunities enjoyed by any other members of the body politic." Only in this way could loyal Northerners "fix our peace upon a rock" and bring the ghastly sacrifices of the war to an end. "Save the Negro," insisted Douglass, "and you save the nation." Moreover, he argued, against the counsels of prejudice, that "white and colored people" could "be blended into a common nationality" and enjoy the "blessings of life, liberty and the pursuit of happiness, as neighborly citizens of a common country."[47]

The energetic and determined Wendell Phillips repeatedly added his arguments to those of Douglass and others throughout 1863 and 1864. In speeches in New York early in 1863 Phillips argued forcefully for justice to African Americans, as a matter of both national self-interest and justice. The "four million of blacks," he noted, were "instinctively on our side, ready and skilled to work." The Union needed "the use of" them, for in a rebel state like South Carolina, "we are not sure there is a white man in it who is on our side." Agreeing with Lincoln, Phillips argued that "the President may do anything to save the Union," but he insisted that for the same reason Congress could pass an act "abolishing slavery wherever our flag waves." Then he went further, and insisted that the North could not "deserve triumph or earn it at the hands of a just God" until "we welcome the negro, the foreigner, all races as equal" and part of "a common nationality."[48]

In speech after speech in 1864 Phillips hammered away at the theme of equal rights for black Americans. Any plan of Reconstruction, he declared, should force all the states, North and South, "to clear their statute books of every distinction between the black man and the white."[49] The approach embodied in Lincoln's ten-percent government in Louisiana was infamously inadequate. Instead of "real freedom," which abolitionists sought, it was in fact giving to the freedmen only the "sort of freedom" that "we are to hope for if the black man be left to the tender mercies either of a Major General or of the white men of the rebel states." Phillips pointed out that General Banks had refused to allow a black regiment that lost half its men before enemy fire to put "Port Hudson" on its flag. His "organization of labor" for the Louisiana freedmen tolerated continued whipping and denial to black men of the right to make their own labor contracts. Whereas Banks told Northerners in a public address that he planned "to prepare the negro" for independence, Phillips insisted that "the negro no more needs to be *prepared* for liberty than the white man." He looked "with contempt on any *preparation* of the negro for justice" and warned Northerners that the Southern whites were "no fit timber to build States with." Not only was giving "the ballot to the negro" "indispensable" to creating loyal states, but it was right.[50]

Reasoning in a similar way, the abolitionist newspaper, the *Commonwealth,* said that it had "no tears to shed" over Lincoln's veto of the Wade-Davis Bill. Though Lincoln's plan for restoration was totally unacceptable, the Wade-Davis Bill also was inadequate, because it was "disfigured by a requisition that none but 'white' persons should take part in the work of Reconstruction." "Until Congress has sense enough and decency enough to pass bills without the color qualification," wrote the paper, "we care not how quickly they are killed." The black leader James McCune Smith agreed that federal policies were inadequate and in practice would preserve "all the wrongs of slavery without its name." Looking to the future, abolitionists and the abolitionist press demanded education and land for the freedmen, in addition to political rights. To avoid serfdom, freedmen must "be made proprietors of the soil in fee simple, as speedily as possible," wrote one man in the *Liberator.* Abolitionists were cheered when Congressman George Julian advocated "an equitable homestead policy" and when Wendell Phillips denounced Lincoln's plan for Reconstruction because the South's large landholders would still be in a position to dominate politics and make freedom "a mere sham." Lincoln, Phillips charged, had "no desire, no purpose, no thought, to lift the freed negro to a higher status, social or political, than that of a mere labourer, superintended by others."[51]

But within Congress many Republicans were not ready to answer the question "What shall we do with the negro?" by supporting equal rights without regard to race. Senator James Doolittle, of Wisconsin, affirmed that he personally could vote for black suffrage, but he said that the "time has not yet come" when African Americans were "educated up to the point where it would be proper to extend to them the right of suffrage in all the States." Senator Lafayette Foster, of Connecticut, agreed that suffrage was not a natural right but a privilege that should be based on "intelligence and moral character." Observing the freedmen who had escaped slavery by migrating to the District of Columbia, he concluded that these men were "by no means qualified to exercise this right," because they were uneducated. Senator Waitman Willey, of West Virginia, likewise concluded that the blacks in Washington, D.C., were "ignorant" and "servile," although through no fault of their own. Lincoln's old political colleague, Senator Lyman Trumbull, of Illinois, rejected arguments for universal equality of rights. To him, the argument that black men should be allowed to vote was equivalent to the notions that women or individuals younger than 21 should be allowed to vote—notions that he considered ridiculous. Trumbull also argued that such controversial questions should not be allowed to divide Northerners while they were fighting to put down the rebellion. The need for unity also required, in the view of Senator John Ten Eyck, that issues of black rights be avoided.[52]

Outside the Republican Party, in the ranks of Democrats and among racist propagandists, the hostility to black Americans remained strong. During 1864, racism would seem to gain ground among the general public, amid deepening discouragement over the military prospects of the Union and a growing desire for peace. These developments would test Lincoln and his policies. They would stimulate his passion for political survival and throw into question his increased resolve to bring about freedom for all the slaves. In a turbulent election year, Lincoln's positions oscillated back and forth, leaving his ultimate stand on the status of black Americans in doubt.

FOUR

POLITICS, EMANCIPATION, AND BLACK RIGHTS

The year 1864 was a presidential election year, and not surprisingly, politics tested the limits of policy. When policies and popularity are in conflict, the resulting collision reveals where a leader really stands. Such political dynamics buffeted Abraham Lincoln as he sought reelection. They tested his resolve on the crucial issues of the war, especially emancipation, and cast light on his priorities. To survive politically, he trimmed and modified his position on emancipation in a way that testified to the abiding strength of white racism.

In the spring and summer of 1864, Abraham Lincoln found himself in grave political danger. Though his conflict with congressional Republicans over the Wade-Davis Bill was serious, he faced greater threats to his political future both before and after his veto of that measure and the subsequent fiery manifesto. First, Lincoln encountered a number of efforts from within his party to deny him renomination for the presidency. No sooner had he evaded these threats, and added to the Republican platform a call for a constitutional amendment prohibiting slavery, than his hopes for reelection began to evaporate before his eyes. Racist assaults from Democrats stimulated the virulent racism that existed in Northern society. Deep discouragement over the course of the war and the administration's apparent inability to bring progress ravaged his popularity. In every state, popular majorities seemed to be turning against him, party leaders were despondent, and Lincoln seemed powerless to do anything about the situation.

Then, after Congress had adjourned, a new and serious problem emerged. Confederate commissioners in Canada succeeded in drawing Lincoln into the open on the subject of emancipation and terms for peace. In a public letter, Lincoln listed emancipation as an outcome the rebels would have to accept in order to have peace. Immediately, a war-weary public reacted negatively to this position, and the result was much backtracking, temporizing, and obfuscation by the president and his allies. Lincoln and the Republicans escaped this crisis, of course. Their deliverance came at the hands of General William Tecumseh Sherman, who marched his victorious army into Atlanta in September. With the fall of Atlanta, the political tide immediately shifted in Lincoln's favor.

But the purposeful confusion about his stand on emancipation would not disappear entirely when political conditions changed. Even after he gained reelection and successfully urged Congress to propose the Thirteenth Amendment, his positions left a cloud of uncertainty over the future of its ratification. Throughout this turbulent political period, Lincoln continued to be far more consistent about amnesty for rebellious Southerners and a conciliatory Reconstruction policy than he was about issues affecting black Americans. Reunion and reconciliation among whites remained his priority. Emancipation seemed to have gained importance in his plans, but substantial confusion remained within his public position on the Thirteenth Amendment. Meanwhile, securing the rights of black Americans slipped further from realization, and a future of limited freedom and racial subordination grew ever more likely.

BEFORE HE COULD SEEK REELECTION, Lincoln first had to fend off a number of challenges from within his own party. These came from the left, from abolitionists and Radical Republicans who were dissatisfied with his slow and hesitant actions against slavery and his inaction on black rights. Personal ambition also played a role, as the first challenge came from secretary of the treasury Salmon Chase. Chase's presidential ambitions burned bright and were of long standing, and he enjoyed an unsullied reputation as a committed foe of human bondage. Through an ally, Senator Samuel Pomeroy of Kansas, Chase allowed his presidential balloon to be floated in February 1864. Lincoln's supporters were ready, however. They quickly spoke out in favor of the president, and Chase soon learned that he had overestimated his popularity both in general and particularly in his native state of Ohio, where his egotistical pursuit of power had alienated many former allies. Even a friend, Benjamin Wade, once observed that Chase's "theology is unsound. He thinks there is a fourth person in the Trinity."[1] To save face, the Treasury secretary had to announce that he was unwilling to be considered for the chief executive's chair.

Chase's withdrawal did nothing to mollify abolitionists and other antislavery Republicans who had reached the conclusion that Lincoln's leadership would never be satisfactory. They continued to agitate for a different nominee, and as it became clear that they could not influence the party, they laid plans for holding their own convention in Cleveland. Among Lincoln's critics were men like Frederick Douglass and African Americans in occupied Louisiana, who charged that Lincoln had worked as hard as anyone could to protect slaveholders' rights. The *New Orleans Tribune* pointed out that General Banks had allowed the state's 1864 constitution to be "framed by men who had no higher principle of action than hatred of their fellows of African descent." A black soldier from Massachusetts rejected Lincoln as "one who, holding anti-slavery principles in one hand and colonization in the other, always gave concessions to slavery when the Union could be preserved without touching the peculiar institution." In a similar vein, Wendell Phillips warned that Lincoln's policy on Reconstruction "makes the freedom of the negro a sham, and perpetuates slavery under a softer name."[2]

Ideas for a rival candidate centered on General John C. Frémont, the famed explorer and 1856 nominee of the Republican Party. At the end of May, the Republican dissidents and abolitionist reformers nominated Frémont on a platform that called for a constitutional amendment to end slavery and "absolute equality before the law" for all men. But Frémont soon alarmed the abolitionists by trying to appeal to Democratic voters, and many withdrew their support. A few months later, after events on the battlefield transformed the political landscape, Frémont would withdraw from the race.[3]

The Republican Party's convention took place in June, and party leaders tried to move simultaneously in two political directions. Adopting the title "National Union Party," Republicans sought to go beyond their party's ranks and appeal to all citizens who favored the Union and were willing to stand behind the national government in its crisis. The nomination of the Tennessee Democrat Andrew Johnson signaled this Unionist goal and Lincoln's desire to work with white Southerners. At the same time, however, delegates to the convention adopted a strongly Republican platform that called for "unconditional surrender" and a constitutional amendment to end slavery. It was known that Lincoln supported the proposed constitutional amendment. He had told New York senator E. D. Morgan, who would give the opening speech at the convention, to "put into the platform as the keystone, the amendment of the Constitution abolishing and prohibiting slavery forever." With this action, Lincoln took his strongest step toward ending all human bondage in the United States.[4]

The president was not going to win reelection easily, however. Not only was emancipation controversial, but many voters were dismayed by the Union's lack of progress on the battlefield, the enormous cost of the war in both lives and treasure, and the abridgements of individual rights that the military and Lincoln had authorized. Moreover, Republicans faced a Democratic Party that was far from moribund or dispirited. The Democrats constituted far more than a respectable but unthreatening minority in the North; they were a well-organized party with clear principles, a strong and stable base of support, and high hopes of regaining power. Indeed, many Democrats believed their fortunes were on the rise, for in 1862 they had captured thirty-five congressional seats from the Republicans. In 1863's elections they had substantially held their own in overall support from voters, though the outcome of various state races had been disappointing to their hopes.[5]

In addition to a storied tradition as the party of Jefferson and Jackson, the Democrats possessed a core of political and social beliefs that long had been shared by a large portion of the electorate. They were against centralization of power and governmental measures that interfered with the lives of individual citizens. In this regard, they saw the Republicans—as they had the Whigs before them—as intrusive and overbearing reformers eager to run other people's lives. They accused Republicans of "political meddling with morals, religion and the rights of distinct communities." Against such cultural intervention, the Democrats pledged to protect individual freedom and limited government. Wartime measures such as conscription, higher taxes, the suspension of the writ of habeas corpus, and military arrests gave them additional powerful reasons to protest against the central government. In prewar days Democrats had pilloried the Republicans as a narrowly sectional party intent on destroying the Union, and now, after three years of war, they accused Lincoln and his party of an intention to punish the South, overturn the Constitution, and destroy state rights. Their frequent battle cry during the war was "The Constitution as it is, and the Union as it was," a slogan that identified their party with sacred traditions now endangered by the Republicans. Finally, Democrats stood against racial equality and for a white man's country. The Republicans, they charged, were ever eager to promote the interests of blacks at the expense of white people. Democrats warned that

Republican ascendancy would lead to the "Africanizing" of America, and this racist theme easily lent itself to vicious and inflammatory rhetoric.[6]

After an initial period of confusion early in the war over what stands to take, the Democrats had found their stride and mounted slashing attacks on Republican policies. They claimed that Lincoln's party had irresponsibly endangered the Union and then embarked on a revolutionary course once war was under way. Repeatedly, Democrats denounced Republican plans to make the conflict "an abolition war—a war for general emancipation" instead of an effort to restore the Union. They charged that the two Confiscation Acts, the abolition of slavery in the District of Columbia, and then Lincoln's Emancipation Proclamation proved that the Republicans were radicals bent on transforming the republic. Backed by the administration, army generals had "put a gag into the mouths of the people," while Lincoln engaged in "glaring usurpation of power" and "palpable and dangerous violation[s]" of the Constitution. Democrats hoped and believed that the Republicans' policies would remove "the scales from the eyes" of anyone who had thought that "the President was a conservative man and that the war was for the restoration of the Union under the Constitution."[7]

Democratic rhetoric often was inflammatory as it denounced Lincoln and upheld tradition. The "Traitor President" had violated the Constitution and sanctioned "Trial by [military] Commissions" in his desire to destroy slavery, according to the *Old Guard,* a monthly New York journal. Lincoln was "a man who loves his country less and the negro more." Through his usurpations, "despotism has enthroned itself in the ancient seats of American freedom," even though the Founding Fathers had fought "against centralized despotic power." The "inevitable result of negro-emancipation," said the journal, "will be to reduce the laboring white man to the *status* of the negro," whereas the Democratic Party "advocates the cause of the Northern laboring man, against the monstrous proposition to turn loose four millions of negroes" to be competitors "in all the labor markets of the country." Lincoln's government "is a REVOLUTION," wrote the editor—a revolution aiming to make African Americans "co-equal citizens with white men."[8]

The "emotive symbols and code words" of the Democrats, notes historian Joel Silbey, "touched a deep chord throughout the Democratic community, from Irish dockworkers in Boston, New York, or Cincinnati, to Southern-born or Southern-descended farmers in the Ohio Valley, to respectable newspaper editors, lawyers, merchants, and bankers in large and small cities throughout the North."[9] Democratic appeals also gained in power when the war went badly—and the news was discouraging in 1864—or when the administration demanded greater sacrifices from the citizenry or infringed people's rights. And for many in the population the race issue was potent, capable of evoking visceral feelings. On this issue the Democratic Party had considerable help from racist writers, theorists, and propagandists, who operated either independently or in close support of Lincoln's opponents.

One of the most persistent and energetic producers of racist theories was Dr. J. H. Van Evrie, in New York. In 1861 Van Evrie had published *Negroes and Negro "Slavery": The First an Inferior Race; The Latter its Normal Condition,* a work whose ideas he repackaged in 1864 in various publications timed to coincide with the national election. Van Evrie presented himself as a physician and an analyst of scientific truths, but he also avowed an important political purpose. He aimed to reach "the day laborer and working man, those who alone or mainly, need to understand the great 'anti-slavery' imposture of our times," which was a "world-wide conspiracy" against the white man's "freedom, manhood and happiness." Through his writing he intended to persuade white workingmen that African Americans were biologically and permanently inferior and that slavery should not be disturbed.[10]

Black people, he asserted in his election-year book, "are a separate species." To diminish the conflict this created with the Bible's story of one common origin for humankind, Van Evrie theorized that "there must have been a supernatural interposition at some subsequent period." Not only did the "grace and majesty" of the Caucasian compared with the "inferiority" of the black body indicate separate species, but "the negro brain in its totality is ten to fifteen percent less than that of the Caucasian." Moreover, African Americans' "relatively small cerebrum" and "comparatively large cerebellum" produced in them a "dominating sensualism." "Intermingling the blood of races essentially different" would lead to "social suicide," he declared, and mulattos could not reproduce beyond four generations. Van Evrie also claimed that black people possessed different "vocal organs" and thus "a corresponding difference in language." Their sexual ardor was "sudden, capricious, superficial, and temporary," and their parental affections diminished so rapidly that a mother became "relatively indifferent" to her child by age 12 or 15, and "at forty she does not recognize it." Van Evrie assured racists that "the strongest affection" a slave "is capable of feeling is love for his master."[11]

In contrast with African Americans, who supposedly had been made to serve, the white race had been created by God for a different purpose; it was the last race to be made and was superior, Van Evrie claimed. "No white heathens have ever been known to exist," whereas no "tribe of the dark races" has ever been discovered "that was not such." America was great, he declared, because whites had refused to mix with blacks or Native Americans, although the mixture of different white bloodlines in the United States would "doubtless" produce "the most powerful and the most civilized people in existence." "It is certain," wrote Van Evrie, "that our own race alone has a history or is capable of those mental manifestations which constitute the materials of history." The Caucasian was able to "live and enjoy the full development of all his powers in the tropics" as well as in other regions, whereas "the negro and other inferior races are absolutely limited to their own centres of existence." Because God had adapted black people's "physical and mental structure, to the tropics," they were meant to produce cotton and sugar there, and consequently the United States should not restrict the taking of slaves to tropical areas.[12]

Drawing political conclusions from his pseudoscientific assertions, Van Evrie wrote that "the obvious design of the Creator" had been that "the negro should be useful, should labor . . . in juxtaposition with the superior Caucasian." It was "the nature of the negro" to be utterly useless "when isolated or separated from the white man." Accordingly, the slave trade was right and moral, slavery was the "normal condition" of African Americans, and "the social order of the South" encouraged the "civilization, progress, and general welfare of both races." There slaves were cared for just as children were raised by their fathers, and the law protected the slave from capricious or cruel treatment. Moreover, because of the natural division of the races, Southern states, with "the largest negro population[,] are the most decidedly and consistently democratic." By contrast, New England states, "with the fewest negroes among them, are the most unsound" and "are certainly behind most of the great American communities in political knowledge." The institution of slavery, Van Evrie declared with political purpose, made "the southern planter the natural ally of the northern farmer." It also was "the leading cause for the successful working of the democratic institutions" and "originated the great American ideas of government embodied in the Declaration of Independence." Free blacks, on the other hand, were unnatural and "destined to extinction."[13]

Van Evrie's writings attracted attention and undoubtedly stirred up racist sentiments, but during the 1864 election they could not compare in impact with a creative piece of political propaganda penned by D. G. Croly and George Wakeman, both of whom worked at the *New York World,* the Democratic Party's leading newspaper. *Miscegenation: The Theory of the Blending of the Races, Applied to the American White Man and Negro* had first been published the previous December as a 72–page pamphlet costing only twenty-five cents. In its title, this small publication coined a new word that soon replaced "amalgamation," the standard term for race mixture. More than that, from spring 1864 through the fall elections, *Miscegenation* excited controversy and served the interests of the Democratic Party so well that, according to Sidney Kaplan, "in the welter of leaflets, brochures, cards, tracts and cartoons struck off by all parties during the Civil War, it stands out as centrally significant."[14]

A clever and deceptive stratagem carried out on two levels accounted for the pamphlet's impact. Writing anonymously, Croly and Wakeman assumed the role of well-educated, committed, and radical advocates of racial equality who argued that racial mixture of whites with blacks would "make us the finest race on earth." All that was needed was "to engraft upon our stock the negro element which providence has placed by our side on this continent." The earnest and straightforward tone of *Miscegenation* was convincing enough to persuade all but the most suspicious reader that abolitionists and emancipationists favored racial mixing and even were eager for it to occur. In itself, this idea was alarming to many voters. But then Croly and Wakeman sent their pamphlet to several leading abolitionists and solicited written comments, many of which were mildly encouraging to the anonymous authors, or incautiously positive. The revelation of these responses could throw gasoline on the flames of racial hate.[15]

The text of *Miscegenation* contained many ideas that would simultaneously charm the abolitionists and alarm Democratic voters. It asserted the "brotherhood" of all races, argued that the war was "a war for the negro," which should end by recognizing his "political, civil, and social rights," and declared that the Republican platform should call for "Freedom, Political and Social Equality; Universal Brotherhood." Similarly, it judged Lincoln's plans for colonization to be defunct and praised the Republican Party for "wisely" admitting "that we must let the negro remain with us, recognizing him as one of the great elements of our strength and prosperity." All of these points were virtually matters of principle for abolitionists and Radical Republicans. Going further, the anonymous authors commented, with apparent tolerance and broad-mindedness, that the most beautiful human beings were a mix of racial types and that the vigor and health of African

Americans would benefit white Americans. More radical, and plainly inflammatory to racists and Democratic partisans, were their statements that "it is desirable the white man should marry the black woman and the white woman the black man," that race mixing would be "of infinite service to the Irish," because "they are a more brutal race and lower in civilization than the negro," and that blacks "are to compete with the white man in all spheres of labor."[16]

Congressman Samuel Sullivan Cox, of Ohio, a Democrat and ally of Clement Vallandigham, publicized this pamphlet on the floor of the House of Representatives, condemning its ideas and flaying the Republicans for promoting such shocking doctrines. Moreover, behind-the-scenes help from Croly and Wakeman, who shared their correspondence, enabled him to assert that abolitionists had "fully decided upon the adoption of this amalgamation platform." He proceeded to name eight prominent abolitionists as individuals who had "indorsed" *Miscegenation*'s scandalous ideas. Cox's speech led to wider discussion of the pamphlet, reviews of its ideas in magazines and newspapers from all parts of the political spectrum, and ultimately its establishment as a staple of political debate throughout 1864. A few Republicans, such as Charles Sumner, had recognized *Miscegenation* as a satire or hoax, and abolitionist newspapers took pains to make clear that they did not promote intermarriage but merely believed that such decisions fell within an individual's right to choose. Politically, however, the damage was done: Democrats had gained the offensive on an issue with emotional power.[17]

The Democratic Party did not hesitate to exploit this advantage. Among its many pieces of campaign literature, one of the most useful and widely distributed was Campaign Document #11, whose title screamed, "Miscegenation Indorsed by the Republican Party." It referred to Republicans as "the Abolition party now in power" and declared that "their object is to unite in marriage the laboring white man and the black woman, and to reduce the white laboring man to the despised and degraded condition of the black man." In support of this assertion, the document charged that Lincoln's party had resolved "that the war shall not end until slavery is abolished." But that position raised the central question, "What is to be the condition of the negro when he has attained his freedom?" According to the Democrats, the Republicans had "already made" their answer — miscegenation — and this horror would be accompanied by other horrors: repeal of laws against intermarriage; Republican presidential electors dancing with colored belles at

Negro balls; the reduction of the Southern states to a condition of "absolute submission"; and "the attempt to raise the colored race to a social equality with the white [which] must result in a conflict of races."[18]

Using quotations from Republican officeholders, Republican journals, and abolitionists, the Democrats attempted to define Lincoln and his party by the inflammatory issue of race mixture. They claimed that Republicans were "wholly favorable" toward miscegenation. In New York City they sponsored a "negro ball" in which "colored belles" were "arrayed in all that gorgeous and highly colored, not to say highly scented, splendor for which the daughters of the Ethiop race are esthetically distinguished." "Read this again, Irishmen and Germans!" the Democrats warned. It was Republicans who believed that African Americans "must be placed on an equality with the white, side by side with the white laboring population, with no prejudice of race working against them, and no right denied them." Under Republicans, "*white men should be employed [as soldiers], because it will save the blood of black men.*" The Republican Party's racial goals were so offensive, Democrats argued, that even Lincoln's postmaster general, Montgomery Blair, had condemned the "Abolition party" for seeking "*amalgamation, equality,* and *fraternity.*" "Miscegenation," concluded this Democratic pamphlet, "is but another pet object of the Lincoln party, of the same stamp with emancipation, confiscation, and subjugation."[19]

As if these racial issues were not problem enough for Lincoln's reelection campaign, the news from the battlefield during the spring and summer of 1864 was discouraging, even grim. In this, the fourth year of a war in which the Northern public had expected a speedy victory, citizens had little or nothing to feel optimistic about. Confederate resistance apparently remained strong. Sherman's army was making agonizingly slow progress from Tennessee into northern Georgia, and Northerners seemed to be waiting in vain for news of some breakthrough. From Virginia there was entirely too much news, for it was news of a sad and depressing kind. General Grant had decided to confront Lee's army and attack it repeatedly. "Whatever happens," he had told Lincoln, "there will be no turning back." And attack he did—with appalling losses—at the Wilderness, Spotsylvania, and Cold Harbor. During one week early in May, Union forces lost 32,000 men killed, wounded, and missing, "a total greater than for all Union armies *combined* in any previous week of the war." In the month of May, Grant's army suffered 44,000 casualties, yet their commander was determined to "fight it out on this line, if it takes all summer."[20] With hindsight, historians would record that Grant understood a grim arithmetic; he had accurately foreseen that the North could replace such huge losses, while Lee's ranks would shrink until surrender was inevitable. During the presidential campaign, however, the interminable lists of dead and wounded soldiers in Northern newspapers constituted a "butcher's bill" that shocked and dismayed the public. War weariness burgeoned with each passing week. Then, in July, a Confederate public relations effort lured Abraham Lincoln into making a statement about his war aims that aroused great controversy and tested the strength of his commitment to emancipation.

Jefferson Davis was keeping a watchful eye on the Northern electoral campaign. Hoping that Southern resistance could outlast Northern will, Davis believed that the defeat of Lincoln could lead to Confederate independence. To encourage Northern desires for peace, he dispatched three commissioners to Canada, at Niagara Falls, a convenient spot from which they might influence sentiment across the border. When the *Tribune*'s Horace Greeley learned of these commissioners' presence, he pressured Lincoln to make contact with them, at least for exploratory purposes. Greeley could not guarantee that the Confederate commissioners had the authority to negotiate peace, but he argued that an "anxiety of the Confederates everywhere for peace" was "beyond doubt." The influential editor, whose views reached a large readership, then "venture[d] to remind" Lincoln "that our bleeding, bankrupt, almost dying country also longs for peace — shudders at the prospect of fresh conscriptions, of further wholesale devastations, and of new rivers of human blood." Lincoln needed no reminder of this fact, or of another point that Greeley made: any widespread suspicion that the president was not eager for peace would do "great harm . . . in the approaching Elections."[21]

Already in political trouble, Lincoln decided that he would let Greeley approach the Confederates, not just to avoid the editor's criticisms, but for the purpose of demonstrating that the South insisted on independence. However, in authorizing Greeley's overture Lincoln released these instructions to the editor and the general public, on July 18, 1864: "If you can find, any person anywhere professing to have any proposition of Jefferson Davis in writing, for peace, embracing the restoration of the Union and abandonment of slavery, what ever else it embraces, say to him he may come to me with you, and that if he really brings such proposition, he shall, at the least, have safe conduct."[22]

With these few words, Lincoln ignited a political firestorm that imperiled his election still further. In the war-weary North, Democratic Party leaders and newspaper editors, and even a good many loyal but despondent citizens and Republicans, scrutinized the letter and concluded that Lincoln had raised the stakes of an already gory contest. After all, Lincoln himself, as well as major Republican organs such as the *New York Times,* had always insisted that the object of the war was to restore the Union. In response to controversy over emancipation, Lincoln and his supporters had always explained that freeing the slaves was a war measure, an instrument to restore the Union rather than an end in itself. On the last day of 1863, for example, the *Times* had reiterated that emancipation and elevation of the slaves were "secondary in importance to the salvation of the Union, and not to be sought at its expense." At the end of April 1864, it had praised Lincoln for having "but one fixed aim, and that was the salvation of the Republic," rather than emancipation.[23]

Yet now, in saying something different, Lincoln seemed to have elevated emancipation to the status of a nonnegotiable war aim. Democrats and critical newspaper editors attacked him energetically. The *New York Herald,* for example, wrote that the Niagara Falls episode had

> rendered very important service to the country in worming out the peace ultimatum of President Lincoln. . . . What is the sine qua non demanded by Mr. Lincoln of the rebellious States as a condition precedent to the re-establishment of peace and the Union? Nothing less than the abolition of slavery. . . . Why has he now taken this extreme ground, when he has always, heretofore, down to the late Baltimore Convention, insisted that the Union is the paramount, while slavery is but a secondary question? . . . Mr. Lincoln is afraid that peace and reunion may come too soon to suit his ambitious purposes and the grasping designs of his party.[24]

Other papers were more scathing in their attacks, and more openly racist. A "typical Democratic editorial" drew this conclusion about Lincoln the abolitionist: "Tens of thousands of white men must yet bite the dust to allay the negro mania of the President." The *Cincinnati Daily Enquirer* charged that Lincoln was dedicated to "depopulating and impoverishing the country" in order to achieve abolition and that he now had admitted that "the war is waged . . . not to restore the Union, but for the abolition of slavery as the main object."[25]

Republicans were sent reeling by the power of this attack. A Buffalo newspaper that had been supportive of the administration now asked "What are we fighting for?" and ventured the opinion that Southerners might have been willing to return to the Union but for Lincoln's surprising statement. Other Republicans, even staunch party men, lamented Lincoln's "blunder," for it had definitely put a powerful new weapon in the hands of his Democratic foes. Henry Raymond, now the incoming chairman of the Republican National Committee, soon warned Lincoln that his political life was in danger. "I feel compelled to drop you a line," wrote Raymond, "concerning the political condition of the country. . . . I am in active correspondence with your staunchest friends in every state, and from them I hear but one report. The tide is setting strongly against us." If elections were held the next day in Illinois, Pennsylvania, Indiana, and New York, reported Raymond, the Republicans would be beaten. "Two special causes" had produced "this great reaction in public sentiment—the want of military successes, and the impression . . . that we are not to have peace *in any event* under this administration until Slavery is abandoned." Raymond begged Lincoln to counter this impression through some "authoritative act." Speaking more directly, the *New London Chronicle* charged that Lincoln's "*propositions are an effectual bar against peace.* HE MUST MODIFY THEM SOMEWHAT, OR HE WILL NEVER BE REELECTED PRESIDENT."[26]

How would Lincoln respond? Even before receiving Raymond's letter, the president had put pen to paper in order to explain his position on emancipation and the war. What he wrote amounted to a classic politician's effort to explain away his earlier letter, to backtrack and regain lost ground. In response to a letter from a Wisconsin editor, a loyal War Democrat who complained that Lincoln's words had left "us no ground to stand upon," Lincoln drafted this language: "To me it seems plain that saying re-union and abandonment of slavery would be considered, if offered, is not saying that nothing *else* or *less* would be considered, if offered." He then reasserted that all of his actions related to slavery had been designed to save the Union, but that it would be treachery to reenslave those who actually had come over to fight for the Union, and that their help in the armed forces was essential. In closing, he wrote: "If Jefferson Davis wishes . . . to know what I would do if he were to offer peace and re-union, saying nothing about slavery, let him try me."[27] The only logical interpretation of these words was that universal emancipation might *not* be a requirement of peace.

Apparently, this letter was never sent. As a skillful and cautious politician, Lincoln may well have concluded that for a president to go on record in this way carried substantial risks. Such a statement surely would have alienated the strongest antislavery elements of the Republican Party, while among conservative voters it might destroy the president's credibility and image of resolve. But Lincoln's decision not to send the letter did not mean that he abandoned the strategy. Instead of sending this message personally, Lincoln simply had others make these arguments for him. Through others' voices he quickly advanced the argument that emancipation might not be a precondition for reunion.

Secretary of State William Henry Seward served as one of the administration's mouthpieces. Speaking in his hometown of Auburn, New York, Seward attacked his party's opponents as "The Allies of Treason." After briefly defending Lincoln's record on military arrests, conscription, and free speech, Seward turned promptly to "the chief complaint against the President." That complaint was "that he will not accept peace on the basis of the integrity of the Union, without having also the abandonment of slavery." To deal with this issue, Seward first denied that there was any interest among the Confederates in obtaining peace on the basis of the integrity of the Union. Next he reiterated an argument that he had made in the past, that as a practical matter the war was settling the issue of slavery by destroying the institution. Finally, he declared that while the rebels continued to wage war against the government, the "military measures affecting slavery" would continue, but "when the insurgents shall have disbanded their armies, and laid down their arms, the war will instantly cease; and all the war measures then existing, including those which affect slavery, will cease also; and all the moral, economical, and political questions, as well questions affecting slavery as others, which shall then be existing, . . . will, by force of the Constitution, pass over to the arbitrament of courts of law and to the councils of legislation."[28]

This formula defined emancipation as a temporary war measure, not as an essential war aim and precondition for peace and reunion. Moreover, Seward's statement that when the fighting stopped, all "questions affecting slavery" would be left to the courts and to "councils of legislation," indicated that President Lincoln would not impose an emancipation policy. Rather, "by force of the Constitution," some questions might be settled by the judiciary, while legislative bodies would settle others. The phrase "councils of legislation" was vague, but it was plural, and it surely embraced future actions by Congress and state legislatures on the Thirteenth Amendment. Under the Constitution's provisions, Southern states in the Union would participate in ratification of a new amendment. Thus, Southerners might gain a voice in the final settlement. In closing, Seward assured his audience that when the Confederates sought peace, they would find a "magnanimous, and humane" reception. Such assurances would tend to give Southerners reason to "try" Lincoln.

The *New York Times* was even more direct, and employed with fidelity the formula of obfuscation that Lincoln had devised in his unsent letter. Repelling editorial criticism from the *National Intelligencer,* the *Times* proclaimed that Lincoln had "*never* '*refused* to receive or consider any proposition looking to peace or Union unless accompanied with the abandonment of slavery.' He has *never* 'prescribed' that abandonment as a '*sine qua non*' of receiving or considering such propositions." President Lincoln, said the *Times,* was a man who used language carefully, and he had meant what he had said to Horace Greeley in 1862, that whatever he did about slavery he did because it would help to save the Union. Then Henry Raymond's paper added: "Mr. Lincoln did say that he *would* receive and consider propositions for peace, coming with proper authority, *if* they embraced the integrity of the Union *and* the abandonment of slavery. But he did not say that he would *not* receive them even if they embraced neither." The strategy of "let Davis try me" was deployed.[29]

Would the strategy rescue Lincoln in the minds of Northern voters? Among the more than one hundred prominent African Americans who attended the National Convention of Colored Men in October 1864 it certainly had the opposite effect. The convention's "Address to the American People" deplored "prejudice against men on account of their color" and sadly observed the "evident" fact that the Republican Party "is not prepared to make the abolition of slavery, in all the Rebel States, a consideration precedent to the re-establishment of the Union." The stance of Republican leaders had shown that "in returning to the Union, slavery has a fair chance to live." After quoting Seward's speech at Auburn, the address asserted: "These, fellow-citizens, are studied words, full of solemn and fearful import. They mean that our Republican Administration is not only ready to make peace with the Rebels, but to make peace with slavery also." Defiantly, the convention delegates declared "We want the elective franchise in all the States," and they reminded Americans that "at the time of the adoption of the Federal Constitution," eleven of the original thirteen states had allowed "colored men" to vote. Would Republicans and Northern whites say that black men were "good enough to use bullets, and not good enough to use ballots? . . . Are we citizens when the nation is in peril, and aliens when the nation is in safety?"

Before adjourning, these delegates formed the National Equal Rights League to fight for black equality.[30]

Black disappointment aside, no one can know whether these Republican tactics of retreat would have reassured whites and saved the 1864 election for Lincoln, for other events intervened. The president's salvation came at the last minute. It is clear that Lincoln himself had virtually given up hope of reelection. On August 23, 1864, he took to a meeting of the cabinet a "Memorandum" on his prospects in the coming election. "This morning, as for some days past," the document read, "it seems exceedingly probable that this Administration will not be re-elected." Above his signature Lincoln added that it would be his duty to cooperate with his victorious opponent, so as to save the Union between the election and the inauguration, for Lincoln believed that any Democrat would win the "election on such ground that he can not possibly save it afterwards." In a strange procedure, he asked the members of the cabinet to sign the back of this document without reading it.[31] Perhaps this was a way for Lincoln to deal with deep disappointment and commit himself to do his duty in the future. Whatever the purpose, it reflected his judgment, and that of most Republicans, that the election was lost.

What saved the day was good news from the battlefield. Southerners had watched with apprehension as General Sherman's army approached Atlanta. South Carolina's Mary Boykin Chesnut had confided to her diary that "Our all now depends on that Army at Atlanta. If that fails us, the game is up." Then, on September 2, 1864, Sherman's troops captured the city. "Atlanta is gone," wrote Mrs. Chesnut. "There is no hope." But what caused despair for Southerners produced joy and an outpouring of relief and optimism among Northerners. With the fall of Atlanta, it was at last clear that the Union would prevail and the rebellion would be defeated. Sherman's victory immediately produced a sea change in Northerners' morale and in their politics. "The fall of Atlanta has produced a general impression throughout the country that the end of the war is near at hand," observed the *New York Herald*. New Yorker George Templeton Strong, recorded in his diary, "It is (coming at this political crisis) the greatest event of the war."[32] With such important good news from the battlefield, and with significant help from the soldiers' vote, which was sometimes obtained in controversial ways, Lincoln won reelection.[33] With a new mandate to govern for four more years and thus to reconstruct a Union that soon would be under federal control once more, Lincoln gained power to move ahead with his policies on emancipation, Reconstruction, and the future of black Americans. How would he proceed?

Ever the guarded and complex strategist, Lincoln moved in multiple and seemingly opposite directions. By temperament, he habitually preferred to avoid an irrevocable commitment to any one detailed course. Instead, he worked to keep his options open. The initiatives that he took after reelection offered encouragement to the slaves but also to white Southerners. His policies revealed that his priority continued to be to lay a basis of cooperation with white Southerners in order to reunite the country. That choice entailed limits on the freedmen's prospects for the future, though Lincoln expressed more clearly than ever before his desire that the country would reach a state of universal emancipation.

Lincoln's first statements after his reelection reflected the complex mixture of his goals. He did not encourage or require progress on blacks' rights as freedmen, but applauded when others chose emancipation. To a group of serenading well-wishers on November 10 he spoke proudly of the fact that the United States had been able to conduct a presidential election in the midst of "a great civil war," and he urged all to join in his resolve "to save our common country." There was no mention of the impact of the election on the future of African Americans. Similarly, when he wrote a few days later to one of his generals in occupied Louisiana, he expressed satisfaction with what black leaders and Radical Republicans saw as a very unsatisfactory situation there. Although a new state constitution accepted emancipation, the legislature that Lincoln's policies had called into being did not extend the ballot to blacks, as the constitution would have allowed. Lincoln did not call on leaders in occupied Louisiana to enact black suffrage. Instead, he pronounced the constitution "excellent" and said that it was "better for the poor black man than we have in Illinois." On the other hand, he told a group of Maryland Unionists that their state's adoption of a "free State constitution was a bigger thing" than Maryland's vote for him in the presidential election. Indeed, he would have chosen "to lose Maryland in the Presidential election to save its free constitution," because elections came regularly but "the adoption of the constitution, being a good thing, could not be undone."[34]

In Maryland's abolition of slavery, however, there was less ground for celebration than Lincoln's words might suggest. Events in the state demonstrated the fierce determination of slaveholders to hold onto their institution and continue their exploitation of blacks. As a Maryland congressman openly acknowledged just before the vote on a new constitution for the state, slave owners manumitted slave children and then "had them bound immediately [as apprentices]." The goal was to "deprive their parents, who were still slaves, of being consulted after their emancipation as to the disposition of their own offspring." The "old apprentice law" was being used as a "legal device that would enable them to secure for a few years more the services of the infant slaves."[35] Union army officers confirmed that "evil-disposed parties" were intent upon "obstructing the operation, and nullifying, as far as they can, the emancipation provision of the new constitution." Their steps to create "forced apprenticeship" had the support of many local officials; "appeals to the courts" were "worse than folly." Consequently, Major General Lew Wallace felt it necessary to issue General Order No. 112 commanding that "special military protection" be given to Maryland's freedmen until the legislature "[made] such military protection unnecessary."[36] These steps were needed in a state within the Union that had just abolished slavery constitutionally.

Defining the status of slavery in a constitutional sense was a matter of great importance. Lincoln and his supporters had always described the Emancipation Proclamation as a war measure, subject to modification by the courts, and even had stated explicitly that war measures would cease with the end of the war. Thus, the status of those slaves covered by the Emancipation Proclamation would become an open question when the war ended, and loyal governments that Lincoln was trying to set up in the South merely had to accept emancipation as understood in this way. Moreover, the proclamation itself had never applied to slaves within the Union, in areas that Union troops had occupied by January 1, 1863, or in Tennessee, which Lincoln had omitted at the suggestion of war governor Andrew Johnson. These facts were widely recognized. The *New York Herald*, for example, had observed, "Short of an amendment of the constitution of the United States, this [abolition by an individual state] is the only way in which the question of slavery can be reached in each of the several States concerned." Lincoln's "tinkering reconstruction experiments," said the *Herald*, "including the abolition of slavery, if adopted to-day . . . may be set aside to-morrow."[37]

Thus, it was significant that Lincoln called for action on the Thirteenth Amendment when he delivered his annual address to Congress in December. The proposed amendment had been defeated in the House before the November elections, and although that same Congress was still sitting, Lincoln urged its members to reconsider and pass the measure. He did not appeal to them on grounds of humanity or justice to the slaves but, in a manner consistent with his earlier emphasis on emancipation, as a means to preserve the Union. The election had showed "almost certainly, that the next Congress will pass the measure," and Lincoln argued that it was wise to send the amendment to the states for consideration "sooner" rather than later. Prompt action was preferable, he continued, because "in a great national crisis, like ours, unanimity" was important, and "such unanimity" could not be attained "unless some deference shall be paid to the will of the majority." As shown by the election, the majority favored the amendment "among the means to secure" the people's common goal — "the maintenance of the Union."[38]

At the end of his address, Lincoln returned to the use of politically slippery language to discuss emancipation and his war aims. The end of armed resistance by the Southerners was "the only indispensable condition to ending the war." Yet Lincoln declared that he "retract[ed] nothing heretofore said as to slavery." Although these positions did not seem strictly commensurable, Lincoln attempted to explain himself. He would not modify his emancipation proclamation, he said, nor "return to slavery any person who is free by the terms of that proclamation, or by any of the Acts of Congress." If the nation's citizens wanted someone to reenslave such persons, "another, and not I, must be their instrument to perform it."[39] These words seemed to stake out Lincoln's minimum position: he absolutely would not return to slavery any bondsman who had gained freedom as a result of the war and whose freedom would be upheld by the courts. His maximum position, then, would be embraced in a constitutional amendment that reached all the slaves and prohibited slavery throughout the United States.

Lincoln's appeal to Congress, as well as Secretary Seward's blandishments, proved effective. With administration support, the Thirteenth Amendment won passage at the end of January 1865 and went before the states. Ratification of the amendment then loomed as a critical issue, for ratification was inextricably intertwined with the restoration of states to the Union. Which states would vote on the amendment?

In his annual message to Congress, Lincoln had approached this question in language that was vague but encouraging to the South. Using the verbal formula developed during the Niagara Falls crisis, Lincoln declared that rebellious Southerners could have peace "at any moment . . . simply by laying down their arms and submitting to the national authority under the Constitution." After a Southern surrender, "the government could not, if it would, maintain" the war. Any remaining questions then would be adjusted "by the peaceful means of legislation, conference, courts, and votes, operating only in constitutional and lawful channels." What, exactly, did this mean?

What would be the role of the previously rebellious states in the established "constitutional and lawful channels"?[40]

Throughout the war the administration had maintained that the Union could not be broken and that the South had not created a separate nation. According to this view, only individuals were engaged in rebellion, and Southern states could not leave the Union. If that were so, then the South surely should take part in the ratification of the Thirteenth Amendment. Moreover, Lincoln's Proclamation of Amnesty and Reconstruction had begun the easy reestablishment of some state governments. After noting that the Supreme Court might modify or declare void his Emancipation Proclamation, Lincoln had encouraged "temporary arrangements," such as apprenticeship, as long as these included recognition of the slaves' freedom and provision of education. Despite mounting opposition and widespread criticism of the Ten-Percent Plan, Lincoln persisted in arguing that the wartime state governments he had created should be seen as legitimate republican governments for their Southern states. Thus, the entire direction of Lincoln's wartime policy on Reconstruction seemed to indicate that the Southern states should have a "constitutional and lawful" role to play in ratifying the Thirteenth Amendment.[41]

In maintaining his support of the ten-percent state governments, Lincoln also extended in his annual message a generous invitation to all white Southerners to take his amnesty oath and become part of the political decision-making process. Although he admitted that Congress held power over "the admission of members," Lincoln noted that the executive had the power to pardon, and he stood by a liberal policy of pardons in his plan for Reconstruction. He told Congress that he was glad that "many [Southerners] availed themselves of the general provision" for pardon that he had promulgated. He indicated that he was confident that "many more" were willing to do so. Moreover, in regard to "special pardons" for those in the excepted categories of leading rebels, "no voluntary application has been denied." Saying that the door had been "open to all," he urged Southerners to walk through it and gain his pardon, lest the time come when that door might have to be closed.[42] Broad participation by virtually all Southern whites in the "constitutional and lawful channels" of the political process would surely affect the results of the ratification process.

The arithmetic that followed from these assumptions was challenging to friends of freedom. There were thirty-six states in the divided Union as 1864 came to an end, and therefore the approval of twenty-seven states, or three-quarters of the total, was necessary to ratify the proposed amendment. If more than nine states opposed it, the amendment would fail. But eleven states had actively participated in the Confederacy (not counting Kentucky and Missouri, which were claimed by the Confederacy but were under Union military control through most of the contest). In the North, Republicans had triumphed in the 1864 elections, and they had reason to believe that they could prevail in most of the Northern legislatures. But the Democrats' nominee, General George McClellan, had carried New Jersey, Kentucky, and Delaware, and ratification was highly unlikely in those states.[43] Thus, it appeared that Lincoln and his party would have to obtain the support of at least five Confederate states — two that would be required even if the North gave unanimous support, plus three more to offset New Jersey, Kentucky, and Delaware.

Clearly this would be no easy feat. Lincoln was counting on ratification by his ten-percent governments in Louisiana, Arkansas, and Tennessee. But these state governments faced mounting opposition in Congress, where Radicals and other Republicans had a number of increasingly strong objections. To the Radicals it was enough that Lincoln's Reconstruction policy lacked any measures to protect the rights of black Southerners or to guarantee to them the right to vote. Radical Republicans feared, reasonably enough, that loyal black Southerners would be subordinated and oppressed by Southern whites left free to reorganize their states on their own. To many other Republicans, in addition to the Radicals, the Ten-Percent Plan had always been unacceptable and at odds with the constitutional obligation to "guarantee to every State in this Union a republican form of government." Many even agreed with the Democrats that such governments would allow the executive to control the supposed states in the occupied South and manipulate them for his electoral or political benefit.[44] Sentiment in Congress clearly was moving in the direction of refusing to seat representatives from these ten-percent governments.[45] If Congress opposed their legitimacy, how could Lincoln expect there to be a clear and uncontested three-fourths majority for ratification of the Thirteenth Amendment? Even if Congress recognized those governments, ratification by two more Southern states would be needed.

A straightforward ratification without coercion seemed impossible. To the extent that Lincoln's thinking can be explained, two explanations emerge from the record. First, Lincoln had always had great faith — an unrealistic faith — in the strength of Southern Unionism. At the beginning of the war, he had expected a resurgence of Unionism that never came. Although he did not want Confederate leaders to come to power, he had refrained from interfering with the actions of his ten-percent governments, and he had formed no policy that would require the exclusion of prominent Confederates from his reorganized governments in the future. Now, with the end in sight, he seemed to feel confident that once the war was over and the influence of the radical secessionists crushed, Southerners would quickly return to their loyalty and devotion to the Union. Second, Lincoln knew that he was willing to be liberal and reasonably accommodating to white Southerners. His desire to convince them that he was fair and to obtain their cooperation had consistently been on display in his policies and in his rhetoric. He expected Southern whites to respond if he offered them meaningful benefits. In the words of William C. Harris, "Lincoln reasoned that his liberal amnesty policy, guaranteeing the rights of citizens, including property except for slaves, and the early restoration of self-government would prevent die-hard rebel resistance and violence."[46]

The *New York Times* in its editorial positions had frequently tracked and reiterated Lincoln's views on policy and issues, and again at the end of 1864 many of the *Times* editorials echoed Lincoln's words. Speaking at greater length than Lincoln thus far had done on key issues of emancipation and Reconstruction, the newspaper may well have signaled many thoughts that the careful chief executive was entertaining but would not make public. In any case, the views of the *Times* were not inconsistent with the policies that Lincoln had announced and defended. For these reasons, its views on Southern whites, emancipation, and the rights of the freed slaves were important and revealing.

Toward Southern rebels the *New York Times* displayed the same tolerance, forbearance, and readiness to reestablish comity that was evident in Lincoln's public statements. In "The Future Southern Feeling Toward the Union" Henry Raymond and his editors rejected the idea that Southerners would be "exceedingly embittered" after their defeat. Most were not fanatics, the *Times* argued, but simply ordinary people who had gone along with their neighbors. Predicting that white Southerners would act "just as honorable but mistaken men in the North would act," the paper predicted that rebels would immediately feel "absolved from duty" to the Confederacy and would "welcome" an "honorable peace." Even in South Carolina, the *Times* contended, there were many "silent loyalists," and "most of the Southern people, whether soldiers or not, will welcome the restored Union" and the return to "wealth and comfort and lawful liberty."[47]

In another editorial the paper argued that some Europeans were mistaken to predict that the postwar North would have to govern a resentful region, as England had to do with Ireland. The South had never been mistreated, the *Times* argued, and its aristocrats had brought on the war and created a population divided in sentiment. "A few years will cool the fever which war has aroused, and under a government like ours, where they will speedily feel themselves with the same rights as their conquerors, and being of the same race . . . with a like past history, they will undoubtedly settle themselves down quietly and contentedly." After General Sherman arrived in Savannah, Georgia, the paper urged aid for the city as "the Way to Restore Fellowship," to illustrate that "brotherhood" was possible, and to "welcome back those who have been estranged from us."[48]

On issues that would be important to slaveholders and Southern whites the *Times* also had much to offer. Asking "What is the North fighting for?" the *Times* answered that it "does not wage war to destroy slavery." That institution would not prevent the North "from making peace tomorrow," and the paper repeated Lincoln's formula that the subject could be left "to future peaceful and constitutional action." In an important addition, the editors then stated, "Nor do we fight to overthrow State rights. The North is still for maintaining to the last iota every right reserved to the States by the Constitution. We want no consolidated Government, and would tolerate none. So far as respects veritable Constitutional State rights, we make no quarrel with the South." Another article described state rights as "the great balance-wheel of our government," enabling "local self-government" to harmonize with a central government exercising national sovereignty. In a country like the United States, with "two or three grand sections . . . there must be reserved to the several parts certain inviolable privileges." These positions certainly signaled friendship to the South, but to make its attitude even more clear the paper denied any Northern desire "to subdue or degrade the Southern people. We want them as our fellow-citizens, not as our subjects."[49]

As for the freedmen, this key Republican newspaper had much to say that would have been reassuring to former slaveholders and to racist whites, both North and South. The editors of the *Times* envisioned, and favored, little immediate change in the condition of black Americans once the war was over and freedom was established. Though it supported the Thirteenth Amendment on the grounds that the war had shown that slavery and the Union could not coexist, the paper worried that too much help for the freedmen would "encourage dependence and idleness" or "sap [the] independence" of "an inferior race." When Wendell Phillips called for full black rights and suffrage for black men in the reconstructed nation, the *Times,* on December 29, 1864, rejected his ideas unreservedly and elaborated views that Southern whites could readily endorse:

> The black masses of the South, of a voting age, are as ignorant upon all public questions as the driven cattle. This benighted condition cannot be changed during the present generation. Few of these adults, even with the best opportunities, will ever learn to read intelligently. . . . To put the ballot in their hands would be not simply a mockery, but a cruelty. . . . [If suffrage were given,] the evils of having admitted such an enormous mass of animal ignorance into our body politic, would inevitably produce a tremendous reaction. It is infatuation to suppose that this negro franchise, thus imposed upon the reclaimed States as a condition precedent to their readmission, would endure.

Surely this condemnation of the idea of black suffrage would have been reassuring to Confederates, but going further, the *Times* remarked that "even if this were otherwise, there are superior interests to be consulted." The central government could not have the right "to declare who shall, and who shall not, vote in any State," for that would give it "absolute authority." The Union that the North had fought to preserve, said the paper, "is a union of States. Destroy the States, or break down their essential powers, and the Union is no longer possible."[50]

In these views and positions, as in Lincoln's policies, there was substantial ground for accommodation with defeated Southerners and little reason to expect substantial change in the rights or social status of freedmen. How the Thirteenth Amendment would be ratified, how far Lincoln would go to encourage reconciliation, how he hoped to navigate the politics of Reconstruction, and what all these things meant for the future of African Americans would become clearer early in 1865. In the month of February, leaders of North and South would discuss peace at the Hampton Roads Conference. There the evolving views of both sections on the persistent and racist question, "What shall we do with the negro?" would be confronted directly.

The Confederate record in this historical period now demands attention. For Southerners, their experiences with the institution of slavery during the war would make the Confederate commissioners to Hampton Roads very interested in Lincoln's overtures.

Based on his observations in Louisiana, General James S. Wadsworth concluded that the government might need to protect freed slaves from white hostility for a few years if freedom were to become a reality. (Library of Congress, Prints & Photographs Division, Civil War Photographs, LC-DIG-cwpb-04579)

This photograph, taken at Antietam, Maryland, on October 3, 1862, shows General John A. McClernand (*right*) with President Lincoln and Allan Pinkerton. Lincoln assured McClernand that with apprenticeship the rebellious states would be "nearly as well off" as if the war had not occurred. (Library of Congress, Prints & Photographs Division, Civil War Photographs, LC-DIG-cwpb-04326)

General Nathaniel Banks organized Lincoln's wartime pro-Union government in Louisiana. That government and Banks's policies proved to be great disappointments to advocates of black rights. (Library of Congress, Prints & Photographs Division, Civil War Photographs, LC-DIG-ppmsca-08366)

Senator Charles Sumner, of Massachusetts, was one of the strongest and most determined advocates in Congress for equal rights for African Americans. (Library of Congress, Prints & Photographs Division, Civil War Photographs, LC-USZ62-128709)

Frederick Douglass demanded equal rights and a fair chance for African Americans. Frequently a harsh critic of Lincoln, he prodded the president to move forward and applauded him when he did. (Library of Congress, Prints & Photographs Division, Civil War Photographs, LC-USZ62-15887)

Though a Democrat, Edwin Stanton, the hardworking secretary of war, wanted to move faster than Lincoln on emancipation. He also favored meaningful, practical improvements in the economic position of Southern blacks. (Library of Congress, Prints & Photographs Division, Civil War Photographs, LC-DIG-cwpbh-00958)

Wendell Phillips was a gifted public speaker who argued for freedom and equal rights for African Americans more strongly and persistently than any other white abolitionist. (Library of Congress, Prints & Photographs Division, Civil War Photographs, LC-DIG-cwpbh-01976)

Dedicated to independence for the Confederacy, Jefferson Davis brought many changes to Southern society. These culminated in his administration's proposal to arm and free the slaves. (Library of Congress, Prints & Photographs Division, Civil War Photographs, LC-DIG-cwpbh-00879)

Vice President Alexander Stephens had become alienated from the Davis administration, but at Hampton Roads his goal was to lure Abraham Lincoln into an armistice. In this way, Stephens hoped, the Confederacy might salvage its independence. (Library of Congress, Prints & Photographs Division, Civil War Photographs, LC-DIG-cwpbh-04320)

Foreseeing inevitable defeat unless the Confederate armies obtained more men, General Patrick Cleburne spoke with rare honesty about the institution of slavery and the aspirations of the slaves. (Library of Congress, Prints & Photographs Division, Civil War Photographs, LC-USZ62-107446)

Recruited from occupied areas of the South, as well as from the North, African American soldiers proved their bravery and made valuable contributions to the Union war effort. (Library of Congress, Prints & Photographs Division, Civil War Photographs, LC-DIG-cwpb-04294)

The Effects of the Proclamation — Freed Negroes Coming into Our Lines at Newbern, North Carolina (*Harper's Weekly,* February 21, 1863)

Twice Speaker of the New York Assembly, Henry Raymond was a founder of both the Republican Party and the *New York Times*. During the war, he led his newspaper, advised Lincoln, and became chairman of the Republican National Committee in 1864. (Library of Congress, Prints & Photographs Division, Civil War Photographs, LC-DIG-cwpbh-03070)

Lincoln's postmaster general, Montgomery Blair, belonged to an influential political family and was a persistent advocate of removing African Americans from the United States and colonizing them elsewhere. (Library of Congress, Prints & Photographs Division, Civil War Photographs, LC-DIG-cwpbh-03263)

PART TWO

Southern Developments

FIVE

SLAVERY, WAR, AND THE SLAVEHOLDER'S MIND

Southern slaveholders gained wealth and power from human bondage, but the institution of slavery made their world complex. Living economically in a world of progress and profit, they were menaced ideologically by an Atlantic culture that increasingly condemned the foundation of their wealth. Loyal to a Revolutionary past that had managed to combine freedom and slavery, they encountered a changing present that steadily grew more hostile to that contradiction. In addition to this ceaseless and dangerous external criticism, internal doubts sometimes surfaced. Asserting that timeless truths supported slavery, slaveholders recalled that their region's position on slavery had changed quite recently. Despite being aggressively self-righteous and confident, they knew occasional fears and insecurities that they tried to hide from themselves. Although deeply religious and reassured by the Bible, they sometimes questioned their own zeal in doing God's will toward the slaves. Theirs was a world in which past and present, home and surroundings, internal and external realities did not meld completely.

This persistent, irritating fact spawned an unremitting effort to justify the slaveholder's way of life. White Southerners needed to repel external criticism and to remove those few, lurking internal doubts that all was well both at home and in the wider world. Feeling instinctively that they were every bit as good as their Northern critics, slaveholders searched for ideas that would support their society and protect them from economic loss or social condemnation. In the intellectual arena, considerable energy went into the elaboration of old, Bible-based proslavery arguments and the construction of new, more aggressive "scientific" or sociological ones.[1] In the routine of daily life, planters and politicians sought an ideology that would serve both personal and social goals. They found an answer: the ideology of paternalism buttressed by convictions of racism and prescriptions of religious duty.

According to the claims of paternalism, Southern slave owners did more than supervise enslaved laborers who produced their wealth. They cared for and elevated an inferior race, treating slaves as members of a plantation family. They gave African Americans the guidance they needed and all the while advanced God's plan for the salvation of Africa and the world. A relationship that rested on coercion became, in the ideology of paternalism, a trust and a benefit, a positive human partnership. Slavery was not exploitation but a mutually beneficial institution. Some claimed it was even a caring connection based on shared experience and familial affection.[2]

Individual Southerners emphasized different aspects of paternalism. Some stressed the idea of the dependency of an inferior race and the stability of an organic society, while others talked most of their religious duty, and still others celebrated the bonds of affection within the "family, black and white." But for all, these efforts involved at least some small measure of self-deception. Holding human beings in bondage fell short of the Golden Rule, and slaves were seen as racial inferiors, not as sons or daughters, brothers or sisters. Slaves certainly made money for their owners, while masters supposedly "elevated" the heathen African while denying him education, marriage, and freedom. Familial bonds did not preclude cruelty or whipping, punishment by slave patrols, or swift suppression of suspected revolts. Such unpleasant facts were known and discussed in Southern society, if infrequently. Thus, in regard to slavery, Southern culture depended on habits of mental avoidance. External denial and internal reassurance were required for slaveholders' self-image and the perceived health of their society.

The experience of the Civil War first undermined and then pierced these mental and cultural myths. Although there was no major slave revolt in the Confederacy, white Southerners feared violent uprisings and endured a progressive loosening of their control over the slaves. In the changed conditions of war, familiar bondsmen and bondswomen began to act in unfamiliar ways. The loyal became disloyal or undependable. Tried-and-true family servants now were recognized as strangers in the house, hiding behind inscrutable masks. War exposed the limited and false foundations of paternalism, and the most convinced paternalists suffered the most painful disillusionment. Dismay, surprise, and a sense of betrayal spread through the plantations' "big houses," as these powerful emotions revealed the extent of slaveholders' dependence on the comforting conventions of paternalism.

Many could not give up the ideas they had relied upon in daily life and used as a shield when facing the hostile outside world. But slowly some Confederates began to revise their conception of reality and tried to accommodate the war's new and troubling facts. Religious leaders were among the first to conclude that something different was required of them. Their belief that God had chosen Confederates as his special and favored people led not to optimistic faith but to anguished reconsiderations, as the wartime signs of divine favor faded. Successive defeats on the battlefield eroded optimism and turned assurance into despair and desperation. Concluding that something must be wrong, a number of pious slaveholding ministers exposed areas of long-hidden disquiet over slavery and urged change. Yet as significant as their actions were in revealing the unpleasant truths of un-Christian exploitation, these ministers urged a conservative course, one far less radical than that which military and political leaders soon would take.

THE MIND OF THE white Southerner was somewhat divided and not totally comfortable with slavery, despite the excuses of racism. In part, this was an inevitable consequence of history, for the various theories holding that slavery was a positive good were of recent vintage and at odds with Southern views that had been ubiquitous only one or two generations earlier. The *Richmond Examiner* was a partisan for the new Confederate nation and a staunch defender of slavery. Yet even its editor discerned "a deep-seated aversion to slavery" that was "lurking in the Southern community." This aversion arose from popular ideas and "teachings which were not desisted from, even at the South, until a few years ago." A British visitor, Sir Arthur James Fremantle, learned from Texas Confederates that "a few years ago, most educated men in the South regarded slavery as a misfortune and not justifiable, though necessary under the circumstances." Ideas that had been so common were not quickly eradicated.[3] The *Richmond Enquirer* frankly admitted:

> If the crisis had come thirty years ago, it would have found our churches and our public men in a condition of dreary doubt as to the justice and beneficence of those institutions, which form the basis of our community. The cant of the "Nineteenth Century," with its impossible "equality" between those races which are not equal by nature, had invaded the Christian Churches, as well as tainted the principles of statesmen;

> and it needed the long strife of parties, and patient investigation of principles to bring the religious world up to the point at which it could recognize and sanction our cause.[4]

After 1830, as Southern society became increasingly hostile to critics of slavery, punishment of dissenters usually suppressed their voices. But religious doubts had never been absent. Antislavery societies had existed in the Upper South into the 1820s and 1830s. And, as Jeffrey Brooke Allen found, "the leaders of organized anti-slavery throughout the South were generally clergymen." Though such clergymen and antislavery individuals were a small minority, they had spoken and worked for their beliefs until roughly thirty years before the Civil War. Moreover, many of them were not racists or antiblack deportationists but men who felt a "repugnance for racism." Holding a "faith in the natural equality of the black man," they had worked for "the education and Christianization of a downtrodden race."[5]

The Friends of Liberty and Equality in North Carolina, for example, published an address to the people in 1830 that condemned slavery as "radically evil" because it was "founded in injustice and cruelty" and "contrary to the . . . religion of Christ." They argued that their "countrymen" had a "duty" to "enlighten and elevate the minds, ennoble the hearts, and improve and elevate the character of the negroes among us." Antislavery views circulated in North Carolina as late as 1860, when a Methodist minister named Daniel Worth was prosecuted for preaching against slavery and distributing Hinton Rowan Helper's book, *The Impending Crisis of the South.* In neighboring South Carolina, leaders had proscribed criticism of the institution. But even there, paternalists who described slavery not as "evil" but as a positive good admitted that religious instruction was, theoretically, necessary. In 1845, future secessionists such as Robert Barnwell Rhett had led a faith-based initiative to promote "the religious instruction of negroes." Their effort, said these planters, was a "*duty* . . . which Divine Providence has placed in our hands, to those whom the same Providence has made dependent on us." Though they maintained that religion would make the slaves more "satisfied with their condition," they also affirmed that "God is no respecter of persons."[6]

The political heritage of the slave South may have been even more influential in maintaining some "aversion" to slavery. The Founding Fathers had viewed slavery as a "necessary evil" rather than a positive good. Moreover, the ideology of human rights that drove their rebellion had spawned the declaration that "All men are created equal" and given rise to much antislavery sentiment in the new nation. As the Civil War approached, Southern radicals tried to make Thomas Jefferson's antislavery views heretical and notorious rather than well known and respectable. But the Revolutionary heritage could not be effaced. In the 1830s, when John C. Calhoun declared slavery "a good—a great good," Senator William C. Rives, of Virginia, denounced Calhoun's "obsolete and revolting" idea and affirmed that slavery was "a misfortune and an evil in all circumstances." When Hinton Helper pilloried slavery as an economic drag on the South, he devoted many pages of his argument to quotations from the antislavery statements of Southern patriots as well as churchmen. For example, George Washington had declared that one of his "*first wishes*" was "to see some plan adopted by which slavery, in this country, may be abolished by law." Helper also quoted James Madison's statement that "It is wrong to admit into the Constitution the idea that there can be property in man," and he noted that James Monroe had called slavery an "evil" that "has preyed upon the very vitals of the Union, and has been prejudicial to all the States, in which it has existed."[7]

Similarly, when Benjamin Hedrick, a professor at the University of North Carolina, attracted controversy in 1856 for opposing the extension of slavery, he defended himself in a Raleigh newspaper by referring to famous Southern patriots. Hedrick reminded readers that his views were neither novel nor unfamiliar. "Opposition to slavery extension," he pointed out, was

> neither a Northern nor a Southern sectional *ism.* It originated with the great Southern statesmen of the Revolution. Washington, Jefferson, Patrick Henry, Madison, and Randolph were all opposed to slavery in the abstract, and were all opposed to admitting it into new territory. One of the early acts of the patriots of the Revolution was to pass the ordinance of '87' by which slavery was excluded from all the territories we then possessed. This was going farther than the Republicans of the present day claim. Many of these great men were slaveholders; but they did not let self interest blind them to the evils of the system.[8]

A few leading Southern politicians continued to voice such ideas into the 1840s and 1850s. In 1845, before the Wilmot Proviso was proposed, Alexander H. Stephens had declared in Congress, "I am no defender of slavery in the abstract." Later, in 1849, President Zachary Taylor, a slaveholder born in Virginia and raised in Kentucky, told Northerners that he "regarded slavery as a great moral and political evil." In 1850, no less a Southern luminary than Henry Clay had declared in the U.S. Senate, "I never can and never will vote, and no earthly power will make me vote to spread slavery over territory where it does not exist." He refused to extend "the everlasting curse of human bondage."[9]

Outside of the political arena, many ordinary Southerners harbored private doubts about the morality and desirability of slavery. Judith McGuire, who was born into the prominent Brockenbrough family of Virginia and married an Episcopal clergyman, was an enthusiastic Confederate, but even she, after observing her slaves, admitted that "the wish for freedom is natural." In 1858, Ella Clanton Thomas, of Georgia, said that "Southern women are I believe all at heart abolitionists." Although she conscientiously studied proslavery writings during the war to strengthen her patriotism, her opinions did not change. "This is a subject upon which I do not like to think," she admitted in 1864, but "taking my stand upon the moral view of the subject, I can but think that to hold men and women in *perpetual* bondage is wrong." Another Georgia woman, Dolly Burge, acknowledged that she "never felt that slavery was altogether right for it is abused by many." Best known, perhaps, are the comments of Mary Chesnut, who suspected that slavery was "a curse to any land." "God forgive us," she wrote, "but ours is a monstrous system, a wrong and an iniquity." Troubled by race-mixing and oppressed by the difficulties of managing slaves, she declared "I hate slavery," and she felt that "every day shows that slavery is doomed the world over." Expressing a similar view about historical trends, Robert E. Lee wrote privately to his wife in 1856, "In this enlightened age, there are few I believe, but what will acknowledge, that slavery as an institution, is a moral & political evil in any Country."[10]

Though not uncommon, such private doubts had little effect on the course of sectional politics. Rather, the intensity of the North-South conflict had produced increasing defensiveness in the slaveholding regime and driven such ideas underground. The slave South ruthlessly silenced and punished dissenters as war approached. Such was the case with Professor Hedrick, who lost his post at the University of North Carolina, and with the Methodist minister Daniel Worth, who fled from that state rather than go to prison. Open questioning of the foundations of a slaveholding society was not permitted, and therefore private doubts had posed no obstacle to the formation of the Confederacy.[11]

Nor had they caused thoughtful and morally sensitive Southerners to be especially troubled, uncertain, or conflicted about politics as secession approached and the war began. Those who had reservations about slavery had lived with them for an extended period and had developed means of dealing with their concerns. White Southerners had no doubt that they were as good as Northerners. The context of the times and the ideology of paternalism gave Southern slaveholders ample reasons to defend themselves against their critics and maintain their self-respect. The discrimination and racism of the North were well known to Southerners, many of whom suspected that they had more tolerance, even consideration, for African Americans than did a large number of their nonslaveholding countrymen. Harriet Beecher Stowe and the abolitionists, complained Mary Boykin Chesnut, "live in nice New England homes, clean, sweet-smelling, shut up in libraries" and distant from slavery, while a number of "good, pious" women that she had known had "strive[d] to ameliorate the condition of these Africans in every particular." She felt that "book-making" that led to fame was "an easier way to be a saint than martyrdom down here, doing unpleasant duty among the Negroes with no reward."[12] Her acerbic comment was representative of widely shared attitudes.

Moreover, white Southerners blamed Northerners for abandoning a national consensus and then proving unfaithful and hostile to the constitutional rights of Southerners. The idea that slavery was a "necessary evil," something undesirable but unavoidable given history and social conditions, had been widely shared in the early years of the nation. Northerners had taken part in the drafting of a constitution that recognized and protected slavery in several important areas, including representation, the return of fugitives, and federal suppression of domestic revolts. The South had remained true to its commitments, many felt, whereas the North had chosen to ignore a clear and common history and assail slavery and slaveholders in violation of sacred constitutional obligations. Robert E. Lee expressed this idea to his wife in 1856 when he arraigned "certain people of the North" for making "Systematic & progressive efforts . . . to interfere with & change the domestic institutions of the South." Such a goal was "both unlawful & entirely foreign to them & their duty." The next year, after the Supreme Court had given its stamp of approval to Southern theories about the territories, attitudes understandably hardened. Protection of slavery in the territories was a Southern right, Mississippi senator Albert Gallatin Brown declared. "The Constitution as expounded by the Supreme Court awards it. We demand it; we mean to have it."[13] To Lee, Brown, and others, Northern unwillingness to treat the South fairly, and not Southern aggressiveness, was the cause of division.

The authors of proslavery arguments had become more creative and more insistent as the Civil War approached. Sociological theories, such as those of George Fitzhugh, presented slavery as the ideal basis for any society. The radical Fitzhugh even suggested that a defense of bondage did not depend on a racial basis for the institution. Supposedly scientific theories argued that Africans were a separate and markedly inferior species and thus needed to be enslaved. Dr. Josiah Nott, of Mobile, Alabama, emphasized the idea of separate origins for the different human races, while Dr. Samuel Cartwright, of New Orleans, stressed the peculiar medical traits of slaves, even arguing that they were susceptible to a disease that made them run away. These new theories found a variety of uses. Politicians, encouraged by Fitzhugh's writings, could criticize the free-labor system and charge that Northern laborers were callously discarded, fired from their employment whenever they were no longer useful, whereas slaves enjoyed steady support and medical care throughout their lives. In sectional debates, public figures occasionally defended the South by alluding to a scientific theory about racial inferiority. On the whole, however, most Southerners justified slavery by referring to the Bible and by discussing paternalism and ideas of racial inferiority.[14]

The biblical justification for slavery was the most familiar to Southerners, and the most venerable. Ministers and other writers continued to develop its tenets throughout the sectional conflict, as Protestant denominations began to split, North versus South, over the morality of slavery. When Southerners read the scriptures, they saw that the Hebrews and the Romans had enslaved other peoples, so they reasoned that the Bible recognized and accepted the institution. The Reverend Thornton Stringfellow, of Virginia, maintained that God had blessed Abraham with many servants or slaves and that patriarchs such as Isaac, Jacob, and Job were all slaveholders. Not only did Old Testament law regulate slavery among the Hebrews and offer no "reproof" to the hereditary enslavement of non-Jews, wrote Stringfellow, but in the "Gospel dispensation," the period of time dating from Christ's appearance on earth, "Jesus Christ recognized this institution as one that was lawful among men." He went on to note the apostle Paul's thoroughgoing emphasis upon subordination in society. It was Paul who had given the instruction, "Servants be obedient to them who are your masters, . . . not with eye service as men pleasers, but as the servants of Christ."[15] To many whites, this biblical testimony was deeply reassuring.

Indeed, some prominent people in the North shared these religious views. John Henry Hopkins, the Episcopal bishop of the Diocese of Vermont, was an unapologetic wartime defender of slavery on religious grounds. In 1861 Hopkins published a brief pamphlet citing biblical support for slavery, and in response to inquiries he republished the pamphlet and followed it, in 1864, with a 376-page book, *A Scriptural, Ecclesiastical, and Historical View of Slavery.* "Slavery was authorized by the Almighty," insisted Hopkins, and no amount of "infidel rationalism" could obscure the fact that the Bible had not changed. In his view, the misfortunes of war had come because Americans, influenced by antislavery ideas, were rebelling against God's divine government. Combining scriptural citation with racism, Hopkins asserted that no one could object to the continuance of slavery as long as the bondsmen "belonged to an inferior race which the *law did not presume to be fitted for freedom at any age.* . . . Such, under the rule of the Scriptures and the Constitution of the United States, is the case of the negro. God, in his wisdom and providence, caused the patriarch Noah to predict that he should be the *servant of servants* to the posterity of Japheth. And the same almighty Ruler, who alone possesses the power, has wonderfully adapted the race to their condition. For every candid observer agrees that the negro is happier and better as a slave than as a free man, and no individual belonging to the Anglo-Saxon stock would acknowledge that the intellect of the negro is equal to his own." The "great mass of slaves," he continued, was not "qualified for freedom," but if the Southern slaveholder owns the slave's labor for life, the slave enjoys "*property for life in his master's support and protection.*"[16]

Another Northern divine who advocated proslavery views was the Reverend Alexander T. McGill, DD, a professor in the Theological Seminary at Princeton, New Jersey. Like Southern slaveholders, McGill called slavery part of God's plan for Africans. He believed in the unity of the human race, but he declared that "Heaven decreed" that Africans would be slaves in the United States. God had a plan for them and for Americans. The Almighty had fixed "the place of each people on the face of the earth," according to McGill, and the racial characteristics of Africans indicated that "God has made [them] to dwell within the tropics of our globe." In the United States they "are strangers and servants . . . here for a special purpose." The "will of God" was "neither a perpetual bondage, nor an immediate abolition," but instead a "schooling of slaves in this Republic." Living "in the bosom of that Christian civilization which speaks the English language and its idioms of regulated liberty," African Americans would become prepared "to carry back to their own land the spoils of a Christian civilization." Southern whites must "be their teachers" and "hasten the tuition." But all Christians,

McGill insisted, should be eager to spread the Gospel and to further "a New Testament exodus" in which the slaves, elevated by their experience in the United States, would return to their native land and become the "redeeming light to Africa."[17]

A prolific Ohio author, David Christy, published similar views in 1862. Christy deplored the "sad errors in religion" that were propagating abolitionism and other reforms. Emancipation "does not necessarily improve the moral and physical condition of the colored race," he argued, but often "has been injurious and ruinous." It was "careful moral training, alone, under suitable constraint" that would "elevate the colored people," and that moral training was going on in the South "with eminent success." Christians therefore had "no justification" for interfering with slavery in the South. The Gospel, wrote Christy, was "a curative remedy for human degradation and indolence . . . capable of lifting the lowly of the race to an elevation where slavery might no longer be necessary." Christ's word was being preached to Southern bondsmen, and as a result the slaves were losing their "heathen superstitions and idolatries," learning to "use the English language," and becoming Christian in numbers far exceeding all the converts of Protestant missions to Africa. Christy argued that "the colored people of the United States alone had made sufficient progress to justify the hope that any portion of the race were capable of carrying back a Christian civilization to the land of their fathers."[18]

Southern ministers developed these same ideas as part of their justification for slaveholding. "The African who is intrusted to our care," proclaimed James W. Miles, an Episcopal priest and professor, speaking to graduates of the College of Charleston in 1863, can only reach his maximum "amount of civilization and development . . . in the position in which God has placed him among us." That same year, the Reverend Thomas Smyth asserted in the *Southern Presbyterian Review* that slavery benefited the black race and "is not in itself wrong." Rather, "God is working out a problem in the physical, social, political, industrial, and world-wide beneficial character of slavery, *as a great missionary agency*" (italics added).[19]

Bishop Stephen Elliott was more explicit and more sweeping in his interpretation of history. The United States had been on its way to becoming the greatest power on earth, but the Civil War had shattered its progress because the nation had sinned in "presumptuous interference with the will and ways of God." The "deeply-laid conspiracy of Black Republicanism threatened to undermine [slavery,] this divinely-guarded institution." Why was slavery so important to God? Elliott argued that the whole world was converting to the Gospel of Christ — except for Africa. To save that continent God needed agents who could act, "through a like physiological structure, through a oneness of blood and of race, to bear the burden of this work, and ultimately, in God's own time, to plant the gospel in their Father-land, after they themselves shall have been prepared, through a proper discipline, for the performance of this duty. And I find this agency in the African slaves now dwelling upon this Continent and educating among ourselves." Thus, "God has committed" to Southern slaveholders the "sublime work . . . of educating a subject nation for his divine purposes." The ruler of the universe had "caused the African race to be planted here under our political protection and under our Christian nurture, for his own ultimate designs." If Southerners carried out their charge, they would "be blessed of him as Joseph was."[20]

Certainly such confident assertions from religious leaders gave Southern whites reason to reject outside criticism of slaveholding. But in addition to these cosmic and rather abstract theories about divine purpose, practical justifications based on racism and ideas of racial inferiority reassured Southerners in their day-to-day routines. African Americans were "cursed with a darkness of skin" and "subjected to the will of superior beings," whites believed, because they lacked the capacity to be independent. "All the experiments that have been tried of the self-elevation of the colored races . . . have been conspicuous failures," wrote one Southerner, arguing that the West Indies "went to ruin" after emancipation. Slaves were a needed but burdensome presence. Usually ignorant and docile, they could become "insolent . . . like spoiled children, simply intolerable." Even the literary and cultivated Mary Boykin Chesnut regarded the black man as "a creature whose mind is as dark and unenlightened as his skin." She also described slaves as "dirty, ugly, and repulsive," and wrote, "It takes these half-Africans but a moment to go back to their naked savage animal nature." Similarly, when some of Catherine Devereux Edmondston's slaves sought permission to marry, she charged them in her diary with undue haste, and concluded, "Cuffee strips off the elegancies & refinements of civilization with great ease." Disapproving of the parenting skills of another slave, she declared, "I do not think negroes possess natural feeling."[21] Such attitudes were part and parcel of a slaveholding culture that justified exploitation by blaming the exploited.

To live with slavery, whites tended to dehumanize the slave. To soften the reality of domination and to function as slaveholders in the face of Northern criticism in a century in which "every day shows that slavery is doomed the world over," they ignored the ugly realities of slavery. Southern plantations were not idyllic communities. Exhausting labor, poor living conditions, and the loss of freedom were every slave's lot. Whipping and sometimes other brutal punishments enforced "good order." Many individual slave owners or their sons exploited black women sexually. Disease and dietary deficiencies took such a heavy toll that few slaves ever reached old age. A huge internal slave trade supplied labor for the Cotton Kingdom by shattering black families. Tearing husbands from wives and parents from children, this trade engulfed a million souls during the 1800s and caused incalculable emotional suffering. Courts defended the prerogatives of owners to "discipline" their slaves, while Southern communities rarely took action against masters known to be brutal or sadistic.[22] Such facts were real but unwelcome to paternalists.

Instead of addressing these facts, slave owners insisted all the more uniformly that they were caring parents for dependent children. Slaveholders commonly spoke of their "family of slaves" or their "family, black and white," and in personal correspondence they often lamented an "irreparable loss" in the death of a "favorite servant." North Carolina's largest slaveholder, Paul Carrington Cameron, illustrated how far such self-deception could go. He reacted to a period of sickness on his plantation by writing, "I fear the negroes have suffered much from the want of proper attention and kindness under this late distemper . . . no love of lucre shall ever induce me to be cruel, or even to make or permit to be made any great exposure of their persons at inclement seasons." On another occasion, he described to his sister his sense of duty: "I cannot better follow the example of our venerated Mother than in doing my duty to her faithful old slaves and their descendants. Do you remember a cold & frosty morning, during her illness, when she said to me, 'Paul my son the people ought to be shod' this is ever in my ears, whenever I see any ones shoes in bad order; and in my ears it will be, so long as I am master."[23]

Similarly, Catherine Devereux Edmondston believed that she treated her slaves well. Yet, she complained, slaves were as presumptuous as their masters were generous. In the South, she wrote, "Cuffy" assumed a great deal, believing that "master must build him a house & give him the where-with-all to make himself comfortable. Ah! Mrs Stowe when you drew your picture you should have put some of the lights of Cuffy's life in it." Mary Boykin Chesnut likewise lamented the sacrifices made each day by plantation mistresses, who were "educated at Northern schools . . . [and] are high-bred, lovely, good, pious." These Southern women were conscientiously "doing their duty as they conceive it. They live in Negro villages. They do not preach and teach hate as a gospel. . . . They set them [the African slaves] the example of a perfect life, a life of utter self-abnegation. Think of [Mrs. Stowe and] these holy New Englanders forced to have a Negro village walk through their houses whenever they see fit, dirty, slatternly, idle, ill-smelling by nature. These women I love have less chance to live their own lives in peace than if they were African missionaries."[24] The concept of paternalism was comforting and reassuring to whites.

Still, fear of slave revolts was never far from the surface, another indication of the emotional complexities of slaveholding. As the sectional crisis intensified, Unionist planters warned that secession might plunge the South into anarchy and violence. One plantation mistress feared such political upheaval because "We have an enemey [*sic*] in our bosoms who will sho[o]t us in our beds." When secession occurred, notes James Roark, "rumors of insurrection raced across the South, and white men scrutinized the conduct of blacks more closely than ever." Even though one planter rejoiced that "abolitionist emissaries" had already "been lynched and expelled from the country," rumors of "'servile insurrection' raced from Virginia to Texas." Tougher laws against "tampering," strengthened slave patrols, heightened vigilance of slaves' passes, and more severe punishments all accompanied the birth of the Confederacy. Bishop Steven Elliott admitted in a sermon that, before the war, Southerners "almost universally believed that domestic insurrection would accompany foreign war, and that we should find our slaves rising 'en masse.'"[25] Though he congratulated his parishioners on the fact that no mass uprising had taken place, the fears of revolt were never extinguished.

When Lincoln issued his Preliminary Emancipation Proclamation, Southerners everywhere denounced what they saw as an attempt to incite revolution. A Tennessee planter believed that Lincoln meant to inaugurate "servile War," and feared "a great loss of property and perhaps of life." The mayor of Savannah viewed the proclamation as an "infamous attempt to incite flight, murder, and rapine on the part of our slave population." Lincoln was trying to convert the "quiet, ignorant dependent black" into a "savage incendiary and brutal murderer." Other Southerners feared that invading Yankee troops would inspire the slaves "to kill their owners & take possession & live as white people," or that the arrival of Northern troops would be a signal to slaves "to rise up against their masters & strike a blow for Union."

Louis Manigault, of South Carolina, denounced the North as "an Enemy of no principle whatsoever, whose only aim is . . . to arm our own Negroes against their very Masters; and entice by every means this misguided Race to assist them in their diabolical programme." In the view of the *Spectator*, a Staunton, Virginia, newspaper, Lincoln was inviting "the servile population of the South to enact the bloody scene of St. Domingo" throughout the Confederacy. Jefferson Davis used his position as president of the Confederacy to condemn Lincoln's proclamation as an attempt to encourage slaves to assassinate their masters.[26]

On countless plantations across the South, planters and planters' wives, especially, feared the possibility of violence. In Alabama, Sarah Espy shuddered at the report of "a most atrocious murder" of an elderly lady and then trembled upon hearing the rumor of "an insurrectionary movement among the negroes of Wills Valley." One South Carolina widow complained that "We know not what moment we may be hacked to death in the most cruel manner by our slaves." Another rendered this sober judgment on her slaves' loyalty: "I fear twould take very little to make them put me out of the way." Reports of assaults by slaves "make woman's blood run cold," declared Hattie Motley of Alabama, while Mrs. M. K. Smith feared "being murdered by negroes at any time they may feel disposed to do so." When Mary Boykin Chesnut learned that a relative had been "murdered by her own people, her Negroes," she "broke down" in "horror and amazement." But her amazement sprang more from the closeness of this death to her family than from disbelief that such was possible. Shortly thereafter, her mother-in-law manifested similar fears when she warned everyone, "Don't touch that soup! It is bitter. There is something wrong with it." She was "terrified," wrote Chesnut, because of "cousin Betsey's fate. She is watching every trifle . . . afraid they will poison us." Hundreds of letters poured into Confederate and state governments from women who implored officials to detail men from military service so that they could control the slaves.[27]

The Confederacy avoided a mass uprising of slave revolutionaries. The South's bondsmen were aware that the men, women, and officials who stayed behind on the home front maintained a heightened vigilance and that the Confederate army was close at hand. Moreover, Southern slaves learned that Union armies were approaching and that the war had become a contest for their freedom. Thus, watchful waiting as the war unfolded made more sense for them than dangerous schemes of revolution. As soon as circumstances were favorable, hundreds of thousands seized their freedom by running to the Yankees. "They all seem waiting on freedom," observed one perceptive Southerner.[28]

The absence of a general slave rebellion, however, did not mean that slavery prospered or that plantation life ran along smoothly in its accustomed channels. To the contrary, every day of the war eroded plantation discipline, disrupted normal routines, and brought troubling changes that surprised, inconvenienced, and discomfited slaveholders. Events outside the plantation stimulated changes within and brought whites face to face with fundamental realities that had been denied and obscured by paternalist ideology.

The character of life on the plantations changed in a multitude of ways. Many of the men who had supervised the plantations or ridden at night with slave patrols were missing, claimed by the Confederacy as soldiers. Women had to assume roles of supervision or discipline that were new and unfamiliar to them. Cotton production declined as government officials urged planters to hold "King Cotton" off the market and switch to the production of food crops that could support the army. Although Lincoln's "Black Republicans" were often far away, Southerners' own government interfered frequently with plantation activities. Military officers descended on farms and unceremoniously seized, or "impressed," needed food, equipment, or animals. When Union raids threatened the loss of territory, the Southern army burned stores of cotton to keep them from falling into enemy hands. Soon Confederate agents claimed one-tenth of nonperishable farm produce under the tax-in-kind, while the government treated slavery even more directly and roughly. First, the military impressed slaves to build fortifications or undertake the heavy fatigue duties necessary to support an army. Then, the Congress enacted laws authorizing levies upon the slave population to support army labor. The government interfered with the very plantations and the institution that it was supposed to protect.

All of these changes and government interventions were unwelcome. Even when planters appreciated the need to shift to food crops, they feared the disruption that this could bring. The slaves were accustomed to work routines with staple crops that kept them busy throughout the year; now they would need to work on seasonal plants, requiring closer supervision at the very time that overseers and male farm managers were in short supply. Slave owners worried that discipline might suffer and the slaves become "demoralized." Impressment of goods by the military was greatly resented, and not simply because this amounted to a seizure of private property with no compensation promised until after the end of the war. Such impressments also fell capriciously on some planters and not on others, depending solely on which farms happened to be close to an army that needed supplies. The Confederate secretary of war conceded that impressment was "a harsh, unequal, and odious mode of supply," and President Davis himself described it as "so unequal in its operations, vexatious to the producer, injurious to the industrial interests, and productive of such discontent among the people as only to be justified by the existence of an absolute necessity."[29]

Even more unwelcome and galling to slave owners was the impressment of their human property. The Richmond administration saw slave labor as a vital resource for the war effort. It initiated its use of slaves by putting some to work building fortifications. Before long, Congress allowed the impressment of slaves for many other functions, including service in hospitals and factories. These steps by their own government shocked and angered slave owners. The government had "no right" to make such a "villainous call," protested one planter in 1861, who saw this as "the beginning of a despotism worse than any European Monarchy." The *Richmond Examiner* sympathized with slave owners and explained that the Southern planter naturally resisted "the shock to the rights of property which is involved" and the loss "of these very slaves for whom he had already fought a long and desperate war." Slave owners also resisted the impressment of their slaves because service in the army often meant that the slaves returned injured, weak, or ill, if they returned at all. The experience of Georgia's Charles Colcock Jones, while extreme, was not unusual. "The sending of our men to work on the Savannah River batteries has been a sad thing to us," he wrote in 1862. "Poor Joe died on the 16th with dysentery (river cholera) contracted there, making two of our best men. . . . Tyrone has been extremely ill; is still in bed. . . . Little Adam is just walking about. July has been very sick, and is barely convalescing. Sam was very sick for a short time." In the following months, neither Tyrone nor Adam regained their health, and when they died the Jones plantation counted four dead out of the seven slaves that had labored for the army.[30]

A more general—and deeper—concern was the loss of control over slaves resulting from the disruption of plantation life. Early in 1862 an Alabama man warned the government that the slaves were developing "a disposition to misrule and insubordination occasioned no doubt from the withdrawal of our male population from their midst." A South Carolina plantation owner, a widow, found her "orders disregarded more & more every day. I can do nothing so must submit." In North Carolina, on the Edmondston plantation, from which Patrick Edmondston was absent only intermittently, a similar deterioration of discipline—and of the submissive habits known as good order—occurred. At first, the Edmondstons became aware of problems on nearby plantations, as the servants whom one woman "left in charge of her house have plundered her shamefully." At that point, Catherine Edmondston remained confident that her slaves would behave well. Soon, however, she noted that her and her husband's absences from the plantation were "telling on the servants; they are getting so awkward, inefficient & even lazy." Then, in July 1862, "rogues" among their servants tried to "break into our Pork House." Since "we never had such a thing before," the Edmondstons were alarmed. Failing to identify the culprits, they whipped two slaves chosen at random, in order "to repress the spirit of disorganization and theft." In September 1863, Catherine recorded in dismay that "All of our negroes have left," and "Negro property is worse than useless for they do no work unless they choose & the owners dare not correct them else off they go." She added: "They keep the Federals informed of everything. . . . As to the idea of a *faithful servant, it is all a fiction*. I have seen the favourite & most petted negroes the first to leave in every instance. So disgusted have I become with the whole race that I often wish I had never seen *one*."[31]

Two large plantations near Lake Phelps, in eastern North Carolina, shared Catherine Edmondston's experiences with the dissolution of order, discipline, and "loyalty." William Pettigrew and Josiah Collins III, who owned hundreds of slaves on adjoining tracts of land, adopted different approaches to the challenge of maintaining control. When Pettigrew's slaves "stampeded" at the approach of Federal forces, with some making their escape to Union lines, he surrounded the slave quarters with troops and forcibly removed his remaining bondsmen to rented land further inland. Josiah Collins decided that it was too difficult to move his 328 slaves, so he resolved to keep them at work under an overseer. The effort was a failure. His slaves began to do as they pleased and declared that they would leave if Collins ever tried to make them move. By spring 1863 the overseer's methods had been reduced to bribery: "I have had to wearke Evry skiam [scheme] to keep them hear. . . . The[y] tore dowan and steal and take any thing the[y] pleas. i can not say a worde. I keepe talking to them[,] have gived off hogs and Cattle to each family [and] by those meanes i have kept them on the lake . . . the[re] are no Dependance in no nigro when the weard freedom is given." To this record of defiant independence the slaves added words of disrespect. "They call you 'Old Collins,'" reported a friend, and the overseer confirmed that "They doo not cear [care] for you at all."[32]

To many white Southerners these personal communications were the most painful disappointment of all, for the reality of slave behavior shattered the fiction of benevolent paternalism. The myth of paternalism had become essential to slaveholders' self-image, and when the slaves denied its reality, they reacted with wounded feelings. Annie Sehon believed that two female slaves who served her were "true," yet one soon ran off to a Federal army camp, leaving Annie to wonder, in pained surprise, about what "changed her so." Judith McGuire was shocked that "Our man Nat . . . to whom I was very partial" had run away. "Some of the servants," she concluded, "are very unfaithful." The Jones family, of Georgia, consisted of devout Presbyterians who had campaigned to bring religious instruction to the slaves in a dedicated, paternalistic manner. Mary Jones, the family's matriarch, felt anger when her granddaughter's nurse helped the Yankees and ran off to them, thus acting "a faithless part as soon as she could." Others among the Jones's slaves also proved "false" and guilty of "ingratitude," prompting Mrs. Jones to reflect bitterly, "My life long . . . I have been laboring and caring for them . . . and this is their return." Another member of the family, speaking out of the depth of the paternalist mentality, was distraught that three slave women had run away "without bidding any of us an affectionate adieu."[33]

Rather than face the destruction of their illusions, some Southerners tried to deny what was being revealed about their relationship with their slaves. The interracial "family" ties of slavery were real, they told themselves, but the Yankees had preyed upon the slaves' weak intellects. Runaways were merely "poor deluded creatures" or "poor deluded wretches," the deceived rather than the deceivers. But for most slave owners the collapse of the paternalist facade brought a painful confrontation with reality. "Those we loved best, and who loved us best—as we thought—were the first to leave us," admitted one Southerner. Louis Manigault agreed that "those we esteemed the most" were often "the first to desert us." By 1864, the honest and intelligent Mary Boykin Chesnut admitted that she did not know her slaves at all. The women who worked in her house were "excellent servants, no matter for their shortcomings behind my back." They labored quietly and seemingly attentively, but their thoughts and feelings remained hidden, inscrutable. "These sphinxes give no sign," Chesnut concluded, that they knew very well what was coming with the end of the war. But if they had spoken, Chesnut was sure what they would have said: "Freedom, my masters!"[34]

FACING THESE TRUTHS on the personal level was a painful task, but some Southerners, principally clergymen, concluded that other truths about slavery must be faced by society. The South's moral discomfort with slavery had always been felt most strongly by a portion of the clergy. A great many ministers, it is true, devoted their efforts to praising and justifying the South's cause. But a fraction of the clergy long had hoped for amelioration of the slaves' condition and greater concern for their religious life. For decades Georgia's Charles Colcock Jones had worked to promote religious instruction of the slaves, as had South Carolina's James Henley Thornwell. Devoted to the ideal of a paternalistic society, Thornwell believed that the Bible was "the *true impregnable*" defense for the Christian slaveholder, but "only when he obeys its directions as well as employs its sanctions." In 1847 he had chaired a committee of the South Carolina Presbyterian Synod that petitioned the legislature, calling on lawmakers to protect the slave family and allow slaves to learn to read. Thornwell published essays in the *Southern Presbyterian Review* urging religious instruction for the slaves, and one of his essays was reprinted under the title *The Rights and the Duties of Masters.*[35]

Ministers like these hoped that the Confederacy would improve on the record of the antebellum South. In December 1861, Reverend Jones used an opportunity to address the general assembly of the Presbyterian Church in Augusta, Georgia, to renew his campaign to bring preaching and religious teaching to the slave population. Slaves, said Jones, "are men, created in the image of God, to be acknowledged and cared for spiritually by us." They needed "faithful, and continued and universal religious instruction" under the direction of patriarchal and devout masters, but instead the South had allowed them to be weak in faith, unlettered, and uninstructed in the Gospel. Thus, declared Jones, the church had "partially only" fulfilled "*her duty to the negroes.*" He challenged the Presbyterian church and other denominations to send missionaries and preach, "until our whole population shall be evangelized, and our whole land be filled with the glory of the Lord."[36]

Another Presbyterian minister, the Reverend Joseph R. Wilson, agreed that masters bore heavy responsibilities from God in their relationship to the slaves. Wilson accepted slavery as "an organizing element in that family order" which God had instituted on earth as part of the "very foundation of Church and State." Slavery was a blessing, if it was "*under proper management, by Christian people*," Wilson emphasized. This meant that slaves were to be Christianized, and in this work, "their earthly masters have something — have much — to do." Indeed, masters would have "to give an account to God at last for the right use of their exalted stewardship over *souls of immortal men*, placed directly underneath their control." Therefore he entreated his listeners to control their tempers, eschew threats, remember mercy, and "treat their servants as they will expect their own Master in heaven to treat *them*."[37]

For many years such pleas had gone unheard. During the years of an intensifying sectional crisis white Southerners strained every nerve to defend slavery against outside criticism, and in that highly charged atmosphere home-grown critics were ineffective and reluctant to press their case, for fear of public condemnation. The establishment of the Confederacy, however, changed the context and encouraged religious reformers. They thought that now, within a Southern slaveholding nation, they would be able to bring the institution into closer conformity with the teachings of Christianity. Moreover, they felt a heavier obligation to act.

The Reverend Benjamin M. Palmer acted under this sense of duty when he delivered an address to South Carolina's legislators. Independence, he told the lawmakers, had "relieved" Southerners "of those embarrassments which a hypocritical fanaticism has interposed." Now, in their own nation, Confederates "shall be able, with greater freedom, to give them [the slaves] God's blessed word, to protect their persons against the abuses of capricious power, and to throw the shield of a stronger guardianship around their domestic relations." Palmer speculated that God's purpose in allowing the war to occur may have been "to chasten us for past shortcomings, and . . . to enlarge our power to protect and bless the race committed to our trust." Palmer even pronounced himself unwilling to insist that "*perpetual* bondage" for African Americans was God's plan.[38] Similarly, Bishop Stephen Elliott told his parishioners:

> Our future destiny is bound up with it [slavery]. As we deal with it, so shall we prosper, or so shall we suffer. The responsibility is upon us, and if we rise up, in a true Christian temper, to the sublime work which God has committed to us of educating a subject nation for his divine purposes, we shall be blessed of him as Joseph was. . . . But if contrariwise,

> we shall misunderstand our relations and shall assume the dominion of masters without remembering the duties thereof, God will "make them pricks in our eyes and thorns in our sides, and shall vex us in the land wherein we dwell."

Elliott also declared that "many, very many, I know, have been insensible to their duty and have neglected the great trust committed to their charge."[39]

Impelled by such feelings, reform-minded ministers in various parts of the South began to work for change. Historian Bell Wiley identified an Episcopal periodical as the first to begin agitating for recognition of slave marriages, in the summer and fall of 1861. Another Episcopal journal endorsed a minister's proposal to prevent the separation of married slaves, and "sentiment favoring legal recognition of slave marriages seems to have spread rapidly in 1862." In November of that year, Reverend Elliott reported with satisfaction to the church's general council that "public sentiment is rapidly becoming sound" upon that subject. In that same month, the Episcopal bishops, adopting some of Elliott's language, issued a pastoral letter to clergy and laity that placed reforms of slavery first on an agenda for action by the church. The pastoral letter declared that next to increasing the number of communicants, "the religious instruction of the negroes" was "the Church's greatest work in these Confederate States." Slaves were "not merely so much property," but "a sacred trust" for Southerners to "elevate . . . in the scale of being" through "ministrations for their benefit and improvement." Urging churchmen to "rush, with the zeal of martyrs, to this labor of love," the bishops urged masters to support not only education but also the "obligation, as Christian men" to protect slave marriages. Southerners could, with "a very little care upon our part," rid slavery of "all necessity for the separation of parents and children."[40]

Baptists seemed to take the lead in urging Confederates to reconsider the laws against teaching slaves to read. In the spring and fall of 1862 two regional conventions of Georgia Baptists urged the legislature to change the law; one criticized the existing legislation as "a disgrace to our civilization and to our country, and to the age in which we live." As Georgia's Baptists discussed the issue in their conventions and publications, the state's Methodists and Presbyterians also began to discuss reforms, and Baptists in other states joined in. The Alabama Baptist Convention in 1863 called for better religious instruction for bondsmen, and Virginia's Appomattox Baptist Association called for legal changes so that slaves could not only learn to read, but also meet together to sing, pray, and exhort. These efforts achieved some success in the spring of 1863 when Georgia's legislature repealed a recent change to the state's legal code that had prohibited slaves from preaching. A proposal to allow blacks to learn to read and write was defeated by Georgia's lawmakers, however. This measure's prospects may have been damaged by the controversy aroused when the Methodist bishop George Foster Pierce advocated slave literacy in unusually strong terms. Declaring that slaves were "immortal beings" whom God would want to be able to read his word, Pierce concluded: "If the institution of slavery cannot be maintained except at the expense of the black man's immortal interests, in the name of heaven, I say—*let it perish.*" That was too much for some members of Georgia's lower house, which refused to act on a bill legalizing slave education.[41]

Efforts to reform slavery accelerated after 1862 as two Presbyterian ministers took the lead in calling for change. James Lyon, an outspoken Tennessean who had opposed secession, served as the moderator of the Southern Presbyterian General Assembly in 1863. That same year, as chair of a committee that had been at work for two years, he delivered a report on the religious instruction of black people. The report, which was published under the title "Slavery and the Duties Growing out of the Relation," went far beyond the one issue of religious instruction. "*Now,*" in the Confederacy, Lyon wrote, "there is neither excuse for not proclaiming, nor pretence for not hearing the truth" about the improvements that must be made in slavery. He cited five areas in which evils "known to all, acknowledged by all, and regretted by all good men" had to be corrected. These were:

—legal barriers to teaching slaves how to read and write;
—absenteeism of planters, which made paternal care impossible;
—lack of legal protection for slaves from the "low, malicious white man" or the "drunken, infuriated master";
—lack of legal recognition for slave marriage and slave families, "an outrage upon the laws of God"; and
—failure to provide religious instruction for the slaves.

Lyon believed that his report was well received, but he admitted that some delegates were "startled at the high ground" he had taken. As a result, it was referred to his committee for another year, and after much discussion, in 1864 it was referred to yet another committee. There it lay when the war came to an end. Lyon had failed to obtain any action, although his proposals for reform had generated considerable public discussion.[42]

Not all the discussion was favorable to Lyon's proposals. The *Southern Presbyterian Review* carried an article in October 1863 that took issue with Lyon's ideas about protecting slave marriages and revealed society's ingrained resistance to change. The anonymous author of this piece agreed that Southerners needed to "look into the private management of our negroes," so that "the inner life of slavery [is] reformed and restored, as far as may be, to the pattern shown us in the Bible." But the article then praised paternalism and developed a theory of slavery as "a *domestic* institution . . . the subject of family government," which contradicted most of Lyon's ideas. By praising the supposedly mild and kind rule of the master as "law-giver" to the slave, this writer declared that legal recognition of slave marriages would destroy the familial basis of slavery and bring slaves under the state. That, in turn, would lead to a "revolution in the status of the slave." He would have to receive property rights and other rights, all of which would be "folly." This article then dismissed the danger of separation to slave families as "greatly overrated" and praised the conduct of white slave owners toward their laboring class as the best in the world. Before concluding, the anonymous author dismissed education for slaves as another step that would vitiate the paternalistic basis of slavery. Those who wanted no change in slaveholding viewed the "fire-side authority" of the planter as laudable and sufficient and believed that shortcomings in planters' behavior were rare.[43]

Another Presbyterian minister, however, joined Lyons in the push for change. The Reverend Calvin Wiley, of North Carolina, had served in the legislature of his state and remained influential in public affairs as the superintendent of public schools. Writing from an overwhelmingly religious, rather than political, perspective, Wiley published a book in 1863 titled *Scriptural Views of National Trials, or, the True Road to the Independence and Peace of the Confederate States of America.* His book provides insight into the thoughts and attitudes of the religious reformers, while simultaneously illustrating the limitations of their approach to the subject of slavery.

Quotations from the Bible dominated almost every one of the more than two hundred pages in Calvin Wiley's book. Religious truths "alone," Wiley declared, could account for "the convulsions and trials" of the Confederacy and "explain *all* national troubles." Yet, though Wiley was quick to assert that "all national as well as all individual suffering" was "the certain result of a violation of the Law of God," he defended slavery in the abstract and adopted a more cautious tone in calling for reforms to the institution. The Confederacy was "a Christian nation," and it consisted of God's chosen people, who honored his word "as the only source of Truth." Yet, clearly the South had done wrong. "*Whatever may be the nature of a nation's cause . . . when it suffers, it is chastened for sin.*"[44]

"*Man is depraved,*" Wiley believed, and though the North's attitude toward slavery had caused the war, something was wrong in the Confederacy. Despite its people's unity and sacrifice, he argued, the nation lacked "healthful energy and proper direction in those spiritual, religious springs, which constitute the vital forces of all communities." Christians had a "*solemn obligation . . . to proclaim in the ears of the whole nation that it has committed offences for which God is correcting it.*" The task before Confederates was to "humble ourselves under the mighty hand of God," recognize "our sins," and "forsake" them.

Then, in an indirect manner, Wiley introduced his view that these sins involved slavery. Because Confederates based their whole "social system on this Word" and called the word as their witness "in our controversy with the nations about slavery," they had an obligation "to construct the whole edifice according to its directions." "*Right now,*" he insisted, was "the time to turn from the offences for which the nation is chastised. We often hear the remark that when the war is over and the better times have come, we will, as men and as Christians, as a Church and as a people, give ourselves to needed reforms." That attitude, said Wiley, "is in fact one of our greatest sins."[45]

Although "the whole continent" had offended heaven "in its conduct towards the African element of society," Wiley charged Southern Christians with failure to speak up and tell the government what God required for the "*duties*" of masters. Bowing to "human opinion, infirmity and passion," and reacting against the "vile and atheistic abolitionists," Southerners had ignored "reforms which the conscience of the whole Church felt were demanded, sternly demanded by the immutable law of God." Entangled in sectional controversies, Southerners had refused to act in a way that might be seen as "a triumph to the free-soilers." Their failure to act was "ridiculous and shameful," especially after the South became an independent nation. Wiley saw no "excuse" to delay further. "It is extremely probable," he concluded, "that God is now chastising the country for its sins in connection with the subject of slavery."[46]

What were these sins? Wiley's answer constituted a catalog of errors and needed reforms. First, there had been "neglect" by the church of its duty to enlighten the public about God's counsel on slavery. It had failed to speak up for the "sacredness" of slave marriages, the protection of the relationship of "parent and child," and the "observance of the Sabbath." In addition, "our slave code is not what it ought to be." Second, Southerners had failed to create a "systematic, efficient, and thorough means for the instruction of the heathen" in the Gospel. The progress in slaves' Christianity that others praised, Wiley argued, was due to "the Providence of God" rather than to "the concerted and persevering efforts of the Church." Third, "conscientious and Christian masters" had failed to restrain "the conduct of hard and cruel proprietors." When there was no control over the conduct of masters, slavery became an "evil," Wiley declared, and society defaulted on what it "owes" to God. Fourth, slave owners had indulged a spirit of revenge against the "poor, deluded negroes" who had run away to support the North. This spirit was especially unjustified because most slaves had remained "quiet and conservative" throughout the war, aiding the Confederacy. Therefore, masters needed to purge the statute books "of every injustice to the devoted slave" who had "so nobly stood by" them in their "hour of need." Concluding his litany of errors, Wiley challenged his "Noble Confederate brethren": "Let us crown our deed *by conquering our own prejudices,* BY DARING TO DO WHAT IS RIGHT, and our triumph will be certain and our history glorious."[47]

Scriptural Views of National Trials was Calvin Wiley's jeremiad calling the Confederacy to account for its sins in the management of slavery. The book's deeply religious character contributed to the movement for reform, as other religious leaders added their voices to the call for change. The Reverend W. B. W. Howe preached a sermon in Charleston in 1864 that stimulated debate in that city's newspapers. Agreeing with Wiley that Confederates were being punished for their "peculiar sins," Howe called on Southerners to allow manumission, education, and legal marriage for the slaves. But he was more conservative than Wiley in arguing that the time for action was after the end of the war. The *Charleston Daily Courier* took a position in support of slave marriages, and Georgia's Baptists called on their state legislature to pass the same reform. Wiley and Lyons remained active, lobbying the governors of North Carolina and Mississippi, respectively, in the closing months of the war and urging them to take action. Lyon even prepared a bill on slaves' "marital and parental relations" that a committee of the Mississippi senate considered and recommended for action at a more "opportune" time.[48]

And yet this accelerating activity, undoubtedly inspired by deep religious conviction, accomplished little. Although white Southerners in growing numbers asked whether God was on their side and questioned the rightness and morality of their laws on slavery, the war came to an end without major revision of the Confederacy's slave codes. As important as religion was to many Southerners, it proved to have less power over lawmakers than practical considerations of military and political need. For in the closing months of the war, the Confederate army and the Davis administration proposed far more sweeping changes to slavery. These proposals, born of necessity and driven by fear of defeat, involved both a new role for male slaves and a general emancipation that would inevitably alter Southern society. As we shall see, however, such radical steps involved the same assumptions of white supremacy that affected policy in the North and led to postwar patterns of oppression.

SIX

HERESY, DOGMA, AND THE CONFEDERATE DEBATE

The Confederacy came into being as a slaveholders' republic. Faced with the election of a "Black Republican" and alarmed by the strength of a party they deemed hostile to slavery, secessionists sprang into action and carried the day. Focusing on one state after another, these "fire-eaters" led the Lower South out of the Union and established a government designed to serve more reliably the peculiar interests of slaveholders. Under the new Confederate administration, they believed, state rights would be respected, the central government would be restricted, slaveholders would be secure, and slavery would be protected. The South's institution of racial slavery was the bedrock on which whites erected their new Confederacy.

But the architects of the Confederate South were looking backward rather than forward; they were anticipating a static government that could resist the dangers of the past rather than meet the challenges of the future. When war engulfed the Confederacy, every aspect of life changed. Established customs gave way to unexpected innovations, pressing crises disrupted daily life, and eternal verities dissolved. By every measure, the Civil War transformed the South far more than it did the North. The armies claimed a higher proportion of men, inflation raged far more virulently, families suffered far more on the home front, and social customs changed more drastically under the pressure of a militarized existence. To the immense surprise of Southerners, the Confederacy became what historian Emory Thomas has aptly called a "revolutionary experience." The revolution that Confederates endured left little untouched. Inevitably, it undermined slavery, the core institution of the new nation.

The military crisis of the Confederacy subjected slavery to a variety of stresses and strains, visiting upon slave owners many unpleasant developments. The traditional expectations of planters had little relevance to a society disrupted and disarranged by war. As the Confederacy struggled to survive, no area of life could remain immune from change, and events began to alter slavery in fundamental ways. Slave owners lost the extensive control that they were accustomed to have over their bondsmen. National priorities began to impinge on what had always been a remarkably local and "domestic" institution. Ultimately, slavery itself came into question, as a result of the Confederacy's crisis, and the political pressures unleashed by war proved far more potent than the promptings of religious conscience.

Two factors influenced the degree to which Southerners would change slavery during the war: the scope of the military crisis and the flexibility of political leaders. In rapid order military demands increased, quickly reaching a point at which government action became necessary to exploit slavery as a vital resource for war. Political leaders then faced a challenge in deciding how many unwelcome changes to make, for altering the fundamentals of slavery threatened both the institution and assumptions of racial subordination. Substantial change to the core of Confederate beliefs meant heresy, whereas adherence to familiar dogma threatened defeat. Events would prove that the slave South possessed only a limited capacity for radical innovation. What capacity there was resided primarily in its military leaders and in President Jefferson Davis. Their determination and realism pointed the way toward change. But white Confederates also proved to be intransigent, loyal to their past and adamant about slavery and white supremacy. In the final military crisis of the Confederacy, political leaders debated proposals to arm and free the slaves. In doing so, they cast light on the nature of their society and the unshakeable core of the white South's racial values.

IN THE ANTEBELLUM SOUTH little had interfered with a slave owner's control of his plantation and his slaves. The region was rural, plantations often were far apart, and slavery as an institution fell very much under the regulation of the individual planter. Using paternalistic arguments, white Southerners described slaves as belonging to their owner's "family," and the planter was the undisputed head of that family, black and white. Although the statute books contained a few mild laws designed to protect slaves from mistreatment, the power of the state primarily supported the slave owner and guarded his investment. Few citizens questioned the behavior of a neighbor toward his slaves, since none of them wanted to endure outsiders' meddling in their own plantation's affairs. The individual slave owner ruled his personal kingdom. On his own property, he functioned as a patriarch or a dictator, a thoughtful ruler or a sadist, according to his inclinations. "The plantation was both the reality and the symbol of what the planters' revolution was all about," writes James Roark, "and its preservation became the touchstone of the planters' wartime experience."[1]

Quickly, the Confederacy's war effort intruded on the planter's separate world. This intrusion went far beyond the armies' claiming the services of many men, taking them away from their plantations. The Confederacy also extended a new arm of control over the plantation through impressment. Military commanders often simply took what they needed, whether that meant horses, wagons, food, or other useful items, including slaves, who were put to work building fortifications, unloading supplies, and performing other heavy labor. At first these impressments occurred without formal legal sanction. Some resources were offered voluntarily. Soon, however, state and national legislation mobilized slave labor for the war effort through the force of law. "The immense demands of armed conflict" with the North were so great "that they could not be borne by whites alone."[2] Governors and officials in Richmond began to look upon the slave population as an essential resource.

In Virginia, for example, army officers and politicians quickly saw that black labor was needed to support the armies and to work in factories, ironworks, railroads, military hospitals, and agencies such as the army's quartermaster, ordnance, niter, and mining bureaus. At first, leaders asked slave owners to volunteer their laborers or to hire them out for necessary tasks. But by the late fall of 1861, free black people had ceased to volunteer, and "the folly of depending upon slaveholders to comply willingly with military requisitions" had become apparent. Faced with continued demands from the military, the general assembly of Virginia therefore passed three laws designed to put black labor at the service of the war effort, whatever the wishes of African Americans or slave owners might be.[3]

The first law created a list of all free black males aged 18 to 50 and defined a method for local justices to select workers to be delivered to the Confederacy, which would pay and maintain them. The next law, passed in the fall of 1862, initiated a census of slaves, so that 10,000 of them (or up to 5 percent of the slave population in any county, city, or town) could be impressed to work on entrenchments or other defenses. Their owners would receive modest pay for the slaves' service from the Confederate government, and the nation was responsible for their food and medical needs. A third law, coming early in 1863, attempted to shield from impressment counties that desperately needed their slaves to grow crops, but this act also established fines for owners who refused to cooperate with impressments.[4]

At the same time, the Confederacy made its long-established practice of impressments legal and tried to improve results while still cooperating with the states. President Davis, rather than the state governor, became the chief enforcer of these impressments. Confederate agents, however, were exhorted to carry out impressments "according to the rules and regulations provided in the laws of the state wherein they are impressed." Nevertheless, by the end of 1863 the new nation needed more slave workmen, so President Davis called for and obtained a more stringent law. As many as one-fifth of a state's male slaves could be taken under the new act, up to a total of 20,000 slaves. The secretary of war soon used this new law to call for 14,500 slaves and established quotas for each state to contribute to this number.[5] By these laws, the Confederacy's Congress and executive branch formally recognized slavery as a resource that could be claimed by the nation in its battle to survive.

Through these means, African Americans came to fulfill many vital functions in the Confederacy. In Virginia alone, thousands of free blacks worked for the government, not merely as laborers but also in skilled positions, such as those of carpenter, machinist, mason, railroad fireman, shoemaker, tanner, or wagon maker. Slaves served the War Department as "butchers, bakers, cattle drivers, teamsters, boatmen, millers, and packers." They labored as shipbuilders, miners, coopers, oilmakers, bricklayers, and blacksmiths. The Tredegar Iron Works, the Confederacy's most notable industrial success story, depended upon as many black workers as white, more than 1,200 African Americans in all. Slaves worked in almost every department of its varied operations. Slaves were especially crucial to railroad maintenance and repair, and thousands kept the roads operating in Virginia alone. Other thousands staffed military hospitals, frequently outnumbering the whites who helped care for wounded soldiers. Near the front lines, the armies depended on slave laborers to erect many of the batteries and defensive works. In the fall of 1862 the War Department had made two requisitions for slaves to construct defenses for Richmond, demanding "almost 10,000 slaves . . . to construct earthworks on the outskirts of the capital." Thousands more were demanded in 1863 and 1864.[6]

The unquestioned authority of the plantation patriarch had disappeared.

No longer were all slaves private property under the exclusive control of the master; the nation was claiming, indeed depending on, the skills and labor of slaves. How far would the idea that slaves constituted a national resource, to be taken and used in preservation of the nation, go? As the prospects of the Confederacy darkened, as military defeats made its position increasingly perilous, the importance of the slave population steadily increased. Before long, it was clear that the South would need to use all of its resources effectively if it hoped to survive in a death struggle against the richer and more populous North. These harsh facts collided with the opposition and anger of slave owners, who did not want to lose control of any of their slaves and bemoaned the risks that government service posed to the health and strength of their slave property. But the reality could not be ignored.

Indeed, a few Southerners had sensed that reality from the first days of the war. Right after the Confederacy's encouraging victory at Bull Run in 1861, Richard S. Ewell had cautioned Jefferson Davis that only one measure could secure victory in what was sure to be "a long, and, at best, doubtful struggle." That measure, Ewell foresaw, was "emancipating the slaves and arming them." A few citizens in the Deep South also had urged the War Department to use the large population of African Americans in the war effort. Since there were as many black Southerners as white ones, noted three petitioners from Mississippi, it made no sense "to attempt the defense of the country with only one of these elements of power." One planter even urged his friend, secretary of war Leroy Pope Walker, to allow him to raise some "negro regiments." Military reverses in the spring of 1862 encouraged a few other individuals to raise the idea of black troops.[7] But these suggestions, coming from a small number of rigorously logical individuals, were faint voices crying in the wilderness. Most white Southerners, dedicated to preserving slavery and their social system, could not even imagine such a heretical idea until the necessity for it became overwhelming.

For a larger number, that time arrived in the last months of 1863. More than a few Southerners then began to propose the radical idea that slaves should be brought into the Confederate armies to swell the number of troops and redress the military imbalance, an imbalance that threatened inevitable defeat. The source and timing of these suggestions reflected the impact of serious military reverses on citizens' morale. Defeats at Gettysburg and Vicksburg in July 1863 had deeply discouraged most Confederates. Though the cause was not yet positively lost, these two reverses were accurately seen as a significant and negative turning point. Moreover, most of the proposals in 1863 came from the Deep South, that is, from areas where the recent success of Union forces had shocked residents and put them in peril. The Federal army's capture of Vicksburg and Port Hudson had cut the Confederacy in two. The Gulf States east of the Mississippi River—and the Richmond government—were now cut off from all Confederate resources west of the river. Also, as part of the Vicksburg campaign, General Grant's army had overrun much of Mississippi. Louisiana and Mississippi were reeling from war's destruction, and citizens in Alabama had good reason to fear the worst.

In the month after the defeats at Gettsyburg and Vicksburg, the general assembly of Alabama urgently called President Davis's attention to the need for more men. "The exigencies of the country" were great, argued Alabama's legislators. The armies had to be increased. Many commissary or quartermaster's department clerks should be sent to the front lines, they declared, along with many of the detailed soldiers whose labor for factories or railroads was not essential to the war effort. In addition, Congress should examine a "modification of the exemption law," in order to "increase the strength of our military force." Turning to the subject of slavery, the worried lawmakers argued that the time for fresh thinking had arrived. "In view of the fact that the Government of the United States has determined to put into the field negro soldiers," they urged that the Confederate Congress consider "the propriety and policy of using in some effective way a certain percentage of the male slave population of the Confederate States."[8] As we have seen, Jefferson Davis promptly asked Congress for authority to use more slave labor.

The language of the Alabama legislators was vague and nonspecific, but others from their region of the Confederacy soon spoke up more directly and pointedly. One of several letters to the War Department even claimed that, "The people are clamoring . . . for the Slaves to be brought into service for defence of our rights and liberties." In early September, 1863, the *Jackson Mississippian* bluntly posed the alternatives: "We must either employ the negroes ourselves, or the enemy will employ them against us." The Union was holding "much of our territory," Lincoln had already brought 50,000 African Americans into "the Federal ranks," and he "proposes to free and arm" the rest "against us." The newspaper estimated that there were "at least six hundred thousand able-bodied men capable of bearing arms" among the Confederacy's black population. The government "must adopt a counter policy" to "thwart the enemy." Believing that African Americans were "affectionate" and "grateful" and could be convinced that the South was their natural home, the *Mississippian* called for a radical change: "If nothing else will do it—if the negroes cannot be made effective and trustworthy to the Southern cause in no [*sic*] other way, we solemnly believe it is the duty of this Government to forestall Lincoln and proceed at once to take steps for the emancipation or liberation of the negroes itself. Let them be declared free, placed in the ranks, and told to fight for their homes and country." Such a step, no matter how destructive, would be better than "the loss of the negroes, the country and liberty." The radical change also would influence European nations, alleviate class resentments in the South, invigorate the cause, and bring success.[9]

In Montgomery, Alabama, the *Weekly Mail* was reaching similar conclusions. Fearing an imminent invasion of Alabama from forces gathering under Grant and General William Rosecrans, the *Weekly Mail* concluded "that it is better for us to use our negroes for our defense than that the Yankees should use them against us." This paper made no mention of emancipation, and it voiced greater disappointment than the *Mississippian* over the effect that arming slaves would have on race relations. Using them in the armies would contradict their normal status "as maintained by Southern statesmen and the Southern people." It would amount to "a practical acknowledgment of equality" and lead to prisoner exchanges that would be "a practical equalization of the races." Any such developments were "revolting to every sentiment of pride, and to every principle that governed our institutions before the war." But, concluded the editor, "we must deal with facts as we find them." Arming the slaves was "a matter of necessity," the "only" means to "checkmate" the enemy. "There is no alternative."[10]

With morale plummeting in Alabama, many of its citizens shared this sense that the military situation was truly desperate. Congressman E. S. Dargan confided in J. B. Jones, the Richmond War Department clerk, his belief that "the people are fast losing all hope of achieving their independence." "Mississippi is nearly subdued," Dargan reported, "and Alabama is almost exhausted." Such desperation caused others, at least a minority, to rethink their purpose. James Alcorn, of Mississippi, a hostile critic of the Richmond administration, told his state's legislature that Southerners had "placed the cause of the war upon a false ground. It was not exclusively to save slavery." The editor of the *Mobile Register* agreed that it was a "mistaken notion" to think that the war was about slavery. "We protest against the theory that this is a war for the negroes," he wrote; "it is a war for constitutional liberty, and the rights of self-government." Although this editor was not yet ready to arm the slaves, he favored making much greater use of them immediately in supporting roles and, if it became clear that "negro soldiers are needed, . . . there is no argument of doubtful expediency to counterbalance the superlative end."[11]

Taking practical steps, Major General Dabney Maury, of the Department of the Gulf, proposed that he be allowed to enlist a company of "creoles" from Mobile. These "creoles" were African Americans, but because of their light skin and social background, they had enjoyed both freedom and higher status than the slaves. Maury argued that they could be added to the Confederacy's forces, and Mobile's congressman supported his proposition. However, the secretary of war, James Seddon, replied that they could not be accepted as soldiers unless they were clearly "disconnected from negroes." As with slaves, the only role open to them in the armed forces was that of laborer.[12] Maury would not be the only general, however, to come forward at this time.

From Major General Patrick Cleburne, of the Army of Tennessee, came the most serious and convincingly argued proposal so far to bring slaves into the army. Cleburne was a distinguished commander, an immigrant from Ireland who had prospered in the South before rising to a high command position on the basis of his merit and gallantry. While in winter quarters in northern Georgia with General Joseph E. Johnston's army, Cleburne and other commanders with whom he worked discussed the prospects of the Confederacy and of their army. The Army of Tennessee was just recovering from its shocking defeat in the battles of Lookout Mountain and Missionary Ridge, and the challenge of a renewed offensive by General Sherman lay ahead. After the commanders' discussion, Cleburne put his conclusions into a report that gained the signatures of thirteen other high-ranking officers, including three other generals.

Cleburne's proposal began with a blunt assessment of the military situation. After almost three years of fighting and despite great bloodshed and loss of treasure, the South had nothing to show for its sacrifices but "long lists of dead and mangled." Long-sought victories had "invariably slipped away," leaving a Confederate nation that was "hemmed in to-day into less than two-thirds" of its territory, while "the enemy menacingly confronts us at every point with superior forces." The consequences of these facts were deeply troubling. "Our soldiers," Cleburne wrote, "can see no end to this state of affairs except in our own exhaustion." Among them the belief was growing that "some black catastrophe is not far ahead of us." Desertions were increasing, supplies were failing, and "if this state continues much longer we must be subjugated."[13]

Turning to analysis, Cleburne cited three causes of the Confederacy's acute crisis. First came "numbers," "the inferiority of our armies to those of the enemy" in the number of troops. Closely related to this fundamental problem was the fact that the enemy could draw on "several sources" for troops, whereas the Confederacy had only a "single source" of men. Lincoln was recruiting from the North's large native white population as well as from immigrants from Europe. In addition, he had announced that "an army of 100,000 negroes as good as any troops" was already in training. By comparison, the South could look only to "that portion of our white men fit for duty and not now in the ranks." A third problem, Cleburne frankly stated, was "the fact that slavery" was no longer an asset, but "has now become, in a military point of view, one of our chief sources of weakness." Not only was the North bringing Southern slaves into its armies, but in the South the institution had become "our most vulnerable point . . . an insidious weakness."[14]

Slavery vitiated Confederates' will to resist in any locality facing a Union invasion, explained Cleburne. Wherever Union forces threatened, "whites can no longer with safety to their property openly sympathize with our cause." Instead, they feared their slaves and soon "take the oath to save property." As a result, they "become dead to us, if not open enemies." Moreover, the Confederate army had to scatter its forces to try to prevent raids on heavily slaveholding areas. Slavery had become "comparatively valueless to us for labor," but of great benefit to the Union army, since the slave population constituted "an omnipresent spy system." The slaves revealed all they knew to Federal troops and helped the North in a variety of ways.[15]

The remedies proposed by President Davis simply would not work, stated Cleburne. Davis had announced a plan to put back into the army all those who were improperly absent, to end substitution (which allowed conscripts to hire a man to take their place), and to send more detailed or exempted men to the front lines. But "experience proves," declared Cleburne, that young boys and old men would not make effective soldiers. Eliminating substitution would only affect those who had wanted to avoid service. Such individuals would be "unwilling and discontented soldiers," and they were sure to view the end of substitution as a "breach of faith." Moreover, as Davis himself had admitted, many exemptions were necessary to the war effort, either agriculturally or economically, and the removal of some exempted men would come at a price. Moreover, Davis's measures would do nothing to create a reserve for the Confederacy, a reserve needed "to meet unexpected disaster or to supply a protracted struggle." Concluding his indictment, Cleburne pointed out that Davis's flawed plan addressed only the first of the Confederacy's three problems; it ignored both the North's recruitment of immigrants and blacks and the fact that slavery had become "an insidious weakness."[16]

The needed remedy was clear, if shocking. Cleburne proposed "that we immediately commence training a large reserve of the most courageous of our slaves, and further that we guarantee freedom within a reasonable time to every slave in the South who shall remain true to the Confederacy in this war." To support his proposal Cleburne drove home his point that the South faced a desperate choice, a choice "between the loss of independence and the loss of slavery." He argued that, in extremis, Southerners would make the right choice. "Every patriot will freely give up the latter—give up the negro slave rather than be a slave himself."[17]

Touting the benefits that would flow from such a revolutionary policy, Cleburne continued to make frank, surprising, and optimistic arguments. England and European nations were against slavery, but Confederate emancipation could cause a "complete change" in "the sympathies of the world." At home, it would deprive Northern whites of their feeling of a "special mission" and blacks of their motive to fight for the Union. The South then could raise "armies numerically superior to those of the North," plus a reserve, and "take the offensive." No longer would Federal troops find "every household surrounded by spies." Instead, the "sympathies" of the African American would "be due to his native South."

Cleburne then honestly acknowledged what few Southerners ever allowed themselves to think: "For many years . . . the negro has been dreaming of freedom." Indeed, he argued, "the hope of freedom is perhaps the only moral incentive that can be applied to him in his present condition." This clear-sighted general maintained that the slaves would fight and that the South could offer more to the black soldier than could the North: a place in "his old home" in the South. Confederates therefore should "immediately" give legal protection to slaves' "marriage and parental relations" and begin enrolling black troops. "The necessity for more fighting men is upon us," Cleburne reminded his superiors, and "we can only get a sufficiency by making the negro share the danger and hardships of war." In closing, he warned of the danger that "this concession to common sense may come too late."[18]

Would Cleburne's bold proposal receive consideration? The controversial nature of such ideas would be sure to arouse debate among Southern whites, but first there was the question whether his arguments would even come before the public. The answer to that question depended upon Jefferson Davis. With Davis, and with his character and views, rested the choice between suppressing such a radical and unexpected proposal or placing it on the political agenda.

Timing was important to President Davis, and in January of 1864 he quickly decided that the time was not right to open what was certain to be a heated and bitter debate. Although General Joseph Johnston tried to quash Cleburne's proposal, on the grounds that it "was more political than military in tenor," another officer who was angered by Cleburne's heresy forwarded the offending document to Davis. "The best policy under the circumstances," concluded the president, "will be to avoid all publicity." Therefore, he had the secretary of war write to Johnston, "requesting him to convey to those concerned my desire that it should be kept private." Davis hoped that "if it be kept out of the public journals its ill effect will be much lessened."[19]

Although Davis acted swiftly, it was noteworthy that he did not attack Cleburne's ideas. Instead he spoke of the dangers of publicity, fearing that discussion of "such a subject" at that time would "be injurious to the public service" because it would damage "unity and harmony." This view reflected the matter of timing and the requirements of his strategy for 1864. All along, Davis's fundamental strategy for gaining independence had depended on the Confederacy outlasting the Union's determination to suppress a rebellion. He had always asserted that the South desired no territorial acquisitions and merely wanted to be left alone. Bitter disappointment on numerous battlefields had reinforced his suspicion that the Confederacy was not strong enough to dominate the United States militarily, and 1863 had brought serious reverses.

Still, as the new year began, there was reason to be hopeful. Northerners too were feeling disappointment. There was growing war weariness over a costly conflict that seemed never to be won, and within the Democratic Party a strong peace wing had materialized that was working to control the party's stands. The 1864 elections were approaching in the North. A staunch Confederate defense had the potential to nourish Northern longings for peace, aid the Peace Democrats, and promote the election of a Democratic president who would declare an armistice. In this way, Davis hoped that the South could gain its independence in 1864. He could not allow a divisive internal quarrel over slavery to ruin the image he hoped to project, the image of a determined, united, and resolute Confederacy strongly resisting the Union armies.[20]

Davis's reaction to the *substance* of Cleburne's proposal was favorable. The Confederate president's views on the future of slavery grew out of his personal experience and his ideas about the nature of slaves and Southern slavery. Both his ideas and his experience were atypical, even nonconforming, in relation to many of his society's conventions and shibboleths. Soon they allowed the Confederate president to move in directions that would seem truly revolutionary to most of the elite. Varina Howell Davis, the president's wife, later wrote that from the beginning of the war her husband had believed slavery was doomed. "I think our slave property will be lost eventually," he had told her, noting that even if the Confederacy secured its independence, an "immense standing army" would be required to keep the slaves in bondage. Perhaps Varina Howell Davis exaggerated, recalling events from a postwar perspective after emancipation had become a fact. But there is no doubt that Jefferson Davis's prior experiences, particularly with his brother, disposed him to think more flexibly than many other prominent Southerners.

Joseph Emory Davis, the president's older brother, had been a father figure and guide for young Jefferson after the death of their father. Already established as a wealthy Mississippi planter, Joseph Davis had secured an appointment to West Point for his younger sibling and later provided him a plantation, Briarfield, when Jefferson left the U.S. military. Briarfield and Hurricane were the family's large plantations, located at Davis Bend, on the Mississippi River, and there the future Confederate president found and participated in an unusual system for the management of slaves, one that undoubtedly influenced his attitudes and practices.[21]

In 1825, Joseph Davis had met and talked with Robert Dale Owen, the social reformer and theorist. Evidently, Owen's vision of cooperation as the key to an ideal society had fascinated the Southerner. Joseph Davis adapted Owen's ideas to his plantations, where he owned more than 200 slaves in the 1830s and 345 slaves by 1860. Relying on good treatment and incentives, Joseph Davis prohibited punishment unless it was ordered by a jury of slaves. An accused individual was always allowed to testify in his own defense, and Davis's role was usually to mitigate the sentences handed out. He gave his slaves opportunities to acquire skills and encouraged them to work for themselves and earn money after completing their tasks on the plantation. Some individuals raised chickens or vegetables, while others cut wood in the swamps. These products were sold either to passing steamboats or to the Davis family and other nearby planters. One slave, Ben Montgomery, established and managed a prosperous store patronized by local whites as well as blacks. He also assisted Joseph Davis with the latter's correspondence and legal briefs, surveyed land and planned levees, designed buildings for the plantation, and managed its cotton gin and steam-powered machinery. Eventually, Ben Montgomery became "the business agent for the entire plantation, relieving his master of much of the routine work."[22]

The "older and more responsible slaves" made up the juries on Joseph Davis's plantation, according to one historian, and Jefferson Davis adopted this practice among his slaves. Whenever a bondsman was accused of wrongdoing, the younger Davis was known always to say, "I will ask him to give me his account of it." Jefferson Davis also allowed his slaves to take as much corn as they needed for themselves and their chickens. He hired doctors and employed a dentist (an unusual step at that time) to come to the plantation from Vicksburg. For recreation, the two brothers loaned guns to their slaves and hunted deer and bear with them. According to his wife, Jefferson believed that "uniformity and gentleness [are] better than severity," and he had his equivalent of a Ben Montgomery in a slave named James Pemberton. Pemberton managed the slave workforce as overseer and took charge of the plantation when Davis's rising political career took him away to Washington. James Pemberton fulfilled this role until his death from pneumonia in 1850.[23]

It is clear that Jefferson Davis was less of a social innovator than his brother, who, in the judgment of one of his bondsmen, "considered slavery an evil that was a vexing problem to get rid of." As the younger Davis gained prominence in Southern politics, he developed a fairly standard set of public justifications for slavery, arguing that it was a positive good. He declared that slavery was the best possible arrangement for supposedly inferior black people and an institution that elevated and benefited nonslaveholding whites. Nevertheless, the conditions and practices on the plantations of both Davis brothers were highly unusual. Suspicious and critical neighbors made sardonic jokes about the Davises' "free negroes" and said that the two brothers would need to widen their cotton rows in order to accommodate the pickers' hoopskirts. The son of Ben Montgomery later told a Northern newspaper, "We just barely had an idea of what slave life was."[24] These facts surely gave

Jefferson Davis a wider perspective on slaves and the institution of slavery than most Southern planters and politicians possessed.

In the closing months of 1864 the flexibility in the Confederate president's thought, as well as his unshakeable commitment to independence, became manifest. After the fall of Atlanta, a dark depression settled over the South, while in the North Lincoln's reelection was assured. "There is no hope," wrote Mary Chesnut, and J. B. Jones called "the loss of Atlanta . . . a stunning blow." The "fondly-cherished visions of peace" that he and other Southerners had held now "vanished like a mirage of the desert." A few weeks later, Jefferson Davis set out on a trip to Georgia, Alabama, and South Carolina. His goal was twofold: to block a rumored effort by Georgia's leaders to meet with General Sherman to end the fighting in their state, and to inspire Confederates to renew their resistance. At this time for cold-eyed realism Davis faced the facts. In Macon, Georgia, he admitted that "two-thirds of our men are absent — some sick, some wounded, but most of them absent without leave." Promising clemency, he urged soldiers to return, warned Southerners about the evils of subjugation, and asserted that "We can defeat the enemy."[25] But Davis's words had no obvious effect. Lincoln would be reelected, and Union offensives would continue. It was time to reconsider Patrick Cleburne's arguments.

The South now had in its ranks only one-quarter the number of men present in the Federal forces, and the head of the Conscription Bureau had reported months before that no more "fresh material for the armies" could be found. In fact, he had recommended that, in light of that reality, "the functions of this Bureau may cease with the termination of the year 1864." Josiah Gorgas, the chief of ordnance, concluded that "There is no help except to use the negroes, giving them their freedom." Others wrote to Jefferson Davis and his administration, some with impatience. "Is it not time now to enlist the negroes?" asked one letter. Henry Allen, governor of Louisiana, advised Secretary of War James Seddon that "the time has come to put into the army every able-bodied negro man as a soldier." Allen persuaded five other governors to join him in a more vaguely worded statement saying that the Union's appropriation of Southern slaves seemed to "*justify a change of policy on our part,*" and that Confederate authorities should "appropriate such part" of the slaves "to the public service as may be required." Late in October a few newspapers, including the *Richmond Enquirer,* spoke out to urge "making [the slaves] soldiers, and giving freedom to those negroes that escape the casualties of battle." It was "necessary" to use the slaves "or abandon the struggle for independence," wrote the *Charlotte Democrat*.[26]

Acting on these unusual and unpopular suggestions, Jefferson Davis broached the subject, but in a politically cautious manner. In his address to Congress on November 7, 1864, he proposed "a radical modification in the theory of the law." Previously, the Confederate government had hired or impressed the labor of slaves, but each bondsmen also bore "another relation to the State — that of a person." These persons should be called to support the war effort. Davis argued that given the training involved in some military work and the dangers of service, it made sense to buy slaves and increase the number of the Confederacy's black military laborers to 40,000. Asking on what terms these Confederate slaves should be held, he then forthrightly recommended that they be freed as a reward for faithful service and allowed to stay in the South, where, he believed, they had a powerful "local attachment." But Davis did not call for arming the slaves and using them as soldiers — at least not yet. The "use of slaves as soldiers in defence of their homes" was, he said, "justifiable if necessary," though he did not view it as required at this time. "But should the alternative ever be presented of subjugation or of the employment of the slave as a soldier," Davis declared, there was "no reason to doubt what should then be our decision." Here Davis used both patriotism and cold logic, for as the *Richmond Sentinel* pointed out, "Subjugation means emancipation."[27]

The cautious wording of Davis's address was deceptive. Soon his administration was quietly orchestrating a campaign aimed at congressional and state lawmakers. The goal was to obtain legislation to arm the slaves, free them after their service, and eventually free their families and allow all to remain in the South. Yet, as radical as this plan was for the Confederacy, it maintained tradition in matters of race. In letters to a number of prominent politicians, Davis's closest adviser, Secretary of State Judah Benjamin, explained what the administration had in mind. For African Americans the principal benefit would be the freeing of black soldiers after they completed their service. After that point, the Davis administration intended and planned to protect white supremacy. "The next step," wrote Benjamin,

> will then be that the States, each for itself, shall act upon the question of the proper status of the families of the men so manumitted. Cautious legislation providing for their ultimate emancipation after an

> intermediate state of serfage or peonage would soon find advocates in different States. We might then be able, while vindicating our faith in the doctrine that the negro is an inferior race and unfitted for social or political equality with the white man, yet so modify and ameliorate the existing condition of that inferior race by providing for it certain rights of property, a certain degree of personal liberty, and legal protection for the marital and parental relations, as to relieve our institutions from much that is not only unjust and impolitic in itself, but calculated to draw down upon us the odium and reprobation of civilized man.[28]

Thus, the administration's proposal would embrace some of the reforms advocated by ministers like Calvin Wiley and James Lyon. But it would combine those reforms with a future status of serfdom or peonage that would last for some unstated period prior to "ultimate" emancipation.

Given the history of the South, this formula suggested indefinite subordination or peonage. Talk of ultimate or eventual emancipation had been a staple of Southern discussions for generations. Southern leaders from the Founding Fathers to Robert E. Lee in the 1850s had expressed vague, nonspecific hopes that slavery would pass away, either in the fullness of time or through the unforeseeable agency of the Creator. Such discussions had never led to action. What was real and practical in Benjamin's vision was the continuation of racial oppression and white supremacy. "Serfage or peonage" signaled a determination to keep African Americans in a status little different from slavery. Those three words were a preview of the postwar Black Codes and the subsequent creation of a system of Jim Crow segregation. Historian Bruce Levine has called them an intellectual and "programmatic bridge" to future racial discrimination.[29]

Aimed at delaying freedom and retaining white control over Southern blacks, the administration's plan embraced racial attitudes that were nearly universal among white Southerners, including those who favored arming and freeing the slaves. General Cleburne, for example, had come to very similar views on his own. About the time he drafted his proposal, he had discussed the future with a Confederate congressman from Tennessee. Although Cleburne "considered slavery at an end," he assumed that economic realities and "wise legislation" would "compel" the former slaves "to labor for a living." Moreover, white Southerners had an opportunity to "mould the relations, for all time to come, between the white and colored races." Rather than waiting for a Yankee victory that would bring "equality and amalgamation," Confederates should act so that they could "control the negroes, and . . . they will still be our laborers as much as they now are; and, to all intents and purposes, will be our servants, at less cost than now." Cleburne's words echoed the ideas that Abraham Lincoln, in the North, had expressed to General McClernand. The assumption that white supremacy was unchangeable infected both sections of the country and would shape the future in tragic ways. In the Confederacy, early in 1865, it would convince many who opposed the administration's plan that no change in slavery was possible.

The primary spokesman in the government's campaign — the most influential voice — would be Robert E. Lee, not Jefferson Davis. It seems likely that the Confederate president chose to stay in the background in order to give his ideas a greater chance of success. Davis was popular as president during the halcyon early days of the Confederacy, but his popularity did not endure for long. Opposition and discontent with his performance had become surprisingly strong as early as 1862, and the winter of 1864–65 would mark the nadir of his influence. With much of the political elite talking about the possibility of shunting Davis aside and replacing him in power with some generalissimo, the president wisely maintained a low profile and left advocacy to General Lee.[30] As the situation of the Confederacy grew more desperate, admiration for Lee increased. As Federal armies closed in, he became the nation's only hope, and very few were willing to oppose him. With Lee's public image virtually above criticism, he was clearly the most effective advocate for a proposal that, despite its racism, was heretical in comparison with prewar beliefs.

A storm of bitter debate and protest broke out in the Confederacy as soon as Davis addressed Congress. With this step, his administration had taken a greater risk and embarked on a larger controversy than anything ventured by Abraham Lincoln during the war. Slavery was essential to society in the minds of many white Confederates. The Davis government was challenging one of the nation's fundamental values and throwing a hallowed institution out the window. In the view of many, the government proposed to abandon or at least seriously compromise the cause for which the South had seceded and gone to war.

Hostile reaction came swiftly. For a host of reasons politicians, editors, and slaveholders condemned and rejected the idea. Some had the temerity to argue — in the face of the Confederacy's desperate situation — that slave soldiers simply were not needed. Representative H. C. Chambers, of Mississippi, praised the "valour, constancy and endurance of our citizen-soldiers."

He claimed that an army composed only of white men would continue to be "a sufficient guaranty of the Rights of the States and the Independence of the Confederate States." Florida congressman Samuel Rogers saw "nothing in the present aspect of our military affairs to justify the hazardous experiment of placing slaves in our armies as soldiers." Congressman William G. Swan, of Tennessee, introduced a resolution that declared that "no exigency now exists, nor is likely to occur in the military affairs of the Confederate States, to justify the placing of negro slaves in the army as soldiers." Some newspapers agreed. The *Richmond Dispatch* unrealistically proclaimed, in November 1864, that the prospects of the Confederacy were "brighter, than they have *ever* been since the commencement of the war." Two months later, when the end of the war was barely ten weeks away, the *Richmond Examiner* asserted that the danger of Southern armies' being overpowered had "passed."[31]

Other opponents chose to argue that the plan's huge negative effects would outweigh any benefits. Congressman Thomas S. Gholson, of Virginia, who opposed the measure on many grounds, pointed out that Southern leaders were hearing "the cries of women and children begging for bread." Since slaves raised much of the South's food crop, why, Gholson asked, expand the army only to have to "disband it for the want of food"? Citing the needs for subsistence, the *Wilmington Journal* also argued that putting slaves into the army would "be worse than a blunder—it would be a political crime." Another negative effect, these critics declared, would be the demoralization of white troops. Representative H. C. Chambers predicted that white soldiers would leave the army if black troops were raised, and Confederate Senator R. M. T. Hunter, of Virginia, asserted that white soldiers could not have "that constancy which should inspire troops in the hour of battle, when they knew that their flanks were being held by negroes." To ask white troops to fight with blacks, wrote the *North Carolina Standard,* was "an insult." Robert Barnwell Rhett, of South Carolina, issued a public letter in which he asked, rhetorically, "Will our soldiery fight beside slaves?" To Rhett, the answer was obviously negative. The *Charleston Mercury* agreed, sneering that its state's white soldiers "will not fight beside a nigger."[32]

Stung by the government's unexpected proposal, some Confederates rushed to claim that it was unconstitutional. Georgia's governor, Joseph E. Brown, insisted that the national government had no "right to impress and pay for a slave" in order "to set him free." To admit such a right, Brown objected, would be to "concede its power to abolish slavery," and "no slave can ever be liberated by the Confederate government without the consent of the States." R. M. T. Hunter agreed that "the Government had no power under the Constitution to arm and emancipate the slaves." The *Richmond Dispatch* called Davis's ideas "totally unconstitutional." The *Galveston Tri-Weekly News* could imagine no "act of the Confederate States Government more unauthorized and more dangerous" than to free slaves for meritorious service. A resolution introduced in the Virginia legislature cited the constitutional provision that "congress shall not pass any law impairing the right of property in negro slaves." It would be unconstitutional, the resolution maintained, for Congress to arm and free the slaves, and it would be unwise for a state legislature to do so. Similarly, the North Carolina House denied that Congress had power "to impress slaves for the purpose of arming them, or preparing them to be armed, in any contingency, without the consent of the States being freely given, and then only according to State law."[33]

Beneath all these objections lay shock and outrage that the Confederate government would attempt to emancipate slaves. For most slaveholders, the purpose of the Confederacy had been to protect slavery. They viewed the administration's proposals as a stunning betrayal, illegitimate and unthinkable. "Slavery was the *casus belli,*" declared a letter to the *Macon Telegraph,* and "every life that has been lost in this struggle was an offering upon the altar of African Slavery." The Confederacy was forgetting "the principles" for which it had been instituted, charged this writer, who added that state sovereignty had been merely "the armor that encased her peculiar institution." "The African is of an inferior race, whose normal condition is slavery," insisted the *Charleston Mercury.* To contemplate freeing him was to render "the base of our institution but shifting sand." The *Richmond Dispatch* agreed: "We give up the whole question when we adopt this measure." The *Richmond Whig* charged Davis with repudiating "the opinion held by the whole South . . . that servitude is a divinely appointed condition for the highest good of the slave." "The existence of a negro soldier," declared the *Richmond Examiner,* "is totally inconsistent with our political aim and with our social as well as political system." A writer to the *Richmond Sentinel* objected that to treat the African American as "an equal partner in the struggle for our rights, would be fatal to the idea which underlies our whole system." "If slaves will make good soldiers," protested Georgia's Howell Cobb, "our whole theory of slavery is wrong." Davis's proposals were "contrary to all our hereditary opinions, policy, and traditions," declared the *Macon Telegraph and Conservative.* A Virginia newspaper warned that freedom would bring equality. Others joined Robert Barnwell Rhett Jr. in predicting the horrors of race-mixing. "The brave soldier who is fighting for the supremacy of his race will have none of it," asserted Rhett. "He wants no Hayti here—no St. Domingo—no mongrels in his family—no miscegenation with his blood."[34]

Opponents also argued that blacks would not fight. South Carolina's William Porcher Miles, who chaired the Military Affairs Committee of the Confederate House, believed that "the negro was unfit by nature for a soldier." The *North Carolina Standard* judged African Americans to be "an unwarlike and comparatively innocent race," while the *Memphis Appeal* branded them "a timid race."[35]

But the dominant sentiment was that to arm and free the slaves would be to abandon the cause. "*We want no Confederate Government without our institutions,*" thundered the *Charleston Mercury.* "Our independence," judged Governor Zebulon Vance, of North Carolina, "is chiefly desirable for the preservation of our political institutions, the principal of which is slavery." And a Texas resident concluded that "independence without slavery, would be valueless." "The South without slavery," he felt, "would not be worth a mess of pottage."[36]

Jefferson Davis no doubt had anticipated fierce opposition, and he was not deterred. Rather, he pressed on, broadening his initiative and then working to develop greater political support. To broaden his plan, he focused on the diplomatic front. Much earlier, after the fall of New Orleans in 1862, Duncan Kenner, a wealthy planter and congressman from Louisiana, had become intrigued with the idea of using gradual emancipation as a lever to gain recognition from England and France. He had proposed his idea to President Davis and Secretary of State Benjamin in 1863, only to have them dissuade him from any action. But at the end of 1864 Davis and Benjamin felt that the time was right. They prepared credentials and instructions for Kenner and sent him to Europe to propose to England and France that the Confederacy would abolish slavery in return for recognition. Kenner's mission shocked ambassadors James Mason and John Slidell, but they helped him arrange to see officials in the two European governments. In conversations with French officials, Kenner found a supportive reaction. The French emperor apparently was willing to grant recognition if England would do so also. But the British government firmly rejected Kenner's proposal, and thus his bid to gain foreign support came to nothing.[37]

While Kenner's foreign mission was under way, the government brought out its most powerful weapon in the domestic battle to gain black troops:

Robert E. Lee. General Lee, an early supporter of raising black troops, needed no conversion to Davis's plan, but to this point he had expressed his views only privately. In October 1864, even before Davis's address to Congress, William Porcher Miles had asked Lee to share his views with the Military Affairs Committee of the Confederate House. Miles was aware that the idea of arming slaves was being seriously considered, and he sought Lee's opinion after explaining that "in urging any measure upon the House the strongest argument we can offer in its support is 'Gen'l. Lee thinks it very desirable.'" Although the text of Lee's response to Miles has been lost, it is evident where the general stood. In a reply dated November 3, 1864, Miles thanked Lee for a "very full and interesting letter in response to mine," and noted, "Your opinion seems mature and decided." Nevertheless, Miles explained that he personally had "considerable misgiving as to the question of Negro troops," and was reluctant to move ahead. Miles doubted the "efficiency" of black troops and was worried about "the effect of such a measure upon our political and social system." He foresaw "violent opposition" to the idea, and thought that even if Congress were to agree, it would be wise "to proceed guardedly and gradually." As an alternative, Miles suggested to Lee that perhaps Congress could authorize the recruitment of 50,000 or 60,000 African American "sappers and miners" and put more blacks to work in the army as "cooks, teamsters, Artillery drivers, etc." With a tightening of the rules on exemptions and detailed soldiers, he asked hopefully, "would not this suffice for the next campaign?"[38]

General Lee knew that it would not. Unlike Representative Miles, who would become a strong opponent of Davis's plan, Lee recognized that the Confederacy was facing its final crisis, and he was willing to make far-reaching changes in order to achieve independence. In the midst of his pressing and distracting military duties, he continued to speak out in favor of arming and emancipating the slaves, and his views became known among political leaders. On January 11, 1865, he expressed himself quite fully to Andrew Hunter, a Virginia state legislator. Lee described "the relation of master and slave," when influenced by "humane laws . . . Christianity and an enlightened public sentiment," as "the best that can exist between the white and black races" in the South. Therefore, he explained, he would have preferred not to disturb the institution, but it had become necessary to use black troops to avert "a greater calamity." Lincoln was emancipating slaves and adding black troops to his powerful armies, and "his progress will thus add to his numbers, and at the same time destroy slavery in a manner most pernicious to the welfare of our people." Southerners should themselves subvert slavery, for "we can devise the means of alleviating the evil consequences to both races."[39]

Without qualification Lee declared, "We should employ [black troops] without delay." He argued that because of their habits of "obedience and subordination" and the white man's influence over the enslaved race, slaves could "be made efficient soldiers." But he also believed that "our chief aim should be to secure their fidelity." As a commander, he wanted to have an army of men whose "personal interest" made them devoted to the cause. "Such an interest," Lee observed, "we can give our negroes by giving immediate freedom to all who enlist, and freedom at the end of the war to the families of those who discharge their duties faithfully (whether they survive or not), together with the privilege of residing at the South. To this might be added a bounty for faithful service." In contrast to those Confederates who argued that the slaves should fight to preserve slavery,[40] Lee realistically pointed out that Confederates could not expect slaves to fight "for prospective freedom when they can secure it at once by going to the enemy, in whose service they will incur no greater risk than in ours." Moreover, he advocated freeing all the slaves. "The best means of securing the efficiency and fidelity of this auxiliary force," Lee wrote, "would be to accompany the measure with a well-digested plan of gradual and general emancipation." Reiterating that these measures would harm the enemy, strengthen the Confederate army, bring "political advantages" to the cause, and make Southern blacks more loyal, Lee urged legislative action "at once."[41]

Lee also renewed his arguments in favor of arming and freeing the slaves to members of the Confederate Congress. His letter to Representative Ethelbert Barksdale, of Mississippi, became public in the last weeks of February, 1865. "Employment of negroes as soldiers," Lee said flatly, was "not only expedient but necessary." The South's white population was simply inadequate. The army needed enough troops "for a protracted struggle," and Union commanders would certainly use the slaves against the Confederacy if it failed to use them for its own defense. After reiterating that slaves would make good soldiers, he wrote, "I think those who are employed should be freed. It would be neither just nor wise, in my opinion, to require them to serve as slaves. The best course, it seems to me, would be to call for such as are willing to come with the consent of their owners." He urged Congress to authorize their enrollment and to empower the president "to call upon individuals or States for such as they are willing to contribute, with the condition of emancipation to all enrolled." Lee predicted that success would silence objections to the policy, and "if individuals still remained unwilling to send their negroes to the army, the force of public opinion in the States would soon bring about such legislation as would remove all obstacles." Lee urged leaving "the matter . . . as far as possible, to the people and to the States, which alone can legislate as the necessities of this particular service may require," that is, legislate to free the slaves. In this way, the administration could evade state-rights objections to national action, and Davis was working closely with sympathetic governors, such as Virginia's William Smith, to secure the appropriate laws at the state level.[42]

Congress proved extremely reluctant to surrender any part of the institution of slavery. As the military situation grew even darker, it continued to delay, to object, and to postpone action. Its behavior prompted an able historian of the early twentieth century to remark that such "dilatoriness . . . is a psychological mystery yet to be solved."[43] But the legislators' psychology was understandable. They were the leaders of a vigorous slave society, and their psychology was that of proud and haughty slaveholders who long had resented criticism and insults of themselves and the institution that was the basis of their wealth and privilege. Only additional pressure from the army and further deterioration of a desperate military situation could force the Confederate Congress to act.

On February 11, 1865, Judah Benjamin wrote to General Lee suggesting that the army could help in overcoming congressional opposition. Some were "asserting" that raising black troops would "disband the army" because Confederate soldiers had a "violent aversion . . . to have negroes in the field with them. . . . If we could get from the army an expression of its desire to be re-enforced by such negroes as for the boon of freedom would volunteer to go to the front, the measure will pass without further delay, and we may yet be able to give you such force as will enable you to assume the offensive when you think it best to do so. If this suggestion meets with your approval, the different divisions ought at once to make themselves heard." Lee readily complied. He ordered his generals to poll their troops and collect information about the soldiers' feelings toward African American troops.[44]

Even before Lee issued that order, some soldiers and units from the Army of Northern Virginia were making their views known, and soon a number of the Richmond newspapers reported that they were being overwhelmed with "patriotick" resolutions from the soldiers. The loyal troops who were still in the field in 1865 were those who had suffered the most and encountered the greatest dangers to establish the Confederacy. They wanted their sacrifice to have meaning; they did not want to lose a war they had struggled so long to win. Thus, it is not surprising that some of the strongest support for arming the slaves came from these soldiers, who knew at first hand how desperately the army needed more troops. A South Carolina regiment, for example, declared that "the liberty of the white man" was more important than "the bondage of the slave, and, if necessary, one hundred thousand negroes should be freed and armed to assist us." "Thomas' brigade" asserted that it would accept black troops "as a necessity and cheerfully acquiesce, preferring, as we do, any and all sacrifices to subjugation." Major General John B. Gordon reported that the men in his corps were "decidedly in favor of the voluntary enlistment of the negroes as soldiers." The *Richmond Whig* informed readers that the Louisiana Guard Artillery "endorses most heartily, and from stern conviction, the policy of arming the colored population of the country . . . with as little delay as possible." Terry's Brigade of the First Virginia Infantry similarly declared that it wanted "independence and separate nationality" and therefore would "hail with acclamation the enrolment into our armies of negro troops."[45]

Not all of the army's reactions were favorable. General James Longstreet let his subordinates know that he thought this measure would sacrifice slavery in the future without helping the army very substantially in the present. General George Pickett also was opposed. Within army units also there was some opposition, ranging from "very few" in General Gordon's Second Corps to a majority of the men in some regiments.[46] But the reports from soldiers mainly emphasized that African American troops were needed, and this message increasingly filled the Richmond newspapers. With such sentiment from the army, and a steadily darkening military prospect, key editors began to bend to Lee and Davis's proposal.

On February 20, 1865, the *Richmond Whig* admitted that the "proposition to put negroes in the army has gained favor rapidly . . . and is known to be favored by nearly all the principal officers." The *Whig*'s editor observed that he was not "very sanguine" about this idea or about emancipation, but said the influence of General Lee was weighing on him. After all, Lee had advocated the arming of slaves "with a warmth he has not, perhaps, exhibited in regard to any other matter of legislation," and the *Whig*'s editor was reluctant to oppose him. The *Richmond Sentinel*, which published Lee's letter to Congressman Barksdale, observed, "With the great mass of our people, nothing more than this letter is needed to settle every doubt or silence every objection." The *Daily Richmond Examiner* lamented that arming slaves was "directly opposite to all the sentiments and principles which have heretofore governed the Southern people," but its editor had previously admitted that "the country will not venture to deny to General Lee, in the present position of affairs, *anything* he may ask for." Citing that duty to support "the leader to whom we already owe so much, and on whose shoulders we rest so great a responsibility," the *Examiner* on February 25 announced: "It may be under protest that we yield to this imperious necessity, but still we yield."[47]

Yet, even as the *Examiner* bowed to the need for black soldiers, it continued to question Lee's views on emancipation, and in this important respect the paper anticipated the behavior of Southern lawmakers. The bills introduced into the Confederate House and Senate addressed only the arming of slaves as soldiers. They said nothing about emancipating them; indeed, their status as property was to remain unchanged. Even so, these bills faced a tough fight and much resistance. One bill was defeated in the Senate early in February. On February 20, the House passed a bill introduced by Representative Barksdale calling for the enrollment of up to 300,000 slaves. Barksdale had emphasized voluntary enlistments, with President Davis asking for and accepting from slave owners the services "of such able-bodied negro men as he may deem expedient." Eventually, however, Barksdale's bill was amended to give the Confederacy the power to call upon each state to provide its share of needed black troops. Opposition still remained strong in the Senate, and not until the Virginia legislature instructed its state's senators to support a measure they personally opposed did this bill pass, by one vote, on March 8, 1865. On March 13 the Confederacy finally had a law authorizing the use of black troops—a law that refused to emancipate a single black soldier.[48]

Jefferson Davis was almost alone among the political elite in believing that emancipation was a desirable, indeed necessary, element of the plan to raise black troops. Using his executive powers, he promptly took steps to graft emancipation onto the legislation administratively. Davis had the War Department issue General Order No. 14, which specified that "no slave will be accepted as a recruit unless with his own consent and with the approbation of his master by a written instrument conferring, as far as he may, the rights of a freedman." As a next step, he redoubled his efforts to work with sympathetic governors to obtain state laws that would contain "liberal provisions" for the reward of black volunteers. Virginia's Governor Smith was Davis's closest ally in this effort, and Virginia was, naturally, the state where the recruitment of black troops could have the greatest effect. Newspapers in Richmond reported that African American recruits were drilling in the city near the end of March. But the war came to an end before this radical and controversial initiative in Southern life could provide any support for General Lee.[49]

What, then, was the significance of the effort to turn 300,000 Southern slaves into Confederate soldiers? Clearly, this unexpected development showed how dramatically the war had changed Southern life, but it also revealed how tenaciously political leaders held onto slavery and how ubiquitously white Southerners defended white supremacy. Only a truly desperate situation could have moved some Southern leaders and slaveholders to consider the prospect of arming and freeing their slaves. As Southerners recognized, arming any considerable number of slaves would, in the words of one opponent, "inevitably be the destruction of the institution of slavery." The Davis administration fully intended to create a postemancipation legal structure that would retain the economic essence of slavery and preserve white supremacy. Its plans foreshadowed the creation of Jim Crow segregation. But to most Southern whites, dismantling the peculiar institution immediately raised the specter of "perfect equality with the white man, socially and politically."[50]

Thus, Jefferson Davis challenged fundamental values of his slaveholding society when he launched his last-ditch effort to replenish the armies and gain independence. His initiative revealed that some Southerners valued independence more highly than slavery and were willing to think of other ways to perpetuate racial subordination and economic servitude. Those individuals were more numerous in the ranks of the army than in Congress, and according to one recent study, they were more common among the citizenry than among the political leadership.[51]

However, there were not nearly enough of them to prevail, for a large majority of the political elite valued slavery above independence. Neither the Confederate Congress nor the Virginia legislature gave any consideration to language in resolutions or laws that would confer liberty on the slaves.[52] Emancipation was rejected; white supremacy was not questioned. The tardy and grudging legislative approval that Jefferson Davis eventually won was permission only to put slaves into the army. There would be no reward for their service, because most political leaders considered freedom for the slaves simply unacceptable. And for *all* members of the Confederacy's political leadership, equality for black Americans apparently was unimaginable. Even Davis's and Benjamin's flexibility stopped there, at arrangements of "serfage or peonage" that would be very much like slavery. The Confederate debate on emancipation revealed the limits of white Southerners' creative imaginations, crippled by racism and the desire to retain the benefits and privileges of slaveholding.

The story of this Confederate debate on emancipation does not end in Richmond, however, for in a strange and illuminating way it became part of the larger national discussion of the racially biased question, "What shall we do with the negro?" As Confederate legislators were considering Davis's proposal for arming and freeing the slaves, they were also learning new details of Lincoln's attitude toward peacemaking and the future of African Americans. The Southern and Northern conversations about the slaves' future came together in the closing weeks of the war, when Southern commissioners met with Abraham Lincoln and William Seward at Hampton Roads, Virginia. There Lincoln indicated how far he was willing to go — "with malice toward none; with charity for all" — in reconciling Southern whites to defeat and reunion. The conversation between Lincoln, Seward, and three leading Confederates showed the limits of the national creative imagination, crippled as it, too, was by racism and the assumption that white supremacy would continue far into the future.

PART THREE

Confluence

SEVEN

THE HAMPTON ROADS CONFERENCE

In the early weeks of 1865 a hunger for peace gripped both the North and the South. For different reasons the people of both sections reached out eagerly for any chance to bring the bloody war to an end. Many Southerners had reached a point of desperation. Dismayed by the losses they had already suffered, groaning under the burdens they were carrying, and pessimistic about their prospects, Confederates were naturally eager to see the fighting stop. The spirits of Northerners, on the other hand, were soaring. Victory now was in sight, but its appearance on the horizon only increased people's eagerness to reach that goal and end the killing.

From the standpoint of the regions' two leaders, there seemed to be no common ground that would allow a settlement. Abraham Lincoln had resolved that there would be no armistice or peace treaty until the South agreed to reenter the Union, and Jefferson Davis adamantly opposed any peace without independence. But Lincoln and Davis were both elected leaders, and they could not be indifferent to the public's will or to popular feelings that now amounted to longing. Each bent to public opinion and decided to explore his options or attempt to turn the longing for peace to his own benefit.

There was no shortage of aspiring peacemakers. In the summer of 1864 James Gilmore, the author and editor of the *Continental Monthly*, and Colonel James F. Jaquess had taken it upon themselves to travel to Richmond and interview Jefferson Davis. Although they failed to achieve any good result, Gilmore now had another idea. He proposed to travel to North Carolina and make an effort to persuade Governor Zebulon Vance to lead his highly dissatisfied state out of the Confederacy. Lincoln disapproved of Gilmore's plan, but he was more receptive to James W. Singleton, of Illinois. Singleton, a Peace Democrat who had the backing of Lincoln's friend Orville Browning, wanted to go to Richmond and probe Confederate opinion on peace.[1]

Both Singleton and Browning learned that the president was willing to show some flexibility in order to end Southern resistance. Lincoln told Singleton that his controversial statement to the Confederate commissioners in Canada had "put him in a false position—that he did not mean to make the abolition of slavery a condition" of peace and that "he would be willing to grant peace with an amnesty, and restoration of the union, leaving slavery to abide the decisions of judicial tribunals." To Orville Browning, Lincoln said on December 24, 1864, that "he had never entertained the purpose of making the abolition of slavery a condition precedent to the termination of the war, and the restoration of the Union." Thus encouraged, Singleton spent two weeks in the Confederate capital and managed to speak with Jefferson Davis, Robert E. Lee, and other leaders. On his return to Washington, Singleton told Lincoln that the Confederates wanted peace, but on generous terms, and would not give up slavery except for "a fair compensation coupled with other liberal terms of reconstruction secured by Constitutional Amendments."[2]

The next and most important initiative came from Francis Preston Blair, the patriarch of the powerful Blair family and a man who enjoyed a close relationship with Lincoln. During 1864 Lincoln had resisted Blair's proposals to visit Richmond, saying that it was too soon. Now the president encouraged Blair, but from a distance. Declining to give his friend any instructions or to be drawn into his plans, Lincoln merely arranged for Blair to be allowed to cross military lines and improvise on his own. Reaching Richmond on January 11, Blair spoke at length with Jefferson Davis, who was also a friend of the family from earlier days in Congress. To the Confederate president Blair proposed the idea of an armistice coupled with an expedition against Maximilian, the Austrian archduke whom France had imposed as ruler of Mexico. This idea was popular with some leaders in the South, including Alexander H. Stephens, vice president of the Confederacy. Stephens believed that any armistice would lead inevitably to Confederate independence. To Blair it seemed that Jefferson Davis had responded with interest; Blair returned to Washington with a letter from Davis offering to appoint a commission that would negotiate "with a view to secure peace to the two countries."[3]

These few words almost destroyed any prospect of a conference. Lincoln was not going to recognize the Confederacy or make peace with it as a separate country. To underline that point, he sent Blair back to Richmond with a statement of his willingness to receive commissioners who would discuss "securing peace to the people of our one common country."[4] At this point Jefferson Davis could have balked, but for reasons of his own the Confederacy's leader chose to persist in encouraging a conference.

Determined to gain independence, Davis saw an opportunity both to satisfy his critics, who claimed that he was indifferent to his countrymen's suffering, and to nerve Southerners to make further sacrifices and fight on. Given Lincoln's stand, any peace effort would surely fail. But by appointing a commission, Davis could appear open to peace and then present to the Confederate public evidence that there was no alternative to continued war. He consulted with Alexander Stephens, who advised that Davis meet with Lincoln personally and that the matter be kept strictly secret. To Stephens's disgust, his advice was "taken as usual in Richmond—disregard[ed] altogether," for Davis publicized the news that a conference was contemplated. Two days later, Stephens again was irritated to learn that he had been appointed a commissioner, along with Assistant Secretary of War John A. Campbell and Senator R. M. T. Hunter, of Virginia. Stephens realized that he had to serve or be condemned as an obstacle to peace, but he felt that he was being used by Davis, and he and Campbell "did not like it." Campbell recorded that President Davis had talked to him about great discontent in the North over Maximilian's presence in Mexico and the idea of a combination of forces against the French puppet. Davis empowered the commissioners to make any treaty except one that would involve reunion with the United States.[5]

As these somewhat unwilling Southerners headed toward Northern lines, it remained uncertain whether they would be able to meet with anyone. In the city of Washington there was much discontent over Blair's peace mission and opposition both to it and to the idea of any kind of conference. Radical Republicans distrusted the Blairs for their conservative views and their persistent influence over Lincoln. They also believed, reasonably enough, that the war soon would come to a successful end and that negotiations ran the risk of compromising away key elements of victory. In the cabinet as well there was dismay and concern over the fact that Lincoln was prone to act on his own without consulting his cabinet officers. Secretary of War Stanton had deprecated Lincoln's decision to send Blair back to Richmond without consulting the cabinet, and Secretary of the Navy Gideon Welles also was worried. Although Welles thought that Lincoln possessed "much shrewdness and much good sense," the naval secretary worried that the president often followed "strange and incomprehensible whims; takes sometimes singular and unaccountable freaks. It would hardly surprise me were he to undertake to arrange terms of peace without consulting anyone."[6] Clearly, Lincoln would face some political opposition if he went forward.

When the three Confederate commissioners reached Union lines in Virginia, General Grant forwarded information about their mission to Washington. The initial reaction of Lincoln and Secretary of State Seward was to refuse to see them. The wording in their instructions about "two countries" seemed unacceptable at first. But Grant, after talking to the Southerners, had become convinced that their desire for peace was genuine, and he used his influence to support their mission. He urged President Lincoln to meet with them and argued that to send them away with no contact would make a bad impression on the public. Responding to Grant's pleas, Lincoln decided, "on the spur of the moment," to attend the conference. His departure from Washington with Secretary Seward "startled Republicans," some of whom saw it as one of those "incomprehensible whims," while others "made no concealment of their anger and apprehensions."[7] Nevertheless, the conference now would go forward, and these five men met aboard ship in Hampton Roads on February 3, 1865.

Historians have debated ever since precisely what was said at the conference. No records were kept of the discussion as it was taking place, and so scholars have had to rely on accounts written later, principally recollections by two of the Confederate commissioners, John A. Campbell and Alexander H. Stephens. According to Campbell, all three Southerners had "recognized the propriety of recording their recollection of what had occurred separately," and Campbell, "shortly after my return home," had written down his account of the meeting, which "was submitted to my colleagues" and received "without objection." Campbell published his memorandum, along with other reminiscences, in 1887. Years earlier, in 1870, Alexander Stephens had published *A Constitutional View of the Late War between the States,* in which he devoted twenty pages to the Hampton Roads meeting. According to Campbell, Stephens had Campbell's memorandum in his possession as he wrote his book. The third commissioner, R. M. T. Hunter, published an article about the conference in 1877, but his account is brief and rather uninformative; resentment of the Union government dominates his essay, and most of the details that would be useful to historians are lacking.[8] Apparently, no other records exist.

The accounts of Campbell and Stephens, however, are very useful. They are fairly detailed and very similar in many respects. The accounts agree in describing the sequence of events and in specifying many details of the discussion. They also agree in portraying a Lincoln who insisted on reunion but seemed eager to be conciliatory and accommodating on other matters, including slavery. Still, much of the significance of what they reported has been ignored in recent decades. One point in Stephens's description of the conference has aroused great objection from some historians, even as equally important facts consistent with Stephens's account have been overlooked.

The meeting began pleasantly, with Lincoln joking that his old friend Stephens was quite a "small nubbin" to emerge from a heavy overcoat and several shawls. According to Stephens's account, there followed references to former, happier days when the politicians had served together in Congress. Then Stephens asked whether there was a way to restore those prior good feelings, and Lincoln promptly insisted that there was only one way: "for those who were resisting the laws of the Union to cease that resistance." Stephens then introduced his idea of a joint intervention against the foreign powers in Mexico, the notion he and Francis P. Blair favored. Although Stephens persisted in trying to explore this idea (and received some help and encouragement from Seward), Lincoln eventually cut off discussion of the topic by insisting that reestablishment of national authority was the "only basis" on which he would consider a settlement.[9]

At that point, John Campbell changed the subject to ask "how restoration was to take place." Lincoln and Seward cited the president's annual address to Congress in December 1864, in which he had named "abandonment of armed resistance" as "the only indispensable condition to ending the war" but had also pledged to stand by his previous acts in regard to slavery. Pressing further, Campbell tried to probe the ambiguities of that statement and explore some of the inevitable legal issues. Seward stated that questions of property would lie with the courts but that he expected Congress to "be liberal" in restoring confiscated property or indemnifying for losses "after the excitement of the times had passed off." When Stephens pressed Lincoln to comment further on the status of Southern slaves, the president described his Emancipation Proclamation as a "*war measure*" that would become "inoperative" with peace. The courts, Lincoln said, would have to decide which slaves had become free and which had not. Seward and Lincoln agreed, incorrectly, that "only about two hundred thousand slaves" had actually begun to enjoy their freedom at that point, as a result of the Emancipation Proclamation and the events of the war.[10]

Then Secretary of State Seward raised an important issue. He observed that Congress had just approved a proposed Thirteenth Amendment, outlawing slavery, and had submitted it to the states for ratification. As this was discussed, Seward gave his opinion that the amendment would "probably not be adopted," since only ten states needed to register their opposition. Stephens explained that Seward's object seemed to be "to impress upon the . . . commissioners that, if the war should not cease, this, as a war measure, would be adopted by a sufficient number of States to become a part of the Constitution . . . [but] if the Confederate States would then abandon the war, they could of themselves, defeat this amendment, by voting it down as members of the Union." When Stephens asked whether the Confederate states would be readmitted to Congress should they cease to fight, Lincoln "promptly" gave his opinion that they "ought to be" and would be, though he refused to make any agreement "with parties in arms against the Government." Lincoln's "own opinion," as Stephens recorded it, was that "when resistance ceased and the National Authority was recognized, the States would be immediately restored to their practical relations to the Union."[11]

R. M. T. Hunter and Stephens, seeking guarantees, then tried to persuade Lincoln that a chief executive could enter into an agreement with a warring party before the end of hostilities, but they made little headway. Instead, Lincoln recounted his policies toward slavery, emphasizing his record of concern for Southern rights. He had been compelled to emancipate in order to save the Union, he noted, and he had always opposed immediate emancipation because of the "many evils attending" it. Then, according to Stephens, Lincoln paused, "as if in deep reflection," before he "used these words, [or words] almost, if not, quite identical: Stephens, . . . if I were in your place: I would go home and get the Governor of the State to call the Legislature together, and get them to recall all the State troops from the war; elect Senators and Members of Congress, and ratify this Constitutional Amendment *prospectively,* so as to take effect — say in five years. Such a ratification would be valid in my opinion." Lincoln advised that the South's "public men" would be wise "to adopt such a policy as will avoid, as far as possible, the evils of immediate emancipation."[12]

Before the meeting came to an end, Lincoln made a number of additional comments that were revealing of his attitude and his plans for policy. When the Southerners complained about emancipation and argued that it would mean suffering for the slaves, Lincoln told a story about an Illinois farmer who had avoided caring for his hogs by planting potatoes on which the animals could feed if they dug them up. Asked what the poor hogs would do in winter, when the ground was frozen, the farmer replied, “Well, let ’em root!” This callous comment evidently was designed to show the Southern commissioners that emancipation could go forward and that Lincoln would not be overly sympathetic to the freedmen — they would have to fend for themselves. Seward and Lincoln also tried to disarm Hunter’s irritated protests that the Union was demanding unconditional surrender, and Lincoln pledged that he would be liberal in his treatment of defeated Southerners. Bringing up the subject of an “indemnity for the loss to owners,” Lincoln volunteered that he was willing to be taxed to pay for such an indemnity, and he assured his listeners that many others shared his views. After about four hours, according to Stephens, the conference ended.[13]

Campbell’s account likewise reports that Lincoln began by insisting that no agreement was possible unless the national authority was recognized; that Lincoln turned aside the idea of uniting to act against foreign intervention in Mexico, despite some interest shown by Seward; and that the president’s December message to Congress was cited as a guide to the future. Similarly, Campbell notes that Lincoln expressed his opinion that the courts would have to decide which slaves had gained their freedom as a result of the Emancipation Proclamation and which had not. On the very important matter of the Thirteenth Amendment and Secretary Seward’s views, Campbell’s account agrees in substance with Stephens’s. According to Campbell, after informing the Southerners that the new amendment had been sent to the states for ratification, Seward described Congress’s action as “a war measure” and said that it was “probable” that the measure “would be abandoned” if the war came to an end. As the conversation continued, Lincoln told his story about the farmer who expected the hogs to root for themselves or starve. Then he and Seward went to some lengths to try to persuade Hunter that the Union did not insist on unconditional surrender or demand humiliation and submission from Southerners. On the contrary, Lincoln promised to exercise his powers “very liberally” and support an indemnity. He added that the laws relating to “confiscation and pains and penalties, had left the matter in his hands,” although Congress controlled the admission of its own members.[14]

There is only one specific item in Stephens’s description that does not appear in Campbell’s account: Lincoln’s suggestion that Georgia ratify the Thirteenth Amendment “prospectively.” That one point has received an excessive amount of attention from recent historians. There is an understandable resistance in American culture to believing that Abraham Lincoln, the Great Emancipator, could have compromised on ending slavery, for emancipation justified the horrendous costs of war and made Lincoln an inspiring and heroic cultural icon. To undermine that point, much has been made of the fact that Alexander Stephens published his book five years after the war came to an end. Some have viewed the passage of time, or a possible Southern bias in Stephens's recollection, as reason not merely to doubt but to reject the accuracy of his account. For example, James McPherson has labeled the idea that Lincoln suggested a delay in ratification of the Thirteenth Amendment "absurd."[15] William C. Harris has argued that Lincoln "could hardly have advised" prospective ratification, which would have "undercut his recent and vigorous efforts to secure congressional action on the antislavery amendment," which he had called "a King's cure." Harris also argues that Campbell's omission of this point "provides further evidence that Lincoln did not make the suggestion on the amendment that Stephens attributed to him." Other writers have simply omitted this specific issue.[16]

The narrow focus on Lincoln's words ignores Seward's role and thus excludes other valuable and revealing evidence. But before turning to Seward's participation, one should recognize that there is additional evidence that Lincoln did, in fact, raise the notion of a delayed or prospective ratification. At the very least, this additional evidence proves that Alexander Stephens specifically understood him to do so and did not invent his story five years later. Such evidence comes from an Augusta, Georgia, newspaper and apparently has not been considered previously.

"Directly after his return" from Hampton Roads, Stephens spoke with the editor of the *Augusta Chronicle and Sentinel.* He gave that editor a detailed account of the conference, and the newspaper relied on Stephens at that time, in February 1865, to argue to the Confederate public that the terms offered by the North "were not dishonorable." Some reactions to the *Chronicle and Sentinel*'s position were harsh. Recalling that he had been "scoffed at and reviled by the administration press of the South" for making such an assertion, the editor, on June 7, 1865, published a detailed account of his conversation with Stephens. Appearing only four months after the meeting at Hampton Roads, this account could not have suffered from the lapse of memory that allegedly affected Stephens's 1870 book.[17]

According to the *Chronicle and Sentinel,* Stephens reported that at one point in the Hampton Roads proceedings Secretary of State Seward suggested to Lincoln that it would be well "to inform these gentlemen that yesterday, Congress acted upon the amendment to the constitution abolishing slavery." Lincoln agreed and then went on to comment on key questions relating to such a proposed amendment. He had been explaining, almost in "the tone of argument," that the South "might do much better to return to the Union at once" rather than risk "the increasing bitterness of feeling in Congress." Then Lincoln added "that there was a question as to the right of the insurgent States to return at once, and claim a right to vote upon the amendment, to which the concurrence of two thirds of the States was required. He stated that it would be desirable to have the institution of slavery abolished by the consent of the people, as soon as possible—he hoped within six years."[18] From this newspaper report it is clear that Stephens returned from Hampton Roads with a definite memory that Lincoln had suggested a delayed or prospective ratification. The *Chronicle and Sentinel* article supports the account given in Stephens's 1870 book and shows that it was not invented five years after the war.

Since no transcript of the conversations at Hampton Roads exists, it is impossible to prove definitively that Lincoln did or did not utter these words. One test of the question rests on Alexander Stephens's veracity. The Southern vice president was a well-known political veteran who enjoyed a good personal reputation. He apparently was respected by Lincoln, his former congressional colleague, who chose Stephens as the recipient of an important letter during the secession crisis.[19] Unless critics of Stephens can demonstrate that he was a liar and his 1865 words untrustworthy, the scales incline toward accepting Stephens's account. In addition, one can evaluate the positions attributed to Lincoln for their level of agreement with his stated policies.

Was Southern rejection of the Thirteenth Amendment conceivable or permissible under Lincoln's established policies? The record shows that it was. In his annual address to Congress in December 1864, Lincoln had stated that the rebels could have peace "at any moment . . . simply by laying down their arms and submitting to the national authority under the Constitution." The war would stop immediately, and any remaining questions then would be adjusted by "legislation, conference, courts, and votes, operating only in constitutional and lawful channels." The Constitution contained no language penalizing or punishing seceded states. Within constitutional channels, the Southern states would presumably have their rights and be able to vote on the amendment.[20]

Moreover, Lincoln's policy on readmitting states was clear. Since December 1863 he had been trying to "revive" the Southern state governments quickly through his Ten-Percent Plan. This plan required no changes in the constitutions or character of Southern state governments and encouraged Confederates to adopt "temporary arrangements" for the freed people. It called merely for a speedy "re-establishment" of state governments once 10 percent of prewar voters had taken an oath of future loyalty and promised to abide by Congress's laws on slavery and the Emancipation Proclamation as interpreted by the courts. All of this suggested that the Southern states could indeed reenter the Union with dispatch. Once restored to the nation, they would be able to vote on a proposed amendment. The distance between this policy and Stephens's recollection that the states would be "immediately restored" was not great.[21]

Lincoln held to this plan and made his position on ratification even clearer after the Hampton Roads Conference. On April 11, 1865, in his final public address, he continued to defend his maligned and unpopular ten-percent government in Louisiana and argued that it should be allowed to vote on the Thirteenth Amendment. Some members of Congress were contending that only the loyal states should vote on ratification. Though Lincoln did not go so far as to commit himself irrevocably against that idea, he disparaged it, saying that "such a ratification would be questionable, and sure to be persistently questioned." On the other hand, he argued, "ratification by three fourths of all the States would be unquestioned and unquestionable."[22] Allowing reestablished rebel states to vote on the Thirteenth Amendment was his preferred, consistent, and public position.

At Hampton Roads, Lincoln acted on his own admonition to the nation to build a peace "with malice toward none; with charity toward all." Even though victory was at hand and the end of the war virtually in sight, Lincoln wanted to reconcile with rebellious Confederates. He offered Southern leaders substantial incentives to rejoin the Union, for he wanted their participation in the work of reunion; he wanted them to take part in and contribute to reunion rather than oppose it at every step. His positions would have been surprising and objectionable to many Northerners, and Lincoln's approach relegated the interests of black Southerners to a subordinate place. But the fact is that the president's actions were consistent with his policies and with his attitude throughout the war — the attitude that reunion was paramount, and emancipation a means to that end.

In addition, Seward's comments on the Thirteenth Amendment were not only consistent with the reports about Lincoln but also very striking, and they have been strikingly neglected by historians. Both Campbell and Stephens attributed to Seward the belief that slavery would *not* be prohibited in the United States by constitutional amendment. Campbell remembered Seward's saying that it was "probable" that the amendment, as a "war measure," would be "abandoned" upon the arrival of peace, and Stephens recalled Seward's trying to lure the Confederates toward surrender by pointing out that they could vote on the amendment, and thus block it, if they promptly laid down their arms. Neither account mentions any objection by Lincoln to Seward's remarks, and neither records any kind of expressed disagreement from the president. Lincoln allowed Seward's comments to stand unchallenged.

Rejection of the Thirteenth Amendment would have been far more significant than prospective ratification or a delay of five or six years. Yet historians have had little to say on this important matter. Could Seward have made such a statement? The existing records of the Hampton Roads Conference indicate that he did. Biographers of Seward have accepted that he did and have not questioned the accounts of Campbell and Stephens. For example, in an early study, Frederic Bancroft concluded that Seward "at least suggested" that the rebellious states could "defeat the adoption of the amendment" by a speedy return to the Union. The best modern biography, by Glyndon G. Van Deusen, affirms that Seward described the proposed amendment as a "war measure" and said that "if the war now came to a close it would not be adopted by a sufficient number of states to become part of the Constitution. He gave the impression that readmitted southern states could by themselves defeat it." Van Deusen added the insightful comment that while Lincoln and Seward "were eager" to see slavery abolished, they wanted this to be accomplished "with the active cooperation of the southern states."[23]

Additional evidence dating from February 1865 rather than from 1870 or 1877 indicates that Seward made such a statement and that the Southern commissioners were powerfully intrigued by it. This evidence comes from letters written in the South immediately following the conference. It shows that word of Seward's suggestion traveled beyond the three commissioners. Confederate legislators also had learned of and were very interested in the possibility that they might reenter the Union and defeat the Thirteenth Amendment.

When Stephens, Campbell, and Hunter returned to Richmond, Jefferson Davis controlled the presentation of their report—as Stephens feared he would—in order to convince his public that the South had to fight on. The commissioners refused to state that only insulting terms had been offered, but Davis then prefaced a very brief summary by them with his own interpretation that "unconditional submission" had been demanded. This irritated the Confederate emissaries. Campbell felt "very much dissatisfied about the whole thing" because he had been attracted by Lincoln's conciliatory remarks. "It *ought not* to have been dropped when it was," Campbell believed. Rather, "terms should have been distinctly offered" by the South in order to continue negotiations. The three commissioners were all well connected in Richmond, and they communicated in private with other Southern leaders, especially members of Congress. Senator Hunter, who fiercely and tenaciously opposed emancipation, evidently reported on the conference to some of his colleagues, and John Campbell definitely discussed Hampton Roads with a number of people, including North Carolina senator William A. Graham.[24]

Campbell gave Senator Graham "a minute narrative of the whole mission from beginning to end." Graham, like Hunter, was a Confederate lawmaker who was determined to hold on to slavery in any way possible, and he acted immediately on the information given him by Campbell. Writing to David L. Swain, a former North Carolina governor and president of the state's university, Graham explained that the Thirteenth Amendment had been proposed, "but that the dissent of ten States could still reject it." He was encouraged by the fact that Lincoln was "apparently anxious for a settlement" and had tried in various ways to demonstrate "his liberality to the South." In a letter to Governor Zebulon Vance, Graham offered these comments: "No one advises the acceptance of the terms offered by Lincoln, but the question is being considered . . . whether reunion, by which ten States may defeat the proposed amendment to the Constitution, & retain slavery, be not preferable to the triumph of his arms, and the subjection of everything to his power." Writing to his wife, Senator Graham said that he agreed with Campbell that "a mission should be sent to Washington to negotiate terms." Senator James L. Orr, of South Carolina, also was "anxious" at this time to begin negotiations "with the enemy to ascertain upon what terms the war could be closed." He condemned Davis for being "too obstinate and supercilious to entertain the proposition."[25] Seward's statement and Lincoln's conciliatory attitude had had an effect in Richmond, if not with Jefferson Davis.

Taken together, the evidence of Hampton Roads documents a readiness on Lincoln's part to conciliate white Confederates, even at the expense of black Southerners. The statements of the commissioners and others present a consistent picture. To the Confederate commissioners Lincoln showed firmness about reunion but also a desire to engage the active participation of Southern whites and an absence of interest in making any speedy improvements in the status of black Americans, once freed. All of this is highly relevant to our understanding of Lincoln, reunion, and the future of African Americans.

WHAT WERE LINCOLN'S MOTIVES and goals at the Hampton Roads Conference? How was he planning to answer the flawed question that so many Northerners were asking: "What shall we do with the negro?" What did this meeting reveal about American society and the national culture? And how did the discussions with Lincoln and Seward affect the Confederacy's debate over slavery, black soldiers, and its racial future?

The last question is the simplest and most straightforward to answer. The racial goals of North and South intersected at Hampton Roads, and the discussions there reverberated in the policy councils of Richmond. In proposing to arm and free the slaves, Jefferson Davis had challenged the fundamental social and economic institution of the South. As a political leader, he took a huge risk that could be justified only by the Confederacy's desperate state, and even then he faced an uphill battle to gain congressional approval. The opposition to any kind of Confederate emancipation was certain to be tenacious and fierce. In historical perspective, it is surprising how many white Confederates were ready to support Davis's plan; such support was evidence of both their desire for independence and their confidence that they could continue to control and exploit a freed black population. But any hint that the North might allow a continuation of slavery was sure to undercut support for Confederate emancipation.

Among lawmakers in Richmond the news of Seward's statements had a significant impact. Reacting to the proposals of the Davis administration, members of Congress were already rethinking the question of Confederate purpose. Had the South seceded to preserve slavery or to gain independence? Should the Confederacy fight on to achieve separate nationality without slavery, or would the sacrifice of slavery leave the Confederates' cause without a purpose and make all their sacrifices futile? Secretary Seward's opinions introduced another possibility into the calculus. Perhaps it would be possible, after all, to hang on to slavery by reentering the Union. Perhaps the sacrifice of independence would allow the preservation of slavery, at least for some years or for some part of the slave population that had not yet been affected by the Emancipation Proclamation.

Within the Confederacy there had always been a portion of the slave-holding class that believed that the greatest security for slavery lay within the Union, under the legal shield of the U.S. Constitution. Even Vice President Stephens had declared in 1860, "I consider slavery much more secure in the Union than out of it if our people were but wise."[26] The possibility of prolonging slavery by reentering the Union stiffened the backs of die-hard conservatives like R. M. T. Hunter and William A. Graham. The idea of ending slavery was already anathema to them, and the sacrifices of war had long since become crushing. Why betray their core beliefs if betrayal was not necessary? Why surrender for Jefferson Davis what they might be able to prolong under Abraham Lincoln? Such thoughts were evident in Graham's letter to Governor Vance, and the letter indicated that other lawmakers were considering the same ideas.

Certainly the bait Seward had dangled before the Confederate commissioners was attractive not just to them but to other Southern leaders and legislators. Given the preexisting opposition to Confederate emancipation, the news from Hampton Roads hardened positions against the ideas of Davis and Lee and probably added some votes to the opposition. By a one-vote margin the Richmond administration ultimately, after long delay, prevailed on a bill to bring slaves into the army, but it failed utterly to obtain any congressional action in favor of emancipation.[27] The hope that Lincoln might allow some continuation of slavery played a role in that outcome within the Confederacy.

What, then, was in Lincoln's mind as the war came to an end and he looked to the Union's future? On that question the president himself provided some additional information and details. Promptly upon his return to Washington he drafted a joint resolution that he hoped to submit to Congress. This resolution was to be part of a larger effort, as Lincoln put it, "looking to peace and re-union," an effort based on incentives designed to gain the cooperation of Southern whites in restoring the Union. As Gideon Welles noted a few weeks later, it was Lincoln's hope that "prominent" Southerners "who had the confidence of the people" would "come together and turn themselves and their neighbors into good Union men." For that reason, his draft resolution proposed that if its terms were adopted and complied with, Lincoln as president would promptly end the war, reduce the armies to a peacetime level, and pardon "all political offences." In addition, he would pledge that all property "except slaves" liable to confiscation would be released from that threat and that "liberality will be recommended to congress upon all points not lying within executive control."[28]

The draft resolution envisioned an end to resistance to the Union's authority and provided an incentive for adoption of the Thirteenth Amendment. Under the terms of the resolution, all the slaveholding states—those in the Confederacy, plus Kentucky, Maryland, and Delaware—would be entitled to share in a gift of $400 million in government bonds, with each state's share proportional to the size of its slave population. Four hundred million dollars was the precise amount of the indemnity that Lincoln had mentioned at Hampton Roads.[29] But there were requirements that would have to be met before states could receive these funds. First, by April 1, 1865, "all resistance to the national authority" would have to "be abandoned and cease." If that condition were met, half of the total, that is, $200 million, would be paid. Second, the remaining funds would be delivered to the states "only upon the amendment of the national constitution recently proposed by congress, becoming valid law" by July 1, 1865. Thus, after the fighting stopped, swift ratification of the Thirteenth Amendment would generate payment of an additional $200 million. The slaveholding states would not have to vote to end slavery, or to end it by July 1, but they could benefit financially by doing so.[30]

Lincoln wanted to end the fighting and persuade the South to reenter the Union. He also wanted slavery to end; therefore he offered a financial incentive to the slaveholding states to ratify the Thirteenth Amendment. It is notable that his plan, respecting state sovereignty, did not involve forcing any state to ratify, and as shown above, this continued to be his approach up to the time of his death. But in accord with his oft-expressed view that slavery was a national problem, he was proposing that the national treasury be used to bring about its solution.

This plan never saw the light of day, however. When Lincoln presented his written proposal to the members of his cabinet, as he noted on the draft document, "these papers . . . were . . . unanamously [*sic*] disapproved by them." The entire cabinet balked at such generosity. Secretary of the Navy Welles was willing to credit the chief executive with the worthy desire of "promoting peace" and did not object to spending what two hundred days of warfare were costing the Union. But he observed that despite Lincoln's "earnest desire . . . to conciliate and effect peace, . . . there may be such a thing as so overdoing as to cause a distrust or adverse feeling. In the present temper of Congress the proposed measure, if a wise one, could not be carried through successfully."[31] The cabinet's united opposition marked the end of Lincoln's plans for an indemnity. It may have suggested to him, as a practical politician, that at some point in the future, if the Confederates did not relent, his policies would have to become more demanding.

To explore more fully how Lincoln may have been thinking about the future, historians have offered some sweeping theories, along with more limited and modest predictions. Ludwell Johnson, who recognized that Lincoln's speeches, though "superficially candid and straightforward," often were complex and "shot through with ambiguity and ulterior meaning," considered possible reasons why the president showed such determination to conciliate the rebellious Southerners. Even after his plan for an indemnity died at the hands of the cabinet, Lincoln authorized General Sherman to give encouraging news to North Carolina's Governor Vance. Sherman was to convey that when resistance ceased, Lincoln would recognize the state governments "*de facto* till Congress could provide others," so that Southerners could "at once be guaranteed all their rights as citizens of a common country." Johnson concluded that this conciliatory approach to peace was grounded in "the political realities" not just of that moment but of the future.[32]

Faced with a steady ideological opposition from the Radical Republicans, who would be unlikely to follow his lead, Lincoln had decided to test what in Johnson's view was "his only other course of action: to build a new conservative coalition which would include Southerners." A "conservative and conciliatory policy of amnesty, indemnity, and speedy readmission of the Southern states" had benefits that were obvious to realistic Confederates. It also could attract at least some Northern Democrats, and Lincoln may have hoped that with moderate Republicans and Southerners included, "the result would be a new Republican party which would strongly resemble the old Whig party." Johnson's interpretation, though admittedly hypothetical, would explain the president's pursuit of such a generous policy on the eve of total victory and "in the face of increasing extremism in his own party."[33]

Johnson is not the only scholar to take seriously the possibility that Lincoln was considering a new political coalition or alignment. The distinguished political historian Michael Holt has analyzed the political dimensions of Lincoln's policies and noted that the president and his party's congressmen "pursued different paths" toward winning the war and strengthening their party for the future. Republicans in Congress followed an anti-Southern strategy that entailed denouncing the South, the slave power's threat to Northerners, and the Confederacy's Northern Democratic allies. Lincoln's approach was "dramatically different," however. Repeatedly, he defended Democratic generals, restrained antislavery commanders like Frémont and Hunter, worked to build the Union Party name and organization, and urged military governors to hold elections quickly in order to speed the reentry of rebel states. The issuance of his Preliminary Emancipation Proclamation actually delayed the Second Confiscation Act, which was due to go into effect in September 1862. His lenient Ten-Percent Policy, and his stubborn adherence to it, led to the remarkable spectacle in 1864 of congressional Republicans "publicly repudiat[ing] the plan of their presidential candidate in order to reaffirm their own antisouthern credentials with the northern electorate."[34]

These congressional Republicans saw and resented the influence that conservatives like Francis P. Blair, Postmaster General Montgomery Blair, and Secretary of State Seward had over Lincoln. They would have deplored the counsel given by another close adviser, Henry Raymond, who told the president that "the Union men of the South must belong to our party—and it seems to me important that we should open the door to them as wide as the hinges will let it swing." But in fact, Holt concludes, Lincoln worked "to build a new coalition" that would include

> proslavery conservatives from the border states, northern Democrats, and former rebels from the Confederacy. This was *not* simply a matter of broadening the base of the Republican party, as some historians have maintained. Rather, it was an attempt to replace the Republican party with a new bisectional organization to be called the Union party.
>
> To state the argument most boldly, Lincoln almost from the moment he was elected set out to destroy the Republican party as it existed in 1860, that is, as an exclusively northern party whose sole basis of cohesion was hostility toward the South and the Democratic party.[35]

Like many questions about Lincoln, what his secret intent for the Republican Party may have been will never be known, but clearly he moved in the general direction described by Holt. In the 1850s, when the dynamics of sectionalism rewarded conflict and division, Lincoln had done as much as anyone to build the new Republican Party. By emphasizing the slave power and the danger it posed to Northern voters, he set his party on a path to success with the Northern electorate. After he took office as the leader of a divided nation, however, his chief responsibility changed, and he inherited the difficult task of unifying the country once more. Lincoln was an experienced and shrewd political operator, and he applied his formidable political intelligence to a changed political landscape. During his presidency, he remained mindful of Republican ideology but showed a consistent determination to hold out an olive branch to the rebels. Even as he adopted strong measures to defeat them, he repeatedly reaffirmed his respect for the role and privileges of states and worked to persuade Southerners that he would not ignore their rights within the Union.

The central fact about Lincoln's course as chief executive was that his policies always gravitated toward the center of Northern politics and straddled various alternatives. They lagged well behind the views of abolitionists and his party in Congress, but moved too rapidly for avowed racists and most Northern Democrats. They held out incentives to Southerners, but also gradually inflicted costs on the rebels when they did not respond or when the weight of Northern opinion demanded action. To Southerners and conservative Northerners he could justly claim that he had tried to avoid harsh measures and had acted only from necessity. Yet when Confederates ignored his inducements and forced his hand, he could prove to more advanced Republicans that he had listened to their ideas. This characteristic of Lincoln's leadership was marked, and it both reflected and furthered another trait that was fundamental to him.

Lincoln the political leader was a man who liked to keep his options open. We cannot *know* whether he was hoping to bring Southerners into a new coalition, but it is clear that his method was to keep various paths available, exploring various possibilities until they were no longer politically viable. Time and time again he refused to commit himself irrevocably to a single direction in policy. This determination to retain flexibility was evident as he shaped his emancipation proclamations, or urged Southerners to respond to his Proclamation of Amnesty and Reconstruction, or vetoed the Wade-Davis Bill, or negotiated at Hampton Roads. At all times, Lincoln labored to preserve his ability to respond to future developments and move in various directions as changing circumstances might suggest. As a result, his policy documents, though presented in graceful and limpid prose, were in fact complex and nuanced in substance. They embraced multiple contingencies. Lincoln was keenly aware that he led a divided nation and governed in a difficult and rapidly changing environment. With an innate conservatism in regard to tactical alternatives, he avoided moving too far or too fast to permit a change of direction, all the while keeping up a steady search for solutions as he surveyed the evolving political landscape. The desire of later generations to see Lincoln in heroic terms has simplified him and his reality and substituted clarity for what was, in fact, subtlety, ambiguity, and contingency.

This does not mean that Lincoln was without a compass. Beneath the facile skills of a talented political operative lay deeper influences that imparted some overall direction to his actions. As president he was influenced by his understanding of his role under the Constitution, his personal belief in what was desirable or right, and his judgment of what was socially and politically possible.

Unlike some legal experts and many in his party, Lincoln held to a belief that the U.S. Constitution forbade interference by the federal government with slavery in the states. As a result, this man who decreed emancipation solely on his authority as commander in chief was also far more of a state-rights president than many tend to remember. Within moments of being sworn in as president, he announced his readiness to support a constitutional amendment that forever guaranteed slavery against federal action in the states where it existed. Because such a prohibition was already "implied constitutional law," Lincoln saw "no objection" to its being made "express, and irrevocable." As a consequence of his view of the Constitution, he favored and repeatedly proposed a method of emancipation that would depend entirely upon state initiative and state choice, even if the federal government might help. For the same reason, he viewed his Emancipation Proclamation as a war measure, a step to be chosen only by the commander in chief, to be justified only by "actual armed rebellion," and to become inoperative as soon as the war itself ceased.[36] Likewise, he told Confederate commissioners that in the judgment of the courts this war measure might apply only to 200,000 black Americans who had actually experienced its benefits. And again, as a result of his ideas about the Constitution, he wanted the rebel states to be restored to their rights swiftly, if not immediately, and to be able to vote on the Thirteenth Amendment.

Lincoln could hold all of these views even though he was antislavery and believed that for one human being to enslave another was morally wrong. In 1837, when the activities of abolitionists were exciting widespread condemnation and Lincoln was just a fledgling state legislator, he had the courage to describe slavery publicly as "founded on both injustice and bad policy." In 1854, when, as a successful lawyer, he reentered politics in opposition to the Kansas-Nebraska Act, he asked whether the African American was a man; suggested that, if so, slavery therefore would be "despotism"; and put forward the idea that "there can be no moral right in connection with one man's making a slave of another." By 1858, he was calling slavery "a moral, a social and a political wrong" and describing the Republican Party as the party whose members "think it wrong" and "propose to deal with it as a wrong." During the war, he famously wrote to a Kentucky Unionist and affirmed that "I am naturally anti-slavery. If slavery is not wrong, nothing is wrong. I can not remember when I did not so think, and feel."[37] In one speech from the late 1850s, a speech that for him was atypical and incautious, Lincoln even appealed to his audience to act more forcefully on the idea of human equality embodied in the Declaration of Independence. "Let us discard all this quibbling about . . . this race and that race and the other race being inferior," he said, "and . . . once more stand up declaring that all men are created equal."[38]

But Lincoln was never an activist or advocate for racial equality. When he reentered politics through his famous Peoria speech, he asked whether the nation should free the slaves and "make them politically and socially our equals." Lincoln's answer was clear: "My own feelings will not admit of this; and if mine would, we well know that those of the great mass of white people will not. Whether this feeling accords with justice and sound judgment, is not the sole question, if indeed, it is any part of it. A universal feeling, whether well or ill-founded, can not be safely disregarded. We can not, then, make them equals." Four years later, in his debates with Stephen Douglas, Lincoln declared: "I am not nor ever have been in favor of bringing about in any way the social and political equality of the white and black races." Speaking before a strongly antiblack audience in southern Illinois, he went on to deny that he favored intermarriage or officeholding and jury duty by blacks. He also said that he believed that the "physical difference between the white and black races" would "for ever forbid" their "living together on terms of social and political equality." Given that such was the case, Lincoln said, "I as much as any other man am in favor of having the superior position assigned to the white race."[39]

To these sentiments Lincoln the president did not raise any determined challenge. While he did not believe that "the negro should be denied everything," as he had said in southern Illinois, he eschewed the role of crusader for racial justice and made little effort to educate public opinion to a nobler view of African Americans. President Lincoln fought tenaciously for the Union, not for racial equality. Throughout his presidency he explained and justified any action against slavery as a necessary means to preserve the Union. When he penned the emancipation proclamations he did not call on his eloquence and remarkable talent with the English language to stir people's hearts or lead them to embrace equality. In those documents, whose language some have likened to a bill of lading, the only reference to moral principles came, briefly, at the end, when he again justified emancipation as a war measure, invoking God's favor upon "this act, sincerely believed to be an act of justice, warranted by the Constitution, upon military necessity." Lincoln largely avoided speaking about improvements in the status of black Americans. Rather than using his high office as a "bully pulpit," he declined the vast majority of opportunities to speak out on race. "Everything I say, you know, goes into print," he said, explaining that he feared making mistakes unless he had carefully prepared.[40]

Although Lincoln praised the contributions of black soldiers, he had almost nothing to say about improvements in their status once the war was over, when they would need to live as free people among hostile Southern whites. On only three occasions, one of them a private communication, did Lincoln broach any idea of moving the freedmen toward equality. The first statement came in his annual address to Congress in December 1862, and that passage was neither bold nor effective. After reaffirming his support for colonization, Lincoln suggested that the country was large enough to absorb freed blacks, and noted that Northern states could always decide "whether to receive them." This was the same speech in which he made the weak argument, immediately ridiculed by Democratic editors, that white workingmen need not fear competition for their jobs, because if freedmen left the South, the total number of positions in the country would remain unchanged. His second statement did not come until more than a year later, in March 1864. Lincoln then sent a letter marked "Private" to Louisiana's governor Michael Hahn in which he said, "I barely suggest for your private consideration, whether some of the colored people may not be let in [to the suffrage] — as, for instance, the very intelligent, and especially those who have fought gallantly in our ranks." When Hahn and the new state government ignored this quiet suggestion, Lincoln did nothing. He said nothing more until his third and final statement, three days before his death. On April 11, 1865, he voiced as a personal preference the idea he had expressed to Hahn. Even then, his words made clear that he would "prefer," rather than require, some limited suffrage.[41]

Compared with these few comments about improving the status of black Americans once freed, Lincoln's remarks to reassure white Southerners about postwar race relations were numerous. Repeatedly, he spoke of his desire to limit the "confusion and destitution" in the postwar South that would result from emancipation and a sudden and "total revolution of labor." Before the private discussions at Hampton Roads about blocking or delaying the Thirteenth Amendment, Lincoln had already publicly and repeatedly dangled before the rebels the appealing prospect of "temporary arrangements" or "apprenticeships" for the freed people. These public statements about apprenticeships clearly referred to measures that looked backward and would minimize the change from slavery to freedom. Lincoln himself told General McClernand that with such "systems of apprenticeship" the Southern states "may be nearly as well off . . . as if the present trouble had not occurred."[42]

Many historians have suggested that Lincoln's interest in colonization ended, or "evaporated," with his Emancipation Proclamation and that his final speech shows that he was looking toward a future of equality. But Lincoln's active support of colonization did not end when he issued the Emancipation Proclamation on January 1, 1863. After the initial Chiriqui project and other Central American possibilities foundered, Lincoln's administration had signed a contract with Bernard Kock. This rather shady promoter had promised to settle blacks on Île à Vache, a small island near Haiti. When Secretary of State Seward uncovered evidence in January 1863 that Kock was a swindler, Lincoln was forced to cancel that contract. But in April 1863 the president again moved forward. He approved a new contract with two New York financiers who were allied with Kock, and they promptly transported five hundred colonists—the first wave of a projected five thousand—to the island. Thus, four months after the Emancipation Proclamation, Lincoln acted on the views that he had expressed to black leaders in the White House: "You and we are different races. We have between us a broader difference than exists between almost any other two races. Whether it is right or wrong I need not discuss, but this physical difference is a great disadvantage to us both. . . . It is better for us both, therefore, to be separated."[43] The effort to promote separation on Île à Vache proved a failure, as things went badly there. It was 1864 when the Interior Department recalled the survivors of a failed project.

That failure undoubtedly convinced Lincoln that no significant movement of African Americans out of the United States was likely soon. But soon did not mean never. Lincoln was not impatient for change, for he had always believed that race was an intractable social and political problem and that a solution would be generations in the making. The fact that freed slaves would be living in the postwar South did not mean that movement of the former slaves outside the United States would not occur eventually or was permanently impossible. Many Americans who wrote about race in this period believed that African Americans were destined to leave the United States, but slowly. Over time, they would gradually migrate to more southerly, tropical regions. Lincoln himself had repeatedly spoken of colonization as a process that was impossible to achieve quickly but could gain momentum with the passage of time and reports of initial success.[44]

A number of fine historians, including Herman Belz and George Fredrickson, take seriously the report of a conversation that Lincoln supposedly had with General Benjamin Butler in April 1865. According to Butler, Lincoln himself asked the troubling question that is the focus of this book. "But what shall we do with the negroes after they are free?" the president asked the general. According to Butler, Lincoln went on to comment, "I can hardly believe that the South and North can live in peace, unless we can get rid of the negroes. . . . I believe that it would be better to export them all to some fertile country with a good climate, which they could have to themselves." In Butler's recollection, Lincoln feared that black soldiers who returned to the South would be "but little better off with their masters than they were before," and that "a race war," or "at least a guerilla war," in the South was possible.[45] This conversation may or may not have taken place, and we can never be sure, for no separate confirmation of it exists.

But it is not necessary to believe that Lincoln continued to favor colonization on the night he went to Ford's Theatre in order to recognize that he had very limited expectations for improvements in American race relations. These limited expectations are the remaining key to understanding Lincoln's approach to the race issue. Like every human being, Lincoln was a person of his time. He was influenced by the depth and breadth of his society's racism and constrained by much conventional thinking on the race problem. As an ambitious politician who never was a zealous abolitionist, he entertained very modest thoughts about positive change in race relations. His behavior as president falls short of the virtues attributed to the mythical, iconic figure of a celebratory national culture because he accepted the persistent reality of an ugly racism that later generations have preferred to gloss over. When in 1861 and 1862 Lincoln proposed schemes for gradual emancipation, he envisioned a process lasting into the 1890s or beyond, with some black people being obligated to serve their parents' masters until well into the twentieth century. When he thought about the post–Civil War world, he imagined a society in which the realities of race relations would change only modestly and slowly, and with difficulty and conflict.

Lincoln wanted slavery to come to an end in the United States, but he did not expect it to be replaced by freedom and equality—not, at least, until generations had passed away. As a practical politician, he had no interest in crusading for a cause so unpopular as racial equality. When he met with the Confederate commissioners at Hampton Roads, he may have been willing to consider a delayed emancipation because he believed that the institution of slavery was dying overall as a result of his war measures and what he elsewhere called the "friction and abrasion" of wartime events.[46] Unquestionably, slavery had been severely damaged by his actions and by the initiative of the slaves themselves. But Lincoln did not expect the realities of life for former slaves to change dramatically and rapidly in the South. Therefore, it mattered little to him whether all the slaves became free immediately or some had to wait a bit longer. All would inevitably experience and have to accept restricted horizons for years to come.

To his credit, Lincoln grasped that slavery and racism had corrupted the heart of a nation "conceived in Liberty and dedicated to the proposition that all men are created equal." But that corruption meant that any solution for a fundamental racial problem would be agonizing and slow. Although Lincoln was against slavery and claimed an "oft-expressed *personal* wish that all men every where could be free," he acknowledged on various occasions that inequality was very resistant to change, if not ineradicable.[47] Although he undoubtedly took pleasure in guardedly and carefully moving a racist country toward universal emancipation, his expectations for racial progress thereafter were very slight. He did not fight for equality or put the amelioration of race relations on his political agenda because he assumed that little change was possible. Only over a long period of time would progress, or separation, occur.

These realities explain a president who at Hampton Roads was willing to bargain away much that was important to blacks in order to conciliate Southern whites. They explain a war leader who took reunion as his primary goal and viewed emancipation as a means to that end. They explain Lincoln's willingness to delay emancipation and his unwillingness to crusade for racial equality or for citizens' rights for black people. In these realities lie unattractive aspects of the national character that are more pleasant to overlook or to subsume in a narrative of unbroken progress. White racism was a central fact of the nation Lincoln tried to lead and reunite, and it was a reality that dominated and constrained his approach to emancipation and postwar freedom. The extent and depth of that racism would be on display in the victorious North only months after Lincoln's death.

EIGHT

1865 AND BEYOND

With the assassination of President Lincoln and the surrender of the Confederate armies, the United States faced a new and uncertain future. The four-year convulsion of killing was over. An enormously destructive war had made some things clear and left other important issues unanswered. The Union would be preserved, for the South was defeated and had lost its bid for independence. In both North and South, most people also accepted the fact that slavery was coming to an end. Abraham Lincoln had adopted emancipation as a tool of conquest, and despite much hairsplitting and various conciliatory offers from the summer of 1864 through the Hampton Roads Conference, two facts stood out: the war had done enormous damage to the institution, and the victorious North expected to see far-reaching change in the "interest" that "was, somehow, the cause of the war." For many months Republicans and their supporters had insisted, more strongly than Lincoln, that the future of the Union could not be safe unless the troubling presence of slavery was removed. During debates on the Thirteenth Amendment even die-hard Democrats had flirted with the idea of putting slavery behind them and their party and embracing universal freedom.[1]

Heading the list of questions left unanswered, however, were two crucial ones: How would the Union, disrupted and damaged by war, be put back together? And what would be the status and role of the newly freed slaves? A reuniting nation now had to deal with this latter question, which had faced the North since early in the war and had arisen for the South in its closing months. Both sections misconceived this question, in terms assuming white control, as "What shall we do with the negro?"

Neither the Constitution nor previous history provided any guidance for putting the Union back together. Similarly, little official guidance existed to suggest an answer for what to do with the freedmen. Lincoln's administration had done little to address this issue, avoiding it silently, consistently, and almost with determination. Emancipation itself had always been explained and justified as a military necessity, a means to preserve the Union. The idea that a few black men might gain the ballot had not been voiced by Lincoln until April 11, 1865, and then only as a personal preference, something to be discussed rather than a policy. Many Republicans were far more convinced than Lincoln that suffrage for all the freed slaves was either desirable or absolutely necessary as a means of protection for former slaves who must live among unhappy former masters. Democratic Party leaders and white Southerners, however, were staunchly opposed. With presidential guidance and advocacy lacking, many Northerners probably had not entertained the idea seriously. These two issues would have to be addressed, and postwar developments made it inescapable that they would influence each other.

Events in the summer and fall of 1865 showed how problematic finding the answers to these questions would be. As Andrew Johnson took up the reins of government and initiated a process of Reconstruction, three Northern states considered the question of the legal and political status of African Americans. While Johnson dealt with defeated Confederates and required them to ratify the Thirteenth Amendment, voters in Connecticut, Wisconsin, and Minnesota decided whether the few black men living among them should have the right to vote. The outcome of these events demonstrated that a racist nation had yet to deal seriously with the question "What shall we do with the negro?" The cause of the war and its ultimate solution in American society remained separated by an ingrained and pervasive culture of white supremacy.

A colossal war had brought about emancipation. Within a few years the refusal of the victors to lose the peace would bring about black suffrage — for a time. But the root of the problem remained the attitudes and assumptions of racial supremacy that characterized most Northern whites and an even higher proportion of former Confederates. Lincoln achieved his major goal: the preservation of the Union. Emancipation arrived as a welcome but also politically problematic by-product. Equality had not been on the agenda, and in the fall of 1865 it would be rejected by victorious Northern states, showing how large a problem remained. The question posed by the war would not be settled by victory or by Reconstruction but would remain to challenge American society through subsequent generations.

THROUGHOUT THE WAR, many Republican leaders had been far in advance of Abraham Lincoln on questions relating to the future of African Americans. In Congress, some had argued early on that it was necessary to free the slaves, bring them into the Union army, and give them the ballot after victory. Reports from the South, such as the reports of army officers and the conclusions of the American Freedmen's Inquiry Commission, had only strengthened these views. At the state level too, there was a conviction among many Republicans that freedom embraced equal rights, in political and civil matters if not in social life. If all African Americans were to be free, these Republicans reasoned, they should also enjoy the right to vote, based on American principles of representative government and human equality. The logic of equal rights was at work, and it impelled Republicans to work for suffrage in their state parties.

Republicans in three Northern states succeeded in bringing the issue of black suffrage before the voters during 1865. These states—Connecticut, Wisconsin, and Minnesota—all had very small numbers of black residents. Connecticut, one of the original thirteen states, was the only state in the New England region that was not extending the right to vote to black citizens at the time. In 1860, it counted 9,000 black residents in a population of 460,000, or less than 2 percent of the total. In the same year, Wisconsin, which had entered the Union in 1848, recorded roughly 1,000 African Americans out of a population of 776,000, and Minnesota, which had entered the Union one decade later, had fewer than 500 black residents out of a population of 172,000. Thus, these two western states were almost entirely white, their African American populations making up far less than 1 percent of the total.[2]

In Connecticut, the prospects for a favorable vote seemed good, at least initially. In July the state's general assembly ratified the Thirteenth Amendment without a single negative vote, and the proposal on suffrage that would go before the people was not unlimited and thus could not be branded as radical. Existing Connecticut law required that voters be able to read and write; by "striking out the word white" in regard to suffrage, voters could extend the ballot to black men, but these new voters would have to be equally qualified and literate before they could exercise the franchise. Proponents of the change also could make an argument that Connecticut should keep up with its neighbors: passing this amendment to the state constitution would remove "an unreasonable and unjust discrimination, which exists in no other New England State."[3]

Republicans also appeared well organized to work for the change. Voices from Connecticut for Impartial Suffrage published a substantial pamphlet summarizing the supportive arguments made by various elected officials, and Republican newspapers in the state featured the issue of suffrage in their daily coverage and urged adoption of the amendment. Equal and impartial suffrage, argued the Republicans, honored the principles of the Declaration of Independence and advanced democracy. The *Hartford Daily Courant* urged voters to "cast our ballots with right, and reason on our side," and to favor "this simple act of justice" that testified to the fact that "all men are born free and equal." The un-American alternative of recognizing "superiority of birth or race," declared the *Norwich Weekly Courier,* meant that "you can build no superstructure except an aristocracy." Republican newspapers also took pleasure in pointing out that in an earlier era black people had helped to adopt the original U.S. Constitution, that Democrats in Maine had come out in favor of black suffrage, and that reports from the South showed that freedmen were working well and making progress despite mistreatment.[4]

The courage and sacrifice of black soldiers who fought to preserve the Union also received well-deserved emphasis. The *Norwich Morning Bulletin* reprinted a speech by the Massachusetts's General Benjamin Butler, who declared, "He who is worthy of handling a bullet in defense of the country should carry a ballot in the government of the country." Military service was rightfully "his certificate of naturalization, his enfranchisement, his citizenship, his qualification to vote everywhere." A Connecticut Republican named John M. Douglas also argued for the rights of the black soldier, asserting that "Milliken's Bend relates his valor. Olustee speaks his lasting praise. Fort Wagner tells a mournful story of two hundred sable men who fell, bearing the honor of New England and the flag of our country. . . . *Be grateful to the black man who has struck a blow in defence of your suffering, bleeding country.*"[5] Such soldiers, the Republican newspapers pointed out, were also respectable residents of the state. The black Connecticut resident was "a man among men," a citizen who supported himself, paid taxes, went to school, and attended church, argued the *Hartford Daily Courant.*[6]

African American citizens of the state also spoke up to defend their rights and interests. In New London, "colored men" met and issued an appeal "to the people of the state." Noting that before 1818 black men who owned enough property could and had voted in Connecticut, these assembled African Americans asked their fellow citizens for "your aid in restoring us to a long lost right." They argued that if men of color "are competent to handle the bullet, in defense of the country, they are also competent to handle the ballot," and they pointed out that black men from Connecticut had fought in the Revolution, the War of 1812, and the Civil War. Without criticizing the immigrants who were coming into the state, these black men observed that they were native-born, and then added: "The colored men of the State of Connecticut are, in general, a law-abiding, industrious, and intelligent class of people; their pecuniary condition is of a fair average; and we challenge close scrutiny to our fitness for exercising the right of suffrage. . . . All we ask is the same tests that are accorded to other citizens." Appealing to the white voters, they sought assistance in regaining "those God-given rights which we all consider so sacred and of such priceless value."[7]

As the summer wore on and the fall elections approached, however, the tone of Republican journals began to change from idealistic and crusading to cautious and defensive. White racism was making its influence felt, as familiar ideas that "This is a white man's government" and "The negro is an inferior race" began to be heard with increasing frequency. A man who wrote to the *Hartford Times* and signed himself "Prejudice" proclaimed with pride, "I am 'prejudiced' against negro voting. I am prejudiced against intermarriages between negroes and whites. I am prejudiced against mixing the bloods of the two races, and of making them, or attempting to make them, *equal.* Nations of mongrel races go to decay and die. I want no South American mixture here."[8]

Uncertainty about the course of Reconstruction also worked against the Republicans in Connecticut. Rocked by the assassination of Lincoln and the sudden change in presidents, voters in the state wanted to feel secure under Andrew Johnson's leadership and were inclined to support his policies. Even Republican papers like the *Hartford Daily Courant* felt obliged to declare that they had "unreservedly" supported President Johnson, "and so shall we continue to do." The *Daily Courant* made clear that it was not allied with any "radical faction" that intended to defeat the president's Southern policy. In the uncharted postwar terrain, people wanted to credit Johnson's assertions that he was building loyal governments in the South, at least until there was undeniable proof that he had failed. Northern whites were not convinced that Southern blacks should vote so soon after slavery. The *Norwich Weekly Courier,* for example, carried a speech by George S. Boutwell, a Republican congressmen from Massachusetts and former governor of that state, who counseled patience in evaluating the president's evolving policy in the South. As Democrats increasingly threw their support behind the president,

Republicans maneuvered with care so as not to seem unsupportive and unpatriotic. While maintaining that nationally prominent Republicans would support the Connecticut suffrage amendment if they lived in the state, newspapers felt obliged to maintain that there was no harm in sustaining "the President's policy [in the South], which is to leave to each State the question as to who shall vote."[9]

On the defensive, Republican papers had to criticize the "'miscegenation' nonsense" and similar racist tactics designed to exploit social fears. The *Hartford Times* charged that if the editor of the Republican *Daily Courant* truly believed his arguments on suffrage, he should welcome black people to "his parlor and his dinner table." In response, the *Daily Courant* calmly observed, "If we do give the negro a vote, we force no one to embrace him," adding that "the natural repugnance between native Americans and the lower class of foreigners" was proof that "social distinctions" would not be threatened. When the *Bridgeport Farmer* charged that Connecticut had been settled for white men and that the national government was for whites alone, the *Norwich Weekly Courier* granted that people had a right to be prejudiced but argued that property or literacy tests for suffrage should be the same for all.[10]

The Republican *Norwich Morning Bulletin* initially made some strong and defiant arguments against its opponents. It charged that the views of the *New Haven Register* amounted to nothing more than "D——n a nigger, anyhow," and the editor of the *Morning Bulletin* deplored the fact that "any white vagabond who couldn't be trusted alone with a ten cent piece, or whom a decent man wouldn't touch with a ten foot pole," was "welcomed to the ballot box," while an "intelligent and respectable" Negro "is forbidden to vote." The *Morning Bulletin* also copied a clever argument from the *New York Post* that pointed out the many contradictions in Democratic racial arguments. Among these were the inconsistent assertions that blacks were lazy and would not work but would steal white people's jobs; that African Americans were cowardly but were dangerous savages; and that Africans could live only in warm climates yet were about to flood the chilly North. Logic did not have the emotional force of fear and prejudice, however. Within a couple of weeks, the *Morning Bulletin,* now on the defensive, was denying that Republicans felt "any maudlin sympathy" for black people or any need to "undertake the mission of elevating the black man." Defending the legitimacy of "social distinctions," by the end of the campaign, this Republican paper was writing that "The republicans of Connecticut will have the good sense hereafter, as they have had heretofore, to regulate all their social relations with the black men in accordance with propriety and good order. They will be their own judges of what is proper, and will not feel bound . . . to propose their sons in marriage to the daughters of the colored persuasion."[11]

The defensive posture of these papers foreshadowed a disappointing result. When Connecticut voters went to the polls at the beginning of October, they defeated the suffrage amendment by a substantial margin. Only 45 percent of the ballots favored black male suffrage, and Republican candidates for office ran well ahead of support for the amendment. In an honest assessment, the *Norwich Morning Bulletin* admitted, "This indicates of course that republicans have voted in considerable numbers against the amendment, or have neglected to vote for it." To explain the defeat, some Republican papers argued that "many good republicans" had been falsely persuaded that "such action would be in opposition to the policy of President Johnson," or that "the vote of Connecticut would be used [by Radicals] to affect the question of reorganization" of the divided Union. But other journals could not deny that the ugly force of racism had done its work. The outcome showed "that many who could not support the copperhead candidates, were yet not rid of that prejudice which belongs properly to a less enlightened age." In a New England state with only a scattering of black residents, racism won "a triumph . . . of prejudice over justice and right."[12]

The lack of a substantial black presence in the population proved equally irrelevant to racial fears and racial hostility in Wisconsin. This western state had considered black suffrage once before, soon after its admission to the Union. In 1849, the idea had won a majority of votes cast on that question, which was one of several on the ballot, but the favorable votes had fallen short of a majority of all participating voters, and therefore the proposition had failed.[13] The 1865 election would show that sentiment in favor of manhood suffrage, without regard to race, had actually weakened, despite the events of the Civil War.

Democrats in Wisconsin waged a campaign against the amendment that sounded traditional party themes. Identifying support for black suffrage with opposition to President Johnson, they argued that supporters wanted to "repudiate" the president's policy and assault both state rights and "the form of government established by the constitution." Democrats believed, wrote the *Daily Milwaukee News,* in "the right of the separate states to self government," and the paper argued that "every man elected to congress" in the South under President Johnson's program of Reconstruction "has the right to a seat" in the nation's capitol. Republican criticisms therefore amounted to an attempt "to destroy state sovereignity [*sic*]." A "centralized" federal government, such as the Republicans supposedly wanted, could "easily slide into a dictatorship," and the Radical Republicans aimed at "Radical domination at the north, and negro domination at the south."[14]

Democratic newspapers warned that the Republicans were "fanatics" and "lunatics" whose ideas would lead sober citizens to wild non sequiturs, such as "the conclusion that women should be armed with the ballot for their protection." A Milwaukee paper extended this reasoning to charge that if blacks gained the right to vote, then the state's Menomonee Indians should too. But such "absurd Isms" were a danger to the people of Wisconsin, warned Democrats. The *Lansing Journal* condemned efforts "to make an inferior rase [*sic*], on whose brow God, in his wisdom, stamped 'inferiority,' equal" to whites. Republicans were attempting "to defy the laws of nature to gratify a crazy theory."[15]

Democrats maintained that as far as the freedmen were concerned, "all that can be done by the north for the abolition of slavery, is accomplished." Beyond that, they argued forcefully that black Americans were undeserving of any further consideration or privileges. Citing speeches by members of the conservative Blair family, they supported Southerners' rejection of black suffrage and agreed with Montgomery Blair, Lincoln's former postmaster general, that black suffrage would create a "mixed, degraded cast[e] of laborers" and reduce white wages. The races, Blair insisted, needed to be separated, and Mexico would be a desirable "place of refuge" for African Americans. Democratic newspapers also suggested that all African Americans were undeserving by printing accounts of Washington Negroes' "unbridled insolence," young ladies in Chicago attacked by "a negro armed with a bowie knife," or supposed idleness and criminality elsewhere. The freedmen, argued the *Daily Milwaukee News,* were the opposite of "moral, honest, intelligent, frugal, industrious, and capable citizens."[16]

Republicans in Wisconsin were not united on the issue of black suffrage, and that fact undoubtedly damaged their cause. U.S. Senator James Doolittle was opposed to black male suffrage and warned that requiring it in the South would lead to a war of the races. The party's candidate for governor, Lucius Fairchild, was a former Democrat turned Unionist, and the level of his support for black suffrage also was open to question. Senator Doolittle succeeded in drafting the state party's platform in a way that avoided the issue. Other Republicans, however, differed with Doolittle both on Reconstruction and on suffrage, and a second "Union Mass Convention" was organized by "the radical and thorough going Unionists of the State." This second convention took a stronger and more combative stand. It came out in favor of equal and impartial suffrage in Wisconsin, demanded that the Southern states adopt the Thirteenth Amendment, and called for another constitutional amendment "to make the representation of each State in the House of Representatives proportionate to the number of qualified male electors of full age in such State."[17] But with Republican newspapers divided also, the party was not in the best position to wage a convincing campaign for black suffrage.

Nevertheless, Republicans argued that four million people should not "be excluded from all participation in the choice of their own rulers," that black soldiers had fought for the Union and earned the right to vote, and that the freedmen faced great hostility in the South and needed continued protection. Republicans declared that the state's African American citizens were "industrious and orderly" and "as intelligent as the average of the population." They called on voters in Wisconsin to support "justice over treason" and to back the men "who helped conquer treason" rather than Democrats, who had been associated with "the disgraceful peace platform" of 1864. Black men also organized to make their views known. In Milwaukee, a meeting was held at which black citizens reaffirmed their loyalty to the nation, documented their sacrifice for the Union, and called for recognition of their right to vote.[18] Republicans also protested that the elective franchise would not turn blacks into officeholders or give them "any peculiar marital privileges." Republicans pointed out that with no more than two hundred potential black voters in the state, it was highly unlikely that any African American would win public office.[19]

But these objections had only modest impact compared to an onslaught of Democratic racist propaganda. Democratic papers kept up stories about idle, worthless freedmen or arrogant black soldiers who abused white men in the South. The Democrats reprinted a satirical piece from a Kentucky newspaper, in which ten years in the future the "enlightened colored statesman, Mr. J. Caesar Crow" would expostulate that white men should be granted some rights, including "the right to marry colored ladies." The freedmen were "ignorant and degenerated," thundered the Democrats, and "the negro is inferior to the Indian." Moreover, they charged that Republicans were holding out "incentives to negro emigration, amalgamation and miscegenation," and they noted that Democrats in the neighboring state of Minnesota were warning of an influx by "the scum of Southern Slavery." After the white police of

Memphis rioted against black citizens, a La Crosse, Wisconsin, newspaper blamed the "outrageous disturbance" on African Americans, who supposedly had declared that they would "rule Memphis, or they would kill every white man in the place." The suffrage amendment, it predicted, would cause "these Memphis niggers to flock to our cities." Quoting an Illinois essayist, the La Crosse paper also argued that national greatness had developed "because the white man was elevated to his true position in the scale of being," and it charged that Indiana Republicans had danced with black "wenches . . . until the gentle perfume was thick enough to cut with a scoop shovel and make into horse blankets."[20]

It is remarkable that Wisconsin's Republicans, facing such inflammatory, scurrilous opposition and hampered by disunity within their own party, avoided defeat across the board. In the fall elections, their candidate for governor prevailed by almost nine thousand votes. The outcome on black suffrage, however, was similar to that in Connecticut. Many Republicans either voted against the proposed amendment or withheld their support. In a state with almost no African American residents, the supposed dangers of black voting and immigration helped produce a majority against black suffrage of more than six thousand votes.[21]

The situation in Minnesota, which was more thinly populated than Wisconsin and had only a miniscule black population, was similar in many respects. There, too, Democrats publicized the views and advice of the Blair family, with a St. Paul newspaper endorsing Frank Blair's lament that the South was being persecuted and that no one should interfere with the right of a sovereign state to determine its electoral laws. Describing Andrew Johnson's policies as "mild, sensible, statesmanlike and patriotic," Democrats worked to make their opponents appear unpatriotic. Republicans, they claimed, were "fanatics." The Republicans supposedly threatened individual liberty with their belief in "an overwhelming, oppressive . . . despotic bureaucracy" and their desire for an "omnipresent, omnipotent, superintending power of the Federal government."[22]

Democratic newspapers continuously featured hostile and biased reports about the freedmen. "Outrages from negro soldiers" were supposedly disturbing the citizens of Shreveport, Louisiana; Southern freedmen were proving themselves to be "worthless" and "thieving"; in Charleston, South Carolina, they were "insolent to a degree unbearable"; a "dangerous Negro" had threatened children in Chicago. Such events were inevitable, according to Democratic newspapers, because African Americans were an "enervated and ignorant race," "unqualified by education," "greatly inferior to the whites," and under the illusion that freedom meant having "plenty to eat and nothing to do."[23]

The platform of the Minnesota Democratic Party denounced opposition to President Johnson and criticized Republicans in Congress for the "revolutionary" idea of excluding Southern representatives "unless elected upon the basis of negro suffrage." It attacked limitations on the freedom of Southern whites and sounded the traditional Democratic note that the party defended individuals' freedom against an overbearing government. Adding some economic issues, the Democrats called for a reissuing of the national debt at lower rates of interest and argued that wealthy investors who owned U.S. bonds should have to pay interest on that income. They also came out clearly against "conferring the elective franchise upon the negroes of this State." Arguing that blacks were inferior and would introduce "an element of disaffection, danger and corruption" into the political system, the Democrats' platform included some inflammatory racial rhetoric. The "social organization" of Minnesota was in peril because allowing black men to vote would make the state "a place of refuge for the scum of Southern Slavery."[24]

Minnesota's Republicans countered with a platform charging that the Democrats were going to "preserve the causes of the rebellion" by keeping the freedmen of the South "in a condition of peonage and serfdom." Not only would such an outcome be "a reproach to the humanity and civilization of the entire nation," but it would violate "the spirit of our institutions," which required that "the measure of a man's political rights shall be neither his religion, his birthplace, his race, his color, nor any merely physical characteristic." Republican editors also argued that African Americans had fought and died for the Union and that "the perfect equality of all men before the laws" was inherent in the principles of the Declaration of Independence and was "the fundamental principle of true democracy." Denial of the vote to freedmen would mean that "the Southern States will gain fifteen representatives in Congress . . . without increasing their voting population." Republicans labeled Democrats "Copperheads" and said that their prejudice against black people might soon lead them to fight against "free suffrage to the foreigner."[25]

However, the Republicans of Minnesota were not strongly united behind equal suffrage for black Americans. At least one Republican newspaper predicted that the suffrage amendment would fail, because, in addition to the influence of Democratic opposition, returning soldiers had seen slavery "in its worst form and the colored men in their most degraded state," and because some Republicans favored an educational requirement for immigrants as well as blacks. General William R. Marshall, the party's candidate for governor, came out in favor of the suffrage amendment. But he also publicly avowed that he "was born in a slave State and had a prejudice against the negro." Marshall argued that "the superior race ought to elevate the inferior" and declared that he was "willing to make the most of the black man's capacities and opportunities." He explained that he could take this position because he had "no fear for his self-respect, and his superiority," and he assured listeners that he would not be "mingling socially with the negro."[26] Such tepid, racist support was probably less than convincing to hesitant voters. A Republican paper similarly defended the party's position by stating, "We don't know of any Republican that is desirous of sending a negro to Congress, or making them Justices of the people, or fear their rivalry in the social circle."[27]

Racist charges put Minnesota Republicans on the defensive, and as the election approached, Democratic journals stepped up their threatening predictions. "If negro voting is allowed," warned the *St. Paul Pioneer,* the Republicans' "next step will be in favor of 'miscegenation.'" The paper also published a letter from a reader charging that the Republicans were ready "to humiliate and degrade" their own race, putting them "below their own negroes" in order to hold on to power. Minnesota's voters should preserve "the government founded by white men for the use of white men," whereas a Marshall administration would make the state "a paradise of darkies." Republicans would "bring in negroes to work on our railroads, to drive our carts, wagons and drays, to jostle white men out of the way, especially the Irish and Germans." "The Degradation of White Labor" would mean that Minnesota became "the Liberia of Free Negroes." Winding up the campaign, the *Pioneer* screamed: "If you wish to have niggers in your schools, niggers at the polls, niggers in the jury box, niggers in your fields, niggers on your public works, niggers gallanting your white girls, niggers corrupted by demagogues, niggers voting, niggers holding office, niggers miscegenating and NIGGERS TILL YOU CAN'T REST—vote the Wendell Phillips [Republican] Miscegenation ticket."[28]

When election day arrived, the Republicans succeeded in electing their nominee for governor, but the suffrage amendment went down to clear defeat. General Marshall won by a healthy margin, testifying to the overall Republican majority in Minnesota. But many of his Republican supporters, like Republicans in Wisconsin and Connecticut, had refused to vote for black suffrage. The total vote on the amendment was substantially smaller than the overall turnout, and only 45 percent of those voting favored it. Within the Republican Party there were many activists who believed in equal rights, but prejudice and fear of social change held in their grip a larger number, both in the party and in society at large. Shortly after Minnesota voted, residents of the Colorado Territory adopted a constitution, and by their votes they also refused to extend the right of suffrage to anyone but whites. In Colorado, the margin in favor of a racial exclusion was overwhelming.[29] Thus, in the first several months after the Union's victory every Northern state or territory that considered black suffrage voted against equality.

WHAT, THEN, SHOULD WE LEARN from the events and policies of the war years and from these elections in the immediate postwar period? An honest, noncelebratory accounting suggests several conclusions.

In the Civil War era, the American people did not make their history in regard to changes in the racial status quo so much as they were made by it. In the North, a sense that slavery was the root cause of the Civil War grew powerfully during the conflict; as Lincoln said in his Second Inaugural Address, the "colored slaves" constituted a "powerful interest" that "was, somehow, the cause of the war." But it was the events of war, rather than any popular consensus, that impelled both North and South to take up emancipation. Abraham Lincoln turned to emancipation in order to win the war and preserve the Union; Jefferson Davis proposed emancipating the slaves in order to gain more soldiers for the cause of Confederate independence. Change came about as the result of overpowering events rather than the wise, creative, and farsighted intentions of political leaders. Indeed, these leaders could claim less credit for accomplishing change than is often given them. Under Lincoln's policies, immediate emancipation for all remained uncertain and insecure in the North even on April 11, 1865, when the course of the war was making it increasingly inevitable. In the South, Davis's promotion of emancipation failed, as the Confederate Congress refused to free a single slave, and administrative actions were too little and came too late to alter the outcome.[30]

Slavery and race were the core problems afflicting the Union, and racism was a deeply rooted cancer in American society. Reluctantly, and under coercive pressures, the nation addressed the issue of slavery, but race was a very different matter. A few—the unpopular minority of abolitionists, some Republican members of Congress, the American Freedmen's Inquiry Commission, and others, such as a number of military commanders who dealt with freedmen in the South—spoke out for the desirability and necessity of racial change, but their voices often went unheard amid the din of battles and deaths.

The nation's elected officials provided little positive leadership on the central question of race and the nation's racial future. The question "What shall we do with the negro?" received far less attention than questions about how to win the war or what to do about slavery. When Jefferson Davis turned to this question in the Confederacy's last months, his administration's answer revealed an explicit desire for long-lasting inferiority and subordination. When, just four days before his death, Abraham Lincoln finally spoke on the issue, he only briefly mentioned a preference for suffrage rights for a few. Although war forced the nation to deal with slavery, the inevitable next question—the society's racial future after slavery—was something that leaders hoped to evade and most citizens wanted to ignore.

Since the Civil War, most Americans also have avoided looking at that era objectively. Despite various historical accounts, popular culture has preferred a mythical version of events, thus depriving the collective historical consciousness of a full recognition of American problems. The burnishing of facts began early. When Lincoln was assassinated, prominent Republicans rapidly turned him into a martyr in order to promote the party's electoral interests. Since then, but in similar fashion, American culture has made Lincoln into an icon in order to inspire progress, banish insecurities, or assuage disappointment over national problems. With the support of too many historians, almost every human virtue has been attributed to him, so that his image functions as a symbol of the nation's inherent virtue and unlimited promise. Lincoln "became the deity of American civil religion," in the words of James McPherson, who has himself taken a very positive view of Lincoln's positions on race. Another recent essayist noted that "the semi-divine status of Lincoln in American history" is a cultural fact. Writers discuss his words with the "exegetical exactitude" that others "give to fine-point disputes about the words and tales of Jesus and his apostles."[31] In scores of surveys Lincoln's name habitually heads the list of the greatest presidents.

When historians have turned from ranking presidents to interpreting the Civil War, their views of Lincoln have followed the abiding concerns of their time. Every historical work is the product of a given time and place, but it is striking how the mythical figure of Lincoln has taken different forms as racial attitudes in the United States have changed. By the early 1900s the once-defeated South had prevailed in that era's struggle over racial opinions, and Northerners came to accept the view that Reconstruction's attempts to make black people equal under the law had been a great mistake. Leading historians "openly assumed the hopeless inferiority of the Negro" and condemned Reconstruction. This interpretation, wrote Don E. Fehrenbacher, "was in perfect harmony with the apotheosis of Abraham Lincoln, who had saved the union and freed the slaves, but who presumably would have opposed Radical Reconstruction." Thus, Lincoln was seen as wise and virtuous to conciliate Southern whites. His racial attitudes were either treated as less important, because blacks were seen as undeserving, or praised for being realistic and *not* egalitarian. Later, with the rise of the civil rights movement and increased concern over racial injustice, the dominant image of Lincoln became that of a tender-hearted "Great Emancipator." Then his antislavery views, his role in freeing the slaves, and his graciousness to men like Frederick Douglass became far more important than his overtures to rebellious Confederates. The Lincoln icon came to emphasize a leader who was unprejudiced and yearned for justice. Thus, the image of Lincoln has changed with changes in public attitudes. Americans have used him as a talisman to further the pressing concerns of different periods.[32]

In recent years, the need to see Lincoln as a racial egalitarian has continued to predominate in popular understanding and in bestsellers that treat him as wise, humane, and virtually without fault.[33] Some writers have acknowledged the ambiguities, complexity, or prejudice in certain of Lincoln's statements, only to argue that Lincoln was purposely obscuring his belief in racial equality for strategic purposes, in order to confuse his opposition. In this formulation, he was actually "a moral visionary" and "fervent idealist" who cloaked his designs in "some very crafty methods" as "an artist in the Machiavellian uses of power."[34] With such arguments every ambiguity, even contradictions, can be interpreted favorably in support of the iconic image. To attribute wisdom, boldness, or modern racial viewpoints to Lincoln, other writers have lavished extravagant praise on his slightest actions while minimizing or ignoring important and consistently held policies. This phenomenon wrenches Lincoln from his historical context, slights his human nature, and impairs our understanding of the nation's history. It sets aside the actual limitations in his policy positions, and for an intelligent understanding of race in U.S. history the proof lies in the policies, not in supposed but secret noble intentions.

This pattern can be seen in James McPherson's recent declaration that "after issuing the Emancipation Proclamation on January 1, 1863, Lincoln never again mentioned colonization." This assertion may be true, for no later public statement about colonization is on record, and Lincoln's reported conversation with Ben Butler is questioned by some scholars. Yet, by suggesting that after January 1, 1863, Lincoln embraced a biracial future for the nation, this statement ignores the fact that in April 1863 he sent hundreds of African Americans to the Caribbean in a colonization effort that ended disastrously, with the government bringing the survivors back in 1864. Similarly, to argue that Lincoln was "the Great Emancipator in history as well as in myth," and to counter arguments that emancipation came as a result of the war or the actions of slaves themselves, McPherson praises Lincoln's "vigorous" efforts to urge Congress to propose the Thirteenth Amendment. Those efforts were very important, but they did not remove the problematic aspects of his approach to ratification. In regard to Hampton Roads, which is simply ignored by some writers, McPherson criticizes a highly respected scholar for giving credit to Alexander Stephens's "absurd claim, made five years after Lincoln's death, that the Union president had urged him in 1865 to ratify the Thirteenth Amendment 'prospectively.'" Yet we have seen that this claim is not absurd but consistent with Lincoln's policy statements and with Secretary of State Seward's unchallenged remarks.[35]

Another example of the iconic approach to Lincoln is the treatment a recent and much praised book by Richard Carwardine gives to his annual address to Congress in December 1862. Lincoln in fact was nearly silent in his public statements about the future place of African Americans in the national society. This 1862 speech was one of only two occasions on which he addressed the issue substantively, and some central but flawed arguments in the speech quickly met with withering critiques from Democratic newspapers. Yet Carwardine's book puts the best possible gloss on Lincoln's words, claiming that he "made a start in educating whites to tolerate a free black population in their midst" and that he challenged racist attitudes "as he had never done before." These words also are true, but they misleadingly suggest that Lincoln was eager to educate whites and determined to combat racism. In fact, his "start" was weak, the challenge was slight, and his comments were notable only by comparison with what little had gone before. Similarly, other historians have portrayed Lincoln as dedicated to racial equality, "intent on readying the public for black suffrage," or working "to prepare public opinion for one more step" toward equality, since he believed that "public sentiment is everything" and "he who moulds public sentiment, goes deeper than he who enacts statutes and pronounces decisions." One author declares that "Lincoln understood that the greatest challenge for a leader in a democratic society is to educate public opinion." Yet the record is clear that Lincoln spoke often about conciliating rebels or colonizing African Americans, and only rarely about rights for the freedmen. His efforts to mold public opinion in favor of racial equality were few.[36]

These facts should neither surprise us nor cause us to condemn Lincoln, whose racial attitudes were relatively enlightened for his day. Instead, the realities of his time — the character of the United States in 1860–65 — ought to claim our attention. Americans need to understand their history, particularly as it relates to the abiding problems and divisions of race. To do so requires putting aside the haze of idealism and uncritical patriotism that surrounds it. To deal intelligently with the present and the future requires an honest understanding of the Civil War and of the way people in that era answered the question (itself freighted with assumptions of racial superiority), "What shall we do with the negro?" Such an understanding would be productive of greater knowledge and insight, for that history can be both sobering and encouraging.

To any observer at the beginning of the twenty-first century, the depth and breadth of white racism in Civil War America compels thoughtful recognition. On the Confederate side, most leaders were determined to preserve slavery, and even after the events of war forced Jefferson Davis and others to consider emancipation, the limits of their imagination of a postemancipation world extended no further than establishing a system of serfdom or peonage. In the North, most Republicans and other Unionists were far from being racial progressives. The ranks of Northerners, it is true, included some abolitionists and advocates of equal rights, but they were few, and their influence weak, until the events of war compelled support for their unusual and unpopular prescriptions for victory. The Republican Party had denied any intention of attacking slavery, and when emancipation came, its leaders excused and apologized for it as a military necessity, an unavoidable incident of war. The party's president feared its sudden impact and socially disorganizing effects. Democrats, meanwhile, repeatedly charged that their rivals were trying to Africanize the North. The charge was untrue, for Lincoln consistently showed more concern for bringing rebellious white Southerners back into the Union than for improving the status of loyal African Americans. After January 1, 1863, surprisingly little sustained attention was given, by Republicans or the public, to the question of the future status of the freedmen. Then, as the war came to an end, Northern voters in three Republican states rejected the idea of black suffrage, even for well-educated or well-qualified individuals. The slow, reluctant, and sideways nature of Northern steps toward progress testified to the power of slavery and racism in the national culture.

Racism's power was glaringly evident as well in the predominant desire of most Northerners to have nothing to do with African Americans. It is possible that, especially after the fall of Atlanta, a majority became comfortable with the idea that freeing the slaves had been a necessary means to defeat the rebellion and preserve the Union. But most Unionists still shared the view of the *New York Times* that black people were grossly inferior, and did not want African Americans to live among them. They opposed the entry of free blacks into their states, and they feared the possibility that large numbers of Southern freedmen would migrate to the North. The majority surely believed, as Lincoln had put it, that "it is better for us both . . . to be separated."[37] A large number probably hoped, as many writers and the Blair family did, that over time the black population would drift out of the continental United States, moving steadily southward into warmer and more tropical regions. In the minds of Northerners, the unsettled West was a land of opportunity for white migrants—as the Republicans had always maintained—rather than for blacks, and the United States was a white man's country.

The dominance of racist attitudes during the Civil War foretold critically important and negative postwar events: the imposition of segregation and racial oppression throughout the South. The predictions of serfage or peonage that had arisen from sources as diverse as Confederate officials, Union generals, and editors of the *New York Times* proved prescient. Within a decade, white supremacy—economic, political, and social—was reestablished in most of the South, and segregation and disfranchisement soon followed. Long after slavery ended, white racism would remain a central problem on the nation's agenda. Later generations of Americans would have to wrestle with the racial issues left unsolved by emancipation.

In the Civil War era and later, most white citizens thought of black people—no matter how long their ancestors had lived in the United States and no matter how bravely they had fought for the Union—as not really Americans.

They were seen as Africans and different, intended by nature to live apart from the white man. Their presence in the nation was a "problem." A writer in the *New York Times* described the African as an "*exotic*—a being whose proper soil and climate is the hot regions of the earth. . . . What useful purpose can the negro work out in the present territory of the United States but that of a servant?"[38] Northerners believed that because black people were different, they did not belong in the white man's country. Confederates believed that their role was to be exploited, as slaves or serfs.

One generation after the Civil War, a Southerner who had gained some insight reflected on the social conclusions flowing from such attitudes. George Washington Cable wrote that the crux of the nation's racial problem was "the idea that [the black man] is of necessity an alien. He was brought to our shores a naked, brutish, unclean, captive, pagan savage, to be and remain a kind of connecting link between man and the beasts of burden. . . . As a social factor he was intended to be as purely zero as the brute at the other end of his plowline. The occasional mingling of his blood with that of the white man worked no change in the sentiment. . . . Generations of American nativity made no difference. . . . He accepted our dress, language, religion, all the fundamentals of our civilization, and became forever expatriated from his own land; still he remained, to us an alien."[39] Cable could have added that the bravery and sacrifice of African Americans as Federal soldiers made no difference either, for these were quickly overlooked in the Civil War era.

As long as whites viewed black people as somehow not legitimate Americans, their claim to equal rights and equal treatment would not be respected. Moreover, it would take several generations for that cultural assumption to be dismantled. The slow pace at which change occurred was evidence of the depth and staying power of racist attitudes. It took generations for white Americans to claim even outstanding individuals—whether W. E. B. Du Bois, Paul Robeson, Richard Wright, Ralph Ellison, Marian Anderson, Duke Ellington, Jackie Robinson, or Martin Luther King Jr.—as their own. The racial attitudes of the Civil War years led easily to the Black Codes, and the readiness with which the rest of the nation allowed the South to disfranchise black people and impose de jure segregation testified to the pervasiveness of assumptions of white supremacy. The slow progress of the legal and political struggle against discrimination in the twentieth century, and the lives that were lost, mark how great a distance had to be traveled.

Popular culture treats the United States as a uniquely virtuous and exceptional nation, whereas a realistic view accepts the inevitable human failures in our society and the wrongs in our history. An accurate approach to the historical record — as opposed to a celebratory gloss — would enable citizens to understand issues better and make decisions more intelligently. And an undistorted view of how Americans in the period of the Civil War thought about the future of African Americans is not discouraging only. It also furnishes grounds for optimism. For it is undeniable that the United States today is a different society, with different cultural attitudes, from the North and South of the 1860s or the 1950s. Change has occurred; progress has been made. An honest, realistic understanding of history can serve as a foundation for progress and patriotism just as effectively as comforting, distorting myths. An accurate view of the Civil War era is essential to that enterprise.

APPENDIX:
A BRIEF, ADDITIONAL NOTE ON A VAST HISTORIOGRAPHY

HISTORICAL TREATMENTS of Lincoln have followed two different paths described, not surprisingly, by race. At various times, both paths have included elements of realism and hagiography. For the first several decades after the Civil War, black scholars and writers tended to praise Lincoln and emphasize his role in emancipation. As racial discrimination gained ever more ground in American society, these writers sought to remind the public that Lincoln had been the Great Emancipator and that the destruction of slavery had been vital to national progress. Individuals such as Charles H. Hunter, W. E. B. Du Bois, Carter G. Woodson, and Benjamin Quarles contributed to this stream of interpretation. Merrill Peterson remarked that "Quarles was a careful historian, yet he could not escape the spell of the emancipation image." Quarles's most important book on Lincoln was *Lincoln and the Negro,* published in 1962.

Later, as the civil rights movement gathered momentum, a number of black authors began to remind readers that previous victories had been flawed and incomplete and that much remained to be done. One of the earliest and strongest of these voices was Lerone Bennett Jr., who in 1968 published an article in *Ebony* magazine entitled "Was Lincoln a White Supremacist?" In that and other works, including *Forced into Glory: Abraham Lincoln's White Dream,* published in 2000, Bennett argued that Lincoln was part of America's racist tradition and had abandoned the freedmen to Confederate rage. Vincent Harding also published an important and critical work, *There Is a River* (1981), which emphasized the contributions that slaves made to their own emancipation. Other black scholars, such as Barbara Jeanne Fields, have carried that argument further, urging a rethinking of the question, Who freed the slaves?

White historians and writers have more uniformly praised Lincoln, but for changing reasons. After the failure of Reconstruction, Northern whites came to accept the white South's view that efforts to change the South had been a terrible mistake and that black people ought not to have gained equal rights. In this mind-set, Lincoln's concern for and conciliation of Southern whites received great praise as a wise and statesmanlike policy. His actions on slavery and race tended to be approved, for their limited character, or deemphasized. Books appearing in the 1920s and 1930s — such as *The Tragic Era,* by Claude Bowers; *The Critical Year,* by Howard K. Beale; or *The Age of Hate,* by George Fort Milton — exemplified this trend. They denounced mistakes in Reconstruction — the supposedly harsh punishment of white Southerners and the supposed folly of enfranchising African Americans—and held Lincoln up as a model of wisdom and charity because of his concern for Southern whites.

In the middle years of the twentieth century, scholarly writing added some criticism and realism to the prevailing favorable views of Lincoln. James G. Randall became the preeminent interpreter of Lincoln in the academy. Known widely for his revisionist thesis that "a blundering generation" had brought about the Civil War, Randall noted Lincoln's lack of control over events, his great interest in colonization, and the limits of emancipation. He judged the "stock image" of the Great Emancipator a myth. When Richard Current finished the last volume of the deceased Randall's biography, he took note of Lincoln's appeals to Southern whites and his omission of substantial efforts to establish civil rights for the freedmen. Benjamin P. Thomas's one-volume biography of Lincoln, published in 1952, also noted some contradictions between popular notions about the Civil War period and the historical record.

In recent decades, some historians, such as David Donald, Herman Belz, and Allen Guelzo, have paid attention to the limitations in Lincoln's policies and to events such as the Hampton Roads Conference. (Their work is noted and cited in chapter 7.) But others, such as John Cox and LaWanda Cox, Hans Trefousse, and Stephen Oates, have portrayed Lincoln as a crusading Radical Republican or a symbol for the civil rights movement. James McPherson's important 1988 book, *Battle Cry of Freedom,* reinterpreted the "Second American Revolution" as a revolution for human freedom, led by Lincoln. Although McPherson has acknowledged (in a review in the *New York Times,* August 27, 2000) that "Lincoln did share the racial prejudices of his time and place," much of his work contributes powerfully to the iconic image of Lincoln. He insists that Lincoln deserves the credit for emancipation and rejects those who argue for the slaves' contribution to that result.

By piling one tribute upon another, McPherson's writing strengthens the hagiographic view of Lincoln and fuels popular culture's skewed understanding of progress and racism in the Civil War era. For example, in a review in the *New York Review of Books,* March 29, 2007, Professor McPherson offered these words of praise for Lincoln:

> He [Frederick Douglass] could not know that at the very moment he was condemning the President as no better than the proslavery Buchanan, Lincoln had decided to issue an emancipation proclamation that would accomplish most of what Douglass demanded. . . . The difference between the two men was one of position and tactics, not conviction. . . . Douglass and many other contemporaries failed to appreciate or even to understand Lincoln's political legerdemain. Many historians have similarly failed. . . . After issuing the Emancipation Proclamation on January 1, 1863, Lincoln never again mentioned colonization. . . . When Lincoln came under enormous pressure in the summer of 1864 to waive his insistence on Southern acceptance of the abolition of slavery as a precondition for peace negotiations, he eloquently refused to do so. . . .

> Douglass also found that Lincoln in person had none of that "pride of race" he had earlier accused him of possessing.

The cumulative effect of such statements is overwhelmingly positive. Yet, as I have shown, they fail to tell the whole story, especially with regard to Lincoln's policies toward slaveholders, state rights, colonization, ratification of the Thirteenth Amendment, or the political strategy used in the summer of 1864. They omit as much as they include. Emphasizing only the positive, Professor McPherson, through his scholarly contributions and many review articles in the *New York Review of Books,* has bolstered the hagiographic, iconic, and oversimplified view of Lincoln. (For more detail on the historiography, see Merrill Peterson's *Lincoln and American Memory,* especially 350, 357, 302, 309. The analysis sketched above differs somewhat from Peterson's narrative but also relies upon it.)

Discussion of Lincoln's actions as president is inevitable in any study of the Civil War. This book, however, is not primarily about Lincoln. Rather, it attempts to examine the way that all Americans, North and South, black and white, dealt with the challenge of racial change during the Civil War. For that reason, it treats books, periodicals, newspapers, pamphlets, sermons, reports of military officers in the field, and other sources, in addition to the actions of those in government. But as president, Abraham Lincoln obviously played a major role. In examining his actions, this book insists on the importance of policy, for policy choices defined results; Lincoln's private comments (which varied), supposed intentions, and rare indications of a preference did not. Lincoln's Proclamation of Amnesty and Reconstruction, his actions during the political crisis in the summer of 1864, the Hampton Roads Conference, and his last speech (reaffirming his stand on ratification of the Thirteenth Amendment) reveal vitally important policy positions that too often are ignored, overlooked, or only superficially analyzed. Attention to these matters recovers the importance of key historical facts and challenges us to reconsider the celebratory themes that dominate the image of the Civil War in popular culture.

In his policies, Lincoln consistently placed a higher priority on engaging and conciliating Southern whites, as an element of saving the Union, than he did on ensuring immediate and total emancipation. Overtures to Southern whites were an integral part of preserving the Union; ending slavery became one of Lincoln's war aims, but emancipating *all* the slaves *immediately* was not an essential part of his policy. Still lower on his list of priorities were steps to elevate the status of the freedmen and ensure their legal or social equality. Lincoln's policies on reunion were remarkably generous to the rebels and remarkably consistent. His policies to aid African Americans were limited, circumscribed, and provisional. To the end of his life, his position on the future of African Americans remained subordinate to the goal of achieving reunion with Southern whites.

These policies reflect the reality of Civil War America. They say something, of course, about Lincoln, but they say much more about the nation in which he lived. They reveal the power of racism in American society. We will never know for certain just how constrained or expansive Lincoln's private views on African Americans were, but we do know what policies he was willing to advance. Even Lincoln's strongest admirers would admit that those policies reflect the limitations on a practical politician who operated within a deeply racist society.

Unfortunately, racism's impact on wartime events was only a foretaste of what was to come. The army officers and observers who had issued warnings about the hostility of Southern planters and their determination to regain power were perceptive. Events soon proved that their fears for the future were justified. The suppression of freedom by white racism was well under way even before the end of Reconstruction, and it would gain power thereafter, culminating in the imposition of a rigid system of segregation and disfranchisement that would last into the 1960s.

NOTES

Introduction

1. Kennan, *American Diplomacy,* 46, 99, 100.

2. Woodrow Wilson, *New Freedom,* 161, 162, 169.

3. A recent example of a glowing analysis of Lincoln, in which he seems always wise and admirable, is the (very readable) volume *Team of Rivals,* by Pulitzer Prize–winning author Doris Kearns Goodwin.

4. Lincoln, *Collected Works,* 8:332–33.

5. For more detail on this point, see Potter, *Lincoln and His Party.*

6. For the enormous changes in the Confederacy, see Emory M. Thomas, *The Confederacy as a Revolutionary Experience* and *The Confederate Nation.* See also Escott, *After Secession* and *Military Necessity.*

7. The two most valuable accounts of the Confederate debate on emancipation are Durden, *The Gray and the Black;* and Levine, *Confederate Emancipation.*

8. This question, and variants of it, cropped up repeatedly in newspapers and magazines such as the *Cincinnati Gazette,* the *Chicago Tribune, Harper's Weekly,* and the *Continental Monthly;* in the correspondence of army officers; and on the floor of the U.S. Senate.

Prologue

1. Lincoln, *Collected Works,* 8:332.

2. "Declarations of Causes of Seceding States: Civil War South Carolina."

3. "Declarations of Causes of Seceding States: Civil War Mississippi."

4. "Declarations of Causes of Seceding States: Civil War Georgia."

5. "Declarations of Causes of Seceding States: Texas."

6. "Speech of E. S. Dargan, Secession Convention of Alabama, January 11, 1861."

7. "Ordinances of Secession, 13 Confederate States of America: Alabama."

8. Dew, *Apostles of Disunion,* 97–99; for the full text of Hale's speech, see ibid., 90–103.

9. Ibid., 57.

10. Ibid., 78.

11. Ibid., 66–67.

12. Ibid., 78.

13. Ibid., 80, 85.

14. Roark, *Masters without Slaves,* 3–8.

15. Warren, *To the Citizens of Beaufort County.* In the slaveholding states of Kentucky and Missouri opinion was too divided for decisive action. The Confederacy would claim these two states and give them representation in the Confederate Congress, but for most of the war they were within Union lines. Lincoln used both force and persuasion to keep Maryland in the Union, and although slavery existed in Delaware, the number of slaves there was so small that loyalty to the Union was never seriously in doubt.

16. Ellis, *Speech of . . . March 9, 1860.*

17. John C. Calhoun quoted in Freehling, *Prelude to Civil War,* 257.

18. The quoted portions of the Dred Scott decision may be found in Finkelman, *Dred Scott v. Sandford,* 61, 69, 73–75; Albert Gallatin Brown's statement was made in Congress on 23 February 1859 and may be found in the *Congressional Globe,* 35th Cong., 2d sess., 1859, 1243. See also Ranck, *Albert Gallatin Brown,* ch. 6.

19. For explorations of this theme, see Wyatt-Brown, *Southern Honor;* and Greenberg, *Masters and Statesmen.* Even a small and sickly figure like Alexander H. Stephens engaged in knife fights with political opponents, and he came close to fighting several duels (see Schott, *Alexander H. Stephens of Georgia*).

20. "Declarations of Causes of Seceding States: Civil War Mississippi"; "Declarations of Causes of Seceding States: Civil War Georgia"; "Declarations of Causes of Seceding States: Texas"; Dew, *Apostles of Disunion,* 86, 96, 41, 26, 46; Frank I. Wilson, *Address Delivered before the Wake County Workingmen's Association.* An attorney, teacher, newspaperman, and writer, Wilson presided over an 1859 meeting of the Wake County Workingman's Association, which, along with the 1860 meeting, was one of "the first labor meetings in the state" (Powell, *Dictionary of North Carolina Biography,* 6:226).

21. "Permanent Constitution of the Confederate States of America," Art. 4; one among the many sources where this document may be found is Thomas, *Confederate Nation,* appendix.

22. Alexander H. Stephens quoted in Durden, *The Gray and the Black,* 7–8.

23. See Escott, *Many Excellent People;* and Michael P. Johnson, *Toward a Patriarchal Republic.*

24. Alfriend, "The Great Danger of the Confederacy," 40.

25. Alfriend, "A Southern Republic and a Northern Democracy," 284, 289; Jeffery, "European Immigration and New England Puritanism," 471; Fitzhugh, "The Revolutions of 1776 and 1861 Contrasted."

26. Alfriend, "The Great Danger of the Confederacy," 40; idem, "A Southern Republic and a Northern Democracy," 285, 289, 286; Jeffery, "European Immigration and New England Puritanism," 471.

27. "True Basis of Political Prosperity," 153–54, 155; "Editor's Table," 181, 182.

28. Hall, *Historic Significance of the Southern Revolution,* 13, 38.

29. Joseph R. Wilson, *Mutual Relation of Masters and Slaves,* 3, 7, 8, 9, 10, 21.

30. Elliott, *New Wine not to be Put into Old Bottles,* 10–11, 14, 11, 12, 14.

31. Moore, *God our Refuge and Strength,* 16, 24, 18.

32. Smyth, "The War of the South Vindicated," 481, 484, 495, 498.

33. Thornwell, *The State of the Country,* 15, 21, 23, 24, 30.

34. Dreher, *A Sermon Delivered . . . June 13, 1861,* 4, 15, 12, 5; Sledd, *A Sermon Delivered . . . Sept. 22d, 1861,* 21; Pierce, *The Word of God a Nation's Life,* 11, 9. The preamble to the Confederate Constitution invoked "the favor and guidance of Almighty God."

35. Elliott, *Our Cause in Harmony,* 9, 10, 14. William Freehling has identified these ideas as a "new disguised heresy, frequent in Upper South polemics" that "built on an old undisguised orthodoxy," the eighteenth- and early nineteenth-century's support for colonization. Colonization "resurfaced as a theological goal" that was "vaguer" and "more evangelical" (see Freehling, *The Road to Disunion,* 2:52–53).

36. Elliott, *Vain is the Help of Man,* 9; idem, *Our Cause in Harmony,* 7; idem, *Ezra's Dilemna,* 9–10, 14; idem, *Funeral Services,* 16–17; idem, *Ezra's Dilemna,* 5.

37. Historians have clearly and accurately explicated the position of the Republican Party. This comment refers only to the inaccurate understanding of events that often prevails in popular culture's version of history.

38. See Gienapp, *The Origins of the Republican Party.*

39. Speech at Peoria, Illinois, 16 Oct. 1854, in Lincoln, *Collected Works,* 2:268.

40. Republican Party platform of 1856, quoted in Donald Bruce Johnson,, *National Party Platforms,* 1:27–28.

41. Commager, *Documents of American History,* 1:363–65.

42. Ibid.

43. Abraham Lincoln, seventh debate with Stephen Douglas, at Alton, Illinois, 15 Oct. 1858, in Lincoln, *This Fiery Trial,* 63–65.

44. The sometimes angry language used in this section — "you . . . denounce us as reptiles . . . you . . . spit upon that old policy" (see ibid., 71) — indicates that Lincoln's goal was more to burnish the party's image with Northerners than to achieve a reconciliation with Southerners.

45. Ibid., 74, 80.

46. Ibid., 80, 78, 76.

47. Lincoln, *Collected Works,* 2:270.

48. Lincoln, *This Fiery Trial,* 86.

49. Foner, *Free Soil, Free Labor, Free Men,* 316. Foner's volume is an invaluable classic.

50. See Potter, *Lincoln and His Party.*

51. Lincoln refused to give his blessing to compromise proposals in the U.S. Senate that might result in the extension of slavery to new areas (see ibid.; and Current, *The Lincoln Nobody Knows,* esp. ch. 4).

52. Lincoln, *Collected Works,* 4:262, 263, 266, 270. For the documents relating to Lincoln's secret role in proposing an amendment to the Constitution, see ibid., 156–57 and note, 158–59.

53. *Douglass' Monthly,* Apr. 1861, 433.

54. Benjamin P. Thomas, *Abraham Lincoln,* 237.

55. Crittenden-Johnson Resolutions, in Commager, *Documents of American History,* 1:395–96.

56. Hofstadter, *American Political Tradition,* ch. 5.

57. Lincoln, *This Fiery Trial,* 35.

58. Lincoln, *Collected Works,* 2:264–65, 250, 265–66.

59. Ibid., 2:266, 501.

60. Ibid., 2:266, 256; Lincoln, *This Fiery Trial,* 57.

61. Lincoln, *Collected Works,* 2:276, 255, 269, 268, 461–62, 467.

62. Ibid., 2:514; Foner, *Free Soil, Free Labor, Free Men,* 290.

63. Lincoln, *Collected Works,* 2:405–6.

64. Ibid., 2:255–56, 409.

65. Smith, *Francis Preston Blair,* xii, 245–46, 251, 320–23. Francis Blair and his sons believed that coexistence between whites and blacks was impossible in the United States, that race mixing would produce a hybrid race incapable of perpetuating itself, and that black people were naturally adapted to tropical regions. Government-assisted migration of African Americans to Central or South America would, they believed, remove the blight of slavery from the United States and enable blacks to establish dominant and friendly governments there.

66. Neely, *The Last Best Hope of Earth,* 41.

1. The North Confronts the Question

1. See Potter, *Lincoln and His Party;* and *Harper's Weekly,* 4 May 1861, 274, and 6 July 1861, 416. The circulation figures are from http://www.spartacus.schoolnet.uk.com/USAharpers.htm (accessed 4 Oct. 2006).

2. McPherson, *Ordeal by Fire,* 267. For a wide-ranging, informative article about the term *contrabands* and Northerners' assumptions about the contrabands, see Masur, "A Rare Phenomenon of Philological Vegetation."

3. *Harper's Weekly,* 6 July 1861, 416; *Atlantic Monthly,* July 1861, 93–94; McPherson, *The Negro's Civil War,* 37, 40–41.

4. Crittenden-Johnson Resolutions, in Commager, *Documents of American History,* 1:395–96; sec. 4 of "An Act to Confiscate property used for Insurrectionary Purposes," *U.S. Statutes at Large,* 12:319; McPherson, *Ordeal by Fire.*

5. Manning, *What This Cruel War Was Over,* ch. 1.

6. *New York Times,* 31 Aug. 1861, 2.

7. *Harper's Weekly,* 14 Sept. 1861, 578.

8. The newspapers are quoted in *Douglass' Monthly,* Oct. 1861, 535–36.

9. *New York Times,* 1 Sept. 1861, 4; 2 Sept. 1861, 4; 3 Sept. 1861, 4; 15 Sept. 1861, 4; 10 Sept. 1861, 4.

10. Ibid., 28 Nov. 1861.

11. Ripley, *The Black Abolitionist Papers,* 5:177. The quoted passages are from Lincoln's Peoria speech of 1854 and his First Inaugural Address; see Lincoln, *This Fiery Trial,* 29, 97.

12. See Berry, *House of Abraham.*

13. Carwardine, *Lincoln,* 189; "The Madisonian Policy," *Chicago Tribune,* 19 Dec. 1861, 2.

14. Lincoln, *Collected Works,* 5:29–31. Delaware was already close, numerically, to being a free state. According to the U.S. Census, in an 1860 population of 112,216, there were 90,589 whites, 19,829 free Negroes, and only 1,798 slaves.

15. Ibid., 5:48–49.

16. Ibid.

17. Ibid., 5:144–46. In the first quotation, Lincoln's original "evils" was replaced by "inconveniences," at the suggestion of his cabinet.

18. *Letter of Hon. Montgomery Blair,* 5–8. Lincoln's relationship with Montgomery Blair, like his relationship with Francis Blair, was marked by mutual confidence. In 1864 Montgomery Blair let Lincoln know that he would resign whenever it would be politically helpful to the president, and after Blair did leave the cabinet, he promptly began making speeches urging Lincoln's reelection (see Smith, *Francis Preston Blair,* 346–47).

19. *New York Times,* 4 Dec. 1861, suppl., 4; 11 May 1862, 3.

20. *Harper's Weekly,* 7 Dec. 1861, 770; 21 Dec. 1861, 802; 8 Feb. 1862, 82; 1 Mar. 1862, 180; 5 Apr. 1862, 310.

21. Ibid., 5 Apr. 1862, 310; 14 June 1862, 373; 28 June 1862, 402.

22. *Cincinnati Daily Gazette,* 25 Apr. 1862, 1; 26 Apr. 1862, 2; 17 May 1862, 2. *Chicago Tribune,* 22 Aug. 1862, 2; 12 Aug. 1862, 2.

23. *Continental Monthly,* prospectus for first issue; Feb. 1862, 136, 225, 226; Mar. 1862, 256.

24. *New Englander* 19, no. 73 (Jan. 1861): 148; no. 76 (Oct. 1861): 911; *New Englander* 21, no. 78 (Jan. 1862): 104, 105, 107, 111; no. 81 (Oct. 1862): 810, 813. On the conservative influence of Yale and its impact on Southern proslavery arguments, see Tise, *Proslavery.*

25. *Douglass' Monthly,* Jan. 1862, 577; Mar. 1862, 614–15; Feb. 1862, 601; Apr. 1862, 626; Jan. 1862, 579; Mar. 1862, 614–15, 618. Ripley, *The Black Abolitionist Papers,* 5:138.

26. Thomas and Hyman, *Stanton,* 232–37.

27. *Douglass' Monthly,* Aug. 1862, 692; July 1862, 675; Aug. 1862, 699; July 1862, 686. Ripley, *The Black Abolitionist Papers,* 5:143, 145. *Continental Monthly,* July 1862, 109. *New York Times,* 20 May 1862, 4; *Douglass' Monthly,* July 1862, 686.

28. Lincoln, *Collected Works,* 5:222–24.

29. *U.S. Statutes at Large,* 12:589–92.

30. McPherson, *Ordeal by Fire,* 397.

31. Whiting, *The War Powers of the President,* chs. 4–6, esp. 107, 109, 114; McPherson, *Ordeal by Fire,* 397.

32. Rafuse, *McClellan's War,* 235.

33. Fisher, *The Laws of Race,* 11.

34. *Atlantic Monthly,* Feb. 1861, 252–54; *North American Review* 92, no. 191 (Apr. 1861): 507–8.

35. *North American Review* 94, no. 195 (Apr. 1861): 509, 503, 511–12, 513, 498–99, 503, 505, 506.

36. *New Englander* 19, no. 76 (Oct. 1861): 841, 843, 842, 845, 839, 910–12.

37. Putnam, *Record of an Obscure Man,* 96–102, 118–19, 167, 90; *Harper's Weekly,* 20 Sept. 1862, 595; Kirke, *Among the Pines,* 93, 27, 73, 57, 82, 90, 19. The *Continental Monthly* stated in its January 1863 issue (p. 128) that sales of *Among the Pines* had reached 30,000.

38. Brace, *The Races of the Old World,* iv, 225–313 passim, esp. 259–73 (quotations from 272 and 260), 439, 451–53, 466–67, 483. Brace's understanding of Darwinism was not perfect, for he did not always take into account the long periods of time involved or the difference between psychological change and what we now understand to be genetic change. For example, he argued that freeborn children in Sierra Leone "have more intelligent eyes, freer bearing, and a more agreeable form" than their parents.

39. *New York Times,* 22 June 1862, 2; Brace, *The Races of the Old World,* 477–78.

40. Van Evrie, *Negroes and Negro "Slavery,"* v, 134, 52, 37, 238, 101, 162, 256, 122, 119, 228, 128, 191, 199, 185–89, 201, 145–67 passim, 134, 20.

41. Sewell, *The Ordeal of Free Labor,* 311, 314–15, 313, 232–37, 317, 324, 312.

42. *Cincinnati Daily Enquirer,* 4 Apr. 1862, 1; 5 Apr. 1862, 1; 6 Apr. 1862, 1. *Cincinnati Daily Gazette,* 3 Apr. 1862, 1. See also *Cincinnati Daily Gazette,* 25 Nov. 1862, 2.

43. *New Englander* 21, no. 81 (Oct. 1862): 799, 786, 808–9, 794, 801.

44. *Continental Monthly,* Feb. 1862, 226. The title of Atkinson's pamphlet was *Cheap Cotton by Free Labor.*

45. Cochin, *The Results of Emancipation,* 17, 291–92, 163, 172, 98, 297, 303.

46. Cochin, *The Results of Slavery,* 98–101, 112–13, 265.

47. *New Englander* 22, no. 83 (Apr. 1863): 355, 356.

48. *North American Review* 96, no. 198 (Jan. 1863): 277, 281–82.

49. *Harper's Weekly,* 28 Sept. 1861, 610. "The President's Proclamation," *Atlantic Monthly,* Nov. 1862, 642. *Continental Monthly,* Apr. 1862, 387; May 1862, 495. *North American Review* 95, no. 197 (Oct. 1862): 530–31. *New York Times,* 12 Dec. 1862, 2.

50. *Cincinnati Daily Gazette,* 17 May 1862, 2; 23 Sept. 1862, 2.

51. Frank P. Blair, *Destiny of the Races.*

52. *Douglass' Monthly,* Oct. 1862, 724.

53. *Continental Monthly,* Apr. 1862, 471, 470; May 1862, 493; June 1862, 660, 662, 727; Aug. 1862, 163–64. See also *Continental Monthly,* July 1862, 68.

54. Lincoln, *Collected Works,* 5:317–19. Twenty of these legislators published their rejection of Lincoln's arguments, saying that his idea was too expensive, that it would encourage rebellious views, and that it would not lessen the pressure for "unconstitutional" emancipation in the rest of the South. Only eight indicated their support.

55. Ibid., 5:370–75, 375n. On 12 September 1862 the founder of the Chiriqui Improvement Company and the secretary of the interior "actually signed a contract providing for coal purchases and a colony to be led by radical Senator Samuel Pomeroy of Kansas" (Smith, *Francis Preston Blair,* 323). The Chiriqui project eventually was abandoned after Honduras, Nicaragua, and Costa Rica objected to it and indicated that they might use force to prevent a settlement.

56. Lincoln, *Collected Works,* 5:370–74.

57. *Douglass' Monthly,* Sept. 1862, 707–8; Ripley, *The Black Abolitionist Papers,* 5:153, 155; *Cincinnati Daily Enquirer,* 7 Oct. 1862, 2.

58. Lincoln, *Collected Works,* 5:342–43, 388–89.

59. Ibid., 5:433–36.

60. *Chicago Tribune,* 24 Sept. 1862, 1; 26 Sept. 1862, 1, with quotations from various newspapers. *Cincinnati Daily Enquirer,* 23 Sept. 1862, 2; 24 Sept. 1862, 2; 25 Sept. 1862, 2.

61. *Atlantic Monthly,* Nov. 1862, 629–32, 641. *Cincinnati Daily Gazette,* 23 Sept. 1862, 2. *New York Times,* 23 Sept. 1862, 1; 28 Sept. 1862, 4; 21 Nov. 1862, 4.

62. *Cincinnati Daily Enquirer,* 14 Oct. 1862, 2; 9 Oct. 1862, 2, 1; 15 Nov. 1862, 2; 3 Dec. 1862, 1.

63. *Cincinnati Daily Gazette,* 23 Sept. 1862, 2; 22 Oct. 1862, 2. *Chicago Tribune,* 26 Sept. 1862, 1. *New Englander* 21, no. 81 (Oct. 1862): 794. *New York Times,* 7 Oct. 1862, 4.

64. *New York Times,* 1 Oct. 1862, 4; 3 Oct. 1862, 4. *Douglass' Monthly,* Nov. 1862, 740. *New York Times,* 24 Oct. 1862, 4; 24 Nov. 1862, 4.

65. *Douglass' Monthly,* Jan. 1863, 774–75.

66. *Continental Monthly,* Nov. 1862, 573, 574, 575, 578.

67. Ibid., Dec. 1862, 730, 731, 733, 734; Jan. 1863, 36.

68. Lincoln, *Collected Works,* 5:530.

69. Ibid., 5:531–34.

70. Ibid., 5:534–36.

71. *Harper's Weekly,* 6 Sept. 1862, 562; 27 Sept. 1862, 610; 1 Nov. 1862, 690; 13 Dec. 1862, 786.

72. *Douglass' Monthly,* Nov. 1862, 741; *New Englander* 21, no. 81 (Oct. 1862): 813, 817–19.

73. *Chicago Tribune,* 2 Dec. 1862, 2; 4 Dec. 1862, 2. *Cincinnati Daily Gazette,* 8 Oct. 1862, 2; 5 Dec. 1862, 2; 25 Nov. 1862, 2; 4 Dec. 1862, 2. *Cincinnati Daily Enquirer,* 7 Oct. 1862, 1 (quoting the *London Times*); 4 Dec. 1862, 2.

74. Lincoln, *Collected Works,* 6:28–31. The areas explicitly exempted from the proclamation were occupied portions of Louisiana and Virginia, the counties that had broken away to form West Virginia, and all of Tennessee.

75. Ibid.; Ripley, *The Black Abolitionist Papers,* 5:184.

76. Lincoln, *Collected Works,* 5:388.

77. *Cincinnati Daily Gazette,* 3 Jan. 1863, 2. *New York Times,* 15 Dec. 1862, 4; 20 Dec. 1862, 4; 28 Dec. 1862, 4; 3 Dec. 1862, 4; 12 Dec. 1862, 2; 24 Nov. 1862, 4; 3 Jan. 1863, 4.

2. War's Proving Ground

1. Berlin, Miller et al., *The Wartime Genesis of Free Labor: The Upper South,* 5, 481–82, 491.

2. Ibid., 367–68ff.

3. Ibid., 551–52.

4. Ibid., 625–38.

5. Ibid., 481–82, 491.

6. Berlin, Glymph et al., *The Wartime Genesis of Free Labor: The Lower South,* 78. Ripley, in *The Black Abolitionist Papers,* gives an estimate of 147,000 Southern black recruits to the Union army (5:273). He also estimates that 70 percent of all Northern black males of military age joined the army, a rate three times higher than that for Northern whites (5:179).

7. Rose, *Rehearsal for Reconstruction.*

8. Berlin, Miller et al., *The Wartime Genesis of Free Labor: The Upper South,* 133–34. For more detail on Dix's proposal and the reactions it evoked, see Voegeli, "A Rejected Alternative." Voegeli also indicates that the number of contrabands sent into Illinois in 1862 is uncertain but probably was not large. Nevertheless, Democratic newspapers charged that Republicans were planning to bring about a black "influx."

9. Interestingly, these events in 1862 did not entirely end discussion of sending freedmen to the North. In 1864, Benjamin Butler wrote to a textile company in Lowell, Massachusetts, offering to supply female black workers for the mills there. Also in 1864, a thousand families from the New York City area applied to hire Negro servants from the South (see Berlin, Miller et al., *The Wartime Genesis of Free Labor: The Upper South,* 190, 204–6; the editors note, on page 206, that "demand for black domestic servants of Southern origin ran high in northeastern cities throughout 1864").

10. Berlin, Glymph et al., *The Wartime Genesis of Free Labor: The Lower South,* 655–765.

11. [Forman], *The Western Sanitary Commission,* 110, 112, 113; Berlin, Miller et al., *The Wartime Genesis of Free Labor: The Upper South,* 142, 148, 161, 173; Berlin,

Glymph et al., *The Wartime Genesis of Free Labor: The Lower South,* 183, 214, 279.

12. [Forman], *The Western Sanitary Commission,* 110; Berlin, Glymph et al., *The Wartime Genesis of Free Labor: The Lower South,* 280, 187. Before the war was over, black people in the Sea Islands complained to Lincoln about promises that they charged Philbrick with breaking. They said that Philbrick had bought eleven plantations for only $1 an acre and promised to sell them to the freedmen. But then he had refused to do so, claiming that they were worth $10 an acre. Philbrick made no sales until 1866, and then he charged $5 per acre (see Berlin, Glymph et al., *The Wartime Genesis of Free Labor: The Lower South,* 297–99, 747, 758, 760, 495).

13. Gerteis, *From Contraband to Freedman,* 50, 76, 85, 104, 105, 76–77, 78. For the second quotation from General Banks, see Perman, *Emancipation and Reconstruction,* 8.

14. Gerteis, *From Contraband to Freedman,* 121–29; Berlin, Glymph et al., *The Wartime Genesis of Free Labor: The Lower South,* 747, 729.

15. Berlin, Glymph et al., *The Wartime Genesis of Free Labor: The Lower South,* 758, 560, 495.

16. Gerteis, *From Contraband to Freedman,* ch. 8, esp. 132–42, 147, 148, and 149, and in ch. 9, 155. For the Treasury Department's regulations, see Berlin, Glymph et al., *The Wartime Genesis of Free Labor: The Lower South,* 539ff.

17. Berlin, Glymph et al., *The Wartime Genesis of Free Labor: The Lower South,* 739, 642–44.

18. Lincoln, *Collected Works,* 6:30, 5:423. African American leaders also were arguing that Northern blacks should be admitted into the army (see Ripley, *The Black Abolitionist Papers,* 5:175–76).

19. *Chicago Tribune,* 4 July 1863, 2; *Littell's Living Age,* 20 June 1863, 556, reprinting an article from the *New York Evening Post* of 29 May 1863; *Douglass' Monthly,* June 1863, 842.

20. *Cincinnati Daily Enquirer,* 8 July 1863, 2; *Douglass' Monthly,* Aug. 1863, 852; Ripley, *The Black Abolitionist Papers,* 5:175–76.

21. Hepworth, *Whip, Hoe, and Sword,* 57, 193. *New York Times,* 11 June 1863, 4; 6 June 1863, 4; 29 Mar. 1863, 4.

22. Berlin, Glymph et al., *The Wartime Genesis of Free Labor: The Lower South,* 555.

23. Ibid., 396.

24. Ibid., 135, 201, 239, 246, 279, 324; see also comments by Edward Philbrick on 182–88.

25. *Facts Concerning the Freedmen;* Berlin, Glymph et al., *The Wartime Genesis of Free Labor: The Lower South,* 142, 146, 148, 149, 209, 217, 214, 297.

26. Berlin, Glymph et al., *The Wartime Genesis of Free Labor: The Lower South,* 417–18, 460, 518, 519, 492, 455, 576, 572–73.

27. Ibid., 691, 693, 729.

28. Ibid., 740, 746, 748, 759, 760, 871.

29. Berlin, Miller et al., *The Wartime Genesis of Free Labor: The Upper South,* 124–45, 152, 181, 212, 217.

30. Berlin, Glymph et al., *The Wartime Genesis of Free Labor: The Lower South,* 137, 268, 329, 521.

31. Ibid., 692–93.

32. Berlin, Miller et al., *The Wartime Genesis of Free Labor: The Upper South,* 124–25, 149, 161, 290; Berlin, Glymph et al., *The Wartime Genesis of Free Labor: The Lower South,* 131, 141, 329, 498, 745.

33. Berlin, Miller et al., *The Wartime Genesis of Free Labor: The Upper South,* 291; M'Kim, *The Freedmen of South Carolina,* in the attached letter to Stephen Colwell, 27, 30; *Facts Concerning the Freedmen,* 6; Hepworth, *Whip, Hoe, and Sword,* 163; Berlin, Glymph et al., *The Wartime Genesis of Free Labor: The Lower South,* 695.

34. [Forman], *The Western Sanitary Commission,* 120; Berlin, Miller et al., *The Wartime Genesis of Free Labor: The Upper South,* 153–54; Berlin, Glymph et al., *The Wartime Genesis of Free Labor: The Lower South,* 693; Waterbury, *Friendly Counsels for Freedmen,* 7, 12, 4; Berlin, Miller et al., *The Wartime Genesis of Free Labor: The Upper South,* 181; Berlin, Glymph et al., *The Wartime Genesis of Free Labor: The Lower South,* 523, 695–96.

35. Berlin, Miller et al., *The Wartime Genesis of Free Labor: The Upper South,* 290; Berlin, Glymph et al., *The Wartime Genesis of Free Labor: The Lower South,* 492, 498, 520, 553.

36. Berlin, Glymph et al., *The Wartime Genesis of Free Labor: The Lower South,* 441–42, 680, 696–97.

37. *New York Times,* 13 June 1863, 1; 10 June 1863, 1; 11 June 1863, 4. *Chicago Tribune,* 10 June 1863, 1; 12 June 1863, 3. *Cincinnati Daily Gazette,* 9 June 1863, 1. *Cincinnati Daily Enquirer,* 10 June 1863, 1.

38. *Chicago Tribune,* 16 June 1863, 2. *New York Times,* 27 July 1864, 1; 13 June 1863, 1.

39. *Cincinnati Daily Enquirer,* 14 July 1863, 2; *Chicago Tribune,* 16 June 1863, 2; *New York Times,* 31 July 1863, 4.

40. *New York Times,* 31 July 1863, 4.

41. Ibid., 11 Aug. 1863, 4.

42. Ibid., 17 Oct. 1863, 1; 12 Nov. 1863, 4.

43. Berlin, Glymph et al., *The Wartime Genesis of Free Labor: The Lower South,* 130, 143, 145.

44. Ibid., 280–81, 246.

45. Ibid., 443, 495, 497, 499.

46. Ibid., 227, 229, 745, 743.

47. Ibid., 745; Hepworth, *Whip, Hoe, and Sword,* 84.

48. *Continental Monthly,* Apr. 1862, 387; June 1862, 659, 660; July 1862, 68; Aug. 1862, 163, 164; July 1863, 13. *New York Times,* 29 Jan. 1864, 4.

49. Berlin, Glymph et al., *The Wartime Genesis of Free Labor: The Lower South,* 520, 553, 555, 576, 572–73.

50. Samuel Gridley Howe was the third member of the commission.

51. American Freedmen's Inquiry Commission, *Preliminary Report,* 8, 5, 8, 12, 3, 24, 12, 10.

52. Ibid., 8, 33, 3, 8.

53. Ibid., 13, 34, 17, 16, 24, 22, 33, 37.

54. American Freedmen's Inquiry Commission, *Final Report,* 15 May 1864, ch. 3, pp. 3, 5, 10, 12. For the text of the *Final Report,* see U.S. War Department, *The War of the Rebellion,* ser. 3, vol. 4.

55. U.S. War Department, *The War of the Rebellion,* ser. 3, vol. 4:11–12.

56. Ibid., 4:13, 14.

57. Ibid., 4:2, 3. For the quotation from the *Weekly Anglo-African,* see Ripley, *The Black Abolitionist Papers,* 5:256.

58. Owen, *The Wrong of Slavery,* 195, 199–200, 201, 228.

59. McKaye, *The Mastership and its Fruits,* 20, 22, 34–37.

60. Hyman, "Johnson, Stanton, and Grant," 90; Berlin, Glymph et al., *The Wartime Genesis of Free Labor: The Lower South,* 576, 584.

3. Amnesty, Apprenticeship, and the Freedmen's Future

1. Frederick Douglass quoted in Boritt, "Did He Dream of a Lily-White America?"

2. Lincoln, *This Fiery Trial,* 195.

3. James G. Blaine quoted in Guelzo, "Defending Emancipation," 313.

4. Lincoln, *This Fiery Trial,* 153; this letter was dated 8 January 1863. On Lincoln's proposals for apprenticeship and compensation, see Lincoln, *Collected Works,* 5:29–31. The closing paragraphs of this letter provide a good example of Lincoln's preference for keeping all his options open. That preference led him to embrace contradictory positions in some of his statements about policy.

5. Lincoln, *This Fiery Trial,* 185, 186, 187. Agreeing with Lincoln about public morale, James G. Blaine later recalled that "at no time during the war was the depression among the people of the North so great as in the spring of 1863" (Blaine is quoted in Guelzo, "Defending Emancipation," 313).

6. Lincoln, *This Fiery Trial,* 164.

7. Ibid., 175, 176.

8. Ibid., 176–77, 178.

9. Ibid., 169; Ripley, *The Black Abolitionist Papers,* 5:265–66. The treatment of black troops did disrupt prisoner exchanges between North and South.

10. "Fellow countrymen" was the phrase used in his First Inaugural Address (see Lincoln, *This Fiery Trial,* 96).

11. Blair, *Speech of the Hon. Montgomery Blair.*

12. Lincoln, *This Fiery Trial,* 182–83.

13. Ibid.

14. Lincoln, *Collected Works,* 7:23. Among the many admiring works that focus on the Gettysburg address are Wills, *Lincoln at Gettysburg;* and Boritt, *Gettysburg Gospel.*

15. Lincoln, *Collected Works,* 7:51.

16. Ibid., 7:54, 51.

17. Ibid., 7:54, 55, 51; Harris, *With Charity for All,* 140–41, 146–47, 149.

18. Lincoln, *Collected Works,* 7:55, 56.

19. See Rorabaugh, *Craft Apprentice;* and Schultz, "Printers' Devils."

20. See Finkelman, "Evading the Ordinance," quotation on 21; and idem, "Slavery and the Northwest Ordinance," quotation on 369.

21. Finkelman, "Evading the Ordinance," 46–47; Bridges, "The Illinois Black Codes," 2–3. Arvarh E. Strickland has pointed out that in addition to those apprenticed or indentured, the U.S. Census recorded 917 slaves in Illinois in 1820, 747 in 1830, and 331 in 1840 (see Strickland, "The Illinois Background of Lincoln's Attitude").

22. Servitude and Emancipation Records (1722–1863), in Illinois State Archives Online Databases, http://www.cyberdriveillinois.com/departments/archives/servant.html. The author gratefully acknowledges the assistance of Karl Moore, of the Illinois State Archives, in identifying and obtaining other useful records.

23. Ibid. The emancipation records in this online database mainly provide evidence that a given individual was, in fact, a free person. Some note that the original record of free status was on file in another county, or that local residents were certifying that an individual was free, or that an individual black person was the child of someone with free status. Illinois state law required such evidence of freedom, along with the posting of a large bond. For discussion of the life expectancy of slaves, see Stampp, *The Peculiar Institution,* ch. 7.

24. Servitude and Emancipation Records (1722–1863), in Illinois State Archives Online Databases, http://www.cyberdriveillinois.com/departments/archives/servant.html.

25. Ibid.; Donald, *Lincoln,* 84–85.

26. Apprenticeship Indentures, Jackson County, Illinois, and Indentures, 1834–1881, Perry County, Illinois, both on microfilm purchased through Karl Moore.

27. Bridges, "The Illinois Black Codes," 3–7.

28. Donald, *Lincoln,* 486–87.

29. Ibid.; Lincoln, *This Fiery Trial,* 193. For accounts of Lincoln's ten-percent Louisiana government that are admiring of Lincoln, see Cox, *Lincoln and Black Freedom;* and McCrary, *Abraham Lincoln and Reconstruction.*

30. Lincoln, *This Fiery Trial,* 194–95.

31. *New York Times,* 11 Aug. 1863, 4.

32. Ibid., 17 Oct. 1863, 1, 6.

33. Ibid., 18 Oct. 1863, 4; 25 Dec. 1863, 4; 28 Dec. 1863, 4; 31 Dec. 1863, 4.

34. Ibid., 18 Feb. 1864, 4.

35. Ibid., 29 Jan. 1864, 4 (two articles), 22 Mar. 1864, 4. See also McPherson, *The Negro's Civil War,* 98–99.

36. Donald, *Lincoln,* 473.

37. *Congressional Globe,* 38th Cong., 1st sess., 1864, 197, 521; Donald, *Charles Sumner and the Rights of Man,* 152–61.

38. *Congressional Globe,* 38th Cong., 1st sess., 1864, 481.

39. Ibid., 817, 837.

40. Ibid., 1438, 1705, 1745, 2242, 988.

41. Ibid., 673.

42. Quoted in Hesseltine, *Lincoln's Plan of Reconstruction,* 105.

43. See www.Classbrain.com, under "Defining Documents," where the text is reproduced from a handwritten copy of the Wade-Davis Bill as originally submitted in 1864 that was found in the Records of Legislative Proceedings, Records of the U.S. House of Representatives, 1789–1946, RG 233, National Archives.

44. Lincoln, *This Fiery Trial,* 200.

45. The Wade-Davis Manifesto appeared in both long and short versions, with some of the text of the latter appearing in the former. These quotations come from the long version, dated 8 August 1864, which may be found, for example, in Henry Winter Davis, *Speeches and Addresses,* 415–26; and Scott, *Reconstruction during the Civil War,* 412–25. The shorter version appeared in many newspapers.

46. McPherson, *The Struggle for Equality,* 221, 226, 242–43; Cheever, *Rights of the coloured race,* 16–17.

47. Douglass, "Present and Future of the Colored Race."

48. Phillips, "State of the Country."

49. Wendell Phillips quoted in *New York Times,* 18 Feb. 1864, 4.

50. Phillips, *Immediate Issue.*

51. Wendell Phillips quoted in McPherson, *Struggle for Equality,* 246, 246–47, 249, 252, 260. For James McCune Smith's remarks, see Ripley, *The Black Abolitionist Papers,* 5:299.

52. *Congressional Globe,* 38th Cong., 1st sess., 1844, 2240, 2245, 1705, 2242.

4. Politics, Emancipation, and Black Rights

1. Benjamin Wade quoted in McPherson, *Battle Cry of Freedom,* 714.

2. McPherson, *The Negro's Civil War,* 306–7; Ripley, *The Black Abolitionist Papers,* 5:277; McPherson, *Battle Cry of Freedom,* 716.

3. McPherson, *Battle Cry of Freedom,* 716.

4. Lincoln is quoted in Current, *The Lincoln Nobody Knows,* 229.

5. Silbey, *Respectable Minority,* ch. 6.

6. Ibid., 25–27.

7. Ibid., 49–52.

8. *Old Guard,* quotations from issues for Jan. 1863, 13–14, 15–19; Feb. 1863, 69; July 1863, 145; Aug. 1863, 213; Feb. 1864, 39.

9. Silbey, *A Respectable Minority,* 28.

10. Van Evrie, *Negroes and Negro "Slavery,"* 134. Van Evrie was closely associated with Chauncey Burr, of the *Old Guard.* The October–December 1863 issue of that journal announced that Van Evrie & Horton had taken charge of the business affairs of Burr's journal so that he could devote himself entirely to editorial affairs.

11. Ibid., 52, 54, 95, 116, 20, 145, 111, 239, 229, 191.

12. Ibid., 9, 48, 14, 22, 78, 86, 249, 251, 255, 268–69.

13. Ibid., 170, 176, 189, 201, 211, 277–78, 307, 309–10.

14. Kaplan, "The Miscegenation Issue," 277.

15. Croly and Wakeman, *Miscegenation,* 11; Kaplan, "The Miscegenation Issue," 284–90.

16. Croly and Wakeman, *Miscegenation,* i, 18, 63, 53, 34, 19, 30, 50.

17. Kaplan, "The Miscegenation Issue," 295–321.

18. *Miscegenation Indorsed by the Republican Party,* quotations from 1, 5, 6, 7, 8.

19. Ibid., 1, 6, 2, 6, 7, 8.

20. Ulysses S. Grant quoted in McPherson, *Battle Cry of Freedom,* 726, 732, 733, 734.

21. Lincoln, *Collected Works,* 7:435; Nelson, *Bullets, Ballots, and Rhetoric.*

22. Lincoln, *Collected Works,* 7:435.

23. *New York Times,* 31 Dec. 1863, 4; 29 Apr. 1864, 4. David Herbert Donald observes that Lincoln's requirement of "'the abandonment of slavery' as a condition for peace talks, was a surprise. It went considerably beyond his own Emancipation Proclamation or any law of Congress" (Donald, *Lincoln,* 523).

24. *New York Herald,* 27 July 1864.

25. McPherson, *Battle Cry of Freedom,* 768–69. *Cincinnati Daily Enquirer,* 23 July 1864, 2; 28 July 1864, 2.

26. *Buffalo Commercial Advertiser,* quoted in *Cincinnati Daily Enquirer,* 29 July 1864, 2; McPherson, *Battle Cry of Freedom,* 769; Henry Raymond, quoted in Lincoln, *Collected Works,* 7:517–18; *New London Chronicle,* quoted in *Cincinnati Daily Enquirer,* 5 Aug. 1864, 1.

27. Lincoln, *Collected Works,* 7:499–501.

28. Seward, *Works,* 491, 502, 503–4.

29. *New York Times,* 18 Aug. 1864, 4.

30. "Proceedings of the National Convention of Colored Men . . . October 4, 5, 6, and 7, 1864," in Ripley, *The Black Abolitionist Papers,* 5:304.

31. Lincoln, *Collected Works,* 7:514.

32. Chesnut, *Diary from Dixie,* 425, 434; *New York Herald,* 12 Sept. 1864; George Templeton Strong quoted in McPherson, *Battle Cry of Freedom,* 773.

33. William B. Hesseltine has written that "without the aid of the military and

counting of soldier votes cast in the field, McClellan would have had a majority in the electoral college." Hesseltine also noted reports of questionable or fraudulent events. "Even the provost-marshal of Grant's army complained that 'all possible obstacles were thrown in the way of a fair soldier vote.'" According to Hesseltine, in Maryland, where a new state constitution was being considered for adoption, soldiers, who were not allowed to vote under the old constitution, provided the margin that "overturned the civilian majority" (Hesseltine, *Lincoln's Plan of Reconstruction,* 130).

34. Lincoln, *Collected Works,* 8:100–101, 107; Harris, *With Charity for All,* 260; Lincoln, *Collected Works,* 8:113.

35. Representative John Creswell, of Maryland, 5 Jan. 1865, in *Congressional Globe,* 38th Cong., 2d sess., 1865, pt. 1:122.

36. U.S. War Department, *War of the Rebellion,* ser. 1, vol. 43, pt. 2:587–88.

37. *New York Herald,* 26 July 1864.

38. Lincoln, *Collected Works,* 8:149.

39. Ibid., 8:152.

40. Ibid., 8:151.

41. As chapter 7 shows, Lincoln soon made this stand explicit.

42. Lincoln, *Collected Works,* 8:152.

43. James McPherson discusses this political landscape in *Battle Cry of Freedom,* 840.

44. Quotation from U.S. Constitution, Art. 4, sec. 3. On fear of executive manipulation, see the language of the Wade-Davis Manifesto, which denounced "those mere shadows of governments" as "mere creatures of his will" (see ch. 3, n. 45 above).

45. Herman Belz has shown that in the winter of 1864–65 congressional leaders seriously explored a possible compromise with Lincoln that would have involved admitting Louisiana, but the compromise fell apart and this measure failed (see Belz, *Reconstructing the Union,* ch. 9).

46. See Potter, *Lincoln and His Party;* and Harris, *With Charity for All,* 260–61.

47. *New York Times,* 24 Nov. 1864; see also *New York Times,* 27 Nov. 1864.

48. *New York Times,* 25 Dec. 1864; 6 Jan. 1865, 4; 16 Jan. 1865, 4.

49. Ibid., 1 Dec. 1864, 4; 15 Jan. 1865, 4. Michael J. McManus has reminded us that during the 1850s some Republicans had emphasized state rights as a tool to oppose the fugitive slave laws (see McManus, "Freedom and Liberty First").

50. *New York Times,* 15 Jan. 1865, and many previous issues, such as 14 July 1863, 4, or 18 Oct. 1863, 4; 27 Dec. 1864, 4; 9 Feb. 1865, 4; 29 Dec. 1864, 4. The *Times* editorial of 29 December captures the racist sentiments that would lead many whites in the post-Reconstruction period to complain of "the Negro Problem." Black leaders would protest accurately but ineffectively that the "problem" was the racist phobias of whites.

5. Slavery, War, and the Slaveholder's Mind

1. On the proslavery argument, see Jenkins, *Pro-slavery Thought;* Stanton, *Leopard's Spots;* Fredrickson, *The Black Image in the White Mind;* and Tise, *Proslavery.*

2. The most committed analyst and most talented theorist of paternalism is Eugene Genovese; see esp. his book *Roll, Jordon, Roll.*

3. *Daily Richmond Examiner,* 19 July 1861, 2; Fremantle, *Three Months in the Southern States,* 42.

4. *Semi-Weekly Richmond Enquirer,* 14 July 1863, 1.

5. See Jeffrey Brooke Allen, "Were Southern White Critics of Slavery Racists?" 171, 170, 190. Finnie, "Antislavery Movement in the Upper South before 1840," emphasizes that the antislavery movement in the Upper South was small and that many of its followers became increasingly antiblack and deportationist in outlook. The point here is not about the size of the minority, but about the fact that such views were held and not unfamiliar. One of the most thorough examinations of the wartime doubts and concerns of religious Confederates is found in Beringer et al., *Why the South Lost.* It also is true that a disproportionate number of proslavery theorists and writers were clergymen, often ministers who had come from or been educated in the North (see Tise, *Proslavery*).

6. Manumission Society of North Carolina, *Address to the People of North Carolina*; *New York Times,* 5 Apr. 1860, 5; *Proceedings of the Meeting in Charleston, S.C., May 13–15, 1845,* 6, 11, 9. For an insightful study of Helper, see Brown, *Southern Outcast.*

7. William C. Rives quoted in Sellers, "The Travail of Slavery"; Helper, *The Impending Crisis of the South,* 193, 199, 200.

8. "Benjamin Sherwood Hedrick," 13.

9. Schott, *Alexander H. Stephens of Georgia,* 61, 104; "Benjamin Sherwood Hedrick," 13. Stephens changed his position and became much more defensive after David Wilmot offered his Proviso.

10. McGuire, *Diary of a Southern Refugee,* 128; Ella Clanton Thomas and Dolly Burge quoted in Roark, *Masters without Slaves,* 89–90; Chesnut, *Diary from Dixie,* 21, 163, 435; Robert E. Lee quoted in Nolan, *Lee Considered,* 11–12.

11. Lefler and Newsome, *North Carolina,* 446; see also Butler and Watson, *The North Carolina Experience,* ch. 9.

12. Chesnut, *Diary from Dixie,* 163.

13. Lee quoted in Nolan, *Lee Considered,* 13; *Congressional Globe,* 35th Cong., 2d sess., 1859, 1243.

14. See Genovese, *The World the Slaveholders Made;* Stanton, *The Leopard's Spots;* and McKitrick, *Slavery Defended,* 34–50, 126–47. See also Freehling, *The Road to Disunion,* 2:35–36, for a differing and penetrating analysis of Fitzhugh's position.

15. Quotations from Thornton Stringfellow's *Scriptural and Statistical Views in Favor of Slavery* (1856), as reprinted in McKitrick, *Slavery Defended,* 88–89, 90, 91,

94, 95. For similar views, see Moore, *God our Refuge and Strength,* 18; and Joseph R. Wilson, *Mutual Relation of Masters and Slaves,* 11–12.

16. Hopkins, *Scriptural, Ecclesiastical, and Historical View,* 8, 48, 31, 33.

17. McGill, *Hand of God with the Black Race,* 7, 10, 16.

18. Christy, *Pulpit Politics,* 615, 621–22, v, iii.

19. Miles, *God in History,* 26; Smyth, "The War of the South Vindicated," 495, 498.

20. Elliott, *Our Cause in Harmony,* 7, 13, 9, 11, 10, 11.

21. *Staunton Vindicator,* 3 Feb. 1860, 1; Smyth, "The War of the South Vindicated," 499n; Chesnut, *Diary from Dixie,* 139, 144, 200, 433; Edmondston, *Journal of a Secesh Lady,* 141, 418.

22. Stampp, *The Peculiar Institution,* ch. 7; Savitt, *Medicine and Slavery;* Walter Johnson, *Soul by Soul;* Genovese, *Roll, Jordan, Roll;* Faust, *James Henry Hammond,* esp. ch. 5; Escott, *Slavery Remembered,* esp. ch. 2.

23. Weldon N. Edwards to Thomas Ruffin, 15 Jan. 1860, in Ruffin, *Papers,* 3:40; Paul C. Cameron to Ruffin, 10 Sept. 1860, ibid., 3:90–91; Cameron quoted in Anderson, "Paul Carrington Cameron as Planter." Cameron's emotions may have been real, but they were to evaporate as soon as his slave children showed signs of independence (see Escott, *Many Excellent People,* 120–21).

24. Edmondston, *Journal of a Secesh Lady,* 130; Chesnut, *Diary from Dixie,* 163.

25. Roark, *Masters without Slaves,* 4, 15, 74; Elliott, *Samson's Riddle.*

26. Roark, *Masters without Slaves,* 74–76; Eaton, *Jefferson Davis,* 144; *Staunton Spectator,* 7 Oct. 1862.

27. Faust, *Mothers of Invention,* 57–59; Chesnut, *Diary from Dixie,* 139, 151.

28. *Elliott and Gonzales Family Papers,* 2 Mar. 1863.

29. Roark, *Masters without Slaves,* 78–79; James Seddon to Jefferson Davis, 26 Nov. 1863, in Confederate States of America, Letters Sent by the Confederate Secretary of War to the President, roll 1, 120–35; *Jefferson Davis, Constitutionalist,* 6:120.

30. Roark, *Masters without Slaves,* 79; Myers, *Children of Pride,* 234, 301, 408. For a valuable overview of Confederate use of slave labor, see Brewer, *The Confederate Negro.*

31. Faust, *Mothers of Invention,* 54–55, 62; Edmondston, *Journal of a Secesh Lady,* 172, 142, 220, 463.

32. Tarlton, "Somerset Place and Its Restoration," 42; B. B. Hinsley to Josiah Collins III, 4 May 1863, and Geo. W. Spruill to Collins, 16 May 1863, Josiah Collins Papers.

33. *Kimberly Family: Personal Correspondence, 1862–1864,* 28 Jan. 1863; McGuire, *Diary of a Southern Refugee,* 128, 171; Myers, *Children of Pride,* 523; Faust, *Mothers of Invention,* 76–77.

34. Roark, *Masters without Slaves,* 83, 89, 84; Chesnut, *Diary from Dixie,* 433.

35. James Henley Thornwell quoted in Freehling, *The Reintegration of American History,* 65.

36. Jones, *Religious Instruction of the Negroes.*

37. Joseph R. Wilson, *Mutual Relation of Masters and Slaves,* 7, 12, 19, 10.

38. Palmer, *Discourse before the General Assembly of South Carolina,* 17, 14–15.

39. Elliott, *Our Cause in Harmony,* 11; idem, *Ezra's Dilemna,* 12–13. Bishop Elliott would later decide that it was best not to move ahead with the reform process until independence had been achieved.

40. Bell Irvin Wiley, "The Movement to Humanize the Institution of Slavery," 208–9; *Pastoral Letter from the Bishops of the Protestant Episcopal Church,* 10–11.

41. Bell Irvin Wiley, "The Movement to Humanize the Institution of Slavery," 209–10; Mohr, *On the Threshold of Freedom,* esp. 248–55 (Pierce quoted on 254). Mohr's account is very thorough and valuable.

42. Bell Irvin Wiley, "The Movement to Humanize the Institution of Slavery," 211–14.

43. "Slave Marriage Law," esp. 145, 146–47, 149, 154, 159, 160, 162.

44. Calvin H. Wiley, *Scriptural Views of National Trials,* iv–v, 31, 159, 188, 48.

45. Ibid., 177, 1–12 passim, 13, 121, 152, 159, 161.

46. Ibid., 187, 188, 189, 191.

47. Ibid., 191, 192, 194, 195, 196, 197, 199, 200.

48. Bell Irvin Wiley, "The Movement to Humanize the Institution of Slavery," 217–19.

6. Heresy, Dogma, and the Confederate Debate

1. Roark, *Masters without Slaves,* 35. For telling examples of the variety of slaveholders and the society's tolerance of all types, see Northup, *Twelve Years a Slave.*

2. Brewer, *The Confederate Negro,* 3.

3. Ibid., 7, 6.

4. Ibid., 7–8.

5. Ibid., 9–10.

6. Ibid., 13, 29, 33, 36, 37, 40, 41, 44, 57, 80–81, 98, 134–35, 142, 144, 145, 147, 151. Clarence Mohr has documented the fact that, in Georgia too, slaves were the lifeblood of industrial transformation, working in many kinds of factories and weapons and munitions plants (see Mohr, *On the Threshold of Freedom,* ch. 5).

7. Levine, *Confederate Emancipation,* 17, 19. The three petitioners from Mississippi evidently were thinking of their state's population when they commented that there were as many black Southerners as white. In the Confederacy as a whole, of course, whites outnumbered blacks.

8. Joint Resolutions of the Alabama Senate and House of Representatives, 29 Aug. 1863, in U.S. War Department, *War of the Rebellion,* ser. 4, vol. 2:767.

9. Levine, *Confederate Emancipation,* 25; Durden, *The Gray and the Black,* 30–31 (quoting the Jackson newspaper).

10. Durden, *The Gray and the Black,* 24–25, 33–34.

11. Ibid., 36, 39, 43–44.

12. Levine, *Confederate Emancipation,* 19. As Levine points out, a few cities, such as New Orleans and Mobile, allowed free black people to serve in local defense units.

13. U.S. War Department, *War of the Rebellion,* ser. 1, vol. 52, pt. 2:586–92. Cleburne's entire report is reprinted in Durden, *The Gray and the Black,* 54–63; the quoted passages are on 54–55.

14. Durden, *The Gray and the Black,* 55–56.

15. Ibid.

16. Ibid., 56–57.

17. Ibid., 58.

18. Ibid., 58–61.

19. Ibid., 65–66.

20. Nelson, *Bullets, Ballots, and Rhetoric;* Escott, *Military Necessity,* 243.

21. For descriptions of practices on the Davis plantations, see Hermann, *Joseph E. Davis;* Eaton, *Jefferson Davis;* Felicity Allen, *Jefferson Davis;* and McElroy, *Jefferson Davis.*

22. Hermann, *Joseph E. Davis,* 43, 53–58.

23. Eaton, *Jefferson Davis,* 39–41; Felicity Allen, *Jefferson Davis,* 115–16. William J. Cooper Jr. views with caution the most positive descriptions of Davis's relations with his slaves because the details were given years after the war. But he also states that the "family tradition . . . does generally fit the available evidence." It seems clear that routines on the Davis brothers' plantations departed from the normal and customary (see Cooper, *Jefferson Davis,* 236).

24. Hermann, *Joseph E. Davis,* 60 (quoting Isaiah Montgomery); Felicity Allen, *Jefferson Davis,* 103; Eaton, *Jefferson Davis,* 39–40.

25. Escott, *After Secession,* 218–19.

26. Levine, *Confederate Emancipation,* 30–32.

27. "Negro Troops and Foreign Rule," *Richmond Sentinel,* 28 Dec. 1864. For the text of Davis's address, see Durden, *The Gray and the Black,* 102–5.

28. U.S. War Department, *War of the Rebellion,* ser. 4, vol. 3:959–60.

29. Levine, *Confederate Emancipation,* 159.

30. For a discussion of the widespread interest in removing Davis, see Escott, *Military Necessity,* ch. 7.

31. Chambers, "Speech of Hon. H. C. Chambers, of Mississippi"; Levine, *Confederate Emancipation,* 42.

32. Levine, *Confederate Emancipation,* 43–44; Chambers, "Speech of Hon. H. C. Chambers, of Mississippi"; Durden, *The Gray and the Black,* 116.

33. Levine, *Confederate Emancipation,* 46; Durden, *The Gray and the Black,* 111, 119, 165–66.

34. Durden, *The Gray and the Black,* 118, 112–13, 110, 108, 124, 184; Levine, *Confederate Emancipation,* 47, 54–55.

35. Levine, *Confederate Emancipation,* 48.

36. Ibid., 57.

37. Durden, *The Gray and the Black,* 147–49; Levine, *Confederate Emancipation,* 18.

38. See Durden, *The Gray and the Black,* 135–37.

39. Ibid., 207–8.

40. For example, Confederate Senator G. A. Henry argued that after serving as soldiers, the slaves should be sent "back to the plantation. . . . The effect of discipline is to tame and subdue—to destroy individuality—to teach the danger and futility of insurrection" (Henry, "Policy of Employing Negro Troops"). Similarly, Representative H. C. Chambers, of Mississippi, argued that if the slave had to be brought into the army, "let him be used still as a slave, without promise of special reward. Let him be made to fight as he has been made to work, as a duty exacted under the authority of his owner" (Chambers, "Speech of Hon. H. C. Chambers, of Mississippi").

41. Durden, *The Gray and the Black,* 208–9.

42. Ibid., 206–7.

43. Stephenson, "The Question of Arming the Slaves," 302.

44. Durden, *The Gray and the Black,* 205; Levine, *Confederate Emancipation,* 114.

45. Durden, *The Gray and the Black,* 218; Escott, *After Secession,* 250; Escott, *Military Necessity,* 135.

46. Durden, *The Gray and the Black,* 217; Levine, *Confederate Emancipation,* 114–15.

47. Escott, *Military Necessity,* 134–36.

48. Levine, *Confederate Emancipation,* 117–18. For details on Virginia's actions, see also Durden, *The Gray and the Black,* 249–50.

49. Durden, *The Gray and the Black,* 268–83, esp. 269, 279, 274–75.

50. Langdon, "The Question of Employing the Negro as a Soldier!" The *Lynchburg Republican* similarly lamented that slave soldiers would "insist, and have the right to insist at the point of the bayonet, upon enjoying all the civil, social and political rights enjoyed by their former masters, on the ground that they had suffered equally all the dangers and responsibilities of the struggle" (quoted in *New York Times,* 10 Nov. 1864).

51. Dillard, "Independence or Slavery." Dillard studied Virginia, Georgia, and Texas, and he concludes that "independence at all costs was the watchword in Virginia and Georgia by the spring of 1865. The Confederacy as Virginians and Georgians had come to understand it meant far more than the preservation of slavery. The conservative revolution of 1861 had in fact become a true revolution" (ibid., 283). Dillard found less willingness to sacrifice slavery for independence in Texas, where the war's immediate dangers were less severe and where slave owners were still profiting.

52. Levine, *Confederate Emancipation,* 117–18, rightly stresses this point.

7. The Hampton Roads Conference

1. Durden, *The Gray and the Black,* 68–71; Donald, *Lincoln,* 523, 556.

2. Donald, *Lincoln,* 559, 556.

3. Ibid., 556–57.

4. Ibid., 557.

5. *Augusta Chronicle and Sentinel,* 7 June 1865; Campbell, *Reminiscences and Documents,* 4.

6. Harris, "The Hampton Roads Conference," 38–40.

7. Donald, *Lincoln,* 557; McPherson, *Battle Cry of Freedom,* 822; Harris, "The Hampton Roads Conference," 46.

8. Campbell, *Reminiscences and Documents,* 5–6; Stephens, *A Constitutional View,* 2:599–619. Four days after the conference, Secretary of State Seward described the meeting in a brief diplomatic dispatch to Charles Francis Adams. Seward's account was clearly designed to give Adams useful responses to foreign inquiries, which were expected in the wake of the conference. Warning that peacemakers often succeeded in ending a conflict before the advantages of a successful war could be obtained, Seward emphasized the firm positions of the administration as the war now continued. The meeting had been "calm and courteous," he said, but Lincoln had insisted on the disbandment of rebel armies and the restoration of national authority before any cessation of hostilities could be considered. Seward told Adams that Lincoln had promised liberality as chief executive but had noted that Congress controlled appropriations and the admission of representatives. As for the Thirteenth Amendment, the position Seward presented for foreign consumption was that there was "every reason to expect" that it would soon be ratified (see U.S. War Department, *War of the Rebellion,* ser. 1, vol. 46, pt. 2:471–73). R. M. T. Hunter's recollections emphasized again and again his belief that the United States had treated the South contemptibly and in a manner that would have been inconceivable to any victorious European nation. Thus, the character of Hunter's account, which seemed to be personal and idiosyncratic, differed from that of the reports of Stephens and Campbell. The only new piece of information that Hunter's account provided was the figure of $400 million for an indemnity for Southerners that Lincoln favored. That figure, as discussed below, received confirmation from Lincoln himself after he returned to Washington (see Hunter, "The Peace Commission of 1865"; Hunter's discussion of the meeting itself begins on page 173).

9. Donald, *Lincoln,* 557; Stephens, *A Constitutional View,* 2:599–608.

10. Stephens, *A Constitutional View,* 2:609–11. The figure of 200,000 individuals was a gross underestimate, since almost 500,000 slaves entered Union lines in occupied areas of the South (see chapter 3).

11. Ibid., 2:612.

12. Ibid., 2:612–14.

13. Ibid., 2:615–18.

14. Campbell, *Reminiscences and Documents,* 11–17. There are other points of agreement in the two accounts, beyond the most important ones summarized here. For example, both also include an exchange between Hunter and Lincoln in which Hunter argued that precedents allowed Lincoln to deal with the warring Confederacy, because Charles I of England had made agreements with Parliament. Lincoln replied that although he was not an expert on history, he knew that Charles I "lost his head."

15. McPherson, "Could the South Have Won?"

16. Harris, "The Hampton Roads Conference," 51. For examples of those who have ignored the issue, see Benjamin P. Thomas, *Abraham Lincoln,* 502–3; Cox, *Lincoln and Black Freedom;* and Paludan, *Presidency of Abraham Lincoln.* Cox's book also provides examples of interpretations that stretch very far in order to be maximally favorable to the idea that Lincoln was a racial egalitarian.

17. *Augusta Chronicle and Sentinel,* 7 June 1865, 2.

18. Ibid. The editor of the *Chronicle and Sentinel* began his account by reminding readers that, "We have before stated that Mr. Davis [has not] communicated . . . the truth" in regard to the Hampton Roads Conference. "Now that the aforesaid Davis has no longer power to arrest and confine persons without the benefit of habeas corpus . . . it may be as well to let the people know the truth." The editor also said that he "felt it a duty" to Alexander Stephens to give his "statement to the public as evidence that when master of his own acts, he hid no part of the truth from any one who asked for it." As noted in chapter 4, ratification of an amendment to the Constitution requires approval by three-fourths of the states.

19. It was on 22 December 1860, that Lincoln wrote privately to Stephens assuring him that there was "no cause" for fears that "a Republican administration would, *directly* or *indirectly,* interfere with their [Southerners'] slaves." It was in this personal letter that Lincoln also made the oft-quoted statement, "You think slavery is *right* and ought to be extended; while we think it is *wrong* and ought to be restricted. That I suppose is the rub." For the text of the letter, see Lincoln, *This Fiery Trial,* 86.

20. Ibid., 215.

21. Ibid., 187, 191–92.

22. Ibid., 226–27.

23. Bancroft, *The Life of William H. Seward,* 414; Van Deusen, *William Henry Seward,* 385–86.

24. See Kean, *Inside the Confederate Government,* 201–2; and Escott, *After Secession,* 223–24.

25. William A. Graham to David L. Swain, 12 Feb. 1865; Graham to Zebulon Vance, 12 Feb. 1865; Graham to Susan Washington Graham, 5 and 18 Feb. 1865; and James Orr to Governor Francis Pickens, 29 Apr. 1865, speaking of his feelings "last winter," all in Bell I. Wiley Papers. Senator Graham's letter to his wife on 5 February gives quite a full account of the conference; in that letter, he stated that he had not yet

spoken with Stephens or Campbell, so it seems highly probable that Hunter was his source.

26. Alexander H. Stephens quoted in Roark, *Masters without Slaves*, 3.

27. See ch. 6 for a fuller discussion.

28. Gideon Welles quoted in Belz, *Reconstructing the Union*, 280; Lincoln, *Collected Works*, 8:261.

29. See ch. 7, n. 8 above.

30. Lincoln, *Collected Works*, 8:260–61.

31. Ibid., 8:261; Harris, "The Hampton Roads Conference," 56.

32. Ludwell H. Johnson, "Lincoln's Solution," 583.

33. Ibid., 585–86.

34. Holt, *Political Parties and American Political Development*, 325, 330, 339–43, 350–51.

35. Ibid., 339–43, 330.

36. Lincoln, *This Fiery Trial*, 95, 119, 151–52. In regard to that proposed constitutional amendment, Seward wrote that Lincoln's role went beyond accepting such a proposal. On 26 December 1860 Seward wrote that Lincoln had suggested (through Thurlow Weed) that Seward introduce this measure before the Senate's Committee of Thirteen, which was trying to find a compromise to save the Union (see Lincoln, *Collected Works*, 4:157n).

37. Lincoln, *This Fiery Trial*, 8, 31–32, 58.

38. Lincoln, *Collected Works*, 2:501.

39. Lincoln, *This Fiery Trial*, 30, 57.

40. Ibid., 57, 152; Lincoln, *Collected Works*, 8:394.

41. Lincoln, *This Fiery Trial*, 148, 193, 225.

42. These representative quotations come from ibid., 188, 153.

43. For examples of historians' views, see Lightner, "Abraham Lincoln and the Ideal of Equality"; Boritt, "Did He Dream of a Lily-White America?" See also Lincoln, *This Fiery Trial*, 130–31; and Vorenberg, "Abraham Lincoln and the Politics of Black Colonization." Vorenberg discounts Lincoln's interest in colonization and interprets Lincoln's actions as motivated by a desire to make emancipation more palatable to the public.

44. Lincoln, *This Fiery Trial*, 29, 126.

45. Fredrickson, "A Man but Not a Brother," 56, 57.

46. Lincoln, *This Fiery Trial*, 126. This statement was made to the border states' representatives in Congress in July 1862.

47. Ibid., 184, 125. The first quotation, of course, is from the Gettysburg Address. The second is from Lincoln's reply to Horace Greeley's "Prayer of Twenty Millions," on 22 Aug. 1862.

8. 1865 and Beyond

1. The quotation, from Lincoln's Second Inaugural Address, may be found in Lincoln, *This Fiery Trial,* 220. See also Vorenberg, *Final Freedom,* 111.

2. U.S. Bureau of the Census, *Statistical History,* 25, 30, 37.

3. *Hartford Daily Courant,* 24, 11 July, 15 Aug. 1865; *Norwich Weekly Courier,* 14 Sept. 1865.

4. *Voices from Connecticut for Impartial Suffrage; Hartford Daily Courant,* 15 Aug., 15 Sept. 1865; *Norwich Weekly Courier,* 20 July 1865; *Connecticut Courant* (weekly edition of the *Hartford Courant*), 7 Oct. 1865; *Norwich Weekly Courier,* 24 Aug. 1865; *Norwich Morning Bulletin,* 16 Aug., 15 July, 9 Aug. 1865; *Hartford Daily Courant,* 16 Aug., 6 Sept., 12 Sept. 1865.

5. *Norwich Morning Bulletin,* 19 Sept. 1865; *Voices from Connecticut for Impartial Suffrage,* point 17.

6. *Hartford Daily Courant,* 15 Aug. 1865.

7. *Norwich Morning Bulletin,* 15 Sept. 1865 (reprinting an article from the *New London Star*).

8. "Prejudice," quoted in *Norwich Morning Bulletin,* 18 Sept., 4 Sept. 1865.

9. *Hartford Daily Courant,* 20 Sept., 26 Sept. 1865; *Norwich Weekly Courier,* 3 Aug., 24 Aug. 1865; *Hartford Daily Courant,* 25 Sept. 1865.

10. *Hartford Daily Courant,* 19 Aug. 1865; *Norwich Weekly Courier,* 31 Aug., 7 Sept. 1865.

11. *Norwich Morning Bulletin,* 6 Sept., 9 Sept., 23 Sept., 27 Sept. 1865.

12. Ibid., 5 Oct., 3 Oct., 6 Oct. 1865; *Hartford Daily Courant,* 3 Oct. 1865.

13. *Daily Milwaukee News,* 12 Nov. 1865.

14. Ibid., 6 July, 23 July, 11 Aug., 16 Aug., 24 Oct., 26 Oct. 1865.

15. *La Crosse Democrat,* 19 Sept., 20 Sept., 11 Oct. 1865; *Daily Milwaukee News,* 7 Sept. 1865; *La Crosse Democrat,* 6 Oct. 1865.

16. *Daily Milwaukee News,* 2 July, 3 July, 22 Oct. 1865; *La Crosse Democrat,* 2 Sept., 13 Sept. 1865; *Daily Milwaukee News,* 4 Aug., 1 Oct., 19 Oct. 1865.

17. *Daily Milwaukee News,* 22 Sept., 4 Oct. 1865; *La Crosse Democrat,* 7 Sept., 20 Sept. 1865; *Eau Clair Free Press,* 21 Sept., 5 Oct. 1865.

18. *Daily Milwaukee News,* 3 Sept. 1865 (quoting the *Janesville Gazette*); *Eau Claire Free Press,* 14 Sept., 21 Sept., 2 Nov. 1865; *Daily Milwaukee News,* 7 Sept. 1865; *La Crosse Democrat,* 12 Oct. 1865.

19. *Eau Clair Free Press,* 28 Sept. 1865.

20. *Daily Milwaukee News,* 1 Oct. 1865; *La Crosse Democrat,* 13 Sept., 6 Sept. 1865; *Daily Milwaukee News,* 11 Aug., 22 Oct. 1865; *La Crosse Democrat,* 11 Sept., 26 Sept., 12 Oct., 28 Oct. 1865.

21. *Daily Milwaukee News,* 22 Nov. 1865.

22. *St. Paul Pioneer,* 1 July, 9 Sept., 7 Sept., 26 July 1865.

23. *Mankato Weekly Record,* 7 Oct., 23 Sept. 1865; *St. Paul Pioneer,* 26 July 1865;

Mankato Weekly Record, 12 Aug., 19 Aug. 1865; *St. Paul Pioneer,* 8 July, 17 Sept. 1865.

24. *Mankato Weekly Record,* 19 Aug. 1865.

25. Ibid., 9 Sept. 1865; *Faribault Central Republican,* 9, 16 Aug., 20 Sept., 24 Oct. 1865.

26. *St. Paul Pioneer,* 21 Sept., 5 Oct. 1865.

27. *Faribault Central Republican,* 11 Oct. 1865.

28. *St. Paul Pioneer,* 13 Sept., 22 Sept., 8 Oct., 10 Oct., 22 Oct., 7 Nov. 1865.

29. *Mankato Weekly Record,* 25 Nov., 18 Nov. 1865. The vote in Colorado was 4,102 to 476.

30. Lincoln, *This Fiery Trial,* 220. As one black soldier put it, he could thank Lincoln "for what the exigencies of the times forced him to do," but this man also "censure[d] him for the non-accomplishment of the real good this accursed rebellion gave him the power to do" (Ripley, *The Black Abolitionist Papers,* 5:278).

31. McPherson, "Liberating Lincoln"; Gopnik, "Angels and Ages," 32.

32. Fehrenbacher, "Disunion and Reunion," 107; see also 114–15. For valuable and more detailed discussions, see Pressly, *Americans Interpret Their Civil War;* and Peterson, *Lincoln in American Memory.* For additional comments, see the appendix.

33. Note, for example, the wholly admiring and uncritical treatment of Lincoln in Goodwin, *Team of Rivals.* The publication of William C. Harris's balanced and thorough book, *With Charity for All,* may signal some change in this pattern.

34. Striner, *Father Abraham,* 1–2. James Oakes, in *The Radical and the Republican,* also argues that Lincoln "chose" the "strategy" of agreeing with Democrats about white supremacy in order to move "race off the table" and further emancipation. Similarly, Lincoln "was once again using racism strategically" to "make emancipation more palatable to white racists" when he lectured the black leaders on their duty to leave the United States. Oakes does acknowledge that this act was "a low point in his presidency." See McPherson, "What Did He Really Think About Race?" for a review of Oakes's book.

35. McPherson, "What Did He Really Think About Race?"; idem, "Liberating Lincoln," 8–9; idem, "Could the South Have Won?" To praise Lincoln in these articles, James McPherson roundly rejected the argument of other scholars that the slaves did much to free themselves or that events proved decisive. Contrast his arguments with this assessment by Ira Berlin: "Reducing the Emancipation Proclamation to a nullity and Lincoln to a cipher denies human agency just as personifying emancipation in a larger-than-life Great Emancipator denies the agency of the slaves and many others, and trivializes the process by which the slaves were freed. . . . Both Lincoln and the slaves played their parts in the drama of emancipation. Denying their complementary roles limits understanding of the complex interaction of human agency and events that resulted in slavery's demise" (Berlin, "Who Freed the Slaves?" 119–20). A considerable number of noted historians, from James G. Randall and Richard Current to David Donald and Allen Guelzo, have either accepted

Stephens's statement or granted that it deserves very serious consideration. The attack on Stephens's account has developed in recent decades as part of the emphasis on Lincoln as the Great Emancipator and moral exemplar. For examples of more realistic treatments of the Hampton Roads conversations, see Randall and Current, *Lincoln, the President,* 4:335; Current, *The Lincoln Nobody Knows,* 237–65, 304; Donald, *Lincoln,* 559–60; and Guelzo, *Abraham Lincoln,* 408–9. Important studies by LaWanda Cox and Phillip Paludan, both discussed in McPherson's 1994 article, make no mention of the Hampton Roads Conference, thus eliding the issue.

36. Carwardine, *Lincoln,* 216; Berwanger, "Lincoln's Constitutional Dilemma," 37; Lightner, "Abraham Lincoln and the Ideal of Equality," esp. 305, 293; Goodwin, *Team of Rivals,* 206.

37. Lincoln, *This Fiery Trial,* 131.

38. *New York Times,* 12 Dec. 1862, 2.

39. Cable, *The Negro Question,* 60.

BIBLIOGRAPHY

Archival Sources

Apprenticeship Indentures, Jackson County, Illinois. Illinois State Archives.

Collins, Josiah, Papers. North Carolina Division of Archives and History, Raleigh.

Confederate States of America. Letters Sent by the Confederate Secretary of War to the President. RG 109, Microcopy M 523. National Archives, Washington, DC.

Indentures, 1834–1881, Perry County, Illinois. Illinois State Archives.

Servitude and Emancipation Records. Illinois State Archives Online Databases. http://www.cyberdriveillinois.com/departments/archives/databases.html.

Tarlton, William S. "Somerset Place and Its Restoration." Report prepared for the Division of State Parks, North Carolina Department of Conservation and Development, 1954. North Carolina Division of Archives and History, Raleigh.

Wiley, Bell I., Papers. Special Collections. Woodruff Library, Emory University.

Newspapers and Magazines

Atlantic Monthly, 1860–65

Augusta (GA) Chronicle and Sentinel, 1865

Chicago Tribune, 1862–63

Cincinnati Daily Enquirer, 1862–64

Cincinnati Daily Gazette, 1862–63

Continental Monthly. 1862–64

Daily Milwaukee News, 1865

Daily Richmond Examiner, 1860–65

Eau Claire (WI) Free Press, 1865

Faribault (MN) Central Republican, 1865

Harper's Weekly, 1860–65

Hartford Daily Courant, 1865

La Crosse (WI) Democrat, 1865

Littell's Living Age, 1861–65

Mankato (MN) Weekly Record, 1865

New Englander, 1861–65

New York Herald, 1864–65

New York Times, 1860–65

North American Review, 1860–65
Norwich (CT) Morning Bulletin, 1865
Norwich (CT) Weekly Courier, 1865
Old Guard, A Monthly Journal; Devoted to the Principles of 1776 and 1787, 1863–65
Richmond Sentinel, 1860–65
Semi-Weekly Richmond Enquirer, 1860–65
Staunton (VA) Speculator, 1860–64
Staunton (VA) Vindicator, 1860–64
St. Paul (MN) Pioneer, 1865
Southern Presbyterian Review, 1863

Other Sources

Manumission Society of North Carolina. *An Address to the People of North Carolina on the Evils of Slavery. By The Friends of Liberty and Equality.* Greensborough: W. Swain, 1830. Documenting the American South, University Library, University of North Carolina at Chapel Hill, 2001. http://docsouth.unc.edu/nc/manumiss/menu.html.

Alfriend, Frank. "The Great Danger of the Confederacy." *Southern Literary Messenger* 37 (Jan. 1863): 39–43. Making of America Digital Library. http://quod.lib.umich.edu/m/moajrnl/browse.journals/sout.html.

———. "A Southern Republic and a Northern Democracy." *Southern Literary Messenger* 37 (May 1863): 283–90. Making of America Digital Library. http://quod.lib.umich.edu/m/moajrnl/browse.journals/sout.html.

Allen, Felicity. *Jefferson Davis: Unconquerable Heart.* Columbia: University of Missouri Press, 1999.

Allen, Jeffrey Brooke. "Were Southern White Critics of Slavery Racists? Kentucky and the Upper South, 1791–1824." *Journal of Southern History* 44 (May 1978): 169–90.

American Freedmen's Inquiry Commission. *Preliminary Report touching the Condition and Management of Emancipated Refugees; made to the Secretary of War, by The American Freedmen's Inquiry Commission, June 30, 1863.* Publication authorized by the Secretary of War. New York: J. F. Trow, 1863.

Anderson, Jean Bradley. "Paul Carrington Cameron as Planter." *Carolina Comments* 27 (Sept. 1979): 114–20.

Atkinson, Edward. *Cheap Cotton by Free Labor.* Boston: A. Williams & Co., 1861.

Bancroft, Frederic. *The Life of William H. Seward.* 2 vols. 1899. Gloucester, MA: Peter Smith, 1967.

Belz, Herman. *Reconstructing the Union: Theory and Policy during the Civil War.* Ithaca, NY: Cornell University Press for the American Historical Association, 1969.

"Benjamin Sherwood Hedrick." Vol. 10, no. 1 of *James Sprunt Historical Publica-*

tions, published by the North Carolina Historical Society, 1910. Available at http://www.archive.org/stream/jamesspruntstudi10nortuoft.

Bennett, Lerone. *Forced into Glory: Abraham Lincoln's White Dream.* Chicago: Johnston, 2000.

Beringer, Richard E., Herman Hattaway, Archer Jones, and William Still. *Why the South Lost the Civil War.* Athens: University of Georgia Press, 1986.

Berlin, Ira. "Who Freed the Slaves? Emancipation and Its Meaning." In *Union and Emancipation: Essays on Politics and Race in the Civil War Era,* edited by David W. Blight and Brooks D. Simpson, 105–22. Kent, OH: Kent State University Press, 1997.

Berlin, Ira, Barbara J. Fields, Thavolia Glymph, and Joseph P. Reidy, eds. *The Destruction of Slavery.* Freedom: A Documentary History of Emancipation, 1861–1867, ser. 1, vol. 1, edited by Ira Berlin. Cambridge: Cambridge University Press, 1985.

Berlin, Ira, Thavolia Glymph, Steven F. Miller, and Joseph P. Reidy, eds. *The Wartime Genesis of Free Labor: The Lower South.* Freedom: A Documentary History of Emancipation, 1861–1867, ser. 1, vol. 3, edited by Ira Berlin. Cambridge: Cambridge University Press, 1990.

Berlin, Ira, Steven F. Miller, Joseph P. Reidy, and Leslie S. Rowland, eds. *The Wartime Genesis of Free Labor: The Upper South.* Freedom: A Documentary History of Emancipation, 1861–1867, ser. 1, vol. 2, edited by Ira Berlin. Cambridge: Cambridge University Press, 1993.

Berry, Stephen. *House of Abraham: Lincoln and the Todds, a Family Divided by War.* Boston: Houghton Mifflin, 2007.

Berwanger, Eugene H. "Lincoln's Constitutional Dilemma: Emancipation and Black Suffrage." *Journal of the Abraham Lincoln Association* 5 (1983): 25–38.

Blair, Frank P. *Destiny of the Races of this Continent: An address delivered before the Mercantile Library Association of Boston, Massachusetts; on the 26th of January, 1859.* Washington, DC: Buell & Blanchard, 1859.

Blair, Montgomery. *Letter of Hon. Montgomery Blair, Postmaster General, to the Meeting held at the Cooper Institute, New York, March 6, 1862.* Washington, DC: Printed at the Congressional Globe Office, 1862. Library of Congress, Rare Book and Special Collections Division, African American Pamphlet Collection. http://memory.loc.gov/ammem/aapchtml/rbaapcbibTitles02.html.

———. *Speech of the Hon. Montgomery Blair (Postmaster General), on the Revolutionary Schemes of the Ultra Abolitionists, and in Defence of the Policy of the President, delivered at the Unconditional Union Meeting held at Rockville, Montgomery Co., Maryland, on Saturday, October 3, 1863.* New York: D. W. Lee, 1863.

Boritt, Gabor S. "Did He Dream of a Lily-White America?" In *The Lincoln Enigma: The Changing Faces of an American Icon,* 1–19. New York: Oxford University Press, 2001.

———. *The Gettysburg Gospel.* New York: Simon & Schuster, 2007.

Brace, Charles Loring. *The Races of the Old World: A Manual of Ethnology.* New York: C. Scribner, 1863.

Brewer, James H. *The Confederate Negro: Virginia's Craftsmen and Military Laborers, 1861–1865.* Durham, NC: Duke University Press, 1969.

Bridges, Roger D. "The Illinois Black Codes." *Illinois History Teacher* 3, no. 2 (1996): 2–12. http://www.lib.niu.edu/ipo/1996/iht329602.html.

Brown, David. *Southern Outcast: Hinton Rowan Helper and the Impending Crisis of the South.* Baton Rouge: Louisiana State University Press, 2006.

Butler, Lindley S., and Alan D. Watson. *The North Carolina Experience: An Interpretive and Documentary History.* Chapel Hill: University of North Carolina Press, 1984.

Cable, George Washington. *The Negro Question: A Selection of Writings on Civil Rights in the South.* Edited by Arlin Turner. New York: Doubleday, 1958.

Campbell, John Archibald. *Reminiscences and Documents relating to the Civil War During the Year 1865.* Baltimore: J. Murphy & Co., 1887.

Carwardine, Richard. *Lincoln: A Life of Purpose and Power.* New York: Knopf, 2006.

Chambers, H. C. "Speech of Hon. H. C. Chambers, of Mississippi, in the CSA House, November 10, 1864." In *Confederate Imprints, 1861–1865,* reel 93.

Cheever, Rev. George B. *Rights of the coloured race to citizenship and representation; and the guilt and consequences of legislation against them: a discourse delivered in the Hall of Representatives of the United States, in Washington, D.C., May 29, 1864.* New York: Francis & Loutrel, printers ... , 1864. Library of Congress, Rare Book and Special Collections Division, African American Pamphlet Collection. http://memory.loc.gov/ammem/aapchtml/rbaapcbibTitles04.html.

Chesnut, Mary Boykin. *Diary from Dixie.* Edited by Ben Ames Williams. Boston: Houghton Mifflin, 1961.

Christy, David. *Pulpit Politics; or, Ecclesiastical Legislation on Slavery, in its Disturbing Influences on the American Union.* 1862. New York: Negro Universities Press, 1969.

Cochin, Augustin. *The Results of Emancipation.* Translated by Mary L. Booth. 2d ed. Boston: Walker, Wise, & Co., 1863.

———. *The Results of Slavery.* Translated by Mary L. Booth. Boston: Walker, Wise, & Co., 1863.

Commager, Henry Steele, ed. *Documents of American History.* 2 vols. in 1. New York: Appleton-Century-Crofts, 1963.

Confederate Imprints, 1861–1865 [microform]: Based on Marjorie Lyle Crandall, Confederate Imprints, a check list, 1955 [and] Richard B. Harwell, More Confederate Imprints, 1957. 143 reels. New Haven, CT: Research Publications, 1974.

Cooper, William J. *Jefferson Davis: American.* New York: Knopf, 2000.

Cox, LaWanda C. F. *Lincoln and Black Freedom: A Study in Presidential Leadership.* Columbia: University of South Carolina Press, 1981.

Croly, David Goodman, and George Wakeman. *Miscegenation: The Theory of the Blending of the Races, Applied to the American White Man and Negro.* New York: H. Dexter, Hamilton & Co., 1964.

Current, Richard N. *The Lincoln Nobody Knows.* 1958. Westport, CT: Greenwood, 1980.

Dargan, E. S. "Speech of E. S. Dargan, Secession Convention of Alabama, January 11, 1861." AmericanCivilWar.com. http://www.americancivilwar.com/documents/dargan_speech.html.

Davis, Henry Winter. *Speeches and Addresses delivered in the Congress of the United States and on Several Public Occasions by Henry Winter Davis.* New York: Harper & Brothers, 1867.

Davis, Jefferson. *Jefferson Davis, Constitutionalist: His Letters, Papers, and Speeches.* Edited by Dunbar Rowland. 10 vols. New York: J. J. Little & Ives for Mississippi Department of Archives and History, 1923.

"Declarations of Causes of Seceding States: Civil War Georgia." AmericanCivilWar.com. http://www.americancivilwar.com/documents/causes_georgia.html.

"Declarations of Causes of Seceding States: Civil War Mississippi." AmericanCivilWar.com. http://www.americancivilwar.com/documents/causes_mississippi.html.

"Declarations of Causes of Seceding States: Civil War South Carolina." AmericanCivilWar.com. http://www.americancivilwar.com/documents/causes_south_carolina.html.

"Declarations of Causes of Seceding States: Texas." AmericanCivilWar.com. http://www.americancivilwar.com/documents/causes_texas.html.

Dew, Charles B. *Apostles of Disunion: Southern Secession Commissioners and the Causes of the Civil War.* Charlottesville: University Press of Virginia, 2001.

Dillard, Philip D. "Independence or Slavery: The Confederate Debate over Arming the Slaves." PhD diss., Rice University, 1999.

Donald, David Herbert. *Charles Sumner and the Coming of the Civil War.* New York: Knopf, 1960.

———. *Charles Sumner and the Rights of Man.* New York: Knopf, 1970.

———. *Lincoln.* New York: Simon & Schuster, 1995.

Douglass, Frederick. *Douglass' Monthly* [1859–1863]. New York: Negro Universities Press, 1969.

———. "Present and Future of the Colored Race." *Douglass' Monthly,* June 1863.

Dreher, Daniel I. *A Sermon Delivered by the Rev. Daniel I. Dreher, Pastor of St. James' Church, Concord, N.C., June 13, 1861: Day of Humiliation and Prayer, as per Appointment of the President of the Confederate States of America.* Salisbury: Printed at the Watchman Office, 1861. Documenting the American South. 2000. http://docsouth.unc.edu/imls/dreher/menu.html.

Durden, Robert F. *The Gray and the Black: The Confederate Debate on Emancipation.* Baton Rouge: Louisiana State University Press, 1972.

Eaton, Clement. *Jefferson Davis.* New York: Free Press, 1977.

"Editor's Table." *Southern Literary Messenger* 37 (Mar. 1863): 180–91. Making of America Digital Library. http://quod.lib.umich.edu/m/moajrnl/browse.journals/sout.html.

Edmondston, Catherine Ann. *"Journal of a Secesh Lady": The Diary of Catherine Ann Devereux Edmondston, 1860–1866.* Edited by Beth G. Crabtree and James W. Patton. Raleigh, NC: Division of Archives and History, Department of Cultural Resources, 1979.

Elliott, Stephen. *Ezra's Dilemna [sic]. A Sermon Preached in Christ Church, Savannah, on Friday, August 21st, 1863, being the Day of Humiliation, Fasting and Prayer, Appointed by the President of the Confederate States.* Savannah: Power Press of George M. Nichols, 1863. Documenting the American South. 2000. http://docsouth.unc.edu/imls/elliottezra/menu.html.

———. *Funeral Services at the Burial of the Right Rev. Leonidas Polk, D. D. Together with the Sermon Delivered in St. Paul's Church, Augusta, Ga., on June 29, 1864: Being the Feast of St. Peter the Apostle.* Columbia: Printed by Evans & Cogswell, 1864. Documenting the American South. 1999. http://docsouth.unc.edu/imls/elliotts2/menu.html.

———. *New Wine not to be Put into Old Bottles. A Sermon Preached in Christ Church, Savannah, on Friday, February 28th, 1862, Being the Day of Humiliation, Fasting, and Prayer, Appointed by the President of the Confederate States.* Savannah: Steam Power Press of John M. Cooper, 1862. Documenting the American South. 2000. http://docsouth.unc.edu/imls/elliott/menu.html.

———. *Our Cause in Harmony with the Purposes of God in Christ Jesus. A Sermon Preached in Christ Church, Savannah, on Thursday, September 18th, 1862, Being the Day Set Forth by the President of the Confederate States, as a Day of Prayer and Thanksgiving, for our Manifold Victories, and Especially for the Fields of Manassas and Richmond, Ky.* Savannah: Power Press of John M. Cooper, 1862. Documenting the American South. 2000. http://docsouth.unc.edu/imls/elliott5/menu.html.

———. *"Samson's Riddle." A Sermon Preached in Christ Church, Savannah, on Friday, March 27th, 1863, Being the Day of Humiliation, Fasting and Prayer, Appointed by the President of the Confederate States.* Macon: Burke, Boykin, 1863. Documenting the American South. 2000. http://docsouth.unc.edu/imls/samson/menu.html.

———. *Vain is the Help of Man. A Sermon Preached in Christ Church, Savannah, on Thursday, September 15, 1864, Being the Day of Fasting, Humiliation, and Prayer, Appointed by the Governor of the State of Georgia.* Macon: Burke, Boykin, 1864. Documenting the American South. 1999. http://docsouth.unc.edu/imls/elliotts/menu.html.

Elliott and Gonzales Family Papers: Personal Correspondence, 1861–1865. Electronic Edition. Documenting the American South. 2000. http://docsouth.unc.edu/imls/gonzales/gonzales.html.

Ellis, John W. *Speech of Hon. John W. Ellis, Delivered before the Democratic State Convention, in Raleigh, March 9, 1860*. Raleigh: "Standard" Office Print, 1860. Documenting the American South. 2002. http://docsouth.unc.edu/nc/ellis/menu.html.

Escott, Paul D. *After Secession: Jefferson Davis and the Failure of Confederate Nationalism*. Baton Rouge: Louisiana State University Press, 1978.

———. *Many Excellent People: Power and Privilege in North Carolina, 1850–1900*. Chapel Hill: University of North Carolina Press, 1985.

———. *Military Necessity: Civil-Military Relations in the Confederacy*. Westport, CT: Praeger Security International, 2006.

———. *Slavery Remembered: A Record of Twentieth-Century Slave Narratives*. Chapel Hill: University of North Carolina Press, 1978.

Facts Concerning the Freedmen. Their Capacity and Their Destiny. Collected and published by the Emancipation League. Boston: Press of Commercial Printing House, 1863. Library of Congress, Rare Book and Special Collections Division, African American Pamphlet Collection. http://memory.loc.gov/ammem/aapchtml/rbaapcbibTitles02.html.

Faust, Drew Gilpin. *James Henry Hammond and the Old South: A Design for Mastery*. Baton Rouge: Louisiana State University Press, 1982.

———. *Mothers of Invention: Women of the Slaveholding South in the American Civil War*. Chapel Hill: University of North Carolina Press, 1996.

Fehrenbacher, Don E. "Disunion and Reunion." In *The Reconstruction of American History*, edited by John Higham, 98–118. London: Hutchinson, 1962.

Finkelman, Paul, ed. *Dred Scott v. Sandford: A Brief History with Documents*. Boston: Bedford Books, 1997.

———. "Evading the Ordinance: The Persistence of Bondage in Indiana and Illinois." *Journal of the Early Republic* 9 (Spring 1989): 21–51.

———. "Slavery and the Northwest Ordinance: A Study in Ambiguity." *Journal of the Early Republic* 6 (Winter 1986): 343–70.

Finnie, Gordon E. "The Antislavery Movement in the Upper South before 1840." *Journal of Southern History* 35 (Aug. 1969): 319–42.

Fisher, Sidney. *The Laws of Race, as connected with slavery*. Philadelphia: W. P. Hazard, 1860.

Fitzhugh, George. "The Revolutions of 1776 and 1861 Contrasted." *Southern Literary Messenger* 37 (Dec. 1863): 718–26. Making of America Digital Library. http://quod.lib.umich.edu/m/moajrnl/browse.journals/sout.html.

Foner, Eric. *Free Soil, Free Labor, Free Men: The Ideology of the Republican Party before the Civil War*. New York: Oxford University Press, 1970.

[Forman, Jacob Gilbert]. *The Western Sanitary Commission; a sketch of its origin, history, labors for the sick and wounded of the Western armies, and aid given to freedmen and Union refugees, with incidents of hospital life.* St. Louis: R. P. Studley & Co. for the Mississippi Valley Sanitary Fair, 1864.

Fredrickson, George M. *The Black Image in the White Mind: The Debate on Afro-American Character and Destiny, 1817–1914.* New York: Harper & Row, 1971.

———. "A Man but Not a Brother." *Journal of Southern History* 41 (Feb. 1975): 39–58.

Freehling, William W. *Prelude to Civil War: The Nullification Controversy in South Carolina, 1816–1836.* New York: Harper & Row, 1966.

———. *The Reintegration of American History: Slavery and the Civil War.* New York: Oxford University Press, 1994.

———. *The Road to Disunion.* 2 vols. New York: Oxford University Press, 1990–2007.

Fremantle, Arthur James Lyon. *Three Months in the Southern States: April, June, 1863.* Mobile: S. H. Goetzel, 1864. Documenting the American South. 2000. http://docsouth.unc.edu/imls/fremantle/menu.html.

Genovese, Eugene D. *Roll, Jordan, Roll: The World the Slaves Made.* 1974. New York: Vintage, 1976.

———. *The World the Slaveholders Made: Two Essays in Interpretation.* 1969. New York: Vintage, 1971.

Gerteis, Louis S. *From Contraband to Freedman: Federal Policy toward Southern Blacks, 1861–1865.* Westport, CT: Greenwood, 1973.

Gienapp, William E. *The Origins of the Republican Party, 1852–1856.* New York: Oxford University Press, 1987.

Goodwin, Doris Kearns. *Team of Rivals: The Political Genius of Abraham Lincoln.* New York: Simon & Schuster, 2005.

Gopnik, Adam. "Angels and Ages: Lincoln's Language and Its Legacy." *New Yorker,* 28 May 2007, 30–37.

Greenberg, Kenneth S. *Masters and Statesmen: The Political Culture of American Slavery.* Baltimore: Johns Hopkins University Press, 1985.

Guelzo, Allen. *Abraham Lincoln: Redeemer President.* Grand Rapids, MI: W. B. Eerdmans, 1999.

———. "Defending Emancipation." *Civil War History* 48, no. 4 (2002): 313–37.

Hall, Rev. William A. *The Historic Significance of the Southern Revolution. A Lecture Delivered by Invitation in Petersburg, Va., March 14th and April 29th, 1864. And in Richmond, Va., April 7th and April 21st, 1864.* Petersburg: Printed by A. F. Crutchfield, 1864. Documenting the American South. 2000. http://docsouth.unc.edu/imls/hall/menu.html.

Harding, Vincent. *There Is a River: The Black Struggle for Freedom in America.* New York: Harcourt, Brace, Jovanovich, 1981.

Harris, William C. "The Hampton Roads Conference: A Final Test of Lincoln's

Presidential Leadership." *Journal of the Abraham Lincoln Association* 21 (Winter 2000): 31–61.

———. *With Charity for All: Lincoln and the Restoration of the Union.* Lexington: University Press of Kentucky, 1997.

Helper, Hinton Rowan. *The Impending Crisis of the South: How to Meet It.* 1857. New York: Collier Books, 1963.

Henry, G. A. "Policy of Employing Negro Troops," 4 Jan. 1865. In *Confederate Imprints,* reel 93.

Hepworth, George H. *The Whip, Hoe, and Sword: or, The Gulf-Department in '63.* Boston: Walker, Wise, & Co., 1864.

Hermann, Janet Sharp. *Joseph E. Davis: Pioneer Patriarch.* Jackson: University Press of Mississippi, 1990.

Hesseltine, William B. *Lincoln's Plan of Reconstruction.* Tuscaloosa, AL: Confederate, 1960.

Hofstader, Richard. *The American Political Tradition and the Men Who Made It.* New York: Knopf, 1948.

Holt, Michael F. *Political Parties and American Political Development: From the Age of Jackson to the Age of Lincoln.* Baton Rouge: Louisiana State University Press, 1992.

Hopkins, John Henry. *A Scriptural, Ecclesiastical, and Historical View of Slavery, from the days of the patriarchy Abraham, to the nineteenth century. Addressed to the Right Rev. Alonzo Potter.* New York: W. I. Pooley & Co., 1864.

Hunter, R. M. T. "The Peace Commission of 1865." *Southern Historical Society Papers* 3 (Jan.–June 1877): 168–76.

Hyman, Harold M. "Johnson, Stanton, and Grant: A Reconsideration of the Army's Role in the Events Leading to Impeachment." *American Historical Review* 66 (Oct. 1960): 85–100.

Illinois Periodicals Online. http://www.lib.niu.edu/perlist.html.

Jeffery, A. "European Immigration and New England Puritanism." *Southern Literary Messenger* 37 (Aug. 1863): 463–72. Making of America Digital Library. http://quod.lib.umich.edu/m/moajrnl/browse.journals/sout.html.

Jenkins, William Sumner. *Pro-slavery Thought in the Old South.* Chapel Hill: University of North Carolina Press, 1935.

Johnson, Donald Bruce, comp. *National Party Platforms.* 2 vols. Urbana: University of Illinois Press, 1978.

Johnson, Ludwell H. "Lincoln's Solution to the Problem of Peace Terms, 1864–1865." *Journal of Southern History* 34 (Nov. 1968): 576–86.

Johnson, Michael P. *Toward a Patriarchal Republic: The Secession of Georgia.* Baton Rouge: Louisiana State University Press, 1977.

Johnson, Walter. *Soul by Soul: Life inside the Antebellum Slave Market.* Cambridge: Harvard University Press, 1999.

Jones, Rev. Charles Colcock. *Religious Instruction of the Negroes. An Address delivered before the General Assembly of the Presbyterian Church, at Augusta, Ga., December 10, 1861.* Published by Order of the General Assembly, 1862. Samuel J. May Anti-Slavery Collection, Cornell University Library. 2006. http://dlxs.library.cornell.edu/m/mayantislavery/browse_J.html.

Kaplan, Sidney. "The Miscegenation Issue in the Election of 1864." *Journal of Negro History* 34 (July 1949): 274–343.

Kean, Robert Garlic Hill. *Inside the Confederate Government: The Diary of Robert Garlick Hill Kean, Head of the Bureau of War.* Edited by Edward Younger. New York: Oxford University Press, 1957.

Kennan, George F. *American Diplomacy.* Exp. ed. Chicago: University of Chicago Press, 1984.

Kimberly Family: Personal Correspondence, 1862–1864. Electronic Edition. Documenting the American South. 2000. http://docsouth.unc.edu/imls/kimberly/menu.html.

Kirke, Edmund [J. R. Gilmore]. *Among the Pines: or, South in Secession-time.* New York: J. R. Gilmore, 1862.

Langdon, C. C. "The Question of Employing the Negro as a Soldier! The impolicy and impracticability of the proposed measure discussed." In *Confederate Imprints,* reel 93.

Lefler, Hugh Talmage, and Albert Ray Newsome. *North Carolina: The History of a Southern State.* 3rd ed. Chapel Hill: University of North Carolina Press, 1973.

Levine, Bruce C. *Confederate Emancipation: Southern Plans to Free and Arm Slaves during the Civil War.* New York: Oxford University Press, 2005.

Lightner, David. "Abraham Lincoln and the Ideal of Equality." *Journal of the Illinois State Historical Society* 75 (Winter 1982): 289–308.

Lincoln, Abraham. *The Collected Works of Abraham Lincoln.* Edited by Roy P. Basler. 9 vols. New Brunswick, NJ: Rutgers University Press, 1953.

———. *This Fiery Trial: The Speeches and Writings of Abraham Lincoln.* Edited by William E. Gienapp. New York: Oxford University Press, 2002.

Manning, Chandra. *What This Cruel War Was Over: Soldiers, Slavery, and the Civil War.* 2007. New York: Vintage, 2008.

Masur, Kate. "'A Rare Phenomenon of Philological Vegetation': The Word 'Contraband' and the Meanings of Emancipation in the United States." *Journal of American History* 93 (Mar. 2007): 1050–84.

McCrary, Peyton. *Abraham Lincoln and Reconstruction: The Louisiana Experiment.* Princeton, NJ: Princeton University Press, 1978.

McElroy, Robert McNutt. *Jefferson Davis: The Unreal and the Real.* New York: Harper & Brothers, 1937.

McGill, Alexander T. *The Hand of God with the Black Race: A Discourse Delivered Before the Pennsylvania Colonization Society.* Philadelphia: W. F. Geddes, Printer, 1862. Library of Congress, Rare Book and Special Collections Division,

African American Pamphlet Collection. http://memory.loc.gov/ammem/aapchtml/rbaapcbibTitles02.html.

McGuire, Judith W. *Diary of a Southern Refugee during the War, by a Lady of Virginia.* 1867. Lincoln: University of Nebraska Press, 1995.

McKaye, James. *The Mastership and its Fruits: The Emancipated Slave face to face with his Old Master; a Supplemental Report to Hon. Edwin M. Stanton, Secretary of War.* New York: Wm. C. Bryant & Co., 1864.

McKitrick, Eric L., ed. *Slavery Defended: The Views of the Old South.* Englewood Cliffs, NJ: Prentice-Hall, 1963.

McManus, Michael J. "'Freedom and Liberty First, and the Union Afterwards': State Rights and the Wisconsin Republican Party, 1854–1861." In *Union and Emancipation: Essays on Politics and Race in the Civil War Era,* edited by David W. Blight and Brooks D. Simpson, 29–56. Kent, OH: Kent State University Press, 1997.

McPherson, James M. *Battle Cry of Freedom: The Civil War Era.* New York: Oxford University Press, 1988.

———. "Could the South Have Won?" *New York Review of Books,* 13 June 2002, 24.

———. "Liberating Lincoln." *New York Review of Books,* 21 Apr. 1994, 7.

———. *The Negro's Civil War: How American Negroes Felt and Acted during the War for the Union.* New York: Pantheon, 1965.

———. *Ordeal by Fire: The Civil War and Reconstruction.* New York: Knopf, 1982.

———. *The Struggle for Equality: Abolitionists and the Negro in the Civil War and Reconstruction.* Princeton, NJ: Princeton University Press, 1964.

———. "What Did He Really Think About Race?" Review of *The Radical and the Republican: Frederick Douglass, Abraham Lincoln, and the Triumph of Antislavery Politics,* by James Oakes. *New York Review of Books,* 29 March 2007.

Miles, James Warley. *God in History, A Discourse Delivered before the Graduating Class of the College of Charleston on Sunday Evening, March 29, 1863.* Charleston: Steam-power Press of Evans & Cogswell, 1863. Documenting the American South. 1999. http://docsouth.unc.edu/imls/miles/menu.html.

Miscegenation Indorsed by the Republican Party. Campaign Document, no. 11. [New York?: N.p., 1864?]. Library of Congress, Rare Book and Special Collections Division, African American Pamphlet Collection. http://memory.loc.gov/ammem/aapchtml/rbaapcbibTitles03.html.

M'Kim, J. Miller. *The Freedmen of South Carolina. An Address Delivered . . . July 9th 1862 . . . .* Philadelphia: W. P. Hazard, 1862. Library of Congress, Rare Book and Special Collections Division, African American Pamphlet Collection. http://memory.loc.gov/ammem/aapchtml/rbaapcbibTitles02.html.

Mohr, Clarence L. *On the Threshold of Freedom: Masters and Slaves in Civil War Georgia.* Baton Rouge: Louisiana State University Press, 2001.

Moore, T. V. *God our Refuge and Strength in this War. A Discourse Before the Congregations of the First and Second Presbyterian Churches, on the Day of Humili-*

ation, Fasting and Prayer, Appointed by President Davis, Friday, Nov. 15, 1861. Richmond: W. Hargrave White, 1861. Documenting the American South. 1999. http://docsouth.unc.edu/imls/mooretv/menu.html.

Myers, Robert Manson. *The Children of Pride: A True Story of Georgia and the Civil War.* New Haven, CT: Yale University Press, 1972.

Neely, Mark E. *The Last Best Hope of Earth: Abraham Lincoln and the Promise of America.* Cambridge: Harvard University Press, 1993.

Nelson, Larry E. *Bullets, Ballots, and Rhetoric: Confederate Policy for the United States Presidential Contest of 1864.* University: University of Alabama Press, 1980.

Nolan, Alan T. *Lee Considered: General Robert E. Lee and Civil War History.* Chapel Hill: University of North Carolina Press, 1991.

Northup, Solomon. *Twelve Years a Slave.* Edited by Sue Eakin and Joseph Logsdon. Baton Rouge: Louisiana State University Press, 1968.

Oakes, James. *The Radical and the Republican: Frederick Douglass, Abraham Lincoln, and the Triumph of Antislavery Politics.* New York: Norton, 2007.

Oates, Stephen. *Abraham Lincoln, the Man behind the Myths.* New York: Harper & Row, 1984.

———. *Our Fiery Trial: Abraham Lincoln, John Brown, and the Civil War Era.* Amherst: University of Massachusetts Press, 1979.

"Ordinances of Secession: 13 Confederate States of America." AmericanCivilWar.com. http://www.americancivilwar.com/documents/ordinance_secession.html.

Owen, Robert Dale. *The Wrong of Slavery and the Right of Emancipation and the Future of the African Race in the United States.* Philadelphia: J. B. Lippincott & Co., 1864.

Palmer, Benjamin Morgan. *A Discourse before the General Assembly of South Carolina, on December 10, 1863, Appointed by the Legislature as a Day of Fasting, Humiliation, and Prayer.* Columbia: Charles P. Pelham, State Printer, 1864. Documenting the American South. 2000. http://docsouth.unc.edu/imls/palmdisc/menu.html.

Paludan, Phillip S. *The Presidency of Abraham Lincoln.* Lawrence: University Press of Kansas, 1994.

Pastoral Letter from the Bishops of the Protestant Episcopal Church to the Clergy and Laity of the Church in the Confederate States of America, Delivered before the General Council, in St. Paul's Church, Augusta, Saturday, Nov. 22d, 1862. Augusta: Steam Power Press Chronicle & Sentinel, 1862. Documenting the American South. 1999. http://docsouth.unc.edu/imls/pastoral/menu.html.

Perman, Michael. *Emancipation and Reconstruction: 1862–1879.* Arlington Heights, IL: Harlan Davidson, 1987.

Peterson, Merrill. *Lincoln in American Memory.* New York: Oxford University Press, 1994.

Phillips, Wendell. *The Immediate Issue: A speech of Wendell Phillips at the annual meeting of the Massachusetts Anti-Slavery Society at Boston*. Library of Congress, Rare Book and Special Collections Division, African American Pamphlet Collection. http://memory.loc.gov/ammem/aapchtml/rbaapcbibTitles02.html.

———. "The State of the Country." In *Speeches, Lectures, and Letters*. Boston: Lee & Shepard, 1862. Making of America Digital Library. 2005. http://quod.lib.umich.edu/cgi/t/text/text-idx?c=moa;idno=ABT7101.

Pierce, George F. *The Word of God a Nation's Life. A Sermon Preached before the Bible Convention of the Confederate States, Augusta, Georgia, March 19th, 1862*. Augusta: Printed at the Office of the Constitutionalist, 1862. Documenting the American South. 1999. http://docsouth.unc.edu/imls/pierce/menu.html.

Potter, David M. *Lincoln and His Party in the Secession Crisis*. New Haven, CT: Yale University Press, 1942.

Powell, William S., ed. *Dictionary of North Carolina Biography*. 6 vols. Chapel Hill: University of North Carolina Press, 1979–96.

Pressly, Thomas. *Americans Interpret Their Civil War*. New York: Free Press, 1965.

Proceedings of the Meeting in Charleston, S.C., May 13–15, 1845, on the Religious Instruction of the Negroes . . . . Charleston: Printed by B. Jenkins, 1845. Library of Congress, Rare Book and Special Collections Division, African American Pamphlet Collection. http://memory.loc.gov/ammem/aapchtml/rbaapcbibTitles03.html.

Putnam, Mary Lowell. *Record of an Obscure Man*. Boston: Ticknor & Fields, 1861.

Quarles, Benjamin. *Lincoln and the Negro*. New York: Oxford University Press, 1962.

Rafuse, Ethan Sepp. *McClellan's War: The Failure of Moderation in the Struggle for the Union*. Bloomington: Indiana University Press, 2005.

Ranck, James Byrne. *Albert Gallatin Brown: Radical Southern Nationalist*. 1937. Philadelphia: Porcupine, 1974.

Randall, James G., and Richard N. Current. *Lincoln, the President*. Vol. 4, *Last Full Measure*. New York: Dodd, Mead, 1955.

Ripley, C. Peter, ed. *The Black Abolitionist Papers*. 5 vols. Chapel Hill: University of North Carolina Press, 1985–92.

Roark, James L. *Masters without Slaves: Southern Planters in the Civil War and Reconstruction*. New York: Norton, 1977.

Rorabaugh, W. J. *The Craft Apprentice: From Franklin to the Machine Age in America*. New York: Oxford University Press, 1986.

Rose, Willie Lee. *Rehearsal for Reconstruction: The Port Royal Experiment*. Indianapolis: Bobbs-Merrill, 1964.

Ruffin, Thomas. *The Papers of Thomas Ruffin*. Edited by J. G. de Roulhac Hamilton. 4 vols. Raleigh: Edwards & Broughton, 1918–20.

Savitt, Todd Lee. *Medicine and Slavery: The Diseases and Health Care of Blacks in Antebellum Virginia*. Urbana: University of Illinois Press, 1978.

Schott, Thomas E. *Alexander H. Stephens of Georgia*. Baton Rouge: Louisiana State University Press, 1988.

Schultz, Ronald. “Printers’ Devils: The Decline of Apprenticeship in America.” Review of *The Craft Apprentice From Franklin to the Machine Age in America,* by W. J. Rorabaugh. *Reviews in American History* 15 (June 1987): 226–31.

Scott, Eben Greenough. *Reconstruction during the Civil War in the United States of America.* Boston: Houghton Mifflin & Co., 1895.

Sellers, Charles Grier, ed. *The Southerner as American.* Chapel Hill: University of North Carolina Press, 1960.

———. “The Travail of Slavery.” In *The Southerner as American,* edited by Charles Grier Sellars. Chapel Hill: University of North Carolina Press, 1960.

Seward, William H. *The Works of William H. Seward.* Edited by George E. Baker. Boston: Houghton Mifflin, 1890.

Sewell, William Grant. *The Ordeal of Free Labor in the British West Indies.* New York: Harper & Brothers, 1861.

Silbey, Joel H. *A Respectable Minority: The Democratic Party in the Civil War Era, 1860–1868.* New York: Norton, 1977.

“Slave Marriage Law.” *Southern Presbyterian Review* 16 (Oct. 1863): 145–62.

Sledd, Robert Newton. *A Sermon Delivered in the Market Street, M. E. Church, Petersburg, Va.: Before the Confederate Cadets, on the Occasion of their Departure for the Seat of War, Sunday, Sept. 22d, 1861.* Petersburg: A. F. Crutchfield & Co., 1861. Documenting the American South. 1999. http://docsouth.unc.edu/imls/sledd/menu.html.

Smith, Elbert B. *Francis Preston Blair.* New York: Free Press, 1980.

Smyth, Rev. Thomas. “The War of the South Vindicated,” *Southern Presbyterian Review* 15 (Apr. 1863): 479–514.

Stampp, Kenneth M. *The Peculiar Institution: Slavery in the Ante-bellum South.* New York: Knopf, 1956.

Stanton, William Ragan. *The Leopard’s Spots: Scientific Attitudes toward Race in America, 1815–59.* Chicago: University of Chicago Press, 1960.

Stephens, Alexander H. *A Constitutional View of the Late War between the States: Its Causes, Character, Conduct, and Results: Presented in a Series of Colloquies at Liberty Hall.* 2 vols. Chicago: Zeigler, McCurdy & Co., 1868 (vol. 1); Philadelphia: National, 1870 (vol. 2).

Stephenson, N. W. “The Question of Arming the Slaves.” *American Historical Review* 18 (Jan. 1913): 295–308.

Strickland, Arvarh E. “The Illinois Background of Lincoln’s Attitude toward Slavery and the Negro.” *Journal of the Illinois State Historical Society* 56 (Autumn 1963): 474–94.

Striner, Richard. *Father Abraham: Lincoln’s Relentless Struggle to End Slavery.* New York: Oxford University Press, 2006.

Thomas, Benjamin P. *Abraham Lincoln: A Biography.* New York: Knopf, 1952.

Thomas, Benjamin P., and Harold M. Hyman. *Stanton: The Life and Times of Lincoln’s Secretary of War.* New York: Knopf, 1962.

Thomas, Emory M. *The Confederacy as a Revolutionary Experience.* Englewood Cliffs, NJ: Prentice-Hall, 1970.

———. *The Confederate Nation, 1861–1865.* New York: Harper & Row, 1979.

Thornwell, James Henley. *The State of the Country: An Article Republished from the Southern Presbyterian Review.* Columbia: Southern Guardian, Steam-Power Press, 1861. Documenting the American South. http://docsouth.unc.edu/imls/thornwel1/menu.html.

Tise, Larry E. *Proslavery: A History of the Defense of Slavery in America, 1701–1840.* Athens: University of Georgia Press, 1987.

Trefousse, Hans Louis. *The Radical Republicans: Lincoln's Vanguard for Racial Justice.* New York: Knopf, 1968.

"True Basis of Political Prosperity." *Southern Literary Messenger* 37 (Mar. 1863): 152–55. Making of America Digital Library. http://quod.lib.umich.edu/m/moajrnl/browse.journals/sout.html.

United States. *The Statutes at Large, Treaties, and Proclamations of the United States of America.* Vol. 12. Boston: Little, Brown, 1863.

———. Bureau of the Census. *The Statistical History of the United States from Colonial Times to the Present.* New York: Basic Books, 1976.

———. War Department. *The War of the Rebellion: A Compilation of the Official Records of the Union and Confederate Armies.* 128 vols. Washington, DC: GPO, 1880–1901.

Van Deusen, Glyndon G. *William Henry Seward.* New York: Oxford University Press, 1967.

Van Evrie, John H. *Negroes and Negro "Slavery": The First an Inferior Race; The Latter its Normal Condition.* New York: Van Evrie, Horton & Co., 1861.

Voegeli, V. Jacque. "A Rejected Alternative: Union Policy and the Relocation of Southern 'Contrabands' at the Dawn of Emancipation." *Journal of Southern History* 69 (Nov. 2003): 765–90.

Voices from Connecticut for Impartial Suffrage. [Connecticut?: N.p., 1865?]. Library of Congress, Rare Book and Special Collections Division, African American Pamphlet Collection. http://memory.loc.gov/ammem/aapchtml/rbaapcbibTitles04.html.

Vorenberg, Michael. "Abraham Lincoln and the Politics of Black Colonization." *Journal of the Abraham Lincoln Association* 14 (Summer 1993): 23–45.

———. *Final Freedom: The Civil War, the Abolition of Slavery, and the Thirteenth Amendment.* Cambridge: Cambridge University Press, 2001.

Warren, Edward Jenner. *To the Citizens of Beaufort County.* N.p.: N.p., between 1861 and 1865. Electronic Edition. Documenting the American South. 2000. http://docsouth.unc.edu/imls/warrenej/warrenej.html.

Waterbury, Rev. J. B. *Friendly Counsels for Freedmen.* New York: American Tract Society, [1864]. Samuel J. May Anti-Slavery Collection, Cornell University Library. 2006. http://dlxs.library.cornell.edu/m/mayantislavery/browse_W.html.

Whiting, William. *The War Powers of the President, and the Legislative Powers of Congress in relation to Rebellion, Treason, and Slavery.* 6th ed. Boston: John L. Shorey for the Emancipation League, 1863.

Wiley, Bell Irvin. "The Movement to Humanize the Institution of Slavery during the Confederacy." *Emory University Quarterly* 5 (Dec. 1949): 207–20.

Wiley, Calvin H. *Scriptural Views of National Trials, or, the True Road to the Independence and Peace of the Confederate States of America.* Greensboro, NC: Sterling, Campbell, & Albright, 1863.

Wills, Garry. *Lincoln at Gettysburg: The Words That Remade America.* New York: Touchstone, 1992.

Wilson, Frank I. *Address Delivered before the Wake County Workingmen's Association: in the Court House at Raleigh, February 6, 1860.* Raleigh: Standard Office Print, 1860. Documenting the American South. 2002. http://docsouth.unc.edu/nc/wilsonfi/menu.html.

Wilson, Joseph R. *Mutual Relation of Masters and Slaves as Taught in the Bible. A Discourse Preached in the First Presbyterian Church, Augusta, Georgia, on Sabbath Morning, Jan. 6, 1861.* Augusta: Steam Press of Chronicle & Sentinel, 1861. Documenting the American South. 1999. http://docsouth.unc.edu/imls/wilson/menu.html.

Wilson, Woodrow. *The New Freedom: A Call for the Emancipation of the Generous Energies of a People.* With an introduction and notes by William E. Leuchtenburg. Englewood Cliffs, NJ: Prentice-Hall, 1961.

Wyatt-Brown, Bertram. *Southern Honor: Ethics and Behavior in the Old South.* New York: Oxford University Press, 1982.

INDEX

DATE DUE
